MAP OF THE HAWAIIAN ISLANDS.

Scale of Miles.

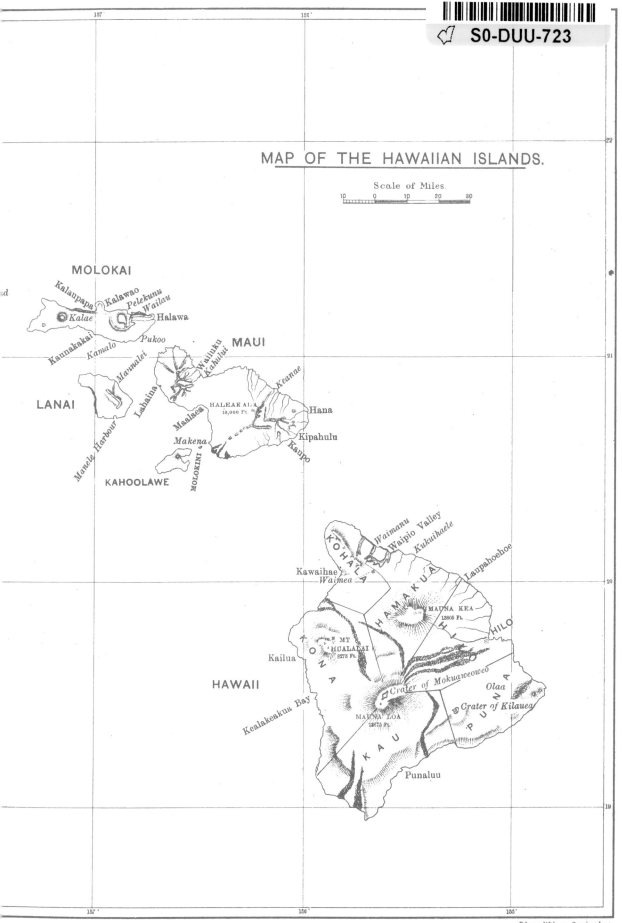

Barefoot on Lava

BAREFOOT
ON LAVA

The Journals and Correspondence
of Naturalist R.C.L. Perkins
in Hawai'i, 1892–1901

Edited by
Neal L. Evenhuis

Bishop Museum Press
Honolulu, 2007

Bishop Museum Bulletin in Zoology 7

Published by Bishop Museum Press
©2007 Bishop Museum Press

Library of Congress Cataloging-in-Publication data

Barefoot on lava: the journals and correspondence of naturalist R.C.L. Perkins in Hawai'i,
1892–1901 / edited by Neal L. Evenhuis.
    p. cm. -- (Bishop Museum Bulletin in Zoology ; no. 7)
 Includes bibliographical references and indexes.
 ISBN 1-58178-061-3 (hardcover : alk. paper)
 1. Perkins, R.C.L. (Robert Cyril Layton), 1866–1955. 2. Naturalists -- England -- biography. 3.
Zoologists -- England -- Biography. 4. Natural history -- Hawaii -- History. I. Evenhuis, Neal L.

 QH31.P246B37 2007
 508.092--dc22
 [B]

2007002631

ISSN 0893-312X
ISBN 10: 1-58178-061-3
ISBN 13: 978-1-58178-061-1

Endsheets: 1899 Map of the Hawaiian Islands from *Fauna Hawaiiensis, Volume 1, part 1*

Printed in China by Everbest

To

Rev. Thomas Blackburn
John Thomas Gulick
Scott Barchard Wilson

*without whose ground-breaking research
in Hawaiian zoology,
R.C.L. Perkins would not have experienced
the Hawaiian Islands*

R.C.L. Perkins on the Dartmoor in south Devon, England. Age 46.

Table of Contents

Foreword

Fauna Hawaiiensis (FH) ranks as a masterpiece in natural history literature of the early 20th century. Published in parts over several years and compiled into 3 volumes, the work covers most terrestrial animal groups in the islands and remains a monumental contribution to our knowledge of the natural history of Hawai'i. Each part was authored by a taxonomic authority, but the fieldwork and collections on which the work was based, were predominately conducted by one man, Robert Cyril Layton Perkins. Perkins also authored several of the fascicles on insects as well as the Introduction. The latter work (Perkins, R.C.L. 1913. Introduction. In: *Fauna Hawaiiensis*. D. Sharp, ed. 1: xv-ccxxvii. Cambridge Univ. Press) is a classic in natural history writing, and in it Perkins revealed an intimate knowledge of the behavior and biology of an incredibly broad range of species. Since he was the last to see many of these alive, his descriptions are all we have to bring these pinned or skinned museum specimens alive. Who was this man who was able to identify to species on sight a large majority of the insects and other organisms he encountered in the field? Entomologists know of him and hold the results of his work in awe. Hawaiian naturalists and biologists in other disciplines know of his work sometimes in disbelief. How could one person become so familiar with such a broad range of taxa? Unfortunately for historians and biologists, Perkins' original field notes and much of the supporting background material for FH were lost, and important information on the locality and provenance of many of his specimens remain unknown.

In this contribution, Neal Evenhuis has compiled and annotated the surviving notes and correspondence of Perkins, including published accounts and a miscellany of unpublished anecdotes by friends and colleagues. This work introduces the man and provides many of the background details that not only explain the person but also place his observations in perspective. On these pages, the reader follows the man in the field, learning his techniques and where and when he collected the myriad of species. We also relive vicariously the numerous vicissitudes, sometimes humorous, of fieldwork in remote places. These details, previously thought to be lost, are now accessible to island biologists and historians.

This work introduces a complex and well-rounded human. Perkins trained in classical languages to become clergy only to have an epiphany and pursue his hobby as an entomologist and naturalist. Subsequently he left the comfortable English countryside to explore the then remote islands where he was to collect and document a largely unknown fauna in often inhospitable circumstances. There he became a legendary collector of natural history specimens, and an astute observer of nature and recorder of the ways of insects and their associated organisms. Knowing him better through these pages only increases the prestige of Perkins and his work.

This work will be especially useful to biologists of all disciplines—not just entomologists—to understand how the Hawaiian Islands looked a century ago. Such understanding is critical in order to appreciate how the biota has changed and continues to change. Perkins witnessed much change during his work, and recorded it with precision and often prescient conclusions. His accurate observations of changes document the timeline and interconnectedness of events that heretofore have been missed or unrecognized. For example, his 1897 note in *Nature* on the nontarget impacts of biological control agents then being introduced to Hawai'i (Perkins, R.C.L. 1897. The introduction of beneficial insects into the Hawaiian Islands. *Nature* 55:499–500) went largely unnoticed for nearly a century.

This tome is timely for all biologists and conservationists outside Hawai'i as well, since much of the world's biodiversity currently faces the processes that Perkins saw and documented in Hawai'i. Perkins realized the urgency of his work soon after his arrival and observed firsthand the rapid changes taking place in the islands. Land use patterns were changing quickly; plantation agriculture was replacing the traditional small scale farms, the human population was becoming more urbanized, and the number of invasive alien species was increasing at an ever increasing pace. These changes continue today on a global scale; therefore, field biologists everywhere will benefit from knowing and understanding Perkins' work. Although Perkins describes a paradise that no longer exists, this compilation is not depressing. The wonder of Hawaiian natural history conveyed on these pages will inspire the reader.

Francis G. Howarth
Bishop Museum, Honolulu
November 2006

Acknowledgments

Numerous individuals gave of their time and expertise in assisting me during the almost ten years of the lifetime of this project. Archival research was made successful with the help of the staff of Bishop Museum Library and Archives (B.J. Short, Judith Kearney, Linda Laurence, DeSoto Brown, Ron Schaefer, Patrice Belcher, Kim Okahara, Duane Wenzel, Betty Lou Kam, Charles O'Brien, Leah Caldeira); Hawaii State Archives, Honolulu, Hawai'i; the Natural History Museum Entomology Library, London (Julie Harvey); Hawaii Agricultural Research Center (formerly Hawaiian Sugar Planters' Association), Aiea (Ann Marsteller); Hawaii Volcanoes National Park Archives (Keola Awong and Helen Bevens); Kona Historical Society, Captain Cook, Hawai'i (Jean Greenwell and Terry Kriege); Oxford University Natural History Museum and Library, Oxford, UK (Stella Bricknell, Darren Mann, Adrian Pont); Torquay Historical Association, Paignton, UK (John R. Pike, Robert A. Perkins [no relation to R.C.L.]); California Academy of Sciences Library, Koebele Collection, San Francisco (Karren Elsbernd, Michele Wellck); Bailey House Museum, Wailuku, Maui (Roslyn Lightfoot); Kauai Historical Society, Lihue, Hawai'i (Mary A. Requilman); University of Hawai'i at Mānoa Hamilton Library; National Museum of Wales, Cardiff (Mike Wilson); and Anita Manning, Waipahu, Hawai'i.

Biographical and genealogical information was obtained with the help of the following: Robert A. Perkins (grandson of R.C.L.P.), Newbury, UK; Christine Faye, Gay & Robinson Sugar Museum, Makaweli, Kaua'i; Karl Ludvigsen, Suffolk, UK; Alisa Vegas, Volcano, Hawai'i; Paul Dahlquist, Waikoloa, Hawai'i; John Massey Stewart, London, England; Derek Palmer, Lydford, Devon, England; E.C. Zimmerman, Canberra, Australia; Anita Manning; and the online information obtained primarily from the Ancestry.com website [www.ancestry.com].

Reviews of various versions and portions of this work were made by the following: Frank Howarth (prologue and glossary); Carla Kishinami (glossary); Clyde T. Imada (glossary); Gordon M. Nishida, U.C. Berkeley (early draft); Anita Manning (early draft); Dan Polhemus, Hawaii State Division of Aquatic Resources (early draft); Marilyn Nicholson, Volcano, Hawai'i (biography). Lucius G. Eldredge provided proofreading and editing assistance in the later stages of the project. Lan Tu provided a keen eye to editing the final draft.

Assistance with transcribing and digitizing the correspondence of David Sharp and Alfred Newton was ably provided by B. Leilani Pyle, Kathleen Hamlin, and Steve Bunting.

Historical accuracy was checked and anecdotal information were provided by Anita Manning and Frank Howarth; and Fred Gregory and his "Post Office in Paradise" website [www.hawaiianstamps.com] is thanked for assistance with Hawaiian postal history.

Locality information and anecdotes were provided by Jim Liebherr, Cornell University and Dan Polhemus.

Anita Manning really started this project. I was inspired by her detailed 1986 account of R.C.L. Perkins and the Sandwich Islands Committee article in the *Bishop Museum Occasional Papers* and was intrigued that no one had delved further into his biography or journals and correspondence. After many frustrating years of failing to find much on his biography or any surviving correspondence from him to Sharp and Newton during his years in Hawai'i, I realized why no one else had ventured into these waters. Numerous tips from Anita on where to hunt, her opening up of her Perkins files with successes and failures in her research on Perkins (the latter was especially time-saving to keep me from re-following dead ends), and her continued support for a successful completion of this project was a boon to my confidence and I am especially thankful to her for that.

Adrian Pont, Oxford Natural History Museum, was extremely helpful with his generous assistance to me during my travels to England to research Perkins's later years in Devon. I thoroughly enjoyed our trips to Gloucestershire, Wiltshire, Devon, and Wales in search of Perkins's later residences and Perkins family gravestones.

And special thanks to my wife Marilyn L. Nicholson for incredibly perceptive comments and her ever-quick to query: "when are you going to finish this thing?" to keep me going.

Prologue

Over one hundred years have passed since the British *Sandwich Islands Committee* sent a skinny young twenty-five year old naturalist, Robert Cyril Layton Perkins, to the Hawaiian Islands. His charge: assess, observe, and collect the fauna there on behalf of the Royal Society and the British Association for the Advancement of Science. During his time in Hawai'i, Perkins collected almost all classes and phyla of terrestrial zoology specimens but specialized primarily in collecting and assessing the bird and insect fauna. The results of his efforts were published in the first monographic treatise on Hawaiian zoology, the folio-sized three-volume *Fauna Hawaiiensis*.

Even before Perkins arrived, the islands had seen a continual increase in urbanization, development of agriculture, and a sustained onslaught of invasive alien species introductions. Surveying such a landscape would prove difficult at best if he were to properly assess the status of native species.

Soon after his arrival in Hawai'i, Perkins recognized the damaging effects of invasive alien plants and animals to the native environment and, through his appeals to the Sandwich Islands Committee and their consequent proposals to funding agencies in England, was able to procure additional funding to do as complete a survey as possible while native insects, birds, and snails were still to be seen. Despite the urgency of collecting before certain species might be erased from the landscape as a result of alien introductions, while he was in Hawai'i he was the unfortunate witness to extreme reductions and even extinctions of certain birds and insects.

Perkins's collecting for the Committee spanned about 7 of the 10 years that the project was in existence (1892–1901), but in that time he amassed one of the best collections of insects and birds from Hawai'i ever to have been assembled by one person. His collecting efforts are legendary: spending months at a time in solitude in rainforests enduring cold nights, drenching rains, muddy tent floors and trails, sopping wet clothes, limited food rations, and few comforts — all to better collect and observe the birds, insects, and other invertebrates he was sent to investigate.

Previously unpublished journals and remembrances of Perkins, supplemented by selected examples of his surviving personal correspondence and those of his associates and colleagues, give us an incomparable picture of the Hawaiian landscape and of what life in Hawai'i was like at the end of the nineteenth century. They are presented here in hopes that they can serve as a guide for some, and an inspiration for others, to help us better understand, conserve, and restore the precious Hawaiian natural heritage for our own enjoyment and the understanding and appreciation of future generations.

Explanation of Format

The corpus of this book is composed of the transcribed journals and remembrances of Robert Cyril Layton Perkins during his 7 years in Hawai'i collecting zoological specimens for the Sandwich Islands Committee in England. Supplementing these journals is correspondence pertaining to these collecting ventures, mostly from his patrons, Drs. Alfred Newton and David Sharp to Perkins. Unfortunately, comparatively few letters have been found from Perkins to others during this time. Letters from Perkins to Newton (mainly dealing with his experiences with birds) have gone mysteriously missing while those to Sharp (dealing primarily with insects he discovered) were apparently destroyed when Sharp was forced to move out of his office in October 1914 and was told what he could not take with him would be destroyed. Sharp notified Perkins of this and asked if he wanted the letters since Sharp had no use for them. If Perkins took possession of the letters, they have not yet been found.

Despite these deplorable losses, information on his experiences in the field concerning birds and insects can be found elsewhere. After leaving the Hawaiian Islands to live in Devon, England, Perkins kept a frequent correspondence with his lifelong friend, George Munro (letters of which contain many reminiscences about birding in Hawai'i). These letters span the years 1901–1955. In 1936, he began corresponding with Elwood C. Zimmerman, who at the time was preparing material for his new series "Insects of Hawaii." These letters deal chiefly with insects and span the years 1936–1952.

Where possible, information supplemental to his journals and remembrances concerning his activities during the period he surveyed for the Sandwich Islands Committee found in these and other correspondence with colleagues is added to give the reader as much detailed information as possible. In many cases, charming anecdotes are found in his personal letters to Munro and Zimmerman that are missing from the more business-like journal entries.

When asked in 1936 to reproduce his journals for the benefit of others, Perkins gathered up what he could find and transcribed into a clean handwritten copy the notes from his original journals that he claimed were written in an almost illegible hand. Doing so almost 40 years after they were originally written, Perkins was able to add information that he had gained since the time he wrote the original journals. Many of Perkins's transcriptions thus included ancillary notes and statements of clarification, which he added in square brackets [ ] to differentiate from his original journal entries. Additionally, the selected correspondence reproduced here also includes parenthetical and ancillary notes that were placed in either parentheses ( ) or square brackets [ ]. In order to keep these marks as in the originals, I have placed my subsequent clarifications or corrections to journal and correspondence entries in curly brackets { }.

All of the transcribed journals and many of the letters transcribed here are deposited in the Bishop Museum Archives. A full list of sources used for this study is given in Appendix I. Additionally, the index lists the people that Perkins or his correspondents mention, which may be of use to future researchers in attempts to find further personal letters from Perkins giving contemporary accounts of his travels and work in Hawai'i.

Many items in the journals, remembrances, and selected correspondence are annotated in footnotes to give the reader further information about people, places, and the animals and plants referred to. A glossary of the more commonly referred to scientific names is presented.

SOCIAL AND ORTHOGRAPHIC CAVEATS

The perception of native Hawaiians by non-Hawaiians in the 1890s is not necessarily in complete congruence with that in existence today. Some who had never set foot in the islands believed that all Hawaiians were "black" in color and were thus referred to as "blacks" without ever having seen one. A subjugative stereotype of Pacific islanders in general was normal for many foreigners at that time and can be found in certain passages in Perkins's journals and the correspondence of he and his colleagues. For example, when Perkins refers to his "native boy" accompanying him on an overnight journey to Hualālai, he is referring to a full grown adult assistant, not a young boy.

There are many spelling anomalies and errors throughout the journals and selected correspondence reproduced in this book and these have been kept as in the original as much as possible to preserve the original writings of Perkins and his correspondents. However, in some cases the misspellings have been corrected or noted when it was found necessary to do so to for clarity of meaning and content. Perkins did not use Hawaiian diacritical marks in his writings and they are omitted here to keep with the authenticity of his orthography. Diacritics are included in footnotes and annotations added by me.

Normal convention is to underline scientific names when writing by hand, but Perkins and his correspondents were inconsistent in doing this. I have kept the names as they are in the original writings, whether underlined or not.

PART ONE

Introduction

Historical Summary

This book will help transport the reader back to a time when life was busy but a bit slower than today and Hawai'i was a much different yet still complex society in which to live and work. Perkins arrived in a world drastically different than the 1000s-year old English one in which he was born and was raised. Hawai'i after western contact was only 120 years old and was enduring the growing pains of trying to adjust to a western way of living forced upon it by the intervention of, at first, crews from trading ships, then missionaries, and later, foreign businessmen. The pristine tropical landscape that welcomed the original Polynesians who came across the vast ocean from the Marquesas in ca. 500 A.D. had long disappeared and was replaced by agriculture and urbanization in much of the lowlands throughout the island chain. This century-old alteration of the Hawaiian landscape was no doubt a tremendous aggravation and disappointment to Perkins and led him to "head for the hills" in order to find the native invertebrates and birds he sought.

The results of Perkins's ten-year labor was the monumental three-volume monograph, *Fauna Hawaiiensis*, a collaborative effort of 23 specialists with an overall introduction prepared by Perkins (see Manning, A., 1988, *Bishop Museum Occasional Papers* 26: 1–46 for a detailed history of the publication of *Fauna Hawaiiensis*). It was the first such compendium ever completed on the animals of the Hawaiian Islands. Hillebrand[1] had, only a few years before Perkins arrival, completed the first manual of flowering plants of the Hawaiian Islands. A detailed study of the animals was long overdue.

---

[1] Hillebrand, Wilhelm B. (1821–1886). A Prussian-born physician, who came to Hawai'i in 1850 to improve his health. During his 21 years in Hawai'i, he not only served as a physician, but as an immigration officer, an agriculturist, and amateur botanist. He was sent by the Hawaiian government on a tour of the Orient to collect plants and animals that would benefit the Hawaiian Islands. He sent back camphor, cinnamon, jackfruit, litchi, mandarin oranges, Chinese plums, Java plums, several kinds of banyans and many other ornamental plants. He was also responsible for the introduction of many species of birds including goldfinches, Japanese finches, linnets, mynah birds, ricebirds, Indian sparrows, and Mongolian pheasants. He additionally brought in a pair of deer from China and a pair from Java. In 1871, he left Hawai'i to eventually return to Heidelberg, Germany. On the way, he spent time in Cambridge, Massachusetts, where, with the assistance of Asa Gray, he began his "Flora of the Hawaiian Islands." Though seriously ill the last 2 years of his life, he was able to finish the first part of the manuscript of his book. With the assistance of his son, it was eventually was published posthumously in 1888.

HONOLULU AT THE TIME OF PERKINS ARRIVAL

Honolulu in 1892 was a relatively normal bustling business center and the governmental seat for the Hawaiian Islands. The governmental system was a monarchy. Originally in place as an *ali'i* (chiefly royalty) system for one thousand years, it evolved into a European monarchy in 1874. That monarchy and the sovereignty of Hawaiians would come to an abrupt end in 1893, when the government of Queen Lili'uokalani was overthrown in a bloodless coup by a group of foreign businessmen and was replaced by a republic. An interim president headed the government until annexation by the United States in 1898, at which time a governor administered the islands.

Honolulu in 1892 was home to over 23,000 residents, including 11,000 native Hawaiians and 3,500 Chinese. The entire Hawaiian Islands comprised a population of 95,400 people that year. Honolulu Harbor (its native name was Kou) was not quite 100 years old (it was developed into a place of anchorage soon after Europeans saw its potential as a harbor in 1794) and was host to a multitude of vessels that came into port each year, carrying over 8,000 immigrant plantation workers, tourists, and new residents from overseas.

Sugar was king in Hawai'i. It had been brought to Hawai'i by Polynesians who planted the cane as a food source around the edges of their *kalo lo'i* (taro fields). In 1825, John Wilkinson started planting sugarcane as a crop in Mānoa Valley on O'ahu. By 1900, there were over 65,000 acres in sugar production throughout the islands. Other major crops that were being exported in the 1890s included rice and coffee. Crops that contributed much less to the overall economy included bananas, pineapples, and oranges. The self-sustaining lifestyle of native Hawaiians living from the products of the land and sea diminished as soon as western contact saw the potential for exports of natural products like sandalwood and introduced crops that would thrive in a lush, year-round warm and humid climate with few natural pests.

Society in early 1890s Honolulu revolved around the new queen, Lili'uokalani, an accomplished musician and songwriter, who was a devout advocate of cultural activities and events. Scientists visiting the islands were treated as dignitaries and were normally taken around by their hosts to meet others of their ilk as well as the leaders of society. The letters of introduction given to Perkins and sent ahead to people such as Charles Reed Bishop,[2] who the Sandwich Islands Committee had hoped would help co-sponsor Perkins's activities, no doubt paved the way for Perkins to meet important and influential people in the islands. Foreign scientists were a distinct novelty not to be ignored and this apparently afforded Perkins the opportunity to meet the Queen only a few days after his arrival.

---

[2] Bishop, Charles Reed (1822–1915). American businessman and financier, Bishop was born in Glenn Falls, New York and arrived in Hawai'i when just 24 years old. A few years after arriving, he started a banking institution and, with partners, was instrumental in some wise land purchases. In 1850 he married Princess Bernice Pauahi Pākī, one of the last of the Kamehameha line; and from then on played an active part in the activities of Hawaiian royalty and education of Hawaii's children. During the reign of King Kalākaua, Bishop was appointed by the King to the Privy Council and was a member of the House of Nobles. Kalākaua appointed him as the President of the Board of Education. After the death of Princess Pauahi in 1884, he built the Bernice P. Bishop Museum as a memorial to her. Bishop was a wealthy and influential landowner and much interested in the doings of the sciences, especially with regard to how the endeavors of Perkins could benefit the building of the collections at Bishop Museum.

Honolulu Harbor area in the 1890s.

Travel on the major islands was primarily by carriage, horse, or in just a few places, rail, the last having been originally introduced to haul sugarcane to the mill or the docks. Perkins favored hiking wherever he could and only used carriages and rails for especially long distances. Travel between the islands was by steamer. Regularly scheduled steamer trips allowed Perkins to travel almost at a moment's notice to virtually wherever he wished throughout the island chain. This ability to travel spontaneously no doubt caused his benefactors some aggravation when attempting to ascertain a location to inform funding agencies. Often, the response by Perkins to requests of where he would go next was simply, "I am uncertain as to my movements." Although steamer trips averaged about $5 per trip (and up to as much as $12 for a one-way trip from Honolulu to the island of Hawai'i), Perkins was given a substantial discount by the Hawaiian government (exact details of which are unknown but some correspondence between Perkins and Sandwich Islands Committee members implied free passage in some cases). This was no doubt one of the most fortunate favors given to Perkins during his stay for had he paid normal steamer fares throughout his stay (during which he took over 60 trips), he would have quickly used up the trifling grant funds given to him by the Royal Society and British Association.

Accommodations for travelers were beginning to expand in the early 1890s. There were inexpensive boarding houses in the larger cities such as Honolulu, Hilo, and Lahaina, and a few hotels as well. During Perkins's ten years in Hawai'i he stayed at the Eagle House, Arlington Hotel, Young Hotel, and the Hawaiian Hotel in the downtown area of Honolulu and the Honolulu Hotel in Waikīkī. Staying at one of these places would normally cost a person about $12 per week.

Aside from these, Perkins also stayed at the homes of people who knew of him through his letters of introductions from colleagues and friends locally who vouched for him. After a short time in the islands and getting his name in the local newspapers, many in Hawai'i would quickly know Perkins's exploits. If someone had a spare room, it would offer a good diversion and the promise of interesting stories to host Perkins in one's home, especially those residing in rural areas who would not normally get visitors.

THE HAWAIIAN POSTAL SYSTEM AND PERKINS

A well-organized and thriving mail system had been in place in Hawai'i since 1851. In 1892, postcards to anywhere within the Universal Postal System (which at that time included North America, Europe, Japan, and Australia) cost 2¢ to mail; 1/2 oz. letters cost 5¢. Postmasters were in all the main towns throughout all the islands and steamers that transported people from island to island also hauled mail on a daily basis. International mail was shipped out weekly. A letter to England missing the weekly steamer would have to wait another week to go out. Mail was to be an important lifeline in Perkins's seven years of living in the field while in the islands. Having Perkins acting as sort of a remote sensor for the Sandwich Islands Committee had its obvious shortcomings: he could and would not know how his benefactors were thinking about a queried subject for at least two months. He would write a card or letter telling them of his adventures as well as his successes and failures in his attempts at collecting but, although mail was on a regular schedule, he would still have to await a steamer on a particular island to take it to Honolulu, where it would then have to wait until Saturday when ships took international mail to England via North America. If all transits went well, a letter could arrive in three weeks in England (but often it was four to five weeks). The return letter from England to Honolulu would take the same time to get back, and then transit to whichever port was nearby where Perkins was stationed at the time. To confound mat-

Envelope showing postmarks of various places in the Hawaiian Islands trying to catch up with a traveling recipient.

Courtesy Fred Gregory

ters, if Perkins was traveling between islands, or if he moved from one island to another after finding out that collecting may not have been all that good at a particular locale, letters from England would be trying to follow him whenever he went. Perkins often left instructions with the Honolulu postmaster as to where letters should be forwarded, but sometimes the letters arrived in a port after he had headed off to another location to collect.

After reading through Perkins's diaries, correspondence, and remembrances, it became apparent that Perkins kept himself very close to this mail "lifeline" wherever he went. He either stayed with or near many of the postmasters in the areas he collected (August Ahrens in Waiʻanae and Archibald Mahaulu in Waialua on Oʻahu; Rudolf Meyer in Kaunakakai and Kalaʻe on Molokaʻi; James Anderson in Makawao on Maui; Fred Hayselden on Lānaʻi; and the Greenwells in Kona on Hawaiʻi). Postmasters knew the land around them into which Perkins would venture, thus they could provide Perkins with the most updated information on conditions that could prove favorable for collecting. When he could not venture away from camp to fetch them himself, letters were often delivered to Perkins's tent by native Hawaiians. Most of the time when they arrived, Perkins would be out in the field, so they left letters in his tent and had instructions to take finished letters back to town to be mailed. Some postmasters, like Meyer, would venture far into the forest to deliver letters at Perkins's camp and to check on how he would be faring, since he often stayed in the forest alone for weeks at a time.

ONE HUNDRED YEARS OF BIOLOGICAL SURVEYS

Scientific exploration of the Hawaiian Islands began as soon as Captain James Cook's ships *Resolution* and *Discovery* set anchor off shore of Waimea, Kauaʻi in January 1778 and the first naturalists stepped onto the shores of Hawaii's beaches to collect plants and animals in the name of his majesty, King George III. Between 1778 and the time of Perkins's arrival, zoological research in the islands derived primarily from naturalists on board the various voyages of exploration that came through the islands. Russian, British, Prussian, American, Danish, and French explorers stopped at Hawaiʻi on their way across the Pacific and contributed greatly to the knowledge of plants and animals of the islands. The discoveries of rare and unusual birds, insects, plants, snails, marine organisms, etc. made by those explorers stimulated great interest among the scientific community.

In the decades subsequent to Cook's arrival, Hawaiʻi became host or home to a variety of persons interested in collecting new and interesting biological specimens. Some collected with the intention of publishing the results in scientific journals and books; others collected to assist visiting scientists or purely for self-interest and curiosity. Some of these early resident collectors included missionaries and other clergy, but some scientists also made their new home in Hawaiʻi where they could have a stable base of operation while researching the botany or zoology of the islands.

Two naturalists with missionary lineages who contributed significant background information on Hawaiian natural history to Perkins before his arrival were John Thomas Gulick, and Sanford Ballard Dole. Gulick specialized in land snails and Dole, better known in political circles as Hawaii's first president and first governor, was interested in ornithology. The Rev. Thomas Blackburn, during his tour of duty in Hawaiʻi, collected numerous insects. Although he only stayed for a short seven years in Hawaiʻi, he is considered by many as "the father of Hawaiian entomology."

Although the age of exploration and world voyages had pretty much waned by the last half of the 19th century, the publications of those who had come to the islands during the first half had created a tremendous desire of scientists to find ways to visit Hawai'i and explore more of the islands' plants and animals. No longer commissioned as naturalists or surgeons on board world voyages, these visiting scientists were instead sent alone or in small groups on behalf of scientific institutions, societies, and museums to help increase the knowledge of the biota of the Hawaiian Islands.

Botanists, geologists, ornithologists, invertebrate zoologists, entomologists, and others were sent to investigate their particular specialty. One of these, Scott Barchard Wilson, a young enigmatic ornithologist from Cambridge University in England came to Hawai'i to collect birds from 1887–1888. Wilson's superb collecting efforts resulted in the lavishly illustrated *Aves Hawaiiensis* he co-authored with A.H. Evans. It was Wilson's collecting that prompted his Cambridge colleague, Alfred Newton, to send Perkins to Hawai'i to complete the task that Wilson had started.

THE EFFECTS OF ALIEN SPECIES ON THE NATURAL ENVIRONMENT

Since the arrival of humans to the Hawaiian Islands, introductions of nonnative plants and animals, primarily to accommodate human habitation, have altered its predominantly lush tropical environment. Unwanted hitchhikers as well as purposeful introductions of plants and animals have caused undue harm not only to the natural environment, but also agriculture, habitation, and the overall quality of life.

Voyaging Polynesians brought various plants and animals forming a corpus of necessary traditional items that were intended to sustain them wherever they landed. In Hawai'i these included domesticated pigs (*pua'a*), bananas (*mai'a*), breadfruit (*'ulu*), sugarcane (*kō*), candlenut (*kukui*), kava (*'awa*), taro (*kalo*), and mountain apples (*ōhia 'ai*), among others.

Despite these initial introductions, it was not until after first contact by Europeans in 1778, that Hawai'i would experience its most devastating environmental changes. The first would be through the introduction of cattle and goats by Capt. George Vancouver in 1793 as a gift to King Kamehameha I. Because Kamehameha declared these cattle *kapu* (taboo), the large bovines reproduced quickly and roamed freely through Hawaiian forests, scraping protective bark and moss off of trees while scratching themselves; while the goats ate the understory vegetation and small shrubs. The trees scraped by the cattle soon died from desiccation, then along with them, many of the insects that called them home and, in domino-like fashion, native birds that relied on those native insects for food, either for themselves or their fledgling young. By 1819, the *kapu* had been removed from the cattle and goats by King Kamehameha II (Liholiho) but by then it was too late. The damage had been done and the lowland and mid-elevation forests would never be the same.

Another environmental disaster to hit Hawai'i less than 50 years after Captain Cook set foot on her shores was the almost total extermination of sandalwood from Hawaiian forests through its harvest for trade. By 1840, the previously lucrative sandalwood trade, sending the aromatic wood to China for incense and fine woodworking, ended due to the depletion of the trees. Today, the small number of surviving solitary sandalwood trees can be found scattered on just a few of the Hawaiian Islands.

By the time Perkins arrived in Hawai'i in early 1892, a silent, but catastrophic event had already occurred that would forever transform the composition of Hawaii's fauna—the introduction of alien ants.[3] Hawai'i did not have any native ants and the presence of only a very few species known during Perkins's investigations in the islands was enough to cause the reduction and possibly even extinction of many defenseless terrestrial and arboreal invertebrates. Although he did not sense any urgency when he embarked on his mission, within his first few months in the islands, Perkins, and as a direct result of his reports to them, the Sandwich Islands Committee, saw the need for a complete survey of the fauna before ants and other introduced alien pests would totally decimate it.

Rats were also a concern to Perkins. Although not mentioned much in his journals, his later correspondence complained of their causing not only the eventual demise of rails on Moloka'i, but also the reduction of species of birds and insects that were dependent on native fruits found in the forests of the Islands.

> "In the years up to about 1900 it was very difficult to get any beetles from the Ie { 'ie'ie} fruits on Oahu, as practically all were eaten & fouled by the foreign rats, as also were all the wild banana fruits long before they were ripe. Nothing surprised me more after returning in 1892 from the Kona forest, where the Ieie had such large fruits, fed on only by the crow & the Ou, to find these all spoilt in this way in the mts. near Honolulu. But after 1900 the Ieie fruits in the latter localities became good & common, & I put this down—possibly quite wrongly—to the mortality amongst the rats which occurred during the rather bad outbreak of plague. At any rate at that time one was continually finding dead rats, not only in the flat country round Honolulu, but also in the mountains nearby. Similarly some of the Staphs, which frequent the Ieie with N. discedens, were not rare after the rats decreased. (Myllaena & Diestota)." *(R.C.L. Perkins letter to E.C. Zimmerman, 20 June 1937, BPBM Entomology Archives).*

The ill-advised introduction of the mongoose to Hawai'i in 1883 to control rats in the cane fields eventually led to the further reduction of the numbers of native birds and was most likely the leading factor in the extinction of the ground nesting rails.

Perkins's concern about the effects of the increasing number of invasive aliens on the Hawaiian environment remained a priority for him throughout his years of collecting for the Sandwich Islands Committee. So much so, that after finishing work for the Committee, he stayed on in Hawai'i and worked for the Territorial Government and later the Hawaiian Sugar Planters' Association (HSPA) as an entomologist. During those post-*Fauna Hawaiiensis* days, he spent most of his time working to find ways to control pestiferous plants and animals established in the islands that were causing damage to forest and agriculture.

---

[3]   One of the earliest documented problems with alien ants in the Hawaiian Islands is given in the diary of Andrew Bloxam when he visited Hawai'i on board the *Blonde* in 1825: "Saturday, May 21, 1825. Employed preserving birds; the ants, I find, make sad ravages with them." *(Bloxam, A. 1925, Diary of Andrew Bloxam, naturalist of the "Blonde" on her trip from England to the Hawaiian Islands 1824–25).*

Biography of R.C.L. Perkins

Unlike other explorers of the 19th and early 20th centuries, R.C.L. Perkins did not leave behind a vast treasure-trove of personal information from which to re-create the lifetime of achievements that he so humbly succeeded in completing. Trying to discover who Perkins was and what he was like is a difficult venture at best. He was by nature a very private man and left little in evidence of his personality. Known photographs of him are few and far between. Still, a picture of this extraordinary man can be painted with broad strokes by way of archival information such as letters to colleagues and friends and the notes and observations of those who knew him during his years in Hawai'i.

EARLY YEARS

Robert Cyril Layton Perkins was born in the quaint village of Badminton, in Gloucestershire, England on 15 November 1866 to Charles Mathew Perkins (born 1838) and Agnes Martha Beach Thomas (born 1843). Service to the Anglican church was pervasive in many family members. His father, an Anglican priest, was the son of the Reverend Benjamin Robert Perkins, long-time vicar at Wotton-under-Edge. A few years after becoming a schoolmaster at Newland, a village near Coleford in Gloucestershire when Robert was born, his father became the Rector at Sopworth. He subsequently moved on to churches in Raglan and Alderley. His mother was the daughter of the Reverend Hugh Percy Thomas and granddaughter of Rev. Percy Thomas, both Rectors of Nash, near Pembroke, West Wales. Robert was the second of five children. His older brother, Charles Mathew, born in 1865, eventually became the Rector at Raglan after his father moved on to Alderley. His younger sisters were Ethel Dene (born in 1871) and Martha "Marrie" Beach (born 1881). His younger brother was Percy G. Perkins (born in 1870).

Living in Newland, young Perkins obtained an early interest in entomology, fostered by the keen interest in nature and entomological collecting of his father and his uncle, Vincent Robert Perkins. Before the age of four Robert collected a specimen of the White-letter hairstreak (*Satyrium w-album*), a rather rare and elusive butterfly in those days. The specimen was pinned by his father and kept preserved. Having subsequently passed down from father (R.C.L.) to son (John), it still exists today in the collection of the Natural History Museum in London. Young Perkins was a natural in the field and this was noticed and encouraged by his father and

Typical cottage in Badminton, England where R.C.L. Perkins was born.

uncle who collected with him both day and night, as well as taking young Perkins to meetings of local natural history societies. He enjoyed his tramps through the forests of England and spent hours studying the Lepidoptera of the local area. Once, his father secured a hornet's nest and placed it in a bell jar next to a window allowing the wasps to come and go, but also allowing a thrilled young Perkins to observe the behavior of the wasps.

SCHOOLING

Despite the avid interest in natural history, especially entomology, that his father had, young Perkins was expected by his family to study the Classics, given that his father and grandfather were rectors in the Anglican Church. When Perkins's father became Rector[4] at Sopworth in north Wiltshire, he sent young Robert to the Merchant Taylors' School in London.[5] He remained at school in London from 1877 to 1885, only coming home for holidays to the rather luxurious environment of the large Sopworth Rectory, complete with a cook and two servants. The rather

---

[4] Rectors of the Anglican Church in England were provided with substantial financial support from wealthy patrons and tithing (the latter usually 10% of the agricultural produce of the lands held by the Church in that area). This "living" or "benefice" could be handed down to family members or sold. Given the generations of Anglican priests in Perkins's family, it is logical to assume that his family were of the more well-to-do class in England and thus could afford servants at home and schooling at Oxford (Anglican membership was required in Perkins's time for admittance to Oxford or Cambridge).

[5] The Merchant Taylors' School was founded in London in 1561 by the Worshipful Company of Merchant Taylors. Its motto "*Homo plantat Homo irrigat sed Deus dat incrementum*" [Man sows, Man irrigates, but God increases] shows the aspirations of its pious founders. Its first school was located on the Thames on Suffolk Lane. In 1875 it moved to Goswell Street in Charterhouse Square in Ipswich with added open space for games, a new addition to the curriculum. Its headmaster at that time, William Baker, by offering the site for games, had hoped to foster a corporate and public spirit among the boys of the School, by drawing them together in common amusements and giving them common interests. It is doubtful whether Perkins was concerned with any games, though, as he does not mention any in his autobiography and Classics was always at the center of the school's curriculum. Only after Perkins left the School were science courses added. In 1891 chemistry and physics classes were added. Biology classes were not added until 1900.

dirty and grimy London school was no match for the friendly forests he was used to in Gloucestershire and Wiltshire. Toward the end of his schooling, there was an attempt to start a natural history society at the Merchant Taylors' School, but it failed.

Perkins left the Merchant Taylors' School in 1885 having obtained a scholarship to Jesus College in Oxford University. During his schooling in London, he completed his studies in the Classics, but he kept up his amateur interest in the sciences—from field observations and book knowledge acquired during his holidays at home at Sopworth Rectory.

At Oxford, Perkins continued his studies in Classics—eventually graduating with a degree in that subject. However, it was his attendance at a public lecture by entomologist E.B. Poulton[6] on insect coloration, which proved to be the turning point that ultimately changed his career. Poulton's lecture not only led to the resurrection of the Oxford Natural History Society, but also was the stimulus that prompted Perkins to join that society. Seeing an opportunity, Perkins conferred with Poulton on his chances at giving up the Classics and taking up science at Oxford. With Poulton's influence, Perkins was allowed to do so. Despite his lack of the basic classes in science normally given to schoolboys, Perkins managed to finish his studies at Oxford successfully in just two years.

Soon after Oxford, a vacancy at the British Museum (Natural History) opened and Perkins applied.

> "When I left college, I was a candidate for a vacancy in the Ent. dept. of the Brit. Mus., but when the head (Dr. Gunther) told me I should not be allowed to work on Hymenoptera I scratched!" *(R.C.L. Perkins letter to E.C. Zimmerman, 17 February 1944, BPBM Entomology Archives).*

> "The interview went like this:
> 'Do you have any interests in insects?'
> 'Yes, I am particularly interested in Hymenoptera.'
> 'Have you made me a collection to show me?'
> 'Yes, but I have none with me to show you because there are many thousands of specimens in the collection. I came here for an interview and could not bring such a large collection.'
> 'Well, young man, if we take you on here, you will not work on Hymenoptera, and you will do exactly as you are told to do.'
> Perkins said that finished things right there!" *(From interview of R.C.L. Perkins by E.C. Zimmerman in August 1949, E.C. Zimmerman letter to N.L. Evenhuis, 20 November 2002).*

Perkins then became a private tutor at Dartmouth, while specializing in the study of the local Hymenoptera, which he continued the remainder of his life. In 1891, while still a tutor, at the urging of colleague Walter Garstang, he answered the request for applicants to go to the Hawaiian Islands to conduct a zoological survey there. In January 1892 he was chosen and asked if he could get his things

---

6   Poulton, [Sir] Edward Bagnall (1856–1943). British-born zoologist and Hope Professor of Zoology at Oxford University, specializing in the meaning of colors of animals. Poulton was a foremost exponent of evolution and was said to be forgiving of his students for almost anything except disbelief in the doctrine of evolution. He was a keen collector and nicknamed by some as Edward "Bag-All" Poulton. Although never producing a *magnum opus*, his scientific reputation was well known and he garnered many awards, fellowships, and the accolades of his colleagues as well as knighthood in 1935 for his contribution to science.

together for a February departure. Without having ever previously left southern England and Wales, the 25-year-old Perkins gathered together literature and field supplies, obtained letters of introduction, and crossed two oceans to begin the adventure of a lifetime.

PUTTING PERKINS IN CONTEXT

Just who was this man who became the first person to survey the zoology of the Hawaiian Islands? Perkins's continual shyness (rarely posing for photographs) and his humble nature (always downplaying his contributions to science) make it rather difficult to describe him or his personality with any sort of accurate detail.

Assistance comes from those who knew him and/or wrote of him. Former Bishop Museum employee and Hawaiian Sugar Planters' Association (HSPA) colleague, Elwood C. Zimmerman, describes an elderly Perkins in the following from his notes made when he met Perkins in England in 1949 and 1950:

> "Perkins was a very small man. He came up to my chin. I suppose about 5'2". Large nose with prominent red veins. Eyes large, whites yellowed. Hair white, bald down middle leaving heavy fringe on sides. white moustached, untrimmed. Claims about 5'6" (was shorter when I saw him) and top weight 104 lbs with clothes on.
>   Rarely sits down; even writes standing up. Numerous medicine bottles in house & a pile of empty mineral oil bottles in outside shed (chronic constipation; says result of work in Hawaii). Drinks warm milk, neither tea nor coffee." (*E.C. Zimmerman letter to N.L. Evenhuis, 20 November 2002*).

An immigration form filled out by Perkins at Ellis Island in New York on 26 November 1911 on a trip made back from England to Hawai'i, has him described as 5 ft. 4 1/2 in. with black hair and brown eyes (*Ellis Island Archives*).

George C. Munro,[7] a close friend of many years related a few anecdotes in unpublished notes concerning Perkins. In these notes, we find the things that are not revealed in either Perkins's re-penned journal entries, his remembrances, or correspondence. Things such as that Perkins was an avid storyteller and had a sense of humor that engendered the friendship and affection of those who got to know him.

> "Perkins had a keen sense of humor and a droll way of telling his stories. We enjoyed his company very much. I once criticised his English. He said it was not necessary to pay attention to his language as few people would know the difference." (*BPBM Archives, MS SC Munro Box 13.2*).

In all of the notes, letters, and published accounts, one thing about Perkins's personality comes through clearly. He was an extremely passionate scientist with an incredible memory and sense of observation. He may have had a droll sense of humor in social situations, but when he put pen to paper, he was all business.

---

7   Munro, George Campbell (1866–1963). Ornithologist; later ranch manager on Moloka'i and Lāna'i and conservationist. Born near Auckland, New Zealand the same year as Perkins (1866), Munro came to Hawai'i as the assistant of Lord Rothschild's bird collector Henry Palmer. The two collected from 1890–1892 starting in Kaua'i and then the Northwestern Hawaiian Islands. In 1892, a year before Palmer left, Munro decided to stay and made a home in Makaweli, Kaua'i. Perkins's visit to Munro on Kaua'i in 1894 resulted in a close friendship between the two; one that lasted a lifetime. Munro hosted Perkins whenever he came to Kaua'i and had a tiny room especially for him. Munro made his diary available to Perkins, who used it to familiarize himself with the localities in which he planned to collect.

Bishop Museum Archives

Robert Cyril Layton Perkins (1866–1955). Picture on left taken 1907. Picture at right taken in 1949.

PERKINS IN HAWAIʻI

Soon after his arrival in Hawaiʻi in the spring of 1892, Perkins went to the Waiʻanae Mountains of leeward Oʻahu to collect. While there he tried riding horses but apparently had a bad time of it and came back to the Eagle House, a boarding house on Nuʻuanu Avenue near downtown Honolulu, sore and chaffed from the experience. Munro related the following:

> "I first met Perkins in Honolulu in April 1892 when I was starting for New Zealand to get married and return to the Islands. He had just come in from Waianae on horseback. He was quite unused to this mode of travel and was skinned for the whole inside of his legs so he told me." (*BPBM Archives, MS SC Munro Box 13.2*).

Perkins himself gave the details of this experience:

> "I had nothing to do with horses previously {previous to his trip to Hawaiʻi Island} & remember my first ride—to Waialua—the next back from there to Honolulu & some days after from town to Waianae! The journey back from the latter place was the day after a torrential rain, the trail deep in red mud, & one of the ordinarily dry gulches was in spate, so when our horses (I had a native with me) were persuaded to jump in, they had to swim & we were wet up to the neck. I always hated riding after those two first trips." *(R.C.L. Perkins letter to E.C. Zimmerman, 14 February 1944, BPBM Entomology Archives).*

In June, after a few months' orientation to Hawaii's fauna on Oʻahu, Perkins traveled to Kona on the island of Hawaiʻi (Big Island) to collect birds. He tried his luck with horses once again; but apparently this also proved a failure.

> "Perkins when he went to Hawaii bought a horse. He rode it once or twice and then abandoned it and did all his mountain travelling on foot. Albert Judd told me an amusing story the Greenwells told him about Perkins's attempts to ride. He was so active on his feet and

a horse is an impediment in forest work he decided he was better without it." (*G.C. Munro notes, BPBM Archives, MS SC Munro Box 13.2*).[8]

After those events, Perkins shunned any offer of riding horses (he did use them for packing in supplies on long trips) and hiked on foot to almost every locality he could. His ability to hike to even the most remote collecting areas amazed everyone, especially the Hawaiians, who were used to visitors and even resident *haoles*[9] using horses or carriages whenever they could. He often had to clear his own trails when making his way to his camps deep in the rainforests.

> "It is hard to realize now the conditions under which I worked, from 1892 to 1897 particularly. Roads were bad, often impassible in wet weather, and I did most of my work on foot. I cut many paths myself single-handed through the densest wet forests, sometimes 8 or 9 miles in length, and lumped tent, guns, and all apparatus and food on my back in such places." (*R.C.L. Perkins letter to T.D.A. Cockerell, October 1924, quoted in* The Nautilus *38(3): 77*).

Lady Luck apparently attended Perkins on a frequent basis. One day while hunting birds in the thick, humid rainforests of East Moloka'i in the summer of 1893, Perkins lost his footing and slipped down a steep slope, eventually ending up more than 2000 feet down into the normally inaccessible Pelekunu Valley. Unfazed about being at the bottom of a nonscalable cliff-like wall of mosses and ferns and slightly bruised and scraped, he walked downstream and across waterfalls until he came upon some native Hawaiians (*kānaka*), who were shocked and could not believe that he was alone in such a place. They kept looking behind Perkins for others. A white man alone in that valley was unheard of.

> "About one-third of the way down I was walking along an apparently good piece, not steep, with bushes on my left and a pali[10] (or nearly) on the right. My gun was in my left hand, the axe in my right. The ridge here was overgrown with fern and I suddenly stepped on nothing, where a landslide had taken place on the right side, unnoticed by me. I naturally dropped both gun and axe and the former rested in the bushes, but the latter fell over the edge I heard it, or stones that it dislodged, striking the bed of the steam below. The ferns I grabbed hold of were stag-horn and tough and I pulled myself up carefully till my chest was well on top and all was well, except for my axe, which I made no attempt to recover. I went slower and carefully after this. Viewed from beneath, it looks like a steep climb up. On reaching the stream I waded down for some distance and then came to a small waterfall and did not know whether to drop down this on spec., to reach the coast. As the fall was smooth and perpendicular I went back, and found I could get further on by going quite high up another ridge and striking the stream lower down. From this point I waded straight down the stream till I came on some kanakas. For a long time I could not convince these that I was alone and when I told them was from Kaunakakai, they, said, no malahini[11] could find his way from there and kept looking back to see if others were coming behind me!" (*R.C.L. Perkins journal entry, 13 July 1893, BPBM Archives, MS Group 141 Box 3*).

---

[8]   The fact that Munro remembered this and other misfortunes with horses by Perkins may have been because Munro and his wife were avid horse riders themselves and were known to win awards for their riding skills at various public events on Kaua'i.

[9]   *Haole* — Hawaiian term for Caucasian people. The term literally means "stranger" but is usually reserved for westerners of pale complexion.

[10]   *Pali* — Hawaiian meaning cliff.

[11]   *Malahini* — Hawaiian meaning newcomer or visitor.

Perkins in his mid-20s and early 30s was an extremely fit man and his successful efforts on foot were a pride to him. Despite the ruggedness of the Hawaiian rainforests, he often arrived at a camp or mountain house before others in his party, who might have even been on horseback.

> "Drove to Waiawa and thence walked up from Mr. Knudsen's house to Halemanu. Mr. K. says the measured distance is 18 miles, but I hardly think it can be as great, elevation about 4,000 ft. ... I left Mr. K's house at 10.15 a.m. and reached the mountain house at 2 p.m. nearly, though Munro told me he thought it would take six hours." (*R.C.L. Perkins journal entry, 7 May 1895, BPBM Archives, MS SC Perkins Box 1*).

A few months after arriving in Hawai'i, Perkins was in the Kona area of the Big Island collecting on the western slopes on Mauna Loa, which are characteristically covered with sharp clinker lava flows called *'a'ā*. This rubble-like ground cover is not only treacherous to any confident footing, but the razor sharp edges of the *'a'ā* can do quick damage to the foot coverings of the uninitiated. It was only a matter of days before the boots Perkins wore were torn to shreds. Instead of spending more of the Committee's scant funds to purchase more boots, he opted to go barefoot while collecting. This proved so successful, that he continued his barefoot collecting throughout most of his sojourn in the wilds of Hawaii's forests, to the amusement and concern of his sponsors and family:

> "... glad we both are to find you writing so cheerfully — even when you are going barefoot. It is well that you mention that fact, for if we ask for any more money we shall be able to make our appeal all the more touching! But I really suppose that boots of some kind are to be had, if you cared to have them, only you possibly may prefer following the practice of old Waterton & G.R. Crotch—who thought them unnecessary restraints." (*A. Newton letter to R.C.L. Perkins, 20 August 1892, BPBM Archives, MS Group 141 Box 3*).

> "This brings me to the question of your want of boots. I do not think it is very wise to go about barefooted because of the risk of getting a serious wound of the feet. Do you think you would like to try the canvas slippers with rope soles that they use so much in the Pyrenees of Spain? They cost very little, {and} will stand a deal of knocking about." (*D. Sharp letter to R.C.L. Perkins, 19 August 1892, BPBM Archives, MS Group 141 Box 2*).

> "By the way I forgot to mention that in the case I dispatched to you there were 2 or 3 pairs of shoes and some other little things sent you by Mr. & Mrs. Perkins." (*D. Sharp letter to R.C.L. Perkins, 13 July 1893, BPBM Archives, MS Group 141, Box 2*).

Once Perkins arrived at a collecting locality deep in the forest or at a remote mountain home, he entered his own special "world" and immediately went to work, collecting birds and insects by day and insects at light by night.[12]

> "Perkins's collector's enthusiasm was so strong that on dark nights when his powerful light attracted many moths and other insects he worked all night, forgetting to eat or sleep." (Munro, G.C., 1956, *Elepaio* 17(3): 19–20).

Perkins preferred collecting alone in the rainforests above the cleared lower slopes as he felt that an assistant would be both an impediment to his work and added expense to his already meager finances. Perkins had to pack in his equipment and food, including even a stove and a supply of oil, as the continuous rain often made

---

[12] In Perkins's time, this method of collecting by light involved the use of a lantern placed near a vertical surface (a wall or a window). The light from the lantern attracted insects and they would land on the nearby vertical surface. The collector would collect the insects as soon as they landed.

it difficult or even impossible to start a fire after a long day of collecting.

"I have done all my rough work myself nearly i.e., cooking, hauling wood, cutting through the dense forests, pack carrying where a horse can't go &c &c for nearly 5 years. I much prefer to camp entirely alone to having natives & nearly always do so. Besides it much lessens the expense which is great enough anyhow!" (*R.C.L. Perkins letter to E.B. Poulton, 27 January 1897, Oxford University Museum of Natural History Library Archives*).

"{When camping in a tent he} made mattresses of Styphelia & put ferns on top to make a bed about 2 feet high. He used to find carabids under the mat after it had decayed a bit. He used Wikstroemia rope to carry his pack in the mountains. He slept in his clothes.

He used an A-tent he got from S.F. after about 9 months in Hawaii. He had no tent on Oahu {1892} but had it with him when he went to Molokai {May 1893}. He often used only a 'fly' canvas. At Walsingham's request, he killed all Lepidoptera with ammonia. He pinned the moths and blew out the wings. He often laid on his belly behind his beating sheet to pin the moths." (*Notes from interview of R.C.L. Perkins by E.C. Zimmerman, August 1949, E.C. Zimmerman letter to N.L. Evenhuis, 23 November 2002*).

"I used an umbrella at first for beating, but smashed up a number, & sometimes had to rig up some sort of a beating cloth as best I could." (*R.C.L. Perkins letter to E.C. Zimmerman, 20 June 1937, BPBM Entomology Archives*).

In his rain-soaked Makakupa'ia campsite on Moloka'i at about the 5,000-foot level, Perkins thought he could solve the problem of muddy ground beneath his tent by digging a moat surrounding the tent. Unfortunately, the rain was so heavy and constant during his three-month stay there that even this did not keep the ground dry; so he often sat on a bed of dried fern fronds over the muddy ground beneath his tent while skinning birds or pinning his insects at night. Fumbling a small insect specimen into the fronds usually meant it was lost forever.

His seriousness when in the field collecting birds, insects, or other invertebrates is probably best exemplified by his terse entry in the Volcano House memoirs book of 25 July 1894 when he visited the Big Island. While others' lengthy handwritten entries above and below his spoke in ebullient terms of the beauty of the area and the majestic views offered by the Kīlauea volcano (erupting constantly making it a sensational vacation spot for visitors), Perkins's entry was very business-like and to the point:

"In two mornings I shot the following birds near the Volcano House: 1. Iiwi; 2. Apapane; 3. Amakihi; 4. Akikiki; 5. Akialoa; 6. Elepaio; 7. Olomao (= Omao = Kamao); 8. Akakane.
— R.C.L. Perkins, for Royal Soc. & British Association, 25 July 1894."
(*Hawaii Volcanoes National Park Archives*).

Despite his fervor when in the field, he remained conservative — possibly too much so — in the numbers of birds and insects he collected, much to his regret in later years:

"A weak point in me as a collector was that I was not such a killer as would have been advantageous! This applies to birds & other creatures as well as insects. I was quite horrified when my friend Henshaw told me that he wanted 'a hundred or two' of the little fly-catcher on the island of Hawaii — the famous 'elepaio' of the old natives, who would not, or at least did not like to kill this bird. They would never shoot a Pueo either, nor would they handle the opeapea (bat) when I shot one. Naturally I killed a very large number of some insect species, because in the field I could not be sure of what were species, but I did not carry this far enough as I now see, in many cases. I could have easily taken thousands of Nysius e.g. in all sorts of localities." *(R.C.L. Perkins letter to E.C. Zimmerman, 21 November 1948, BPBM Entomology Archives).*

Perkins's love of Greek and Latin traveled with him to Hawai'i. In addition to keeping himself entertained in the evenings of camping alone in the Hawaiian rainforests by reciting Greek and Latin poetry, his first diaries were written in Latin.

PERKINS AND THE BISHOP MUSEUM

At the time of Perkins's arrival in Hawai'i in March 1892, the Bishop Museum had just recently opened its doors to the public (June 1891). Perkins was quick to make arrangements to see the collections housed at the Bishop Museum and had already made contact with its founder, Charles Reed Bishop, upon his arrival in the islands. He also contacted its first curator and later first director, Dr. William T. Brigham,[13] a Harvard University Professor with interests in anthropology, botany, and ornithology. Perkins visited Brigham and the museum on various occasions in the first years he was in the Islands to check bird and insect specimens.

Bishop's support of Perkins was in distinct contrast to the jealousy that Brigham had for Perkins in the later years that Perkins worked on the *Fauna Hawaiiensis.* While Bishop was supporting the fieldwork of Perkins financially and additionally asking Brigham to assist with getting Perkins a gun and a dog, correspondence showed that Brigham had little good to say about Perkins to his Hawai'i colleagues and employers (even calling him "boy" in his letters to Bishop). Bishop was more laudatory of Perkins's abilities and at one time called Perkins "the best naturalist to have ever visited these islands" and felt that he was a far superior collector than the bird collectors Wilson or Palmer (Kent, H.W., 1965, *Charles Reed Bishop, Man of Hawaii*, p. 205). Brigham gave Perkins little help, never acknowledged his merit, and had little or no interest in his entomological or ornithological endeavors:

> "He could give me no information at all about the birds, nor about the insects and knew nothing of Blackburn's fine work here. This was as I expected, for he was in communication with the Committee before I was sent out, when it was hoped the museum here would participate, and wrote to them that he had been all over the islands, that it was no use sending out an entomologist, as there were no native insects, but only a few American species." *(R.C.L. Perkins journal entry, 28 October 1892, BPBM Archives, MS SC Perkins 141 Box 1)*

Brigham's declaration to the Sandwich Islands Committee of Hawai'i having no native insects was an incredibly naïve claim. Hawai'i is today known to be home to over 5200 species of insects found nowhere else in the world.[14]

---

[13] Brigham, William Tufts (1841–1926). Curator and first director of the Bernice P. Bishop Museum in Honolulu. Best known as an ethnologist specializing in ancient Hawaiian worship, Brigham was born in Boston and graduated from Harvard University with a Master's degree in 1865. He taught botany at Harvard and also taught at O'ahu College before coming to the Bishop Museum in 1889, where he was appointed curator and led some of the Museum's first scientific expeditions. During his "colorful" tenure at the Museum he had ongoing and often heated disputes with Trustees leading to his resigning a few times (always ending in him relenting and coming back). In addition, he was belligerent with staff, a social and racial bigot, and a misanthrope. Despite these shortcomings, he became the Museum's first director in 1897 and remained in that position until he retired in 1919 when Dr. Herbert Gregory became the Museum's director. During his retirement, he maintained an office at the Museum where he continued his work as emeritus director until his death in 1926.

[14] Eldredge, L.G. & Evenhuis, N.L., 2003, *Bishop Museum Occasional Papers* 76: 1–28.

Brigham's often vitriolic and erratic behavior resulted in him threatening to quit the Museum a number of times. During these episodes Bishop and a few others beseeched the advice of others in the operation of the museum. Perkins's advice was sought at that time and he gladly offered his opinions, though couched in careful terms so as to avoid conflict with Brigham. Bishop wrote of Perkins to Museum Trustee, the Rev. Charles McEwen Hyde on 22 January 1897:

> "You know that Mr. Perkins is about to leave the islands. He is thoroughly scientific, and may have some views about the Museum and what should be its aim, that may be of value, and that he may be willing to express to you and the other Trustees. He may not be willing to oppose openly any of Mr. Brigham for he is very modest and loves peace." (*Bishop Museum Archives, MS Pauahi, C.R. Bishop letters, Kent Coll. Book 13*).

During one of Brigham's fits later that same year and again quitting the Museum, Perkins was briefly considered as a possible replacement for Brigham, having been supported strongly by George Munro and David Sharp. Trustee Hyde inquired about Perkins's interest in the position. Perkins politely refused a directorship on the grounds that he had no experience in ethnology but said he could be useful in dealing with the zoological matters.

> "When he {Brigham} resigned on one occasion Dr. Hyde came to me & asked if I would take his place & I told him at once that the Museum was primarily an ethnological one & that I was no ethnologist but was capable of directing any zoological work, & could do so under an ethnologist. Dr. Hyde for some reason was offended at this & began his reply to me 'as you will not help us'. Of course Brigham did not keep to his resignation & I never expected him to do so!" (*R.C.L. Perkins letter to G.C. Munro, 20 May 1948, BPBM Archives, MS SC Munro Box 13.3*).

A few years before the Brigham resignation episode above, some unfortunate comments by Smithsonian hymenopterist William Ashmead regarding what he considered poor care of the insects in the Bishop Museum caused a rift between Brigham and Perkins that would never be repaired.

> "Ashmead's criticism of the handling of the insects at the Museum was ill advised as it appeared in the daily newspapers. I dont wonder that Brigham was enraged! Dr. Hyde came to me & said he wanted me & Koebele,[15] as being the only entomologists, to go and examine the collections & report to the trustees & I went very unwillingly with him & Koebele. Brigham was very rude & showed us nothing & we made no report. After this he cordially detested both myself & K.! & in fact he had no use for entomologists anymore & dont think I ever visited the Museum again, though during my earlier years of collecting I went there frequently, besides reporting to him at the end of any lengthy trip to the other islands." (*R.C.L. Perkins letter to G.C. Munro, 20 May 1948, BPBM Archives, MS SC Munro Box 13.3*).

Perkins's work for the Sandwich Islands Committee came to an end in late 1901 but he stayed on in Hawai'i in the employ of the territorial government and finally the Hawaii Sugar Planters' Association. Before his employment with the terri-

---

15 Koebele, Albert (1852–1924). German-born, Koebele came to work for government entomologist C.V. Riley in Washington, DC in 1881, then soon moved to California, where he garnered fame for his work in the biological control of *Icerya purchasi*, the cottony cushion scale, a major pest of citrus. As a result of not getting along with his government colleague Daniel W. Coquillett, then also in California, Koebele resigned and went to work for the Hawaiian government in 1893. He met Perkins in 1895 and joined him on many field trips on O'ahu as well as other islands. Subsequently, while on the staff of the HSPA he became successful in finding biological control organisms in south Pacific countries to bring back to Hawai'i to help control pests of Hawaiian agriculture. He traveled to Australia with Perkins in 1904 in search of biological control agents of cane pests to bring back to Hawai'i.

torial government, Perkins had a brief stint as a schoolteacher for the Pauoa Public School in Honolulu, where he was considered a "superior teacher with a wonderful memory and a keen mind. He was nicknamed by his students 'Birdie'"[16] (Kent, H.W., 1965, *Charles Reed Bishop, Man of Hawaii*, p. 207).

PERSONAL LIFE IN HAWAI'I

One of the biggest mysteries about Perkins was his social and personal life during and after his trips to Hawai'i. Few of his personal letters survive. He married Zoë Atkinson, daughter of prominent Honolulu resident, Alatau Atkinson, superintendent of public schools in Hawai'i and editor of the Honolulu newspapers the *Hawaiian Gazette* and *Hawaiian Star*. Zoë, born in England in 1868 before the Atkinson family moved to Hawai'i, was the eldest of the four Atkinson girls. The girls were well-known socialites by the time Perkins arrived in Honolulu. Zoë had been a teacher in Hawai'i since 1887 and was headmistress at the Pohukaina Girls School adjacent to 'Iolani Palace. Along with her sisters, she got positive reviews for acting in various operas at the new Opera House in Honolulu. In 1891, Zoë became a social coordinator for Queen Lili'uokalani. The Queen often wished to show her thanks to various people for gifts she had received and Zoë organized grand royal receptions and galas in their honor, some featuring piano recitals by Zoë. Perkins must have made a lasting impression with his antics at a royal reception after meeting the Queen, as told by Munro:

> When presented to the Queen {he} fell over chairs when backing away (*BPBM Archives, MS SC Munro Box 13.2*).

Even his wedding to Zoë in 1901 involved some shenanigans. Again Munro relates the story:

> "Zoe was determined that her father would not beggar himself to give her a wedding as he had had to do with the others.[17] He had practically to invite all of the old missionary and plantation crowd. So she and Perkins played a trick and found him called suddenly to England and he had to rush out to Haleiwa Hotel where she was at the time and get a Hawaiian parson to wed them. He would be saying "aye" when he didn't know what the parson was asking him." (*BPBM Archives, MS SC Munro Box 13.2*).

Perkins added a few more details about a rather last-minute decision to get married:

> "Our marriage was determined on very suddenly as it took place here {Waialua} on Friday night & we only made up our minds the day before! We came out because Mr & Mrs A. were staying here already & they knew nothing about it until I arrived at noon on Friday to make the necessary arrangements, my wife coming on the evening train, then we were

---

[16] Although lifelong friends with G.C. Munro and having had over 10 years worth of correspondence with Sharp and Newton and his colleagues at HSPA, all letters from Perkins to his friends and colleagues were invariably signed "R.C.L. Perkins." He was known to his colleagues as "Perkins," but a few letters from friends, relatives, and in-laws give evidence that he had a few nicknames: "Perks" was one and his brother's children knew him as "Uncle Bob." Zimmerman referred to him as "Perk."

[17] Her sisters: Kapiolani ("Lani") Atkinson, who married British Navy Lt. (later Captain) Frederick K.C. Gibbons in October 1895 and lived in England; Mary Kathlccn ("Mollie") Atkinson, who married Samuel Wilder, Jr., son of the owner of the Wilder Steamship Company, in July 1896; and Ethel May ("Maisie") Alatau Atkinson, who married lawyer Arthur Morgan Brown (listed as "Marshall of the Republic" in the marriage announcement of the *Hawaiian Gazette*) in August 1897 and eventually moved to Hilo on the Big Island.

married at once in the hotel by the kanaka farm!" *(R.C.L. Perkins letter to George Munro, 6 October 1901, BPBM Archives, MS SC Munro Box 13.4).*

During his relationship with Zoë, Perkins was conspicuously absent from the various public social affairs that Zoë attended, many of which made the pages of the local newspapers. Zoë and her sisters were among the most eligible bachelorettes in Honolulu. Their attendance at tennis events at the Pacific Club; socials and teas at the homes of prominent Honolulu businessmen, government officials, and foreign dignitaries; and the numerous weddings of the Honolulu social elite were all noted in detail in the newspapers, even including what gowns they wore. Perkins may well have been "out of his league" in pursuing the attention of the popular young Zoë since those mentioned in the local papers as being seen with her were eligible bachelors of notable rank in society, business, and government. Despite his apparent popularity in the local press (the papers frequently kept up with the various travels of Perkins and let their readers know where he was off to next or where he just arrived), it was undoubtedly not proper for a young woman of such high social station to be seen with a field biologist who might have just wandered in from the muddy rainforests after trying to catch moths or ground beetles.

"{Zoë} was a very good dancer & had by the Queen's request got together a group of young Honoluluites to dance the old-fashioned minuet (?spelling!) in the palace or palace grounds. I do not know the names of most, if any of the performers, except Zoë, as in my earlier collecting days I had no contact with Society Folk!" *(R.C.L. Perkins letter to Mrs. E.C. Zimmerman, 4 January 1950, BPBM Entomology Archives).*

In spite of the apparent differences of social status between the two, they did indeed get together, obviously got along quite well, and Perkins was even able to devise a way to mix business with pleasure in order to have some time together with Zoë —theoretically without the hovering of journalists. Although he may have thought that he would avoid the nosy Honolulu newspaper reporters by making arrangements to be on neighbor islands with Zoë, the news items still appeared, though tactfully withholding an explicit association between the two. On at least two occasions, Zoë and Perkins were spotted at Kīlauea's Volcano House and mention was made in the gossip pages.

Perkins became engaged to Zoë Atkinson in April 1896 and he told friends and acquaintances:

Mr. Perkins called this afternoon and announced his engagement to Miss Zoe Atkinson *(Christina Greenwell diary, 6 April 1896, BPBM Archives, MS Document 343).*

Whether planned or not, the engagement was a bit protracted. A little less than a year after he announced his engagement to Zoë, Perkins returned to England (March 1897) to work on his collections of the last five years and sort specimens to send to specialists, not knowing for sure if funds could be secured to allow him to return once again to Hawai'i.

After a few years in England, funds were indeed obtained, and in May 1900 Perkins arrived back in Hawai'i and finished his collecting for the Committee in little over one year. It was near the end of that eighteen-month sojourn (October 1901) that he finally married Zoë.

Perkins and Zoë had four sons. Their first, Robert (January 1903–May 1903), died in childhood in Hawai'i from ptomaine poisoning. The second son, Richard (1904–1985), was born in Hawai'i, while the third, Charles Mathew (1905–1989) was born on board ship while Zoë was en route to England. The youngest, John Frederick ("Jack") (1910–1989), was born in England.

Richard became an excellent photographer of ships in England, worked for a time as assistant editor of *Jane's Fighting Ships*, and eventually donated his collection of negatives to the National Maritime Museum. In the 1950s he and his wife Dorothy lived with Perkins and took care of him during his last years when he became bedridden.

Charles, a design engineer by profession, studied at the Massachusetts Institute of Technology and soon after completing his studies spent some time in Honolulu with the Oahu Plantation from the late 1920s till the early 1930s. He was seriously injured in a car accident in Hawai'i and travelled to England to recover at his father's home in Devon. He later moved to Cleveland, Ohio and then Royal Oak (near Detroit), Michigan, and finally retired to Phoenix, Arizona. Charles was chief engineer with the Fuller Manufacturing Company in Michigan in the 1950s and introduced a new transmission design in 1963 to wide acclaim. He retired in 1973 but stayed on as a consultant to that company and its successor Eaton (K. Ludvigsen, *in litt.*).

John, youngest of the Perkins sons, followed in his father's footsteps—becoming a hymenopterist (specializing in Ichneumonidae) —and worked at the British Museum (Natural History). At his retirement in 1973 he was Deputy Keeper of Entomology.

AFTER *FAUNA HAWAIIENSIS*

The extensive experience Perkins had gained while in the field in Hawai'i during his work for the Sandwich Islands Committee made him a logical choice by the Territorial Government to appoint him as Assistant Entomologist for the Board of Commissioners of Agriculture and Forestry in 1902. While there, he worked with Albert Koebele on biological control options for *Lantana*, which was a serious weed in the open areas of the islands. It is interesting to note that, as today, even in those times visitors considered the sight of the colorful lantana blossoms a thing of beauty and not an invasive pest as did residents of the Islands.

> "The ride to 'The Pali' was glorious .... Taro patches, running streams of pure water, and high elevations of land on either hand ... the way was bordered with flowers, and the deserted places with lantana blossoms, yellow and purple intermixed, as thickly as sometimes the fields of New England, when clad in their autumn robes of white-capped buckwheat bloom." *(*Burnett, C. 1892, *Land of the o-o*, p. 152*).*

However, it was his capture of a cane leafhopper at a light in his room in Waialua in 1900 while collecting for the Sandwich Islands Committee that led to his next job. That capture and his identification of further specimens and a resulting report in November 1902 of the seriousness of this highly injurious insect to sugarcane led to the establishment of a Division of Entomology in the Hawaii Sugar Planters' Association (HSPA). Perkins was selected as the first Superintendent of that division and under his direct supervision were three entomologists who were later to become legends of Hawaiian entomology: Otto H. Swezey,[18] G.W. Kirkaldy,[19] and F.W. Terry.[20] Additionally, two consulting entomologists were also attached to this division, Alexander Craw and the famous biocontrol entomologist, Albert Koebele, the latter who worked closely with Perkins after their first meeting in 1895. Perkins and Koebele traveled together collecting insects on many of the Hawaiian Islands and went to Australia together in 1904 to secure potential candidates for use as biological control agents against the sugarcane leafhopper in the islands.

When first employed by HSPA, Perkins lived on Bates Street, not too far from the first place he spent the night in 1892—the Eagle Hotel—which was located at the time a few blocks away on Nuʻuanu Avenue. A few years after returning to live in England, he was told that his old Bates Street home was being occupied by legendary Bishop Museum anthropologist, Kenneth Emory and his wife. It is a distinct coincidence that the same residence would be called home by Hawaii's preeminent zoologist and next by Hawaii's preeminent anthropologist. The Bates home still stands today, with some external modifications to the original. In 1906, Perkins moved to a home on Kewalo Street—a short walk from the HSPA headquarters—where he lived for another three years.

Perkins began his work for HSPA with the establishment of its Division of Entomology in 1904. He continued working for HSPA and living in Hawaiʻi but after 1906 began taking six months leave each year to go back to England. Ill health finally forced him to move from Hawaiʻi to England in 1909. There was talk of the chance at a job opening at his *alma mater*, Oxford University, but it never came to fruition. He also was considered for David Sharp's position at Cambridge but Perkins thought the pay too meager to accept.

Perkins always had an avid interest in Hawaiian entomology but had little regard for Hawaiʻi as a place to live or rear his children. Ironically, although he and Zoë taught while in Hawaiʻi and Zoë's father was at one time the superintendent of the

---

[18] Swezey, Otto Herman (1869–1959). Swezey was employed by the Hawaii Sugar Planters' Association in 1904, becoming the first American to be employed by a private company. He remained with them until his retirement in 1933. While in the employ of the HSPA, he became curator of entomology at the Bishop Museum and founded its entomology section in 1907. Along with Kirkaldy and Terry, the three worked on leafhoppers and their natural enemies.

[19] Kirkaldy, George Willis (1873–1910). Hemipterist. Kirkaldy was a passionate worker and prolific writer, publishing more than 40 papers on Hawaiian Hemiptera in the short 7 years he was in Hawaiʻi. He broke a leg falling off of a horse in 1909 and had several unsuccessful operations to reset the leg in Honolulu. While vacationing in San Francisco, he took the opportunity to try again to reset the leg in hopes of having better doctors there. The operation was successful at first. Unfortunately, gangrene set in and he later died from the infection.

   Perkins did not have much good to say about Kirkaldy and his views are best summarized in later correspondence: "Kirkaldy when he came out to the islands as one of my assistants under the Board of Agriculture had no idea of the value of specimens. He thought that anything he had described was finished with! I told him the specimens were far more valuable than anything he or I wrote in the F.H.! & he realized this later when he was at work on his Supplement & when I went over to England in 1907 he asked me to examine a large number of his types contained in the collection that Sharp kept there, some of these having certainly suffered while in his possession." (*R.C.L. Perkins letter to E.C. Zimmerman, 1 November 1948, BPBM Entomology Archives*).

[20] Terry, Frank Wray (1877–1911). Born in England, Terry worked briefly at the British Museum (Natural History) as a preparator in entomology. He was employed at the Hawaii Territorial Board of Agriculture in 1903 and was transferred to HSPA at the same time as Perkins (1904) working there on economic entomology until his untimely death in 1911. While on vacation in England in the summer of that year, Terry contracted pleuropneumonia. He died a few months later in the care of his aunt in New York City.

public schools in Hawai'i, Perkins did not have a favorable opinion about the educational system in the islands.

"I am tired of the islands in many ways, but particularly because I miss the society of the kind of people one meets all the time in a place like Cambridge or Oxford. Moreover, I should like to get the children out of the country while they are still small. I have no belief in the education, or anything of that sort out here." (*R.C.L. Perkins letter to G.C. Munro, 2 April 1908, BPBM Archives, MS SC Munro Box 13.4*)

Ironically, many years later in England he reminisced pleasantly and possibly with tongue-in-cheek about the "good old days" of Hawai'i:

"I certainly liked the old Hawaii best when the side walks (or at least many of them) were made of raised boards, often with holes in them through which one might put ones foot, & the street cars were drawn by mules." (*R.C.L. Perkins letter to Mrs. E.C. Zimmerman, 10 January 1950, BPBM Registrar Archives*).

He returned to Hawai'i a few times after 1909, the last was a trip alone for a few months in the summer of 1912 to complete his work on the introduction for the *Fauna Hawaiiensis.*

"That 'Introduction' was a very hurried piece of work & I wrote a good deal of it on the steamers when on a visit to England; also from this hurried writing there are several things that need correction. The proofs were sent to me to Honolulu {when he was not there, but in England}, but before I returned the final proofsheets, the work had been printed, so the corrections were never made." (*R.C.L. Perkins letter to E.C. Zimmerman, 17 February 1944, BPBM Entomology Archives*).

Despite the letters to colleagues and friends in which he mentioned a possible return visit to Hawai'i after the 1912 visit, he never did. Although no longer in Hawai'i, Perkins was still kept on the HSPA payroll as a consultant until his death. During World War II, when funds could not go directly from the US to England, his paychecks were instead funneled to him via Australia so that he could continue his work for HSPA during that time.

Moving back to England was no small chore. Packing up all of the books, insects, and other things that Perkins had acquired during his sojourn in Hawai'i plus all of the belongings that Zoë owned, including the royal gifts given to her during her employ under the Queen, would require many large packing crates to travel the distance across two oceans as well as the transcontinental trip via rail across the United States. Added to these personal belongings and collections were the almost 2,500 thick wax disks that formed the large collection of pre-electric phonograph records, especially those of operas, that he and his family so loved to listen to on their Gramophone.

"I got a Grammophone {sic} some time ago. I have quite a lot of records. As we have no musical instruments in the home, it is a source of a good deal of pleasure to us, to listen to the songs played by others." (*R.C.L. Perkins letter to George Munro, 20 May 1903, BPBM Archives, MS SC Munro Box 13.4*).

As he had done successfully for all of his shipments of collected specimens during his work for the Sandwich Islands Committee, Perkins used Wells Fargo for this "final" shipment from Hawai'i to England. Upon arrival, Perkins examined the contents of the crates. As he had expected from his years of experience in using this company, nothing had been damaged in transit.

In November 1909, soon after arrival in England, Perkins and family moved into the Devon area and lived at Park Hill House in Paignton, a substantial multi-story residence with numerous rooms, servant's quarters in the rear, and a small fruit orchard.

> "We leave this house {Derwent, Cleveland Road, Paignton} in two weeks, when my address will be Park Hill House, Paignton, Devon. I have taken that house for three years for my family and it has been a good deal of expense furnishing it. It has a lovely fruit garden, the best in Paignton, peaches, nectarines, grapes, etc. are there this summer by the cart load, while pears, apples, and small fruits are still more plentiful, so it will be nice for the children next year." (*R.C.L. Perkins letter to W.M. Giffard, 25 October 1909, BPBM Archives, MS Group 141 Box 3*).

> "The house is old, which is all the better, as they don't build these thick walls now-a-days to keep out the cold and it has all the modern conveniences in the way of bathrooms, etc. ... I like having lots of empty rooms for laboratory work, my collections, fishing rods, etc." (*R.C.L. Perkins letter to W.M. Giffard, 14 November 1909, BPBM Archives, MS Group 141 Box 3*).

The Devon area was no doubt the place of choice for Perkins for many reasons: it was relatively near to his father's residence in Alderley in Gloucestershire (whom he visited often); it was near some of his favorite boyhood haunts in Gloucestershire (Sopworth, Wotton-under-Edge, Badminton); and it had a wealth of streams that proved to be a major requirement for his daily routine: every morning Perkins would head out to a local stream and bring back fish for the breakfast table.

Soon after arriving in Devon, Perkins became a member of the Torquay Natural History Association in Devon and was a contributor to its journals and attended the local meetings. He was also a member of the Teign Natural History Club there. Much of his work subsequent to *Fauna Hawaiiensis* dealt with the aculeates of England, especially the bees and sawflies of the Devon and Gloucestershire areas. While living in Paignton at Park Hill House, Perkins returned to Hawai'i on at least three occasions. He arrived at Ellis Island in New York on 15 April 1910 from Liverpool on the *Lusitania*. The notation on the immigration form stated that he was on his way to the Young Hotel in Honolulu. A letter from Perkins to W.M. Giffard has him in Waikīkī on 23 December 1910, possibly from the same trip. A second trip had him arriving at Ellis Island on 26 November 1911 via the ship *Teutonic*. He noted on that immigration form that he was visiting his sister-in-law, Mrs. A.M. Brown in Hilo at that time. His third trip was during the summer of 1912 when he came to Honolulu for a few months to complete the writing of the introduction for *Fauna Hawaiiensis*.

After slightly over ten years at Park Hill House (seven years more than he had originally thought), the family moved into a quaint two-story red-brick house on Thurlestone Road in Newton Abbott a few miles away, which was their home for the next 23 years. Although not having the land for a large garden of fruit trees, which was one of Perkins's great pleasures, this home was however within reasonable walking distance to nearby rivers, where he often fished.

The Perkins family at their Newton Abbott home in the 1920s. Left to right standing: Zoë, Charles, Richard, R.C.L. Sitting: John ("Jack").

Her three sons having previously moved out to attend school, start families, or begin jobs, Zoë died in November 1940 after being invalid for the last eight years of her life due to a stroke from diabetes. Diabetes was apparently common in her immediate family as her brothers Robert and Alatau ("Jack") Atkinson also had it, both of whom preceded her in death. During Zoë's last years, Perkins and his son Richard dutifully tended to her daily medical needs. Despite her stroke, she learned to write left-handed and continued to embroider until the end.

Perkins remarried in 1942 to Clara Jessie Senior (née Dowse), whom Perkins described as "a cool & collected little woman & very charming & does everything for me & Richard." In addition to being a great help to Perkins around the house, Clara was active socially and wrote community plays in which she sometimes acted. In 1943, not long after their marriage, they moved house from the rather urban Newton Abbott across the Dartmoor Forest to the more rural Lydford where they put up residence in a much smaller and humble home called "Downside." Housing construction having been severely restricted during WWII, the house and land were purchased in severe disrepair.

> "My son {Richard} got the garden (about 1/2 acre) now into fine condition with fruit trees — it was a neglected waste when we came here in 43 — & such vegetables as we need, while we also have some lawn & also very nice flowers. The bungalow itself is badly in need of much repairing — in fact in parts almost falling to pieces." *(R.C.L. Perkins letter to G.C. Munro, 21 March 1948, BPBM Archives, MS SC Munro Box 13.3).*

> "With almost 3/4 acre of garden to this small house in 3 years we have only been able twice to get a man to help for half a day's work." *(R.C.L. Perkins letter to E.C. Zimmerman, 14 October 1945, BPBM Entomology Archives).*

During World War II, Perkins not only lost Zoë but also lost his resident help to the war effort, although one of his servants from his Newton Abbott house came

Neal Evenhuis

Thurlestone Road home in Newton Abbott. Photo taken in 2003.

to "Downside" to assist once or twice a week. However, he and Clara were not completely alone at "Downside" during those years as they had the company of Perkins's eldest son Richard. At the time, Richard was extremely ill having contracted intestinal tuberculosis, losing 50 lbs or more. During the war years and continuing for a few years afterward, Perkins and his family were privileged to receive packages from friends in Hawai'i containing goods that otherwise were difficult or impossible to get in England due to rationing.

> "I remember that at the end of the first five years of camp life (more or less) I never wanted to see corned beef or tinned salmon again! Now tinned salmon is a luxury, as that of the quality we used to get in Hawaii takes a lot of points for a 1 lb. tin—when one can get it!" *(R.C.L. Perkins letter to G.C. Munro, 21 December 1947, BPBM Archives, MS SC Munro Box 13.3)*

The gray, stucco-sided, single-story "Downside" home had a large garden area in back, a small lawn out front with a long driveway, the front yard bordered on all sides with tall flowering bushes and hedges, a closed-in front sun porch [on the two side walls were hung two yellow Hawaiian feather lei formerly belonging to King Lunalilo's grandmother (Princess Miriam Kalakua Kaheiheimaile) given to his wife Zoë by the former (1892) postmaster H.G. Crabbe[21] many years before]. Perkins always held memories of his years in Hawai'i dear to him, especially with regard to the fauna and flora. In addition to various Hawaiiana in the house, he had two of Scott Wilson's bird portraits framed above his bed. "Downside" also had a

---

[21] Crabbe, Horace Gates (1830–1903). Postmaster in Honolulu during the time Perkins was in Hawai'i, Crabbe was born in Philadelphia and lived in Washington D.C. where he was one of the select few to witness the first telegraph message. He arrived in Honolulu in 1848 as a clerk for the Boston merchants S.H. Williams & Co. and was appointed court chamberlain to Lunalilo when he became King. He was elected to the House of Nobles during Kalākaua's reign but soon abandoned it for his mercantile pursuits. It was no doubt during his term as court chamberlain to Lunalilo that he acquired the feather leis of Lunalilo's grandmother.

Neal Evenhuis

"Downside" in Lydford, Devon, England. Photo taken in 2003.

separate room Perkins called his "little bug room." Unfortunately, his almost constant ill-health did not allow him to do much work in the "bug room" or even allow him to go outdoors to fish or collect as he did almost daily in earlier years. His doctor encouraged him to sit in a comfortable lounge chair out in front of the house on sunny days, but Perkins, the prideful and formerly active field worker, considered this an insult and refused, saying that only people "near death" did this. Through post-war rationing and constant ill-health, Perkins lived at "Downside" for the next eight years before moving back across the Dartmoor to "Woodcot" in Lustleigh two years after Clara died on 13 May 1949. In Lustleigh he lived with Richard and, after his son's marriage in 1952, Richard's wife Dorothy, who both tended to him till his last few days. Perkins gave a brief description of the Lustleigh home:

> "I know the country round this place very well as a collecting ground. It is a small village with a few shops. Our abode is on a steep slope—practically mountainous!—above the village, on the way up to a well known beauty spot called Lustleigh Cleave. On the top of the Cleave one looks down into what in Hawaii one would call a considerable gulch, with a small stream at the bottom & on the other side, dense woodland with the moor {Dartmoor} beyond. I saw the local Dr. on my arrival here. He said 'no going down or up hill for you'. Consequently I have not been outside our gate here, nor had I for a long time at Lydford." *(R.C.L. Perkins letter to G.C. Munro, 7 October 1951, BPBM Archives, MS SC Munro Box 13.3).*

In late 1954, Perkins moved with Richard and Dorothy to a small cottage in Bovey Tracey called "Wotton," the name no doubt harkening back to his days of youth and his pleasant visits to Wotton-under-Edge in Gloucestershire.

Despite his not returning to Hawai'i after 1912, Perkins continued his interest in

Hawaiian entomology and ornithology and answered numerous queries with detailed reminisces of the places he visited sometimes many years earlier. He had many correspondents and was as prompt as his health could allow in his responses. He was also glad to determine material for others and was especially keen to encourage and help young students of Hymenoptera.

"His memory of things Hawaiian was extraordinary, and he spoke to me as if he had just returned from the islands."(*E.C. Zimmerman, 2002, in litt.*)

"I am now feeling my age very severely & my memory is not good for recent affairs but remains excellent for former times, so that if they are still standing I could I am sure pick out the exact tree on which some particular capture was made." (*R.C.L. Perkins letter to E.C. Zimmerman, 14 February 1944, BPBM Entomology Archives*).

"He had a most acute vision and a remarkable visual memory. This greatly aided his flair for both field and taxonomic work. In the latter he had a faculty for observing and selecting characters which vary little within a species and thus making identification simpler." (J.F. Perkins, 1961, *Dict. Natl. Biogr., 1951–1960*, p. 807).

During his work for the Sandwich Islands Committee, Perkins was humble, to the point of being rather insecure, about his efforts and made apologies for failures that he was sure would lead to his recall. He was often consoled by his patrons in England assuring him that all was well despite the inevitable shortcomings of collecting. If either Newton or Sharp has misgivings of Perkins's abilities at the beginning of his work, the results he brought back from his extensive collections after a few years worth of work in the field won them over.

"I always uphold the outdoor observer provided that he be a trained man, & of course no one will doubt your training why you must be the best authority on the ornithology (indeed the zoology in general) of the Sandwich Islands & a far better one than ever there has been before, or perhaps will ever be again." (*A. Newton letter to R.C.L. Perkins, 17 July 1896, BPBM Archives, MS Group 141 Box 2*).

The monumental contributions to zoology by Perkins in a career that spanned six decades did not go unnoticed to others as well. He was awarded a Doctor of Science from his *alma mater*, Oxford University, in 1909. He was given the Gold Medal from Linnean Society in 1913 during the term of presidency of his friend and colleague, E.B. Poulton; and he was nominated and was made a Fellow of the Royal Society in 1920. He was also a co-founder and the first president of the Hawaiian Entomological Society in 1906 and was elected as an Honorary Fellow of the Royal Entomological Society of London in 1954.

Perkins's ill health forced him to move back to England in 1909 and he often complained to his correspondents of frequent sicknesses that kept him from his work and keeping up with his many correspondents. His later years in England were unfortunately extremely painful, suffering from what was later diagnosed as fibrocitis.

"For some weeks I suffered tortures of pain beyond description, day & night, & the drugs given me to allay the pains had no effect at all in diminishing these. I should have been only too pleased to have been put to death during that time. I do not even now know what was the true cause of all of this, & even now I can only crawl about the house slowly & feebly, sleep badly, eat little & am only skin & bones!" (*R.C.L. Perkins letter to G.C. Munro, 11 June 1951, BPBM Archives, MS SC Munro Box 13.3*).

In addition to this constant pain, he also endured frequent and mysterious illnesses that were probably a consequence of his years alone in the cold and humid high-elevation rainforests and bogs of Hawai'i, sometimes without eating for days at a time. Despite these afflictions, he always seemed to manage to get out to fish.

> "I had three dangerous illnesses last winter, one after the other, but during the summer have forced myself out fishing for trout & wading in the rivers, which is no doubt reckless of me at my age, but I have always been careless in such matters!" (*R.C.L. Perkins letter to Hale Carpenter, 18 September 1942, Oxford University Museum of Natural History Library Archives*).

> "Perkins's collector's enthusiasm was so strong that on dark nights when his powerful light attracted many moths and other insects he worked all night, forgetting to eat or sleep. I am sure that this, and the daily tramping through the mountain bogs with feet almost never dry, going to the limit of his strength, affected his nervous system and accounted for the later mysterious painful illnesses which afflicted him till shortly before his life ended, in late September, 1955, close to the end of his 90th year. He suffered tragedy near the end by his eyesight deteriorating in a single night so as to prevent his reading or writing." (Munro, G.C., 1956, *Elepaio* 17(3): 20).

Munro knew well of Perkins's afflictions since he too suffered some of them. In one letter to Perkins, he offered a potential remedy:

> "I wonder if I have discovered something. I remember hearing you speak of your toenails rotting off with the Molokai mud. Did you ever find anything out about that, that is the infection that caused it? Recently a lady friend told me of a trouble she had with her foot and said that her doctor told her it was an infection from mud and that it was difficult to cure on account of the difficulty in getting disinfectants for it. Another lady offered me a sulfur face cream for the epidermus on my neck. I didn't use it for that and suddenly decided that my foot trouble was perhaps from black nails. I tried it and by Jove it began to clear up right away. Unfortunately the mixture is not sold here. It is Nac Prescription Cream 'contains volatized sulfur - penetrates pore deep - guaranteed to kill the pimple germ.' As I remember it your troubles were laid to the conditions imposed on you by the hard forest conditions, and not seeing to it that you heeded your mother's instructions about airing your sheets." (*G.C. Munro letter to R.C.L. Perkins, 28 June 1936, Natural History Museum, Entomology Library Archives*).

It was ironic that Perkins was as fit as he was during his collecting years, but suffered as he did after his collecting years.

> "{He} did not know what it was like to be sick during his collecting years, but was unwell since the first world war. {He} had a calcified cyst on his liver and was operated on in Honolulu by Dr. Hoffman while Judd looked on. He could work long hours. Got glasses in 1912 {for reading only} but discarded them. In June 1948 his left eye "went", and that was his good eye. Was extremely active until 75 when he ruptured himself climbing up a stream bank through an alder thicket when fishing. Could spend 12 hours at a time fishing in cold streams in Devon." (*E.C. Zimmerman letter to N.L. Evenhuis, November 2002*).

Perkins corresponded frequently with his old friend Munro until he became too feeble to write and finally went quite blind.

> "I myself have sad news to relate, 2 or 3 months ago I was reading again Dr. Buck's book on the Polynesian migrations, which he sent me a good time ago. I read about 100 pages overnight and on the next day opened the book to go on with it and to my horror, could not read a word although it is in good print. I am now blind to any print even to the largest headlines in the newspapers. You may imagine what a blow this is as the year before I was

quite able to catch minute insects and name them." *(R.C.L. Perkins [via Richard Perkins] letter to G.C. Munro, 12 December 1952, BPBM Archives, MS SS Munro Box 13.3).*

His last handwritten letter to Munro was dated 17 July 1952, when Perkins was 85 years of age. From then on, his son Richard would write the letters that were to go out to Perkins's many correspondents and he would read letters aloud to Perkins that were addressed to him. Refusing to ever be put in a hospital or nursing home, Perkins died of old age at home in Bovey Tracey in Devon, England on 29 September 1955.

Perkins fishing on the river Bovey near his home in south Devon. Age 74.

Robert A. Perkins Family Album

Background to *Fauna Hawaiiensis* Collecting

After having interest in the status of the fauna of the Hawaiian Islands stimulated by the recent Hawaiian Island collecting efforts of Rev. Thomas Blackburn[22] (insects), Rev. John Thomas Gulick[23] (snails), and Scott Barchard Wilson[24] (birds), the British Association for the Advancement of Science (BAAS) appointed a committee in 1890 to report on the status of what was known in Hawai'i zoologically and to investigate any perceived deficiencies.

A Committee was formed that consisted of the following scientists: English geologist and naturalist, William Thomas Blanford (1832–1905); then director of the British Museum (Natural History), William Henry Flower (1831–1899); preeminent biologists and co-editors of the *Biologia Centrali Americana*, Frederick Du Cane Godman (1834–1919) and Osbert Salvin (1835–1898); geologist and explorer Henry Haversham Godwin-Austen (1834–1923); zoologist and author of the recently (1889) published *A Naturalist in North Celebes*, Sydney John Hickson (1859– 1940); well-known Cambridge ornithologist Alfred Newton (1829–1907); ornithologist and editor of the scientific journal *The Ibis*, Philip Lutley Sclater

---

[22] Blackburn, Reverend Thomas (1844–1912). Thomas Blackburn was born in Islington, England in 1844 and educated at the University of London. He was ordained as a priest in 1869 and went to Hawai'i to become senior priest and chaplain to the Bishop of the Episcopal Church there from 1876–1882. He collected and described insects, mainly beetles and aculeate Hymenoptera, from Hawai'i and was the first resident of Hawai'i to publish on the entomology of the islands (1882). He was transferred to South Australia in 1882 where he was rector at Port Lincoln and later Woodville. He later became Honorary Canon of Adelaide. His works on Australian beetles remain to this day primary references followed by virtually every Australian coleopterist. He died in Adelaide in 1912.

During his tour of duty in Hawai'i, Blackburn was chiefly preoccupied with clerical duties but was still was able to travel to all the main islands (collecting on his home island of O'ahu every 2 weeks), collecting numerous insects from each (except Moloka'i). Many years after his move to Australia, he put up for sale much of his collection, of which some were purchased by the British Museum (Natural History) in London, while keeping the bees and the beetles—to be worked on by him or assisted by David Sharp. Although he only stayed for a short seven years in Hawai'i, he is still considered by many "the father of Hawaiian entomology" primarily for laying the groundwork for future entomologists in the islands. In his letters to Perkins, Sharp would find fault with Blackburn, if for nothing else, the fact that he did not stray too far off of road or trail to collect his insects. In striking contrast, Perkins, went to great efforts to travel far inland to make his collections.

[23] Gulick, John Thomas (1832–1923). Gulick was born in Waimea on Kaua'i, the son of the Reverend Peter Johnson Gulick, who had come as a missionary to Hawai'i in 1827. Although he followed in his father's footsteps and missionaried in Japan, he was born with a strong love of natural history and pursued his passion for it whenever he could. Gulick specialized in land snails and, using his substantial collections and observations, developed a Darwinistic theory of natural selection to explain the incredible variety of hundreds of species of Hawaiian land snails, especially in the endemic O'ahu genus *Achatinella*.

[24] Wilson, Scott Barchard (1864–1923). Born in Wandsworth, England, Wilson graduated from Magdalene College at Cambridge University. He was influenced in ornithology by Alfred Newton and then by Cambridge ornithologist Hans Gadow, with whom he traveled to Portugal. In 1887 he was asked by Alfred Newton to collect birds in the Hawaiian Islands. He collected numerous birds in two year's worth of rigorous collecting, which resulted in the "*Aves Hawaiiensis*," co-authored with Arthur H. Evans and including fourteen species new to science. Wilson was often moody and sometimes depressed, which affected his work in later years. He committed suicide at the age of 69.

(1829–1913); and Cambridge entomologist and recent (1885) co-author of *Memoirs on the Coleoptera of the Hawaiian Islands*, David Sharp (1840–1922).

In addition to the fact that the BAAS was already sending scientists out to many different parts of the world to ascertain the status of various faunas and floras (e.g., surveys were ongoing in the West Indies and a field station was being set up in Italy), scientific curiosity following in the footsteps of Blackburn, Wilson, and Gulick captured the attention of the BAAS and was the fuel that helped influence its decision to give the Sandwich Islands Committee an initial grant of £100.[25]

Flower, the committee chairman, acted quickly and the new Committee decided to send a naturalist to the islands to collect as many zoological specimens as possible and have them sent back to England where they would be examined and reported upon by competent authorities. An experienced ornithological collector, Lionel W. Wiglesworth[26] volunteered to go immediately, but the Committee opted to seek additional funding after realizing that the £100 grant would not be sufficient to complete the task they had envisioned.

Realizing that additional funding would be necessary to adequately sponsor such an adventure, Newton approached his 22-year-old Cambridge student of birds and well-known man of means, Walter Rothschild.[27] When he was told that the spoils would be split three ways (Cambridge, British Museum, and Rothschild's own museum at Tring),[28] Rothschild immediately refused. He figured if this were the case, why fund the expedition and only get one-third of the catch when he could easily have his own collectors go there and reap the fruits of the entire hunt for himself.

By January 1892 the Committee had £300 in hand and, from a field of 20 applicants, selected young Robert Cyril Layton Perkins to be its collector in the Hawaiian Islands.

However, months before this while the Committee was still searching for additional funding, Rothschild wrote to his field collector—who was at the time collecting in the Chatham Islands near New Zealand—to pack up his gear and go to the Hawaiian Islands. Rothschild had acquired the services of Henry C. Palmer,[29] who

[25] Equal to roughly $10,700 in the current value of US dollars (for 2006). The rate of exchange of pounds sterling to dollars in 1890 was $5 to £1 and an 1890 US dollar equals $21.38 in 2006 rates.

[26] Wiglesworth, Lionel William (1865–1901). A British ornithologist who published a few works on the birds of Polynesia and other areas of the South Pacific. He died of dysentery in Fiji.

[27] Rothschild, [Lord] Lionel Walter (1868–1937). Although born into the famous Rothschild banking family, Rothschild had a stronger interest in natural history and in building his museum at Tring. He specialized in birds and Lepidoptera, the latter occupying the majority of his time subsequent to the bird collecting by his team of collectors and Perkins in Hawai'i. He spent an obligatory time working at his family's bank, but soon left it to spend the rest of his life working at Tring.

[28] In fact, Rothschild was approached early on by his old professor, Newton, to assist in the funding of this expedition. Rothschild refused since he was in no way interested in funding an expedition in which the spoils of victory were to be split among various institutions such as Cambridge University and the British Museum or the Bishop Museum in Honolulu.

[29] Palmer, Henry C. (fl. 1890–1894). A New Zealand or Australian sailor/ornithologist. Very little is known of this interesting character in bird collecting lore. He was sent to the Chatham Islands by Rothschild to collect birds, but soon after was sent to the Hawaiian Islands with George C. Munro in December 1890 to collect birds there. He spent months in the Northwestern Hawaiian Islands and worked his way down the chain, ending his stay in the islands a little after Perkins arrived. The two only overlapped for a few weeks in the area of Waialua on O'ahu in 1893 (Evenhuis, N.L., 2001, *Hawaii Biological Survey Reports* 1: 3). He was said to have been murdered in the goldfields of Australia a year after his departure from the Hawaiian Islands.

was joined in Hawai'i by George C. Munro, who collected with him. Palmer spent four years in Hawai'i (1890–1893) and brought back for the Tring museum a total of 1,832 skins of birds, among them 10 species new to science.

Newton felt that Rothschild intended to monopolize the credit and glory associated with the new bird discoveries that were to be made in the Hawaiian Islands and was sparing no expense to get there first. Just a few years prior, Newton had taken young Rothschild (then 22) "under his wing" as a student while at Cambridge and allowed him to spend countless hours in his office silently assimilating the information on ornithology in the books in Newton's library as well as from Newton's conversations. It was no doubt the shock of Rothschild's leaving Cambridge before finishing his schooling (he only spent two years there) and that normally hard-to-get expedition funds were always at Rothschild's disposal allowing him to do as he pleased to acquire specimens for his museum at Tring would be the wedge placed between the two (the Tring Museum ironically opened its doors to the public the same year Perkins arrived in Hawai'i). Rothschild had, before the Sandwich Islands Committee was formed, proposed a joint venture to the Chatham Islands and the Sandwich Islands with Newton. Newton apparently forgot that he had refused the offer and instead thought that Rothschild was trying to get someone to the Sandwich Islands before anyone else in order to acquire the birds that Newton wanted so desperately.

Correspondence from Newton to Perkins shows that the former was hopelessly caught up in this imaginary "war" of bird collecting, which affected his relationship with Rothschild in the years to come. Newton's attitude toward Rothschild and his collectors was unsurprisingly infectious and had apparently stoked the fires within the young Perkins as well—so much so that in a few cases, Perkins appeared almost paranoid when another potential "birder" would show up in the islands and asked Newton for background on the person or advice on what to do. An almost futile task since it would take months for the mail to travel from Perkins to Newton and back before Perkins could get any answer to his enquiries. An example of Perkins's skittishness is when a German "professor" arrived in the islands to do some biological work. Perkins told Sharp about being alarmed at the presence of this unknown person. Sharp forwarded the letter on to Newton:

> "... but he {Sharp} informed me, when enclosing your letter {of 4 June; six weeks earlier}, that he had written to you, telling you not to be unhappy about the German "Professor"—I am much of the same opinion. I wish you had mentioned his name, but I have written to an old friend of mine at Bremen {Hartlaub} —whence the man appears to come—to ask about him. I think he will most likely turn out to be no "Professor" at all, since you say he has no English, & according to my experiences all German Professors speak it." (*A.F. Newton letter to R.C.L. Perkins, 17 July 1896, BPBM Archives, MS Group 141 Box 2*).

> "In my last letter I told you I had written to a friend at Bremen enquiring about the man from that place whose goings on had alarmed you. This morning I have the reply & I copy here what my friend says—'After an absence of about 7 weeks I am back in Bremen where I found your letter. The Professor is Prof. Schauinsland,[30] the director of our museum. He has got leave for a year and the 3 principal stations of his voyage are Laysan, the Sandwich

---

[30] Schauinsland, Hugo Hermann (1857–1937). German naturalist and one-time director of the Bremen Übersee-Museums. He spent three months in the Hawaiian Islands in the summer of 1896, mainly on the Northwestern Hawaiian Island of Laysan. Some of the results of his expedition were published in the 1899 book *Drei Monate auf einer Korallaninsel*.

group and New Zealand. Now Dr. Schauinsland is <u>all but a systematic zoologist</u>! He knows little or nothing of ornithology. What he hopes to do in yonder localities are biological studies, for instance the development of the young in the eggs of <u>Diomedia</u>, <u>Tachypetes</u> &^{c} (Laysan)! He is entre nous soit dit not a great cannon and I fear his ornithological discoveries will be = 0. Nevertheless he is collecting and 'Ein blindes Hahn findet Zuweilen eine Perle'." (*A.F. Newton letter to R.C.L. Perkins, 28 July 1896, BPBM Archives, MS Group. 141 Box 2*).

Newton's final response to Perkins's request for information about this "visitor" would arrive in Perkins's hands at least another three weeks after his final letter of 28 July, making it almost 3 months before receiving an answer to his initial concern of 4 June — after the visiting professor had already completed his trip to the islands and had returned home!

History of Perkins's Journals

During his three sojourns in Hawai'i for the Sandwich Islands Committee and the eventual publishing of the results of his collecting in the *Fauna Hawaiiensis* series, Perkins periodically kept hastily scribbled notes and handwritten journals of his collecting and associated activities. Previous researchers of Perkins and I have made searches in museums, archives, and libraries, but no originals of these journals have been found except one during this study: a typescript of his original May–June 1893 Moloka'i journal, the handwritten version of which he sent to the Sandwich Island Committee, which was located in the Archives of the Zoological Society of London.

Stories vary as to the eventual fate of these original journals and diaries, even from Perkins himself. Perkins says they were in a deplorable condition ("all but illegible") and some were destroyed soon after he gleaned what he needed for his "Introduction" to *Fauna Hawaiiensis*.

> "After I wrote the 'Introduction' to the Fauna Haw. I destroyed most of my diaries, the note books often containing a mix up of accounts & other matters, as well as collecting notes. Some of these were accidentally preserved & I enclose excerpts from two of my collecting trips to the Kauai Mts." (*R.C.L. Perkins letter to G.C. Munro, 8 September 1932, BPBM Archives, MS SC Munro Box 13.3*).

E.C. Zimmerman, who visited Perkins at his "Downside" home in Lydford, Devon, England in August 1949, stated:

> "Perkins's first trip notes were kept in Latin. These were lost during one of his parents' house moves." (*E.C. Zimmerman letter to N.L. Evenhuis, in litt.*)

> "In regard to Perkins's field notebooks, I may say that the others (that is, those missing from the Bishop Museum collections) were burned in a fire at Perkins's home (together with other material that would have been of use to us now)." (*E.C. Zimmerman letter to A. Manning, in litt.*)

Perkins's wrote to Zimmerman the following regarding the loss of the diaries and other papers:

> "I have also written a brief sketch of all my other chief collecting trips, of which the complete diaries were left in my father's house years ago & not recovered. This will give an idea of the exact localities I visited & the time spent in these. Of various short trips for a day or two to different islands I have no record. Thus I crossed Molokai to Lanai on one

or more occasion or from the former to Maui, & also made similar brief trips from Honolulu to other of the islands, but these were I think mostly to spy out the land rather than for serious collecting." *(R.C.L. Perkins letter to E.C. Zimmerman, 31 October 1937, BPBM Entomology Archives).*

"In destroying old papers & letters I frequently come across notes on Haw. Insects written long ago & of no further importance." *(R.C.L. Perkins letter to E.C. Zimmerman, 4 October 1948, BPBM Entomology Archives).*

Perkins did not start a journal until a full three months after his March arrival in Hawai'i (the first entry is 20 June), no doubt in response to a letter with a specific request to do so by Sharp.

"Of course any observations on the habits or distribution of the creatures that you may make, and that you may publish will be quite your own gift to the scientific world, so I shall say nothing about them, but if you have time to make any jottings in note-books however imperfect I recommend you do it as such memoranda even when of the most imperfect nature are very useful afterwards in enabling the mind to recall exactly the conditions one wishes to describe." *(D. Sharp letter to R.C.L. Perkins, 21 May 1892, BPBM Archives, MS Group 141 Box 3).*

Copy of a Perkins's handwritten journal page dealing with his second Moloka'i trip.

> **Table 1.** List of Perkins journals and remembrances[31, 32]
>
> *Journals*:   *Island*
> June 20–September 10, 1892   Hawaiʻi
> October 24–November 5, 1892   Oʻahu
> May 11–June 29, 1893   Molokaʻi
> July 9–September 25, 1893   Molokaʻi
> January 5–February 23, 1894   Lānaʻi
> March 6–May 12, 1894   Maui
> May 15–June 16, 1894   Kauaʻi
> July 4–July 14, 1894   Lānaʻi
> July 20–August 15, 1894   Hawaiʻi
> December 19, 1894–January 1895   Hawaiʻi
> April 9–May 22, 1895   Kauaʻi
>
> *Remembrances*:
> "Kau & Puna VI (part)—IX (part) 1895"
> "Kauai, Oct. 1895"
> "Collecting on the slopes of Mauna Kea from Hilo. 1895"
> "Waianae Mountains, Oahu—February 1896"
> "Hawaii Kona— March 1896"
> "West Maui & Haleakala in V 1896"
> "Molokai—June 1896"
> "Kauai—July & August 1896"
> "Kau & Puna VIII & IX– 96 (partly in each month)"
> "Haleakala Maui—October 1896"
> "January 1897 & February 1897"
> "Collecting in 1900–1901"

However, despite continuous pleas of Sharp and Newton to keep them and the Sandwich Islands Committee informed of his activities in a timely manner, Perkins still did not religiously keep entries for every day in the field. There are many gaps of days, weeks, and even months when he did not keep journals (most often this is apparent with regard to his Oʻahu collecting that occurred in between travel to other islands).

As rare as the Oʻahu journals must have been, it is all the more unfortunate that in one case, his December 1892 notebook was stolen while he was staying at the Kawailoa Ranch cabin in the hills near the north shore area of Oʻahu.

> "Towards the end of my stay in the Kawailoa mountain house one day, during my absence in the higher forest this house was entered and much of the contents was carried off, including food that I had taken up. Also my notebook, paper, watch and other things disappeared with these. Fortunately my specimens were not interfered with in any way, so the loss was not serious." (*Perkins journals: Oʻahu October–November 1892, BPBM Archives, MS SC Perkins Box 1.1*).

---

[31] A complete list of the "later" diaries that Perkins claimed were either lost or destroyed is found in correspondence from Perkins to Munro. All are accounted for in the above table by "remembrances" except the following: "Olaa and Kilauea December 1896"; "Waianae Coast January 1897"; "Kauai January and February 1897"; and "March 1897" [the last in which Perkins added: "collected a little in mts. round Honolulu before leaving for England – staying a while in California, Arizona, Mexico, New Orleans & Washington on the way back." (*R.C.L. Perkins letter to G.C. Munro, 16 August 1936, BPBM Archives, MS SC Munro Box 13.3*).

[32] In addition, Perkins wrote an eighteen-paged abridged version of his travels in a letter to E.C. Zimmerman in 1944 in which additional details are mentioned that are not written elsewhere (diaries, remembrances, or correspondence). (*R.C.L. Perkins letter to E.C. Zimmerman, 14 February 1944, BPBM Entomology Archives*).

Perkins promised to send some of his journals to Newton and Sharp to help increase chances of continued funding from the Royal Society. The first of these, a summary of bird collecting in Kona, was sent to Newton in 1892 soon after Perkins returned to Honolulu after collecting for a little over five months on the western slopes of Mauna Loa on Hawai'i Island. This summary so thrilled Newton that he quickly submitted it for publication in *The Ibis* without Perkins's approval or a proper checking of the proofs.

> "I have now to thank you for yours 16th Oct^r, to get which was an unexpected pleasure, and a still greater one has been affected by the notes of your diary ... which I have read with interest and delight. They are capital, and I thank you heartily for them. I should like to send them straight off for publication in 'The Ibis'." (*A. Newton letter to R.C.L. Perkins, 12 November 1892, BPBM Archives, MS Group 141 Box 3*)

The errors that Perkins found in the article years later caused him grave concern, even as late as 1936 when he was transcribing his surviving notes and writing his remembrances; lamenting the fact that the names of two bird genera were switched throughout the article, all unbeknownst to him [the generic names were added (incorrectly) by Newton (who subsequently apologized to Perkins in later correspondence) before sending them to *The Ibis*].

Among some of the first of Perkins's journals sent to Newton were those that concerned his first few months on Moloka'i in the summer of 1893. They were much appreciated by Newton who said the entries were quite tantalizing:

> "I have read the pages of your Molokai journal, & hardly know how to express my admiration for your perseverance in working on under so many & great difficulties. Your narrative enables me to realize as I have never before done the vast amount of energy required for zoological exploration in such a country & in such weather." (*A. Newton letter to R.C.L. Perkins, 12 August 1893, BPBM Archives, MS Group 141 Box 3*).

When one reads the information contained in these journals it is apparent that Perkins's purpose in writing them was much the same as a business report to a client of how the funds were being spent. Perkins was on a contract to collect, and his journals were a written record of his collecting and observations. Perkins had for the most part not intended them as a travelogue nor to be written for a general audience. Instead, they stand as a permanent testimonial to his tremendous collecting efforts and results, and his incredible fortitude and energy in successfully reaching some of the most inaccessible and remote places in the Hawaiian Islands. The many crates packed full with specimens that were sent back to Cambridge University would physically prove his worth to the Committee as a field collector but the journals would supplement the specimens with biological observations that could not be placed on the tiny scraps of paper he had used to indicate locality of the specimens he collected. What Perkins may not have realized at the time was that his writings would include some of the best personal observations of biological information ever assembled for birds and insects of Hawai'i. Their loss would be irreplaceable. Although this fact may have escaped Perkins, it did not go unnoticed by his colleagues.

In 1936, Bishop Museum Trustee Albert F. Judd, Jr.[33] and Perkins's life-long friend George C. Munro convinced him to make copies of whatever journals and notes he could find for the Bernice Pauahi Bishop Museum Library in Honolulu. These were sent at various times as he completed writing them up. After finishing his last batch, he wrote to Zimmerman:

> "This is just to notify you that I have sent off to the director of the Museum {Bishop Museum} some accounts of other collecting trips that I made in Hawaii which almost complete the account of the work I did there when collecting for the 'S.I. Committee.' Only one of these is an actual diary—that of my trip to Halemanu, Kauai, in search of the bird Phaeornis palmeri. The rest I have taken from brief notes I made before I wrote that hurried "Introduction" to F.H. from the fuller diaries that were not preserved. I could have amplified these a good deal from memory & from my correspondence with Dr. Sharp & Prof. Newton, but have not done this. These notes may be of interest to entomologists & ornithologists in the islands, as some guide to where I went & what object I had in view, but there is nothing of general interest in them.
>
> I made a good many lesser trips to all the islands, usually for a few days e.g. to Hamakua, Hawaii, Waimea, Hawaii, S. Kona, to W. Maui, Lanai, &c. sometimes mere stopover visits at ports called at by steamers on the way to or from Honolulu, usually for some special purpose, or sometimes merely to spy out the land & its prospects. I have no records of these, though I remember some of them very well." *(R.C.L. Perkins letter to E.C. Zimmerman, 17 November 1937, BPBM Entomology Archives).*

For the most part, two sets of these "copies" exist: one in the Bishop Museum Archives, Honolulu, the other in the Natural History Museum, London. However, even among these, there are two different versions that exist for some trips, each written for a specific audience. For example, the journal entries for the trip to Kaua'i in 1894 and another in 1895 exist in two forms. One version is an abridged version that lists parenthetically and in an abbreviated form anything to do with insects. As stated by Perkins on the copy in the BMNH, the abbreviated 1895 version was meant for Perkins's birding friend, Munro.

> "Diary of collecting at Halemanu, Kauai. This is from the original diary; a copy taken from this, but a little different, was used in sending an account of the trip to G.C. Munro a short while ago, but I may also have left out some facts concerning insects. The account sent to Munro was one taken from original diary sent back to England in 1895." *(BMNH Entomology Archives).*

The other version for each comparable dated entry is complete for all taxa collected or observed. For example, where an entry might have said "(beetles collected)" in the abridged version for Munro, the complete version includes all the details on every insect species, host plant, etc. that was probably in the original diary notes from which Perkins was transcribing these copies.

The existing copies of Perkins's journals and remembrances are in twenty-three parts. Some of the remembrances have titles that are similar to titles of other published notes such as his bird-collecting experiences in Kona in 1893 (*Ibis* (6) 5: 101–112) and his insect-collecting experiences on the slopes of Haleakalā in 1895 (*Entomologist's Monthly Magazine* (2) 7: 190–195).

---

[33] Judd, Albert Francis, Jr. (1874–1939). Bishop Museum ethnologist and Bishop Estate Trustee. Son of Hawaii Supreme Court Justice, Albert F. Judd.

Perkins was a fairly prolific correspondent during his 7 years collecting for the Committee (almost 170 letters just to Sharp and Newton), but this did not necessarily translate to him also being a prolific journal writer. Examining the copies of the surviving transcribed journals shows that his proclivity toward journal writing was correlated somewhat with the length of solitude he had at any given place of collecting and his success at a particular locality. He was most prolific in his writing during the 6 months he lived virtually alone in the forest on Moloka'i in 1893. He was least prolific in his journal entries when he was on O'ahu, no doubt because of the various nightly social diversions "in Town" as he would call his stays in Honolulu. He dramatically reduced his journal writing on his second and third trips to the Islands since he viewed these trips more as those to fill in the gaps of places and things he had not yet collected. Moreover, reports of his progress on these trips were not as necessary as they had been during his first trip, which were written to secure grants from the Royal Society and BAAS to allow continuance of the Perkins's collecting in the Islands.

PART TWO

First Expedition (1892–1894)

Preparations for the Trip
January–March 1892

In January 1892, R.C.L. Perkins was chosen by the Sandwich Islands Committee to be its collector in the islands. David Sharp[34] was chair of the committee and Perkins's chief advisor in terms of general collecting, especially with insects. Professor Alfred Newton[35] was Perkins's main advisor with regard to bird collecting.

Meetings with specialists, learning specific collecting techniques for various types of organisms (Sharp called these "dodges"), gathering up collecting equipment, securing reference material to take along, obtaining letters of introduction for his traveling in Hawai'i, saying his good-byes to family and friends, etc. all had to be crammed into the span of just a few weeks in January and February — before he would set sail for New York. The 26-year-old Perkins was making arrangements for the adventure of a lifetime. It was admirable that the Committee would put their faith in so young a man, but all the more amazing, since Perkins had never before this left his home of England and therefore had no experience collecting in exotic locales.

At this time, Sharp took the opportunity of sending a letter of notification to Charles Reed Bishop of the Committee's selection of Perkins and gave a rather bland testimonial that would essentially serve as a letter of introduction to Bishop for Perkins:

> I have now to tell you that the Committees . . . have, within the last week selected from the various candidates who offered their services, Mr. Robert C.L. Perkins, B.A. of Jesus College, Oxford, and this gentleman will proceed to Honolulu, via San Francisco, with as little delay as possible. I accordingly have to bespeak on his behalf the valuable assistance of yourself and any of your friends whether private persons or members of the Hawaiian

---

[34]   Sharp, David (1840–1922). Entomologist. Sharp was curator of the zoology museum at Cambridge University and specialized in the taxonomy of beetles during the existence of the Sandwich Islands Committee. In his correspondence with Perkins while the latter was in Hawai'i, Sharp was often the one who would comfort Perkins and give him sound advice on how to handle situations that were of concern to the young traveler.

[35]   Newton, Alfred (1829–1907). Ornithologist and Cambridge professor of zoology. By the time Perkins ventured out to the Hawaiian Islands, Newton was already near retirement and had concluded his world travels with regard to scientific expedition in his endeavor to find new birds. Newton therefore looked upon Perkins's collecting as a vicarious pleasure—or misery—depending on the successes or failures of Perkins during his years collecting for the Sandwich Islands Committee. The tone of his letters to Perkins could often cause the young collector much discomfort as he tried his best to please his patron from afar.

Government, which I hope will regard favorably the important enquiry with which he is entrusted. Although I had not previously known Mr. Perkins, I feel sure from the testimony of others well qualified by personal acquaintance with him that I may safely recommend him to your notice and consideration—and I may add that he will perhaps stand in greater need of such attentions as you may be so good as to bestow upon him for I understand that he has never visited a foreign country.

Mr. Perkins's instructions are to lose no opportunity of collecting examples of all classes of fauna—though he will be directed to a few special points. It is impossible for me at present to say how long he will stay in the islands. The belief of the Committee is that the proper investigation of their zoology would require his residence for a couple of years, but the funds as yet at our disposal (£300) are manifestly insufficient for so long a period. We intend however to apply for a renewal of grants, I should state that Mr. Perkins renders his services gratuitously—his actual expenses alone being defrayed by the Committee—and this fact will, I trust, dispose all who are in a position to assist him the more readily to further his object." (*A.F. Newton letter to C.R. Bishop, 9 January 1892, BPBM Archives, MS Group 141 Box 3*)

He was given £50 by the Committee for the trip to Hawai'i and £100 for the work "as long as it will last." Having secured all of his supplies, reference literature for his expedition,[36] and a final detailed letter from Newton listing the bird species he could expect to find on each island, Perkins departed Liverpool, England on 17 February 1892 on board the White Star Line's *Majestic*.

The 10,000-ton *Majestic* had her maiden voyage only a few years before in April 1890. She was built as the White Star Line's main hope to win back the Blue Riband (the award given to the ship that crossed the Atlantic the fastest) from a rival line's ship. It took one year for the *Majestic* to win the award, which she held for quite some time. Three years after the voyage on which Perkins was a passenger, the captain of the *Majestic* would be none other than the ill-fated John Edward Smith, who in 1912 was the captain of another White Star liner, the *Titanic*, when it was sunk by an iceberg. Ironically, it was the *Majestic* that would be the White Star Line's replacement ship for the *Titanic* after that tragic voyage.

The *Majestic* averaged about 20 knots during its cross-Atlantic runs and would reach New York in about 6 days. After almost a week on the frigid Atlantic waters, Perkins arrived in New York on 24 February and, rather than stopping to rest and possibly meet fellow zoologists at the American Museum of Natural History, instead quickly transferred to rail for another week-long trip, this time across the Appalachian's rolling hills, the American heartland's plains, the Rockies, and finally the Sierra Nevada Mountains to San Francisco.

After arriving in San Francisco, Perkins made his way to the docks at the base of Folsom Street and boarded the Oceanic Steamship Company's liner *Mariposa* on 3 March for the final sail across the vast Pacific Ocean to Honolulu.

---

[36] Perkins did not specifically list the literature he took with him. However, from subsequent correspondence and results of archival research, I have been able to locate a few of the works he took with him: Hillebrand's 1888 *Flora of the Hawaiian Islands*, Byron's 1826 *Voyage of the H.M.S. Blonde to the Sandwich Islands, in the years 1824–1825,* and Blackburn & Sharp's 1885 *Memoirs of the Coleoptera of the Hawaiian Islands*. Upon his arrival he secured a copy of Lorrin Andrews's 1865 *Dictionary of the Hawaiian Language* and received the parts of Wilson & Evans's *Aves Hawaiiensis* as they came out.

The *Mariposa* was one of four ships in the Oceanic Steamship Line. The others were the *Alameda*, the *Monawoi*, and the *Australia*. The *Mariposa* was one of the more popular steamship liners that made the voyage from San Francisco to Honolulu, and then on to Samoa, and Sydney, Australia. On board, Perkins would find all the newest conveniences at his disposal.

> "The *Mariposa* is most richly and tastefully furnished throughout and arranged with a special view to the comfort and convenience of her passengers. The staterooms are all elegant and complete, electric bells and electric lights are all in each room and fine hair mattresses on woven wire springs covered with the cleanest of linen, occupy each berth. Fresh water is supplied from running tubes and rooms are all ventilated. The dining room is fitted with elegantly carved tables around which are placed revolving chairs, softly cushioned. Every luxury the appetite could crave is almost daily offered or obtainable, the Company priding itself on the manner in which, in the special regard of food, their guests are cared for. The social hall affords opportunity for gatherings of the fairer sex and contains a grand piano.... The smoking-room is the recourse of the sterner sex and offers all the accommodations required." (*Paradise of the Pacific* 6: 70).

The *Mariposa* left the docks at 3:00 p.m. and sailed through the Golden Gate and out into the Pacific for its 2100-mile journey.

In the early morning after a little over a seven days at sea, the *Mariposa* came within sight of the windward cliffs of Moloka'i and the Kalaupapa[37] leper colony, where the "unclean" mentioned in the narrative below were kept segregated from the rest of the population.

> "In the early morning of the day of arrival, while coming along the windward of Molokai and under the lee of Oahu, the tourist will be shown the segregated but comfortable home of the 'unclean' of Hawaii; the bald, rounded, summit of Koko Head; the rugged, fire-burnt, weather-scared outlines of the extinct volcano Diamond Head; then the cocoanut palm's of the King's grove, the glistening surf-bound beach of Waikiki, and finally the entrance to Honolulu harbor." (*Paradise of the Pacific* 6: 66).

Close to mid-day on Thursday 10 March, the *Mariposa* entered Honolulu Harbor. As it approached the wharf, it would be boarded by the harbor pilot who rode the vessel to the dock. The steamer was tied down and the gangplank put in place for departing passengers. After almost three weeks of travel from Liverpool, R.C.L. Perkins had finally arrived in the Hawaiian Islands.

---

[37] The Kalaupapa leper colony was, at the time of Perkins's sojourn in Hawai'i, at its highest in numbers of people (over 1,000). The colony started in 1866 when the first 10 people with leprosy were dropped off at the mouth of nearby Waikolu Valley. The arrival of Father Damien in 1873 and complaints by residents in the settlement and at the top of the *pali* overlooking the settlement, including Board of Health representative Rudolf Meyer, led to changes that offered more provisions and better living conditions for the residents. Experiments with medication led to the use of sulfa drugs that eventually made the disease no longer contagious. In 1969, the laws of exiling leprosy patients to Kalaupapa were abolished; but many residents chose to live out the remainder of their lives there. It is today a National Historical Park.

SELECTED CORRESPONDENCE

Cambridge, England
20 January 1892
Robert Cyril Layton Perkins

Dear M[r]. Perkins,

Professor Foster has sent the enclosed from the United States Legation about your luggage getting through the States. You may keep the letter as it may be useful to you.

I am glad to see from it that you will probably be able to get through N. America without any Custom's expense.

I also enclose the copies of letters of introduction for you: these copies may be useful for you after you have got rid of the originals.

If I can be of any assistance to you while making your preparations I hope you will let me know.

Yours very truly
D. Sharp.

Magdalene College
Cambridge, England
25 January 1892
Robert Cyril Layton Perkins

Dear M[r]. Perkins,

I here with enclose the promised copy of my letter to M[r]. Bishop, that you may know exactly what I have asked him to do on your behalf.

You will no doubt have received from D[r]. Sharp the reply from the United States Legation to the application which I got from Prof[r]. Foster (one of the Secretaries of the Royal Society) to make, and I hope you will have acted on the hint there in contained as to consulting the United States Consul General in London.

D[r]. Sharp has shown me the duplicates of the letters addressed by the Hawaiian Chargé d'Affaires to his Government, and (though some of the details are inaccurate) their tenor is all that could be desired.

I would here recapitulate some of the points which I especially mentioned to you when you were here, and it may be convenient to take them in the order of the different islands.

1) Niihau. We seem to know nothing of any peculiar species which this island may possess. The scarlet Vestiaria and the crimson Himatione sanguinea are found there (& indeed on every island) – but we know not whether there is any green Himatione, or any Hemignathus.

2) Kauai. Nothing new may be expected there, for Mr. Knudsen,[38] who lives on the island, and Wilson have probably exhausted it in that respect. But it has two peculiar species of Hemignathus, and 2 of green Himatione – none of them being common in collections.

3) Oahu. It is to this island that the remains of the forest upon it that I would particularly direct your attention in the first instance. It was here that Townsend[39] and Deppe[40] stayed and things they got have not been obtained since – especially its Hemignathus lichtensteini, the larger of the two species, to be looked for, as the type specimen now at Berlin is the only one known to exist in collections; but the smaller one, H. lucidus, is clearly as rare, and the two peculiar species of green Himatione, H. chloris and H. maculata not less so. The possibility of the last being only the young of supposed "H. flava" is a point to be ascertained – the real locality of H. flava (a conspicuously coloured bird – bright yellow below) having yet to be determined. It is the straight-billed species – for you will remember what I told you of the species of green Himatione being distributed "by pairs" (a straight & curved bill one) on almost each island. There is said to be a patch of forest only some 15 miles from Honolulu that I hope you will not be long in visiting. Another patch is said to be further off. Oahu possibly is, or was, the abode of Acrulocercus apicalis, the black long-tailed bird, with white tips to its tail feathers – but the real locality of that species is not known to me. Specimens are very rare.

4) Molokai. Here there is said to be no Acrulocercus but it may be the locality for A. apicalis just mentioned. No Hemignathus is known, and only one species of green Himatione (H. kalaana) which has a curved bill. Of course there ought to be a straight-billed one as well. But here also is Loxops flammea, the largest species of a real flame colour. Wilson got only 3 or 4 specimens.

---

[38] Knudsen, Valdemar (1820-1898). Norwegian born, Knudsen came to Hawaiʻi in 1851 and settled in Waiawa, Kauaʻi. As was common for most non-Hawaiians in the mid-1800s he learned the local language in order to survive in the rural Kauaʻi country; and helped fellow foreigners when they arrived in the islands to also learn the language. Knudsen had an interest in natural history, especially botany and ornithology. His home near Kokeʻe, Halemanu, was host to many visiting naturalists and residents alike. Newton was wrong about the island being "exhausted" of bird collecting since Rothschild's collectors were in in the early 1890s able to secure the new Kauaʻi ʻŌʻō, missed previously by others.

[39] Townsend, John Kirk (1809–1851). Born in Philadelphia in 1809, Townsend was schooled as a physician, but became an ornithologist at the Philadelphia Academy of Natural Sciences. In 1834 he joined naturalist Thomas Nutall across to the Pacific coast. After a successful expedition hunting birds and mammals in the west and a quick sojourn to the Hawaiian Islands, Townsend was back in Vancouver and once again boarded a ship for Hawaiʻi. He arrived in January 1837 and stayed another three months before heading for Tahiti and South America. While in Hawaiʻi he hunted in Nuʻuanu with Ferdinand Deppe and collected the rare Oʻahu Kipi (Hemignathus lichtensteini), which was the subject of Newton's obsession in wanting Perkins to catch it.

[40] Deppe, Ferdinand (1794–1860). Prussian zoologist and traveler. Originally a gardener, he was recommended in 1821 by the director of the Zoological Museum in Berlin to make a collecting trip to Mexico on behalf of the Prussian Count von Sack. He quickly learned how to collect and skin birds and mammals and studied books on the zoology, botany, and geology of South America in preparation for his trip. His collecting in Mexico spanned the years 1824–1832. He stayed on as a commission agent and a few years later sailed to Hawaiʻi. In Hawaiʻi, he met and accompanied Townsend in Nuʻuanu Valley in 1838 to help capture the only known specimen of Hemignathus lichtensteini, and soon after was tricked out of all he had earned as a commission agent and sailed back to Germany a broke man. He died in oblivion in 1860.

5) Lanai. This has 2 species of green Himatione – one a curved & the other straight-billed. No Loxops, Hemignathus or Acrulocercus are known.

6) Kahoolawe. Nothing whatever is known of this! but it is probably unproductive in the bird way.

7) Maui. No green Himatione known, but Wilson obtained a single specimen of what looks like a deeply saturated H. sanguinea which he has called H. dolii. Other specimens of course wanted. Acrulocercus nobilis, the one with the very long curled tail feathers is said to be here as well as on Hawaii. That however is questionable. No Loxops, no Hemignathus known.

8) Hawaii. This being the largest is the most important island, but the chance of your being able to investigate it properly is I fear contingent on a renewal of our grants, & we must not expect too much. The very extent of the island, coupled with its mountainous character and its being clothed with forests that are in some places extremely dense, will make its investigation a work of a long time, and for these reasons it is my own opinion, though not necessarily of the Joint Committee which I have had no opportunity of ascertaining, that you would do well to leave it alone, until we are in a better financial position. Although it has been again & again visited by collectors, there is yet good hope that novelties may be discovered there, and of course much to be made out in regard to the distribution of species which are not new, for some of them are said to be exceedingly local. Of the most interesting is the Chaetoptila angustipluma of which you saw in my office at the museum the only specimen I believe has reached Europe. There is one at Philadelphia & others I understand in Mr. Bishop's collection at Honolulu – but these are all that are known and the belief is that the species is extinct, like Drepanis pacifica (the beautiful black & golden yellow bird) – but it is not easy to understand why this should be. The precise locality at which specimens were obtained is not known and therefore there is nothing more definite to guide your search, but the rediscovery of the species would be a matter of considerable interest; and, as it is one of the few purely Meliphaginae forms existing in the islands (Acrulocercus is the other), and example in spirit would be important and desirable. But in any event the tongue should be preserved. Another supposed extinct species is the little rail (Pennula ecaudata or millei) which used to be found by one, or perhaps more of the mountain lakes, and there I venture to hope it might still be discovered – unless indeed the rats have finished it off, which I cannot think is likely, for I doubt their frequenting such elevations in great numbers. And here I may say that both on this and on the other islands, the possibility of meeting with rare or new things seems to be the greatest on the hill tops – so that the higher you go (always excepting perpetual snow) the better chance of success. It appears quite possible that Chloridops kona – the exaggerated green finch you saw – one of which Wilson only obtained a single specimen – may occur more frequently at higher elevations than those at which he worked – and this possibility is increased by what I hear of Mr. Rothschild's collection having gotten some 20 or 30 examples at no great distance from Kona (on the western side of Hawaii) the place where Wilson discovered it. Mr. Rothschild's men are said to have found also another new finch of which the male is red & the female is green or brown – but I know nothing more about this, & there may be a mistake, and their

bird prove to be only the Carpodacus [house finch, linnet] (which has been imported from America) wherein the sexes differ in this way. The two peculiar species of
Hemignathus & the two of green Himatione from Hawaii are pretty well known,
but it is the smaller and less brilliant species of Loxops (L. coccineus) which is still
very rare & the duck Anas wyvilliana.

I think these are the chief points on which I dwelt. In a general way the species of
Fan tailed Flycatcher (about which there is so much uncertainty) Chasiempis
regain attention, and then there is the wonderful "Fringilla anna" which you will
see in M[r]. Bishop's Collection – the real whereabouts of which is unknown.

I understand from D[r]. Hickson[41] that you will not take your departure before 10th
Feb. so that I shall have time to write you again. In the meantime I hope your
preparations are progressing favorably & remain

Yours very truly
Alfred Newton

Cambridge, England
30 January 1892
Robert Cyril Layton Perkins

Dear M[r]. Perkins,

I thank you for your two postcards and am glad to find that you had been so careful
as to take note of most of the points in which I had especially dwelt – nevertheless
you may find what I wrote in some manner useful to you if you will preserve it.

I had been in hope of sending you an introduction to a M[r]. Greenwell who used
to live at Kona in Hawaii but I am sorry to hear of his death from his brother who
is the well-known archaeologist and Canon of Durham.

I doubt not however that M[r]. Scott Wilson will be able to give you an introduction to some of the sons, as well as to other persons who may be of use to you –
and I am glad to hear you are in communication with him. Pray make a point of
seeing him.

I enclose a note from M[r]. Vredenburg[42] to whom I am also writing today. He

---

[41] Hickson, Sydney John (1850–1940). Treasurer of the Sandwich Islands Committee from 1892–1912. Hickson
proved to be a very valuable source to Perkins whenever he needed more funds to be able to continue his work or
travel in the Islands.

[42] Vredenburg, Wilmot Laurence Andrade (–1909). Colorful son of an officer of the British consulate with
an avid interest in birding as well as many other things. He arrived in Hawaiʻi as supercargo. After arriving in
Honolulu, he quickly moved to the Big Island to hunt wild cattle and pigs on the slopes of Mauna Kea. While a
resident of Waimea, he was soon hired to manage a sugar plantation in Puakō in 1899. When that proved a fail-

seems to be a man of considerable ability, though occupying but a humble position, and is, M^r. Wilson told me, an admirable bush man.

If there is anything else I can do for you before you start, pray let me know, and I shall be at all times glad if you will write to me as to your doings – indeed it is absolutely necessary for a renewal of the grants that either D^r. Sharp or I (or both) should be kept fully informed by reports from time to time – and the sooner the better.

Deliver me to be
Yours very truly
Alfred Newton

---

ure he was hired by the Parker Ranch to manage their Waiki'i section of the Ranch. He also taught school at the Waimea School, brought the first car to Waimea, and was often the center of merry-making at parties with his expertise of many musical instruments. He often carried a loaded pistol at his side and this proved to be his doom in 1909. After killing a wild pig and bending down to get it, his gun fell out of its holster and went off, the bullet firing directly into his heart.

First Months on Oʻahu
10 March–3 June 1892

Perkins arrived in the Hawaiian Islands on Thursday 10 March 1892. His arrival was apparently noteworthy enough to make the local press:

> "Mr. Perkins has lost no time in pursuing his journey, as he arrived here by the steamer *Mariposa* yesterday. Honolulu is becoming a meeting place for scientists. There are here now Professor Marcuse[43] of Germany and Preston[44] of the United States investigating the vagaries of the earth's axis, and Mr. Perkins to make a thorough examination and report of the zoology of the group." (*Daily Bulletin*, 1892).

His letters of introduction from England and, through them, his acquaintanceship with Charles Reed Bishop no doubt assisted him in meeting people who could assist him in his endeavor and influence his associations with others during his employment in the islands. On Tuesday 15 March, only a few days after his arrival, he was received by Queen Liliʻuokalani [*Paradise of the Pacific* 5(March): 5]. This meeting, and no doubt others in those first few days in the Islands helped Perkins make the necessary contacts to begin his collecting efforts in a short amount of time.

Among those with whom he met in those first few weeks on Oʻahu was Albert Jaeger, a botanist and forester in Hawaiʻi, who mentioned to Perkins that on the royal expedition of 1885 to Nihoa he had collected a finch.[45]

> "Early in 1892 I visited Mʳ. Jaeger (?spelling of name) in Honolulu. He told me that he got a thick-billed bird (captured by hand) on Nihoa & I have some idea that Wilson, whom he knew, obtained it from him. He told me Brigham was on the trip but declined to go ashore. As B. told me he was very seasick on boats perhaps that was the cause! I remember my

---

[43] Marcuse, Adolf (1859–1918). German planetary scientist who visited Honolulu from June 1891 to May 1892 as part of his research on noting variations in latitudes in correlation with the earth's axis. The results of his trip were published in 1893 "Ergebnisse der Expedition nach Honolulu zu Untersuchung der Polhöhenänderungen." *Astronomische Nachrichten* 131: 297–302.

[44] Preston, Erasmus Darwin (1851–1906). American planetary geologist. He was employed at the time by the U.S. Coast and Geodetic Survey. He was in Honolulu assisting Marcuse with observations of latitude for his study.

[45] If this story proves true, it is interesting, since this species (the Nihoa Finch) was not described from this specimen but was described much later (1917) from specimens collected in 1916. Wilson did describe a finch in 1890, but this was not the Nihoa Finch; it was the Laysan Finch.

visit to Jaeger's very well, as one of his sons walked up one of the big coconut trees & brought us down—I was with a friend—green nuts, the only time I saw the trees climbed in this way. M^r. J. was largely concerned in getting Koebele to the islands & we talked mostly of this. It was before I started collecting myself." *(R.C.L. Perkins letter to G.C. Munro, 26 May 1944, BPBM Archives, MS SC Munro Box 13.3).*

Perkins gave a summary account of his first few weeks collecting in his introduction to the *Fauna Hawaiiensis*:

"I arrived in Honolulu early in 1892 and during the spring months collected chiefly in the Waianae range of Oahu, partly on the eastern and partly on the western side of these mountains, but more successfully on the latter. Except for an odd day or two I did not attempt the Koolau range, which was the scene of most of Mr. Blackburn's entomological field-work." (Perkins, R.C.L., 1913, *Fauna Hawaiiensis* 1: xxxii).

His first collecting trip was to go out to Waialua, where he stayed at the house of the postmaster there, Archibald Scott Mahaulu, which previously was the home of the Emerson family. Perkins's initial collecting experiences were collecting on the slopes and ridges of the eastern side of Mt. Ka'ala (up to about 3,000 feet—going beyond this elevation would have proven difficult as the climb beyond 3,200 feet is comprised of precariously steep cliffs), no doubt following what is now called the DuPont trail, the only trail there in those days; and testing the situation on the north shore of O'ahu where he learned about the Hawaiian fauna and met the many hunters that frequently came to Waialua to shoot waterfowl. After returning to Honolulu for a few days, he decided to move on to the drier leeward side of the Wai'anae Range. In April, after his Wai'anae trip, he made a second excursion out to Waialua. These first few excursions were already enough to alert Perkins to the problems with introduced ants, as is evidenced by the response of Newton (*vide infra*) to Perkins's first letter to him from the field.

Perkins gave a more detailed summary of these first months on O'ahu in later correspondence:

"My first trip after reaching Honolulu was to Waialua in iii.92 & during part of this month & I think part of April I stayed in the house of Mehaulu {= Mahaulu} & collected (mostly on foot from there) only in the nearest parts of the Waianae range up to 3000 ft. I was not very successful as birds were scarce & of these I took only a few specimens; I carried a gun as always, the distance to any good collecting was considerable & of course all was strange to me, so that I spent a lot of time in places that later I should have known to be unprofitable. Returning to Honolulu I visited Waianae & stopped at a small dairy, run by a Portugese, some miles above Waianae. Birds were scarce & common species I shot at few or none, but I collected over a good deal of ground up to 3000 ft & did quite well with insects, particularly Micro-lepidoptera. I also collected to the head of Makaha Valley, a large part of which was then filled with Lantana, beneath which it was necessary to crawl along pig trails, though the lower part had an open path." *(R.C.L. Perkins letter to E.C. Zimmerman, 14 March 1944, BPBM Entomology Archives).*

Perkins's insect collection labels indicate that he collected in the neighborhood of Honolulu in between his collecting in the Wai'anae range and his trip to Kona. In April and May he collected in "forests" near Honolulu and also along a ridge on the Kōnāhuanui side of Nu'uanu Valley.

Based on the amazing detail of species identifications he made by sight and of the general knowledge and habits of the birds and insects he wrote about in his first few journal entries while in Kona in June 1892, Perkins probably used these first three months on O'ahu as a time to meet fellow naturalists, learn as much as possible about the fauna and their biologies, catch up on the literature, and then go out and see what he could find—improving on his attempts until he was satisfied with the results. Waialua, the Wai'anae mountain range, and areas near to where he was staying (the Eagle House in Honolulu) such as Nu'uanu Valley apparently became his training grounds with regard to insect collecting.

During this period, he also made an effort to learn about the Hawaiian flora. He was apparently an excellent student as all of his journal entries are replete with the names of host plants and trees in which insects and birds were found nesting, roosting, or feeding. He most always included the Hawaiian name for plants, birds, and other living things he came across in his travels. Some names he may have learned from his birding predecessor Wilson, but no doubt he also learned many Hawaiian names from local guides while in the islands.

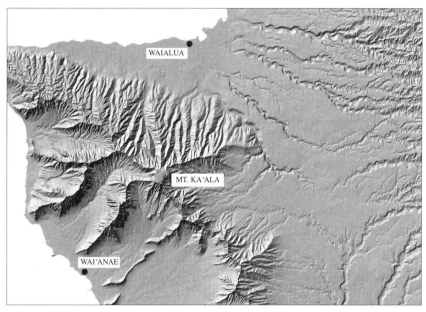

 Map of O'ahu with detail showing Perkins's March and April 1892 collecting areas in the Wai'anae range.

JOURNALS AND REMEMBRANCES

[I kept no diary of my two first trips into the country on Oahu in April and May 1892.[46] The first was to Waialua, where I stayed at Mehaulu's {= Mahaulu's}[47] but collected only in the Waianae range and the ridges of Kaala.[48] I saw but four species of birds — the Elepaio, Apapane, Iiwi and Amakihi, nor did I do very well with the insects, everything being of course strange to me. After a return to Honolulu I went out to Waianae, and stayed for some time in a small unoccupied dairy house belonging to the Waianae Plantation, and for two or three days with August Ahrens,[49] the manager. The dairy was below the forest and on the edge of some quite swampy ground. I saw no birds other than those I had found on the other side of the range, but did fairly well with the insects. When I reported the number of species of Lepidoptera that I obtained on this trip, Dr Sharp wrote back to me that it was evident that the known species of these would be greatly increased if I should be so able to visit all the islands, the number found in so short time in so small an area being unexpected by him. Ahrens himself was interested in entomology to some extent, and showed me specimens of the cane-borer[50] and a few other beetles that he had collected for a friend in Germany. He begged me to get him a few beetles from the mountains for this friend, but I was only able to supply him with a few kinds. On the whole for a beginner I did fairly well on this trip and gained a good deal of information as to the best sort of localities for the native insects.]

---

[46] Perkins actually was first in the field on Oʻahu in March as is indicated by his label data of 26 March on Mt. Kaʻala, 1500 ft. and his later correspondence that indicated he traveled to the east side of the Waiʻanae range up to about 3000 feet.

[47] Mahaulu, Archibald Scott (1863–1939) was postmaster of Waialua and district judge.

[48] Further details of Perkins's activities around Waialua and the Waiʻanae Range are found in correspondence: "... I was staying at Waialua at the ranch home—formerly I believe the Emerson family lived there—which was near the place where later the 'Haleiwa hotel' was built. On two occasions I tramped from there to that part on the E. side of the Waianae range which is opposite to Wahiawa of the Koolau range (that made a pretty hard days work!)." *(R.C.L. Perkins letter to G.C. Munro, 21 December 1947, BPBM Archives, MS SC Munro Box 13.3).*

[49] Ahrens, August (1856–1917) started with the Waianae Plantation in the 1880s as a sugar boiler and became Manager by the time Perkins arrived in the islands. He was also the school agent for the Waianae district until 1897. The Waianae Plantation on the leeward side of Oʻahu had sugar, coffee, and dairy lands under its control.

[50] Its common name is actually the New Guinea sugarcane borer [*Rhabdoscelus obscurus* (Boisduval)].

SELECTED CORRESPONDENCE

Magdalene College
Cambridge, England
19 March 1892
Robert Cyril Layton Perkins

Dear M^r. Perkins,

This will find you I hope safely arrived, and prospering in your undertaking. We have had no news of you since you left England, and I need not say we shall be glad to hear from you.

I am today sending you six copies of the last number of "Nature" containing an article by me on the ornithology of the Sandwich Isles, and I hope that by distributing these copies in likely quarters you may excite greater interest in your investigations. I would suggest your taking steps to have part or parts of it, if not the whole, reproduced in one or more of the island newspapers. The more public notice is taken of your doings and the more attention is drawn to your objects the more likely are you to succeed in attaining them.

I have been much disappointed at the publication of my article being so long delayed. I had hoped it would appear within fortnight of your departure, and to have speedily followed your arrival at Honolulu; but it seems to have been "crowded out" of "Nature" until now. With best wishes I remain

Yours very truly,
Alfred Newton

Magdalene College
Cambridge, England
21 April 1892
Robert Cyril Layton Perkins

Dear M^r. Perkins

I was very glad this morning to get your letter from the "British Club, Honolulu"[51] bearing an Oahu postmark 26 March[52] & thusly to know of your safe arrival — a few days previously I presume; but neither the day of your arrival nor of your writing is

---

[51] Currently called the Pacific Club. This establishment for businessmen in Hawai'i was founded in 1851 and is one of the oldest continuing organizations in Hawai'i. It served as a safe haven for British arriving in the Islands in its early days.

[52] This postmark does not indicate the date upon which Perkins actually wrote this letter. On 26 March, Perkins was on Mt. Ka'ala in the Wai'anae Mountains (as indicated by label data) and did not return to Honolulu until April. International mail went out every Saturday and 26 March 1892 was a Saturday. Based on the letter from Newton of 30 April (below), it is most likely that Perkins wrote this letter on British Club stationery either in Honolulu a few days before he traveled to the Wai'anae Mountains to collect or had the stationery with him while in the Waialua area and wrote while in the field and had the letter mailed from Waialua.

given. It is satisfactory to learn that in such matters your operations are likely to be facilitated, and I trust that before very long they will be of such a kind as to induce an extension of assistance. I shall be most anxious until we get fresh news of you, and I trust some may reach us before 3^d May, on which day I rather think the question of a renewal of the grant from the Government Fund will be virtually decided. I understand that at the last meeting of the Board it was opposed, and our fate is therefore uncertain. If a promising report should be in the meantime received from you all may go well, otherwise I have my fears.

I think it is very likely that the Bishop Collection[53] may contain a good many specimens of birds that have been introduced into the Islands, and that naturally you would not have seen at Cambridge or elsewhere – but you may be sure that pretty nearly all you get on Oahu will be worth having (except of course such widely spread species as <u>Vestiaria coccinea</u> & <u>Himatione sanguinea</u>) for Wilson made no regular attempt to collect on that island or I suspect he would have got other green species of <u>Himatione</u>, the two peculiar species of <u>Hemignathus</u> & perhaps <u>Acrulocercus apicalis</u>.

I am just now at Lowestoft[54] for a few days, but return to Cambridge almost immediately – meanwhile I forward your letter to D^r. David Sharp – and wishing you well I remain

Yours very truly,
Alfred Newton

I hope you will have received the 1/2 dozen copies of '<u>Nature</u>' containing my paper on the ornithology of the S.I. & have been able to distribute them to advantage.

Magdalene College
Cambridge, England
30 April 1892
Robert Cyril Layton Perkins

Dear M^r. Perkins,

Your letter of the 7th {April} reached me two days ago (thus taking only 3 weeks) & has given me great pleasure – for I think that as a first excursion in a strange country your trip to Waialua was as successful as one has any right to expect – even as regards the birds – while your letter to D^r. Sharp concerning the insects & things in general, which he has shown me seems to have more than satisfied him, and (though I am not sure of it) perhaps he is less easily pleased than I am! The Portugee you bribed was faithful, and duly posted your letter at Waialua as you will in due time learn when you get the answer to it that I wrote on the 21st.

<hr>

[53] The Bernice P. Bishop Museum in Honolulu was founded in 1889 by Charles Reed Bishop as a tribute to his late wife, the Princess Bernice Pauahi. It contained artifacts of Hawaiian royalty as well as natural history specimens from throughout Polynesia. From these noble yet humble beginnings, the museum today has grown to house more than 22 million natural history specimens from throughout the Pacific region..

[54] Located in Waveney District, Suffolk, eastern England, on the North Sea. Lowestoft is the most easterly town in England. It is an important fishing center as well as a popular resort.

You seem to have gone to the right place, and on your return thither on your way from Wainae {= Wai'anae} to Kahuka {= Kahuku} you will probably find it more profitable than it first appeared. As to the yellow Himatione you got I refrain from a decided opinion till I see it – still from what you say of its having a curved bill it ought to be chloris. Wilson never got a really yellow specimen anywhere and the only one I have seen is one of Townsend's which they sent to us to look at from Philadelphia – & appeared to us to be the adult of maculata in full plumage. It is quite possible that both species have a yellow phase, and perhaps indeed all the other green species as well. Here I may mention that Townsend in his book[55] (p. 269) under date entry 15 Jany. writes – "Several days ago M^r. Deppe and myself visited Nuano {= Nu'uanu} Valley, where we hired a native house, in which we are now living. Our subject has been to procure birds, plants, &c., and we have so far been very successful. I have already prepared about eighty birds which I procured here"[56] – a little further on he says it was five miles from Honolulu, commanding a fine view of the harbour & shipping. There is no Nuano marked on my map, but doubtless you should find the place easily enough if you don't already know it – but it would naturally be altered, being so near the capitol {sic}, in the course of time, & might have a poor collecting station now.

You are quite right as to the differences between Himatione & Hemignathus – the latter has the lower mandible perceptibly not to say much shorter than the upper. To find out whether either or both of the two Oahuan species of Hemignathus still exists is a great point – Wilson got neither, and of the bigger species H. lichtensteini, the only specimen known is that at Berlin. Of the smaller one, H. lucidus, we have 2 or 3 of Townsend's specimens here. These two species & the Oahuan Acrulocercus whichever it be (& I expect it is apicalis, with tail feathers tipped with white) are about the best things to be got in the bird-way there.

I dont remember Wilson having told me of the devastation caused by the "mynahs" – but I can well believe it – only I thought they had not been forest haunting birds, keeping rather to the cultivated portions. I suppose you have satisfied yourself that they do interfere with the native species – people who are not naturalists take up such strange ideas on subjects of this kind – even in England there are men who say that the Red-legged Partridge drives away the Gray bird. About Chasiempis it is useless for me to form any opinion – It is as puzzling a question as I ever had to do with – & I dont see how it is to be cleared up except through the evidence of observers on the spot.

I am glad you have got a good guide, though guides are at the best an encumbrance, however necessary they may be at times – & of course they often are. It is something that the Gov^t. gave you a permit to shoot & they offer you a cheap passage to the other islands – but, though it is a matter on which you must use your own discre-

---

55 Townsend wrote a book in 1839 entitled "Narrative of a journey across the Rocky Mountains, to the Columbia River, and a visit to the Sandwich Islands, Chili, etc.," which gives a description of the vegetation and bird fauna when he and W. Deppe visited in 1838.

56 Perkins wrote to Munro: "It is curious that Bloxam found birds scarce on Oahu (1825) while Townsend and Deppe 10 years later found them very plentiful & much more so than on Kauai but I suspect that the latter naturalists were much better collectors." (*R.C.L. Perkins letter to G.C. Munro, 26 May 1944, BPBM Archives MS SC Munro Box 13.3*).

tion, I am not at all anxious that you should leave Oahu – especially after what you have written to D^r. Sharp & myself of the extent of the forest there, and the time it would take to explore them. Wilson certainly did not do them as much as he might – and Hawaii is so big a place, that you would be so to speak, lost in it besides the fact that so far as I know Rothschild's man {Palmer} has been working the best districts or what are believed as such. I have good hopes of the £200 grant from the Government Fund of the Royal Society being renewed, so good indeed that after talking the matter over with D^r. Sharp yesterday we came to the conclusion that D^r. Hickson might safely remit you another £100 and he is to be instructed accordingly. We shall of course be glad to receive the first fruits of your labours – pray be careful how you send them. I think I mentioned to you that I had heard from M^r. Vredenburg of Waimea & in his letter which was dated 24 Feb. he said was sending (I suppose by post) a box with some insects – but alas! the box has not turned up & I fear it may have been "confiscated" in passing through America, as it certainly ought to have reached here by this time.

I was sorry to notice in your letter to D.S. you said it was impossible to collect birds & insects on the same day – I have certainly known collectors who were able to look after both. He bids me to thank you for your letter which he will reply in a few days.

I think I have now touched on every point concerning which you have written me, and once more I thank you for your letters. Remaining

Yours very truly,
Alfred Newton

Not the least pleasant news you sent Sharp was that you felt so "fit" – pray you keep so. You will find ants most annoying & requiring every caution to be taken against their injuring your collections.

Magdalene College
Cambridge, England
21 May 1892
Robert Cyril Layton Perkins

Dear M^r. Perkins,

I thank you for your letters, bearing the postmark "Honolulu April 20", and written, I suppose, a couple of days before. I am very sorry that the packet with 6 copies of 'Nature' had not reached you, & I fear it may have been stolen in transit. I have asked Macmillan to post you another six and to register the packet, so I trust you may get it. It is of course very annoying to me that the first miscarried, though I hope M^r. Bishop will have received that which I sent him separately. After what you tell me of the behavior of Rothschild's collectors, it is of the highest importance that the distinctly scientific and public nature of your mission – contrasted with the spirit in which they go to work – should be well understood by all persons in the islands, & I think that my article in 'Nature' would help to accomplish this.

I wrote to you last on the 30<u>th</u> April in reply to your letter of the 7<u>th</u> of that month – & there told that the place where Deppe & Townsend stayed to collect birds was in the Nuano {Nu'uanu} valley, only 5 miles from Honolulu. Of course it does not follow that the things they got would be found there now – in fact the presumption is to the contrary – & I quite approve of your going to the westward & northern ranges – but I do hope the two species of Hemignathus will in time reward your researches – & also that you may get the Oahu Acrulocercus, whichever it may be. I find Wilson thinks that A. apicalis (the one he did not get) is on Maui, but whether he has good ground for that belief I don't know. Your former letter I sent him to read, & he returned it remarking that he thought you were making a good beginning – which indeed was my own opinion as I told you, though I wish this last letter had reported things secured as well as seen.

I am glad to inform you that we have obtained the wished for renewed grant from the Royal Society (£200) which was voted 3 days ago – & I hope we may in due time get the other £100 from the British Association but there will be a fight for it as there always is & much (I may say everything) will depend on what we hear & receive from you between this and the middle of July. Still the money we have already got ought to enable you to work Oahu very fairly, & may pay for a subsequent visit to Maui & Hawaii but I fear the size of the latter will prevent your attacking it very successfully. Hickson has, I believe, remitted you another £100 for current expenses – at least we instructed him to do so, & he said he would.

I dont know that I have anything else to say to you. In your movements you must be guided chiefly by what you think best. I always place confidence in a man until he does something to shew that he is not worthy of it, & I should not be writing to you in this way if I thought you were doing anything of the kind. You do not mention your health, so I trust it is good, and with my best wishes for your success I remain

Yours very truly
Alfred Newton

D<u>r</u>. Sharp has just sent me a letter to enclose with my own for you, & I have read what he says – I wholly agree with him about the balance of notes made at the time. I don't know where his 5000 silver pins[57] are but I suppose he will put them in a separate letter. I hope you will mount them all & do not be afraid of asking for more when they are used up.

---

[57] Perkins in later correspondence explained the use of these silver pins: "When I went out to the islands there were no good pins for small insects comparable with the rustless, stainless steel ones we now use, but Sharp introduced the silver wire ones (about 9 p.c. alloy) which did not rust nor verdigris like the ordinary ones. These pins were very soft & I found that while one could pin certain Carabidae with these, the points always turned when one tried to pierce the species with convex elytra such as fugitivus, fascipennis, &c." *(R.C.L. Perkins letter to E.C. Zimmerman, 18 August 1937, BPBM Entomology Archives).*

University Museum of Zoology and Comparative Anatomy
Cambridge, England
21 May 1892
Robert Cyril Layton Perkins

Dear M^r. Perkins,

I duly received your letter of 7.4.92, but have not replied to it before, as I thought by waiting a letter I might get another one from you in reply to one I wrote you about two months ago asking you, as soon as you had sufficient knowledge to do so, to inform the Committee as to the sums of money that you think may be necessary to carry on the exploration satisfactorily, and also as to the time & so on that you suppose may be required. I daresay I shall receive information on these points shortly.

I was most pleased to hear that you had arrived safely in the islands and that you had made a first expedition with satisfactory results as to the insects (though I would have liked to have known that the large dragon-flies had been captured as well as seen). Your Clytarlus & Lucanid I am most pleased to hear of, but of course can say nothing of their novelty till I see them.

I think we have enough money in hand to carry on matters till the meeting of the British Association (and to bring you back of course if that should unfortunately be necessary); and we propose making an application to the British Association for another sum: but now that we have a collector in the islands, it is necessary if we expect to get a grant from the Association that we should be able to point to results achieved, because there is always a keen competition for the small amounts of public funds that can be devoted to such purposes. The Association meeting is earlier than usual this year, it meets (at Edinburgh) on the 3rd August, and we must have our report ready quite a fortnight before that; I hope by that time we may have received the results of your first month or two's work, but if you should not have sent us anything, I think you will just about have time after the receipt of this letter to send us an account of your doings so that we may act accordingly. Independent of the Committee I look personally with great interest to what you may think of the prospects of doing good work in the islands and what results in specimens you think there may be. Of course any observations on the habits or distribution of the creatures that you may make, and that you may publish will be quite your own gift to the scientific world, so I shall say nothing about them, but if you have time to make any jottings in note-books however imperfect I recommend you do it as such memoranda even when of the most imperfect nature are very useful afterwards in enabling the mind to recall exactly the conditions one wishes to describe. Great interest is in the details of the Sandwich Island fauna and I have little doubt myself that our own interest will continue to increase. I observe in the last part of the P. Boston Soc. that it is stated that Mr. Gulick has got the Achatinellidae in the act of evolving by segregation into more numerous species! and that the Bostonians are so taken with the idea that they have constructed a model of Oahu, and are sticking the specimens on the model in the spots that Gulick says he caught them in so as to illustrate his views.[58]

No doubt when you come back loaded with information as to the local conditions {of the} fauna generally your opinions will be of much value. At any rate I am sure they will be looked forward to by zoologists with much interest.

If we can do anything to assist you in getting as complete a sample of the fauna as possible, please do not hesitate to ask us, for I am sure the Committee find you going ahead well, they will be most anxious to assist you & to keep the {illegible} going, so do not fear swamping us with material, we can do with a great deal of that. In the birds I presume what you have learned from Prof^r. Newton that discretion & knowledge what to look for are of more importance than they are in the invertebrates. You mentioned lizards in your letter to me, they will be of much interest, and especially from different localities and islands.

I was most pleased to hear you are in good health and spirits, and I hope these will continue, and your efforts to make us acquainted with all the beasties of the islands will be highly successful. With this letter I send you 5,000 of the silver pins of various sizes, if you want more or anything else, please let me know.

With best wishes in hoping to hear from you soon

I am yours very truly
D. Sharp.

PS: I do not mean that you should publish anything now. I am only speaking of the advisability of your making memoranda now for your own future use.

Museum
Cambridge, England
28 May 1892
Robert Cyril Layton Perkins

Dear M^r. Perkins,

Your letter of May 5th reached me on the 26th inst., a week less than usual on the road, the time of transit being usually apparently four weeks. In it you allude to sending off some specimens but you do not say by what route, whether by same mail or what. They have not arrived here and I do not know whether I ought to be uneasy about them or not.

---

[58] This relief model of O'ahu was built by malacologist Alpheus Hyatt (1838–1902), curator of the Boston Society of Natural History and founder of the Woods Hole Marine Laboratory, in order to better understand the geographical relationships of the *Achatinella* species upon which Gulick had written treatises.

The entomological items of news of course interest & please me very much. You have put three questions to me, to which I will first reply. 1. Whether you should buy a tent? This must be left entirely to your own discretion; the treasurer sent another £100 to be placed to your credit at the Bank in Honolulu about a fortnight ago, and I have received a grant of £200 recently from the Royal Society, so that we have funds in hand to go on for some time. Of course the Committee would like them husbanded to the best of your ability because it appears to me that two or three years are required at least for our purposes, and it will be difficult to procure the funds for the latter part of the exploration; as regards this point I shall feel much obliged if you can put me in a position to inform the Committee what sum you find you must have to carry on the exploration satisfactorily; we must have some knowledge of this kind as all arrangements have to be made long beforehand, so we must know what is the least we can do with so as to ensure providing that.

The second point is whether you should at present stop in Oahu or go to Hawaii? As to this we must again leave it to your discretion. You know the ways & means, & the advantages and disadvantages of going from island to island frequently much better than we do over here; and as regards looking after things specially, that is practically limited to the ornithology, & you have received as to what instruction Prof^r. Newton can give you.

The third point you enquire about is whether you ought to neglect one group for another. Here again we leave you complete powers for decision; of course I must not recommend to neglect any one group for another, more so by doing you might in the long run very much limit the results you attain. But I admit I should like to see you do well in the other groups beyond entomology and should be most particularly pleased to find you were able to settle the ornithological points Prof. Newton especially pointed out to you.

I am afraid there has been miscarriage of some of our letters to you, could you give us any better address than Honolulu?[59] I think if you were to make arrangements with some person or institution where we could address you & who would constantly send on to you or take good care of letters it would be better.

It will give me the greatest pleasure to assist you in any small matters that I can over here; and I shall write to your father as soon as the specimens you sent off arrive. I think from what you say I had better try to get you some fine pithe for the finest pins for you to stick into instead of cork. Be sure and use plenty of carbolic {acid} in your boxes & things, it is I know from Blackburn's experience the only way of keeping things from spoiling. I sent you 5000 pins by last mail; if you want more of any one size shortly please let me know which size and how many; perhaps a specimen

---

[59] Letters to Perkins by Sharp and Newton were invariably addressed simply as "R.C.L. Perkins, Honolulu, Hawaii" and would be delivered to the general post office in Honolulu, where Perkins could pick them up when he was in town. He gave instructions to the Honolulu postmaster where letters could be forwarded when he traveled to other islands. Upon arriving at each destination of his inter-island travels, Perkins would have to make contact with the postmaster there to ensure that his letters would be received and possibly taken to him in the field if he desired, or picked up from the postmaster. Since many of the "rural" postmasters in those days often had letters received at their normal place of occupation, folks coming to pick up letters could be a boon to their business (e.g., James Anderson, the postmaster in Makawao, Maui, was the manager of a grocery store).

would make {illegible} still safer. I have already mentioned that the treasurer sent another £100 to your credit at the Bank at Honolulu about two weeks ago.

I shall see next week if I can make out a list of known species of Leps for you. Of course you wont neglect the large things that come in your way unless you are quite certain that they are no good. The big Elater[60] you speak of is of great interest, scarcely any specimens are known of it (<u>Chalcolepidus albertis</u> is its name) and it is a point of dispute as to whether it is distinct from a South American species or not; a knowledge of its variation is essential to settling such point. So also with regard to the common large Longicorn,[61] how much it varies is very important.

As regards to the want of success in turning over stones, this mode of collecting varies greatly according to circumstances, especially in hot climates; the sun heats the stones so greatly that if something is found under them it is buried in the ground or at the roots of the plants at the edges of the stones; on the other hand at different seasons & circumstances things might be found freely even under quite small stones. I found in some situations in Spain that digging at the edges of quite large rocks where there was vegetable matter was very successful when {illegible} could be found under stones, and the things in such cases go down quite deep till they come to the first layer of damp or cool soil. In the south of France one finds all sorts of small insects under large stones deeply imbedded & requiring two to turn them over, especially when such stones are situated in partially shaded spots, and are of a somewhat bad conductor of heat character.

I intend to reserve the Aculeate[62] Hymenoptera, so that you may if you please have the opportunity of working them out when you come back. There are two or three genera of large Orthopteran described from the islands, but I think nearly all are known by only one specimen; and this applies even in the case of the large dragon-flies. In regard to the Thysanura and Collembola of which you speak it is most diffi-cult to preserve specimens well; you might try a few in glycerine as well as in spirit; they are very interesting & owing to their belonging to an entirely apterous order are of special importance in the Sandwich Islands. Diptera are not much got in warm countries except by catching them in a net specially. The insect you mention with curious front legs as possibly a Mantid is more likely I fancy to turn out a mantispid (Neuroptera), or if it has a beak a bug of the family Emesiidae, which singularly resemble small Mantids.

With all good wishes possible, and hoping the specimens will soon come to hand, I am

Yours very truly
D. Sharp.

---

60 Elater — entomologist's slang for Elateridae.
61 Longicorn — beetles of the family Cerambycidae.
62 Aculeate — a type of Hymenoptera including bees, vespid wasps, and sphecid wasps; many aculeates in Hawai'i are solitary, that is, not living in colonies.

Kona, Hawai'i Island
4 June–14 October 1892

Although in his letters Newton pleaded for Perkins to stay and collect on O'ahu to get rare birds, Perkins instead felt that his chances of capturing rare and good numbers of birds and insects would be better on the island of Hawai'i than on O'ahu and he therefore made arrangements to visit its Kona coast within three months of having arrived on O'ahu. On Friday 3 June he boarded the Inter-Island Steam Ship Company's *W.G. Hall* for the 30-hour trip from Honolulu to the island of Hawai'i. Leaving Honolulu at 12 noon, the steamer made stops along the way at the ports of Lahaina on Maui and Kawaihae on Hawai'i Island before sailing a bit more south and arriving off shore of Kealakekua Bay at roughly 6 pm on Saturday 4 June. There is no dock in Kealakekua Bay, so Perkins, along with others that went ashore there, debarked by way of a longboat.

Little is known of his activities soon after arriving, but since he had not yet purchased a tent he no doubt made rooming arrangements at the Yates boarding house (the only boarding house) near the Greenwell home (elevation roughly 1500 ft.) in the Ka'awaloa district upslope of the famous Captain Cook monument. Perkins probably spent a few days or so after his arrival collecting at the lower elevations (an insect label from 6 June is from Kealakekua), then he spent time making arrangements for his food, equipment, and lodging for collecting higher up on the slopes of Mauna Loa. With letters of introduction preceding him, he contacted the Greenwells, asked permission to collect on their lands, and arranged for an assistant to accompany him. Since Perkins lists Pulehua[63] as a return address in his correspondence and mentions it frequently in his journal entries as a base of operations, no doubt the Greenwells allowed him to stay in the ranch house of that name while collecting in the upland area.

---

[63] Contemporary maps at the time Perkins collected in this area have this locality spelled as "Puu Lehua" (referring to the hill of that name); however, the name "Pulehua" actually refers to the act of liming trees for birds and the spelling with one "u" is correct (Jean Greenwell, pers. comm.). The name refers to one of the Greenwell ranch areas up slope (at about 4600 ft.) from their house at Kalukalu (1500 ft.). Pulehua is most likely the locality from which Perkins made collections in the surrounding forests labeled on specimens and in his journals as "Kona 4000 ft". Dr. George Trousseau built the house in 1873 when he was a physician to the Hawaiian royal court, and used it as a sheep station. Henry Greenwell purchased it in 1879. Before acquiring the "Pulehua" name, it was known as "Dr. Trousseau's mountain cottage" and was a popular place for birders to use as lodging and a center of collecting in the surrounding forests. Scott Wilson had stayed in this house during his time in the Kona area and recommended to Perkins that he do likewise. The first specimen of the *palila* (*Loxioides bailleui*) was collected here by Théodore Ballieu (1828–1885), who was French consul in Hawai'i from 1869–1878. The ranch house burned down in 1987, and all that remains of the buildings now is the butter house.

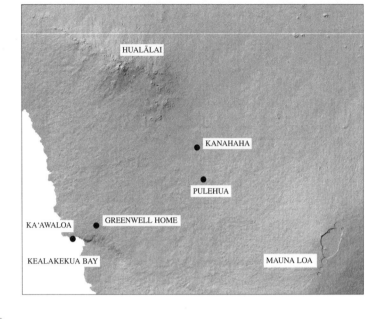

Map of Hawai'i Island with detail showing Perkins's collecting areas in the Kona area.

JOURNALS AND REMEMBRANCES

So far in Oahu I had seen very few birds and none of those which Professor Newton was most anxious for me to obtain, viz., <u>Acrulocercus apicalis</u>, and the Oahu species of <u>Heterorhynchus</u> and <u>Hemignathus</u>. Consequently I thought it would be advisable to visit some district of the islands where the birds were known to be numerous in species and individuals, so as to become better acquainted with their habits than seemed possible on Oahu. On this account I left Oahu for Kona, Hawaii in June 1892, and stayed there for several months. Here, I was helped in every possible way by Mrs. Greenwell and her two elder sons who were managing the ranch. Mr. Greenwell[64] had died some time before I came to the islands and

---

[64] Henry Nicholas Greenwell (1826-1891) arrived in Hawai'i (from England via Australia) in 1850 and was one of the first coffee plantation owners on the island of Hawai'i in addition to his being a cattle and sheep rancher. In 1868 he married Elizabeth Caroline (née Hall) (1841–1934) in Montserrat and soon returned to Hawai'i to continue his agricultural interests. The two had 10 children, 6 sons and 4 daughters. After his death in December 1891, his sons Arthur and William Henry, took over ranching responsibilities. Perkins seems to have made friends with the Greenwells on his first visit and usually visited them on subsequent trips to the Kona area. The Greenwell whom Perkins mentions here as being associated with the fisherman's fly "Greenwell's Glory" was William Nicolas Greenwell (1822–1919).

it was only later that I learned that his brother was the well-known archaeologist and Canon of Durham Cathedral, whose name is known to every trout fisherman as perpetuated in the famous trout-fly 'Greenwell's Glory'.

On June 20th I made my first note concerning my collecting, though still very unfamiliar with the Hawaiian fauna. I had then been collecting for some time in Kona, as is evident from my remarks on birds on July 1st.[65]

June 20[66]

At 4000 ft. I found nine specimens of a species of Chalcididae forming a circle round the exit of a burrow in a dead tree-trunk. Their antennae were kept in rapid movement and they were crossing these, each with its neighbour. The exit hole was that of some beetle, probably occupied by some Aculeate, and I imagine that the parasites, all males, were assembling in expectation of the emergence of the female. [A crude sketch made of these 9 males, regularly arranged round the edge of the hole, as if looking into it, would indicate a species of Eupelmus.]

June 25

Collected down to Kaawaloa,[67] as I am going down to the steamer landing at Kealakekua to-morrow. I took some interesting spiders, a Clytarlus, a small, gnat-like predaceous bug, and at the start (4000 ft.) a beautiful black and white Tineid on a Koa trunk. Also Aculeate Hym., Odynerus with a humped back, pug moths,[68] Neuroptera, &c. [The Tineid was Hyposmocoma exornata.]

June 26–27

Went down to the steamer landing. {Collected on the beach.}

June 28

Walked up to Pulehua. Collected a large black Eucnemid but only dead specimens, and some Cossonids on the way up.

---

[65] Although his first published note on insect collecting is 20 June, Perkins evidently made notes on earlier bird collecting in Kona or else referred to his memory, because his article in *The Ibis* concerning his bird collecting in Kona refers to incidents no doubt before 20 June: "In the lower forest the oo (*Acrulocercus nobilis*) was a common bird, frequenting, as is well known, the lofty lehua-trees, especially when growing in the rough lava. Save its antipathy to the red birds (*Vestiaria*), its habits are difficult to observe, as it usually keeps very high up in the trees. Its peculiar cry, rather more like "ow-ow" than "oo", is very curious, and it would readily respond and even approach when I imitated its voice. The young bird is without the tufts of yellow feathers beneath the wings. I strongly suspect it builds in holes in the trunks of the lehua-trees at a great elevation, as my native assistant and a white boy, who was with him at the time, assured me that they saw one of these birds enter such a hole two or three times, but that they could not possibly climb up, though they made the attempt. This was about the middle of June—at the same time that I obtained the young, which certainly had not been long out of the nest." (Perkins, R.C.L., 1893, *The Ibis*, (6) 5: 109).

[66] Perkins's collection number for insects taken on this day (No. 213) indicates he also collected at the 2500-ft elevation in this area. It is possible that Perkins collected downslope from where he was staying (at Pulehua) and worked his way back upslope to the 4000-ft elevation of Pulehua during the day.

[67] Ka'awaloa was the district in which Perkins spent most of his time while on Greenwell land. It refers specifically to the area on the coast where Cook's monument is located; but also pertains to the general group of residences in the Kealakekua area in which the Greenwell's had their residence (Kalukalu) and other farmers and retailers resided (located about 1500 ft in elevation). Perkins did collect around Cook's monument, but if the specimen labels have "1500 ft" they pertain instead to the area near the Greenwell home of Kalukalu.

[68] Pug moths — moths of the family Geometridae.

June 29
Collected down to the lower dairy,[69] but before 11 a.m. it turned out very wet; I got a few Elaters, black and brown forms, and 2 larger and 2 smaller Xyletobius. There was a very minute oval beetle in an evil smelling fungus, a number of a species of Cis and 2 or 3 Staphs.[70] I spent most of the day searching tree-trunks for the black and white Tineids of which I took several of 2 or 3 species. The following tineids looked the best: (1) a unicolorous bronzy species; on the wing, 3 specimens (2) a larger species with black fore wings and a rather broad white bar across near the apex; on tree trunk [Heterocrossa latifasciata] (3) a greyish white species with black V-shaped mark near centre of each fore wing.

June 30
Went upwards to 5000 ft. I brought back a number of beetles, but little I think new to me, except perhaps Cis and 2 spp. of Staphs. There are: Proterhinus about 20, Staphs two from dry dead wood of Koa, one with a red head, perhaps Oligota; Cossonidae shining, metallic, four [Oodemas]; Cis about two dozen, of three species; Elaters about 2 dozen; Xyletobius or allies about 50. Spiders about a dozen and a half; Hym. Aculeate two dozen specimens. Hemiptera 14 (3 or 4 species); Lepidoptera 25. A fine 'lacewing'[71] new to me, blackish-bronze with red head and tip of abdomen — 3 specimens. Also about a dozen of an ant-lion.[72] I saw no birds that I cared to shoot at.

July 1
Went out with gun and net with native boy. Took a small Eucnemid under bark and Cossonidae from that of fallen trees. An elongate testaceous species of Nitidulid with black markings at sap beneath Acacia bark, and a Staph with it. A few of the large Xyletobius on dead standing trunks; male and female sent as No. 26 Cis &c in fungi and under bark.[73] The two males of {No.} 26 were pursuing the female, and when the latter stretched its wings to fly I boxed the three. These Xyletobius fall to the ground at once when alarmed. I collected two species of Geometers[74] from Acacia trunks, and a pair of a Tineid in cop.[75] Also a Chrysopid, an Odynerus and a Crabro. At night a fine Noctuid with minute central white dot surrounded with black on fore-wings, and a large Tineid.

While examining a fallen tree-trunk for beetles I heard quite near me the peculiar whistled song of the big Finch.[76] It is quite different from that of any other bird

---

[69]   The Greenwells had a number of dairies on their lands below Pulehua. Perkins could have been referring to one of these dairies or to the one at Nahuina. Gaspar's Dairy, which appears on current maps, was not in existence in 1892.

[70]   Entomologist's slang for Staphylinidae. Perkins's collecting notes for this day (No. 279) indicate these staphylinids were also collected from the fungus.

[71]   From the description, this appears to be a specimen of the family Chrysopidae in the order Neuroptera.

[72]   Family Myrmeleontidae (Neuroptera), ant-lions.

[73]   These specimens no doubt are a part of Perkins's collection Nos. 301, 308, 328, and 338, which indicate that they were collected at the 4000-foot elevation, probably near Pulehua.

[74]   Moths or caterpillars of the family Geometridae.

[75]   An abbreviation for the Latin *in copula*, meaning a male and female taken while locked together during mating. An uncommon and quite useful catch for association of the sexes of a species that might otherwise be difficult to associate due to the different appearance of males and females.

[76]   This refers to the Koa Finch (*Rhodacanthis palmeri*). This collected specimen corresponds to Perkins's collection number 347 in the Bishop Museum's vertebrate zoology collection.

here. Advancing gently I got sight of it in easy range and soon had it in my hands a fine male bird. I had no idea of the beauty of this species, as I had seen only a couple of specimens in a glass jar of alcohol, shot for Scott B. Wilson by Henry Greenwell, and not yet sent off. These appeared dark and colourless in the liquid. [Here a brief description of the colour of this bird is omitted.] The beak is very strong but rather less so than that of <u>Chloridops</u>. This specimen, as I noticed on gathering it had the characteristic smell so strong in the green <u>Himatione</u>. [i.e., <u>Chlorodrepanis</u>] though rather less strong than in this.

It is most curious that the so-called Fringillidae should have the same odour as the Drepanids, which have very different food. I have noticed it in both <u>Loxioides</u> and <u>Psittacirostra</u> and Wilson can hardly have failed to do so in the case of these common birds. Later we obtained two more adult males and what I took to be the female of the Finch, but the latter proved to be an immature male. It is a green bird, so as to be more like <u>Chloridops</u> in colour. The more powerful beak of <u>Chloridops</u> is natural, as it is able to break the hard dry drupes of the Bastard Sandal[77] and extract the embryo, and I cannot do this with my tooth. The other feeds on the unripe pod of the Koa cutting this up into pieces of considerable size which are swallowed thus and so found in the stomach. It also feeds on small caterpillars. I also shot the male parent and a young female of <u>Chasiempis</u>. I feel sure now that there is only one species on Oahu. This, however, is quite distinct from the one here.

July 2

After skinning birds I went out to look for more of the Finch, though it was raining fast. I soon shot a male which had come down into a Sandal-wood[78] tree and subsequently saw two more in Koa trees. Excepting a moth new to me I collected no insects, and it is necessary to give one's whole attention to this bird when one is after it. On my return I shot four of the Californian quail {*Callipepla californica*} for food.

July 3

Went out for birds and got one <u>Chloridops</u>, one Koa finch and couple of short-billed <u>Hemignathus</u> [i.e. <u>Heterorhynchus</u>]. The latter works especially the dead wood of the Acacias,[79] tapping loudly with its beak, like a wood-pecker. Its food consists of wood-eating caterpillars, and other Xylophagous[80] insects, especially beetles.

July 4

I went upwards towards the East my boy carrying the gun. While collecting some insects I came on a pair of <u>Chloridops</u>, only a few yards from me and shouted out for the gun, but he was some distance away and when he arrived the cartridge missed fire and the birds flew away. We saw no others. I took a single small

[77] Bastard sandal or bastard sandalwood (*naio* or *'a'aka*) (*Myoporum sandwicense* A. Gray).

[78] Sandalwood (*'iliahi*) (*Santalum freycinetianum* Gaud.).

[79] Acacias = *koa* [*Acacia koa*].

[80] Wood feeding or wood eating.

species of Clytarlus at 5000 ft. and a few species of Cis and Xyletobius with Brachypeplus and Proterhinus as before. We got back late, being lost in the fog and rain. After dark I collected 3 Noctuae[81] at flowers [The flowers of sandal and bastard sandal were both attractive to moths in Kona.]

July 5

Out all day after Chloridops and the Koa finch but we got neither, nor did we even hear either. While waiting about for these I found that the right food plant for the larger Clytarlus [i.e. Plagithmysus blackburni] is the 'Mamani' {= *māmane*} and by searching I got a dozen or more specimens. They run very quickly up the trunks and occasionally take flight. Two pair were in Cop. I found them only on three of the trees examined and these were at some distance apart. I pinned up a few Diptera, and collected some spiders and the larger Xyletobius.

July 6

I collected the whole way down to Kaawaloa, as I wanted food. Pyrameis atalanta and other Lepidoptera. Below Holokalele[82] I collected a dragonfly new to me, Sympetrum?

July 7

Collected in the forest at about 2500–3000 ft., where the Oo was chiefly found. Now the flowers of the Ieie are mostly withered, and I could only find a few Brachypepli and Staphylinids on this plant.

July 8

My thick porpoise-leather shooting boots are now worn to bits by the lava, and I walked up to Pulehua bare-footed. At night a few Noctuae at flowers as usual.

July 9

After birds. Got one female Koa finch and a young male of Loxops and the short-billed Hemignathus [Heterorhynchus]. A few beetles &c. Not a good day.

July 10

Washing clothes &c. Later I went out and collected about two dozen Microlepidoptera.[83] after which it rained heavily and myself and net were wet through, but I did fairly well.

July 11

After the desired birds all day, but saw only one Koa finch, not attainable. I

---

81 Cutworm moths of the family Noctuidae (Lepidoptera).

82 Actually spelled Holoka'alele, elevation 2,500 ft. (762 m). It was known at the time to have ponds; thus, a good place to look for dragonflies and damselflies. The area has always been a marshy flat area in the middle of the sparse forest (J. Greenwell, pers. comm.).

83 Microlepidoptera = very small moths. These usually need special treatment including pinning and processing in the field —which includes blowing on pinned specimens from behind to spread the wings, then placing them on a pinning medium to keep the wings spread— or else they are virtually impossible to identify properly.

watched the Hemignathus with short beak [i.e. Heterorhynchus] with much interest.[84] When I first sighted it, it was ten yards off, but I easily crept up nearer without frightening it. I kept it under observation for a full half-hour. It was creeping
along the fallen tree trunks turning now towards the right and now towards the left
in its search for food, and looking around for this in all directions. At times it
inserted the upper mandible in small holes in the wood while the tip of the lower
rested on the surface of the bark the beak being agape, at times the upper one was
thrust beneath the loose bark and portions prised off. The neck is very strong but
very flexible and aids greatly in this work. The tongue reaches to the tip of the
upper mandible and well beyond the lower and is no doubt used in securing some
of the wood-boring insects. The blows of the bird's beak on the bark of the trees
are audible at a long distance, like those of our woodpeckers. Not much in insects
to-day.

July 12
Out after birds all day, going over to Nahuina.[85] Got two Chloridops, a male and
female. Heard only one Koa finch, but got no sight of it. The stomachs of the
Chloridops were filled with the small white embryos of the bastard sandal, appearing at first sight like a mass of little white maggots. Caught two fine Noctuae at
night. [A brief description of one of these, omitted here, shows that it was Agrotis
neurogramma; the specimen not being recorded in F.H.[86] was probably destroyed
in the mail.]

July 13
I shot only a Loxops and two short-billed Hemignathus [i.e. Heterorhynchus]. I
wandered a long way in the forest without taking particular notice of the way and
got back with difficulty after dark to Pulehua.

July 14
Killed 3 Chloridops, 2 male, 1 female, and saw one Koa finch, but not in range.
Under a little stone I found a single small Carabid.

---

[84] Perkins gives further details of this observation in the Aves chapter of his *Fauna Hawaiiensis*: "On the 11th
of July, 1892, in the high forest of Kona I first had the opportunity of watching one of these birds
{*Heterorhynchus*} in pursuit of food, and I was able to examine all its actions for a long time and at a very short
distance, both with the naked eye and with field-glasses, I have little to add to the account then written, after similar observations of many other individuals. The bird in question was an adult male in fine plumage, and when
first seen was about 10 yards off, but showed no fear when I approached it more closely. It was visiting one after
another of a number of fallen tree-trunks, large but smooth-barked examples of *Acacia koa*. Along each of these
it proceeded from one end to the other, peering now over the right side of the trunk and now over the left, so that
in a single journey it searched both sides of the tree without retracing its steps. The upper mandible is thrust into
small holes or cracks in the wood, while the point of the lower presses on the surface of the bark, and in this manner the burrows of wood-boring insects are opened out. So too it thrusts its upper beak under loose pieces of bark,
resting the lower one on the surface, and breaks off fragments of the bark, under which its food is concealed. The
upper mandible, though so slender as to be slightly flexible, is very strong, and this flexibility of the beak aided
by the extreme flexibility and strength of the neck no doubt greatly assists the bird in exploring and opening out
the burrows. In extracting and capturing its prey it also employs the thin brush-tongue, which can be extended to
the length of the upper mandible. At frequent intervals it gives several blows to the trunk, the sound of which can
be heard at a considerable distance. These blows are dealt with great vigour and with the beak wide agape, so
that the point of both mandibles comes in contact with the surface at the same time." (Perkins, R.C.L., 1903,
Fauna Hawaiiensis 1(4): 427-428).

[85] Nahuina — a ranch on the Kona coast belonging to the Greenwells. Primarily a dairy.

[86]   F.H. = *Fauna Hawaiiensis.*

July 15

Three Elepaio, male female and young skinned, with yesterday's Chloridops. Afterwards collected some Lepidoptera including a Pterophorid new to me.

July 16

I worked as far as to Nahuina but did badly. Except a single specimen of a Brachypeplus, which I think is new to me, there was nothing of interest.

July 17

Went out for birds, but did nothing with these. The insects were better. The small Staph with red head, two Clytarli from Koa, species new to me, with male and female dissimilar [C. nodifer] and Proterhinus, Brachypeplus, Cis, Xyletobius &c as usual. A Hemerobiid with spotted wings is certainly new [There is no record of this in 'F.H.' and I suppose it was amongst the specimens that were broken in transit to England]. Besides these I collected some Myriapods,[87] spiders and slugs. A very minute bronzy Tineid is certainly new.

July 18

Walked down to Kaawaloa with gun, returning to Pulehua in the afternoon. I wanted to get a native duck, but failed. I caught a P. atalanta on the way down. It is much rarer here than P. tammeamea.[88] Staphs and Brachypeplus from Freycinetia, (above 3000 ft.) a large green bug on the bark of Koa tree [Coleotichus[89]], one Chloridops and a few commoner birds. Most of the insects caught to-day I packed in sawdust at Kaawaloa and left down there.

July 19

Went out specifically for the Koa finch. I heard several in the course of the day, but got no sight of any of them. Took a Carabid under a small stone.

July 20

No birds. Small larvae of Deilephila abundant; the apex of the caudal horn is cleft. On lichen a green and black spider exactly resembling the surface on which it rested, could not be beaten for similarity; one large and one small Clytarlus, the latter on Koa. Collected also some Psocidae.

July 21

I collected insects down to Kaawaloa — Coleoptera, Lepidoptera and Aculeate Hymenoptera. Left there towards evening and reached Pulehua late, the last four miles in the dark.[90]

July 22

After birds. I only heard one Koa finch and got no sight of it. One short and one long-billed Hemignathus, all males in good plumage. Two large species of Pro-

---

87   Centipedes and millipedes.

88   *Pyrameis tammeamea.*

89   *Coleotichus blackburniae.*

90   The distance from Ka'awaloa (the Greenwells home in the sense of Perkins) to Pulehua is roughly 8 miles. Thus, some of Perkins's daily hikes while collecting down to the Greenwells and back to Pulehua would be a round trip of 16 miles or so.

sopis one black with white collar, the other with red abdomen. [N{esoprosopis} setosifrons and paradoxica.]

July 23
Sunday. I walked down to the Greenwell's and returned at night.

July 24
Three Chloridops and a male Loxops obtained. Collected some Aculeates and beetles. Eristalis tenax and another foreign Syrphid [Xanthogramma] are common up here. I took a small male Crabro in cop. with female Mimesa!

July 25
Two Chloridops collected; one large and one small Clytarlus and a number of Hemiptera. The flat metallic beetle of which I had taken one before from Maile, I now collected singly on Koa [Parandrita konae.]

July 26
Went down to Kaawaloa to look for the duck (A. wyvilliana) of which I shot one. Saw several of the Haw. buzzard.[91] I stayed down here as it was too late to return.

July 27
An extremely hot day and a hard walk up. On the way I found a rather large Brachypeplus beneath bark, the larvae also numerous in the wet decaying mess, and a Hym. parasite running amongst these [?Proctotrupes hawaiiensis]. A fly with spotted wings [Drosophila hawaiiensis] is common at the sap which exudes from the trunk of Acacia koa.

July 28
Skinned buzzard. No special insects to note.

July 29
Collected down to Kaawaloa. Nothing noteworthy.

July 30
(Sunday) Did not collect.[92]

July 31
Went up to Holokalele on purpose to get Odonata, but almost directly after I got there it poured with rain. I was therefore only able to get very few specimens. These were of two species, male and female of one in cop.

---

91   This the native Hawaiian hawk, or 'io (*Buteo solitarius*). "Buzzard" is a British term for many birds of prey or scavengers that have a similar hovering flight pattern. The Aves chapter of *Fauna Hawaiiensis* by Perkins also listed the common name of *Buteo solitarius* as "Hawaiian buzzard" rather than "Hawaiian hawk."

92   This entry is at odds with Perkins's numbered insect collection (No. 305), which is dated as 30 July and "Kona, 5000 ft." Sundays were a day off for Perkins and Perkins's diary says he went up to Holoka'alele the following day, hence the label data for No. 305 is probably in error.

August 1

Up to Pulehua again and then on to Kanahaha.[93] Beetles and again the Hemerobiid with spotted wings were collected. A very variable Capsid bug swarms on some of the bushy trees round here.

August 2

After birds. No finches, but saw four Chloridops and one buzzard. Nothing else of note.

August 3

Skinned birds and went out to look for Koa finch. Heard none at all. A small Clytarlus brought in with the firewood.

August 4

Only a single Loxops. This Loxops was chasing off the straight-billed Himatione [Oreomyza mana] from a Koa tree, driving it from branch to branch. Previously I had seen the Apapane driving off a male Loxops. Collected chiefly Aculeates and Lepidoptera.

August 5

Went from Pulehua to Hualālai[94] and collected to about 6000 ft. Birds were not plentiful nor any of them species of note. Insects more numerous than I expected. I got some new Lepidoptera and beetles. There were two Tortricids on Koa; and a very small Tineid, almost entirely white, seemed very distinct. Five Staphs. from a dead dry Koa branch and three of a large brown Anobiid; the small flat bronzy beetle [Parandrita]; one from Koa and one from Ohia. Two small Clytarlus, Brachypeplus, Proterhinus &c as previously, but I hope some may be different species; also Neuroptera &c.

August 6

(Sunday) Stayed down at Kaawaloa.

August 7

Collected up to Pulehua. Nothing special. Bred a Tachinid fly from green larva of a Noctuid. Two of the larger [Plagithmysus], one of the smaller Clytarlus.

August 8

A bad day with a number of heavy showers. Nothing special except a large Tortricid.

---

[93] Another part of the Greenwell ranch upslope and north of Pulehua. Primarily a sheep ranch belonging to Dr. Trousseau (*vide supra*) before it came into the hands of the Greenwells. Perkins's collection No. 321 for this date indicates that Hymenoptera and Diptera were collected at the 6000-foot level.

[94] Hualālai is an active volcanic mountain (summit 8000 ft), last erupted in 1801. It is doubtful that Perkins on this date actually walked all the way to the mountain itself and then made his way back down to Ka'awaloa where he stayed the night. It is more likely that he hiked "toward" Hualālai (i.e., north) and did collecting at the 6000 ft level in the saddle area between Mauna Loa and Hualālai, then made his way down to Kaawaloa later that day or early evening. Although Perkins's journals mention collecting to about 6000 ft, the insects for this date (collection Nos. 293, 310, and 344) are labeled as "nearly 5000 ft," "5000 ft," and "about 5000 ft."

August 9
Collected Neuroptera, Hymenoptera, Diptera, Hemiptera and beetles; a rather good day. A rather good Brachypeplus, no. 23 was found beneath smooth bark of Koa trunk, amongst small fungi growing there, together with its larvae [Orthostolus sordidus] and where the wood beneath the bark was covered with a white layer of hyphae there were two species of Cis, one, larger and new to me [C. bimaculatus] the other the smallest I have yet found and so variable in colour that I collected a large number. From a dead branch very high up in the tree I collected a number of Trichopterygidae and some other beetles beneath the bark. I took a Crabro carrying its prey, one of the shining aeneous Sarcophagidae, which are clearly natives [Dyscritomyia or Prosthetochaeta sp.]. A heavy shower in the afternoon. One Chloridops female.

August 10
Went to Kanahaha, Aculeates being the chief object. Collected also some moths and a few beetles &^{c}. At noon there was a heavy shower. One Chloridops.

August 11
Still no Koa finches to be heard. Collected a very sluggish Staph. beneath bark, with Cossonids; at first sight they appeared to be dead specimens [Thoracophorus blackburni]. The crow[95] has now come higher up and is feeding greedily on the ripe Pohas now that the Freycinetia below is past fruiting.

August 12
Skinned a Crow and then went to Kanahaha. Collected various insects, including a Dermestid which has some superficial resemblance to some of the Xyletobius [Labrocerus sp.] A few Lepidoptera in the evening, amongst these a Pterophorid.

August 13
Sunday. I took a few Lepidoptera and shot a bat[96] at nightfall.

August 14–15
Went across to Hualālai with my native boy. Stayed during the night at about 8000 ft., but did not get much sleep as it was very stony where we stopped and quite a hard white frost in the night.[97] I saw no bird worth shooting and collected few insects, chiefly Hemiptera, Lepidoptera and some Psocidae, which were numerous. We spent the morning on and about the summit and did not get back till late, there being much mist on the plateau between the mountains which made it very difficult to find the way across to Kanahaha.

August 16
I did not do much and my boy went off home for a time.

---

[95] Hawaiian Crow, or ʻalalā (*Corvus hawaiiensis*).

[96] *Lasiurus cinereus semotus*, the native Hawaiian hoary bat.

[97] Perkins gave more details about this in later correspondence: "When I slept out in the open on the flat when one begins the steep ascent from the plateau to the top of Hualālai from near the end of the Judd Road, across from the Greenwell's former sheep station (called I think Kanahaha) the ground was similarly white with frost (in August!)." (*R.C.L. Perkins letter to G.C. Munro, 29 November 1949, BPBM Archives, MS SC Munro Box 13.3*).

August 17
Not a very successful day, though I caught some moths towards and during the evening.

* * * * *

[After this date no regular records were kept as there was only one page vacant in my small note-book and there was naturally little to record.[98] On this page I noted:]

August 28
A small and excessively sluggish weevil occurs on the underside of rotting, fallen Koa branches, to which damp earth sticks. They are very difficult to detect, resembling little lumps of dirt. [This species was <u>Acalles</u> <u>tuberculatus</u>.]

August 30
Started out with the intention of collecting above the forest and sleeping out for the night. After going a long way it rained heavily and we were very wet, so I thought it better to return. We got back after dark with difficulty. I collected two small Clytarli but did not wait to do any serious collecting.

September 2
I shot a single Koa finch, <u>R{hodacanthis}</u>. <u>palmeri</u>. It was a male. [I must now have been informed from England of the name of this bird, as the scientific name is not used previously.][99]

September 10
I collected a small beetle, very unlike anything I have seen in the islands, by sifting dead leaves at the foot of a big Koa tree (4000 ft.) It is probably not a native. [<u>Lathridius</u> <u>nodifer</u>].

* * * * *

[During the latter part of September and until I left in the first part of the following month I did more collecting at a lower elevation, i.e. from 2000–3000 ft. There is no doubt that, so far as insects are concerned, this rain-belt with a far greater variety of those trees that endemic insects frequent than the higher forest, would have proved much more profitable than the latter, where most of my collecting was done. But as the birds <u>Chloridops</u> and <u>Rhodacanthis</u> occurred only in the higher forest and were specially wanted by Prof. Newton for the Cambridge Museum, most of my time was spent there, till I could obtain a series of skins.

Almost the last day of my collecting, in October {13th–14th},[100] I found the

---

98 However, he collected anobiid beetles on 25 August labeled "Kona, 4000 ft." [= Pulehua] (collection No. 314 in the BPBM entomology collection).

[99] In fact, Perkins did not know the species before he left for the islands. Rothschild described it in August 1892.

[100] Perkins also referred to a bird observation on his last day in Kona: "Instead of the shivering wings of *Phaeornis* you see a quicker, more jerky movement in *Chasiempis*; but only the day before I left Kona, I saw the latter put on a genuine shiver exactly like that of *Phaeornis*, and the position in both species while these movements are performed is, as above stated, exactly the same." (Perkins, R.C.L., 1893, *The Ibis* (6) 5: 111).

Longicorn Plagithmysus vicinus on Pelea in the wet belt, and noted that trees of ohia and Wauke were also attacked by beetles of that genus, though I obtained no specimens at this time and only that of the Ohia [P. bilineatus] on a later occasion, when I failed to find the Wauke trees, I had noticed before.]

[The following note was on a loose piece of paper enclosed in the note-book:]

Hymenoptera. There are two very abundant species of Crabro at 4000 ft. The larger preys commonly on a fly of the genus Sarcophaga having a reddish tail, but sometimes on a large green metallic fly, which is much less common. These Crabros I have seen swarming round a dead and stinking cow, having been attracted by the thousands of blow-flies about it. The smaller species I found carrying a daddy-long-legs[101] to its nest and the Mimesa was found carrying the same fly. Altogether there are about half-a-dozen species of Crabro here, some of these I have only seen in the rain belt. Two of the species at 4000 ft., and also the Mimesa burrow in the dirt, and I noticed that a number of them begin their burrow at the edge of a stone and then dig down beneath this, so that the nest is kept drier than would be the case if it were uncovered. The red-tailed Crabro I found only in the wet belt (2000–3000 ft.) and the species down there seem to burrow in dead wood. [These were tumidoventris var. leucognathus and N. rubrocaudatus.] The species of Odynerus are numerous, probably about a score of distinct forms and have varied habits, except that all store up small caterpillars in their cells. Some burrow in the ground or form their cells in the holes in the lava, while others inhabit burrows in dead trees. A few I expect are not constant in these habits, for I found burrows of the Mimesa on level ground, and also took it entering holes in dead tree-trunks — probably the exit-holes of wood-eating beetles.

The bees of the genus Prosopis excepting two or three smallish species, which burrow in the ground at 4000 ft., are not very abundant, though there are about eight species here. There are three larger species, of which one with a red abdomen makes its cells in dead tree trunks of the Mamani, and another with white collar and black abdomen I found entering a burrow in the trunk of a bastard-sandal tree. Both these species visit the flowers of the latter and of the true sandal and of course the Ohia. The other large species has a more pubescent abdomen, and I only saw it in the wet-belt. I noticed numbers flying very high up about dead tree-trunks still standing and all out of reach. A fairly large species very different from the above occurs round Cook's monument on the coast, together with one (or more?) smaller species.

It is remarkable that the Ichneumonidae seem scarcely to be represented at all unless by imported species with the exception of the Ophion group.

The most interesting parasitic Hymenoptera are the small 'Oxyura' which are numerous in individuals, winged species throughout the forest and a wingless form at 4000 ft. These 'Oxyura' are certainly Aculeate.

---

[101] Crane flies of either the family Limoniidae or Tipulidae.

Some of the Chalcididae are rather fine species and have been found on dead wood frequented by beetles and wood-eating caterpillars and also about borings in wood where bees or wasps made their cells, but only a few types of this extensive group have come in my way here.

[It is evident that after finishing my collecting in Kona in 1892, I wrote a short general account of the insects I found there. Probably I had the intention of sending this to one of the English entomological publications. I can now find only the account of the Hymenoptera as given above, but on the cover of the book is a rough estimate of the number of species obtained, not only of these, but also the number of those in each of the other orders — the total given being 310.

A general account of the birds observed there was sent to Prof. Newton, who forwarded it for publication to "The Ibis" (Jan. 1893). Unfortunately I had no literature to consult when the notes were written, nor were any proofs sent out to me, so that some errors in this paper were left uncorrected. Thus the names Psittacirostra and Loxioides are transposed throughout and all that is said of the former applies to the latter and vice-versa. Should the 'Ibis' paper ever be referred to by others, it is necessary that attention should paid to this point.

When I first arrived in Kona the great Ohia trees at an elevation of about 2500 ft. were a mass of bloom and each of them was literally alive with hordes of the crimson Apapane and scarlet Iiwi, while, continually crossing from the top of one great tree to another, the Oo could be seen on the wing, sometimes six or eight at a time. The Amakihi was numerous in the same trees, but less conspicuous, and occasionally one saw the long-billed Hemignathus. Feeding on the fruit of the Ieie could be seen the Hawaiian crow commonly and the Ou in great abundance. The picture of this noisy, active and often quarrelsome assembly of birds, many of them of brilliant colours was one never to be forgotten. After the flowering of the Ohia was over the great gathering naturally dispersed, but even then the bird population was very great.]

SELECTED CORRESPONDENCE

Cambridge, England
15 September 1892
Robert Cyril Layton Perkins

Dear Mr Perkins,

Your letter from Kaawaloa of date 6.8.92 is to hand and I am glad to hear you are prosperous. It is satisfactory to find you get all our letters as at first that seemed not the case.

The occurrence of <u>Vanessa</u> <u>atalanta</u> in the islands seems to me very extraordinary and I entertain some doubts about it. You say it is very wild, but here it is the one of the finest of butterflies, & can be caught by any child without difficulty. I fancy therefore that it may prove to be a closely allied species; of which several are known, though some think these to be only races.

If the small Clytarli you report differ in form of the femora they are in all probability distinct species. I should not be surprised at 12 to 20 species of that division off the genus turning up in the islands. The Xyletobii you sent from Waianae are extremely interesting: there are six or eight new ones, but mostly only one or two specimens: you have now got the dodge[102] of getting them it is evident, and if the different islands have different species that group will run to 870 or 1000 species in all probability! Please keep any you get coupled[103] separate as you did before. It is very difficult to find the very smallest things in so much sawdust; & I think it will be well to send you some very small glass tubes: if you would like them please let me know & I will write to the homeopathic for some. Please let me know your wants long before they arise: at present all you have asked for is a dozen small boxes.

The flattened Hawaiian beetle yet turned up by Blackburn is <u>Brachypeplus</u> <u>infirmus</u>; your description however does not agree with that so yours is probably new, & we must perpetuate a joke and call it <u>subinfirmus</u>. I expect you will much increase the Brachypepli in species. <u>Proterhinus</u> you do not seem to do well in, perhaps you have not got into a good locality for them yet. I suppose there is no hope of your getting the larvae? The very small rare Staphs you mention are no doubt <u>Oligota</u> or <u>Liophena</u>. The big brown <u>Xyletobius</u> will be <u>Holcobius</u> <u>major</u> or a new one.

Have you got any more <u>Machilis</u>? That one you sent from Hawaii {Perkins corrected this to "Waianae" in this letter} seem to be extremely peculiar, but there is only one ♂ in what you sent. I have from Blackburn a specimen of allied genus even larger than the <u>Machilis</u> you sent. I think the best way is to put them in spirit, with one or two pinned to shew scales.

As regards the labels on the Lepidoptera I know Lord Walsingham[104] will be most particular to preserve the locality for every specimen. I shall hope that they wont reset more than necessary; if I were a Lepidopterist I should have very few set specimens in the ordinary way. The two or three Proctotrupids you sent are excessively interesting; if you get any idea of their habits or what species they are connected with please preserve it. I hope you will do something in other groups besides the insects; otherwise naturalists will think I am selfish in getting an entomologist

---

102   Dodge — a slang term referring to any particular hunting or collecting technique used to secure prey by a collector in the field. Many invertebrates have specific habits and need specialized techniques to hunt for them before they can be observed and/or collected.

103   Coupled — referring to collecting insects that are coupled in the act of mating, thereby assuring association of the sexes, which can sometimes be difficult in species where males and females appear quite different to the eye.

104   Walsingham, [Lord] Thomas de Grey (1843–1919). The 6th baron of Walsingham, Thomas de Grey was well-known in scientific circles for his work with microlepidoptera (moths). He was also widely known as a crack cricketer. The de Grey family resided at Merton Hall, built in 1613 in the Norfolk countryside.

sent to the islands, who wont get anything else. I am told nothing is known as to Sandwich Islands spiders scorpions & so on.

I do not think the aculeate Hymenoptera will offer much difficulty as to species if you get plenty of specimens.

By the way, that beetle of Munro's from Hawaii is a Cossonid! Fancy that being descended from a common ancestor (I think we might say very uncommon sort of ancestor) with [Dryophthorus?]. You have sent three or four species of Oodemas – the brassy weevils – from Waianae but I should like to see more specimens. I dont think I shall write a paper on the Waianae lot as there is but little new amongst them except the Xyletobii & of these only one or two of each.
It is very interesting to hear that you have got so few introduced species on Hawaii: you must try a little about Hilo or some of the one or two small towns to see if there is not more near them.

Prof^r Newton is away just now or I am sure he would send you a kind message; nobody good {sic} be kinder than he is though you have not found a new Hemignathus or Chloridops yet.

In your first lot your Xyletobii are out of all proportion in comparison with other things. One of the polished Mirosternus with golden pubescence on each side is also new; indeed nearly all the Anobiids you got at Waianae are new. Kindest regards.

Yours very truly
D. Sharp.

Hillingdon, England
16 September 1892
Robert Cyril Layton Perkins

My dear Mr Perkins,

Your letter of the 10th August reached me this morning, and I am glad to have once more good news from you – only you do but {sic} say which letters of mine you have got. I left Cambridge at the beginning of last week to take a holiday till about the end of the month – and just before I came away we had received your box, about which I wrote to you by the next mail. I had also written to you of other matters – still more important – namely the length of time you were pre-pared to stay in order that we may know whether to apply for more funds for you. Concerning all of this you will no doubt let us know in good time – meanwhile I am delighted to have such good evidence of your welfare as your letter contains – your long walks, your cave-dwelling & all the rest of it.

I am sorry that being away from home I can't answer all your questions as I should like. My memory is so very bad that I can't trust it on many points – and therefore what I now reply must be taken with all reserve. I will send you another list of S.I. birds when I get home, but surely that which was given in my article in 'Nature' (copies of which I believe you eventually got) ought to help you? It gave all the land-birds then known, & their distribution in the islands, and I can't remember that the M.S. list I drew out for you did more.

The smaller Hemignathus is bright coloured enough – I dare say in life it looks very bright – but I have no knowledge of the big one being ever entitled to be called "yellow" – but then I am well aware of the brilliance often displayed by a bird in the bush not being borne out when the poor thing is in your hand – & I could fancy that in a favourable light H. obscurus even might glow. I cant say as to the straight-billed Himatione being yellow – nor can I give you the localities for Loxops – though I seem to have written about that in one of my later letters to you. It is certainly a scarce bird – Wilson, I think, did not get a half a dozen specimens & one of those, he spoilt after he got it home. I am not a believer in {illegible} being animals – if you can convince me to the contrary pray do so, & I shall gladly acknowledge my error.

Everybody said Phaeornis was a flycatcher till Gadow looked at its guts, which he said placed it near the thrushes (I am wrong to have written {illegible}). According to him it is a more generalized form than true thrushes. He is a great upholder of guts as giving the most valuable taxonomic characters, but I always tell him that he will find that they break down in some particular case, just as all the other "single" characters do, and perhaps this may be the particular case. It is an ingenious notice of yours that Chasiempis has run to colour and Phaeornis to music. Far be it from me to say that it is not so – only bear in mind that a theory is not necessarily true because it is neatly {illegible} and explains some facts. Do conceive some theory or 2 or 3 theories to explain the common odour that is so remarkable. Can't you bottle us a little of the stink that we may enjoy it too?

It is most refreshing to me to read of your climbing heights & sleeping in draughty caves with no blanket but the hoar frost! It must have been very uncomfortable, but I can't bring myself to say that I am sorry you should suffer such hardships, for I know what pleasure it will give you to think of it in after years!

We shall be glad to hear before long of the dispatch of another box – but I especially want to hear where Acrulocercus apicalis lives, & whether both species of Oahuan Hemignathus exist.

I am glad you have fallen in with a bat. I rather think 2 spp. have been said to occur – but I don't trust my memory. With all good wishes believe me

Yours very truly
Alfred Newton

I want to know why Chaetoptila became extinct, if extinct it is.

O'ahu
14 October 1892 – April 1893

If not earlier, it was no doubt becoming evident to Perkins by now that from the tone of Newton's letters to him, this man was obsessed with Perkins finding a specimen of the rare O'ahu *'akialoa (Hemignathus lichtensteini)* that Townsend and Deppe had gotten years before and was only known from one specimen. Finding that rare bird is most likely why Newton did not want Perkins to leave O'ahu earlier in the year—when Perkins was writing Sharp and Newton that he thought it might be better to go collecting on some of the other islands. Although Perkins probably knew his search on O'ahu would offer little reward with much labor, he nevertheless made a special expedition for it upon his return to O'ahu from Kona in October of 1892. What happened on this trip was just another unfortunate episode in futility in the bird-catching travails of Perkins while hunting without a dog or human companion.

> "On those early weeks of collecting I was really trying to get the Oahu <u>Hemignathus</u> & <u>Heterorhynchus</u> & the Oo. The collecting of either of these would I am sure have pleased Prof.ʳ Newton more than a new sp. Scott Wilson got none of these & Newton could not bear to think that other Museums had specimens of these & Cambridge none! My not getting either of these at one time I think might have led to my recall. All I could say was: if you find that Rothschild's collectors, who are better equipped than myself & are two in number with nothing to collect except birds succeed, I will allow that I have made a failure of things. Afterwards he quite forgave my failure but I never dared to tell him that I was sure I saw a pair of the <u>Hemignathus</u> not far from where Deppe & Townsend collected it & that I killed one of these but could not gather it! I might have had orders to keep on Oahu till I got one!" *(R.C.L. Perkins letter to E.C. Zimmerman, 3 January 1950, BPBM Entomology Archives).*

In an earlier letter to Zimmerman (1944) Perkins gave a brief account of his collecting during this period:

> "After shipping the Kona collection, I did some collecting in the mountains near Honolulu, chiefly from Kalihi to Manoa, & then went on to Waialua where I occupied a mountain house belonging to the Kawailoa ranch, & was in that neighbourhood until the spring of 1943 {error = 1893}. It was a very wet season in the mountains & the rains exceptionally heavy & the insect collection poor. But I was mainly in search of birds. Prof.ʳ. Newton had set his heart on getting specimens of the old Oahu birds — its Oo, <u>Hemignathus</u> & <u>Heterorhynchus</u> — very few examples of which were extant, & seemed even more keen on this than on the discovery of new species. Scott Wilson had heard some report of one or

other of these at Halemano {= Helemano}, but I went through the mountains from there to the Waimea Valley without even hearing much less seeing any of these. I had become acquainted with the songs & cries of the allied species in Kona, which, no doubt, those of the Oahu species would have resembled." *(R.C.L. Perkins letter to E.C. Zimmerman, 14 February 1944, BPBM Entomology Archives).*

In a later letter, Perkins recalled his collecting in the mountains near Honolulu during this period:

"In 1892 when I first went up in the mts near Honolulu the moth {*Margaronia exaula* [= *Stemorrhages exaula*]} was abundant there flying wildly by day (there was much Maile on the trees & it might have bred on this?). Can it be that this moth led one of the early navigators to record the presence of a (?) green Colias, which was not caught. I believe there are green coloured Colias in the Arctic region, which might have been seen there by this recorder & the moth mistaken for one!" *(R.C.L. Perkins letter to E.C. Zimmerman, 14 June 1950, BPBM Entomology Archives).*

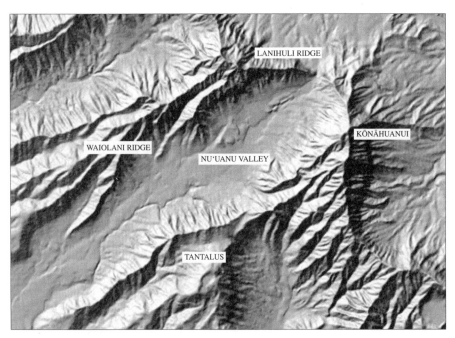

Map of Oʻahu with detail showing Perkins's collecting areas in the Nuʻuanu Valley area. Downtown Honolulu is at the mouth of the valley.

Journals and Remembrances

On my return from Kona in October 1892 I again made an attempt to obtain some of the old Oahu birds, which no one had collected for many years. It had become known to me that these had been obtained in Nuuanu Valley and as on either side of the valley were the two highest peaks in the Koolau range, it seemed possible that the birds might have been confined to this neighbourhood. A survey of the valley itself gave little hope of success, the changes being very great from the original condition described by one of the old naturalists many years before: "the last 3 or 4 miles thro' a thick wood, whose boughs overhanging the path form a dark and gloomy shade ... the dark cliff on right and left contrasted with the variety of trees and plants at the bottom and on each side of the narrow path."[105] I was certain that, if any of the birds formerly obtained still existed round Nuuanu, they would be found on the ridges. I therefore started a systematic search of the main ridge on the Waolani side of the valley and the side ridges leading up to this from the valley, and later made a similar search on the Konahuanui side. There were more birds on the Waolani side than the other, but only three species in any number, the Elepaio, the Apapane and the Amakihi. The Iiwi occurred, but was quite rare. On one occasion I saw what I had no doubt was a pair of <u>Hemignathus</u>. This was on one of the two occasions when I stayed all night on the ridge, hoping that either towards evening or early in the morning birds might show up in greater numbers. That night there was a very heavy thunderstorm and much rain and I started to go still higher up the ridge as soon as it began to get light, being very wet and cold. On a very narrow part of the ridge a pair of green birds flew across in front of me one just behind and in pursuit of the other, which squeaked as it flew. This darted across the ridge and down the Nuuanu side, the other alighted in an Ohia bush on the ridge, but evidently was about to fly on, as it swayed on the branch. I had no doubt at the time that this was the rare Akialoa of Oahu and when I shot, feathers were blown back towards me as the bird fell over the very steep side of the ridge in the direction from which it had come. I spent hours in searching for this bird amongst the thick brush, but without success, and another attempt on the following day, when with a cane knife I largely cleaned a steep broad strip of the undergrowth for many yards down from where I had shot the bird, was also

---

[105] This is Perkins's paraphrasing of the comment made by the first western naturalist, Andrew Bloxam, in 1825 (this version was compiled by Maria Graham from Bloxam's journals but were not his exact words): "The path which leads to it {the pali} from Honoruru winds along the beautiful and fertile valley of Anu Anu {= Nu'uanu}, and thence ascends gradually, for eight miles, through a cultivated and populous district, separated, by a pretty stream, from a thick wood, which we crossed, completely sheltered from the mid-day sun, and found ourselves suddenly on the brink of a precipice some thousands of feet above the grassy plain below." (Byron, Lord, 1826, *Voyage of the H.M.S.* Blonde *to the Sandwich Islands, in the years 1824–1825*, p. 140).

A later version taken directly from his journals goes into more detail: "After we had gone four or five miles the huts and cultivated plots became scarcer and we entered into a thick wood, the shade of which was very grateful in keeping off the powerful rays of the sun. Our path was very narrow, and in some parts muddy and bad, in other places very slippery over a reddish clay. We scarcely saw a single bird though we heard several in the thickets around." (Bloxam, A. 1925, *Diary of Andrew Bloxam, naturalist of the "Blonde" on her trip from England to the Hawaiian Islands from 1824-25*).

By the time Perkins had arrived in the valley in 1892, the ground had been stripped bare by the introduction of cattle and goats and was primarily grassy until one got to the top. "Found Nuuanu mostly tall Hilo grass. Lots of Dracaena near head & mixed native trees with much dense Hau." *(R.C.L. Perkins interview with E.C. Zimmerman, August 1949, E.C. Zimmerman letter to N.L. Evenhuis, 20 November 2002).*

Bishop Museum Archives

Lanihuli ridge at the head of Nuʻuanu Valley on Oʻahu

a failure. On a number of days afterwards I hunted around Waolani, and once more I spent a night in the open on the ridge, but never again saw anything that could be mistaken for a <u>Hemignathus</u>.[106]

While searching for this bird I had another stroke of ill-luck, for one day under a detached stone I found a fine, large grossly punctured Carabid. When I had turned out my captures of the day in the evening, I was called away to the telephone, leaving the insects on my table against the open window. On my return after a consid-

---

[106]   Perkins recalled this again in later correspondence: "The night I slept! on the high ridge & in the early morning saw the Akialoa (♂ chasing ♀) as I supposed, I shall not easily forget, as there was a terrific thunderstorm & very heavy rain & of course I was soaked to the skin having no shelter. It is just possible as this was so close to Deppe's locality that the bird was very local on Oahu. Otherwise it is strange that neither Palmer nor myself saw any sign of it in the much finer forests towards the other end of the Koolau Range. It is also strange if no Oahu thrush was obtained by Deppe & T. & perhaps this may yet be found to exist wrongly named as one of the allied species in some museum." *(R.C.L. Perkins letter to G.C. Munro, 26 May 1944, BPBM Archives, MS SC Munro Box 13.3).*

erable delay, I found most of these had disappeared, and a great stream of the ant Pheidole was coming and going through the window and carrying off their booty. I could not recover my Carabid, which I have little doubt was Deropristus blaptoides, a single specimen of which was captured by Blackburn on a ridge across the valley from where I found the individual referred to.

* * * * *

[I found on loose sheets a portion of a diary made at this time and written in pencil as follows:]

October 24
Started before 7 a.m. up Nuuanu Valley. Two miles or more before the pali I crossed the valley on the left of the road. The ground is very uneven and full of holes, in part covered with dense guava scrub,[107] Hau &c. The grass here is thick and tall and very thick at the roots, so that it is as laborious to walk through as deep mud. I took a ridge up, on which nice healthy Koas were growing, but here I saw no birds except a pair of Chasiempis, an adult male and a young one. The rain was very heavy and my (supposed!) waterproof bag got wet inside and the male Elepaio, which I shot, was soaked. The young one had lost its long tail feathers and was not worth shooting. The other when dried out has made a good skin. In the stem of some dead tree I got an Oodemas, a Dryophthorus with strongly raised carinae on the elytra and a larger species without these.

October 25
Started up the valley very early and crossed to the left side a little beyond the halfway house.[108] Here I went up by a Koa-bearing ridge and made slow progress, as there was a tangled mass of ieie vines over much of this ridge. Collected a red-spotted Odynerus and a couple of black, shining species. A Hydrophilid was common under some very wet fallen wood. Here I saw no birds except Elepaio and Himatione sanguinea. Higher up I did some insect collecting taking 4 or 5 dozen Carabidae, several species, including a solitary minute Cyclothorax, also species of Heteramphus and an Oodemas. Mimesa was numerous, but I only caught one male. I took 5 species of Lepidoptera, the best a large Tortricid [Archips longiplicatus, recorded in F.H. as 27.x.92] and a beautiful little Tineid, deep-black and white in colour. Flying round the Ohias was the small Lithocolletid? with blue transverse stripes [Philodoria splendida] previously found at Waianae. Here too I saw the Himatione with curved beak, but did not shoot any. One of these was following a fine male H. Sanguinea, from bush to bush. The latter was constantly coming to rest and then singing, but each time that it moved on, the green bird followed. Several times the Sanguinea flew at the other and drove it off, but it persisted in returning and following.

---

[107]   There are two species of fruit-bearing trees called guava in Hawai'i: common guava (*Psidium gujava*) and strawberry guava (*Psidium cattleyanum*). Both are considered serious forest pests. The latter was introduced to Hawai'i in 1825 and has since become one of the dominant low-elevation trees in Hawaiian forests, displacing native trees, forming dense thickets, and preventing native understory plants from growth.

[108]   The Nu'uanu Half-Way House was a well-known stopover for those traveling across the *pali* to or from Honolulu. It was located in Nu'uanu Valley about 4 miles from downtown Honolulu and 2 miles from the *pali* summit. In the late 1880s it was managed by the Union Feed Company's stable foreman, Timothy B. Arcia.

October 26

Did not go mauka,[109] as it was very wet. I started work on my insect boxes. There was a thunderstorm this evening.

October 27

Went along the same ridge as on the 25ᵗʰ, but instead of climbing on this by a side ridge from far up the valley I began far down the valley. It was very hot and uninteresting until I got far up. At about 1500 feet I took male and female of the red-bodied Prosopis in cop. and a few specimens of Crabro and Odynerus. At 2000 feet as I could see the rain clouds coming lower I did some insect collecting — some Cis, several species of Proterhinus and of Brachypeplus, one of the latter a single specimen of large size and with black elytra new to me. I also took Xyletobius, minute Oligota?, Oodemas a small Cossonid with golden pubescence [Deinocossonus] and a pair of a fine metallic Carabid [Derobroscus politus] I also collected two small moths, probably Lithocolletids, one the Ohia species, as on the 25ᵗʰ, the other, allied to it, on a different tree, containing many mined leaves, though I saw but one moth. [Philodoria auromagnifica; the date in 'F.H.' 25.x is an error for 27.x.92]. It now came on a very heavy rain, with recurrence of yesterday's thunder, but I continued collecting getting some Carabidae, Heteramphus, a large Brachypeplus in decaying, wood, wet and very rotten, though the tree still stood, ?a Lobeliad. The pale yellow larvae were numerous in the mush beneath the bark [Orthostolus robustus and ?O. nepos] with a single specimen of 2 spp. Staphylinids. The small earwig found on Hawaii is also here [Labia pygidiata in 'F.H.']. I took also land shrimps,[110] whitish slugs, a Planarian, and spiders.

I saw a great many fly-catchers, in one case the parents with their two young ones. Some of the latter are very bright brown in colour. I saw one in which the spots at the base of the wing were white the more apical series of these still brown. This bird had acquired the penetrating whistle of the adult, but not perfectly. The birds were very tame and if one was near by, and especially if a young bird, it would come right close up to examine the intruder. They will perch without fear on a branch only a yard distant, following after one as one moves on, keeping up a querulous chattering till their curiosity is satisfied. Hearing this, other specimens on the precipitous sides and in the gulches below respond with their loud, clear whistle. The adults are generally rather more wary, but even these sometimes come quite close up. Himatione sanguinea were singing around, and the squeak of the green Himatione [i.e. Chlorodrepanis] could be frequently heard, but no sound or sign of Hemignathus. I did not shoot at any bird to-day. As on the 25ᵗʰ. I stayed so late listening for birds, I nearly had to sleep out, not getting back till after dark. I also collected winged and wingless species of Oxyura [Sierola and Sclerodermus] and I brought down some land shells.

---

[109] *Mauka* — Hawaiian word meaning "toward the mountains." After spending time in the islands, it becomes quickly evident that conventional directions of north, south, east, and west are meaningless. It is much easier to refer to directions as *mauka* (toward the mountains) or *makai* (toward the ocean).

[110] No doubt referring to amphipods or isopods.

October 28

I did not go up into the mountains, but visited Prof^r Brigham at his house.[111] He could give me no information at all about the birds, nor about the insects and knew nothing of Blackburn's fine work here. This was as I expected, for he was in communication with the Committee before I was sent out, when it was hoped the museum here would participate, and wrote to them that he had been all over the islands, that it was no use sending out an entomologist, as there were no native insects, but only a few American species. A small Agrion was abundant in his garden and the female of a <u>Megachile</u>, no doubt foreign [<u>M</u>. <u>Schauinslandi</u> Alfken].

October 29

I did not go up the mountains, as I had to work all day at my boxes. [I had lately received a letter to the effect that the Committee hoped my Hawaii material would be soon arriving in England, so that a report could be got out in time for an application for a further grant of money. I had not been notified to this effect in due time. Consequently I determined — greatly against my better judgment — to send the many pinned insects I had accumulated by mail. To do so I had to cut down all boxes to half the size, and could find no one in Honolulu who would do this. As a result of this a large number of these specimens were more or less damaged in the mail and some, no doubt, entirely destroyed. In consignments sent as freight,[112] not a single specimen, even of the most delicate pinned insects, was ever damaged in the least, but they took some months to make the journey].

October 30
Sunday.

October 31

Went up the valley beyond the Halfway House, and then up a ridge on the Konahuanui side. A tiring and hard climb through much Ieie. There were three species of land shells on this ridge and some <u>Dryophthorus</u>. On the top I saw one of the blue-black species of Agrion, no doubt one of those of which I found two species of nymphs[113] in the lilies[114] here. I could not catch specimens in my hand. I got a <u>Brachypeplus</u> new to me and also a very distinct new <u>Clytarlus</u> [<u>P</u>. <u>solitarius</u>] and I picked up a <u>C</u>. <u>microgaster</u> [<u>Callithmysus</u> <u>microgaster</u>]. Also the usual beetles, Carabids, <u>Oodemas</u>, <u>Cis</u>, <u>Proterhinus</u> &c. Found a solitary caterpillar of a sphingid (on Kopiko) bright green in colour, head retractile, short, stumpy form, with sparse yellow shagreen dots, yellow subdorsal and infraspiracular lines, the

---

111 The Brigham house was replete with a plethora of antiquities and books dealing with Hawaiian and Pacific cultures and was most likely a welcome site for Perkins, who immersed himself in not only knowledge of the natural history of the islands but also took a personal interest in its cultural history as well. In the first few years of his working in Hawai'i, it is possible that Perkins might have visited Brigham whenever he returned from the field; however, after the 1895 falling out with Brigham over the directorship of the Bishop Museum, Perkins did not visit either Brigham or the Bishop Museum.

112 Wells Fargo was the company that Perkins contracted to do the shipping of his specimens. He was so impressed with their service — no loss of specimens during his seven years collecting in Hawai'i — that he contracted them to also move his household belongings when he moved back to England in 1909 (R.A. Perkins, pers. comm.).

113 Nymphs — immature damselflies; naiads. One of the damselfly species referred to here that inhabits the leaf axils of *Astelia* is *Megalagrion koelense*.

114 Lilies — *Astelia*.

caudal horn bifid at tip. Prosopis fuscipennis, Chalcids, Hemiptera &ᶜ. Only common birds, chiefly H. sanguinea. Did not shoot at any.

November 1
Went up Pauoa Valley on to Konahuanui.[115] Nothing of special note. Collected some Aculeates and the usual beetles. A pair of a small Oodemas cut out of a hollow dry twig look different [O. ramalorum] one male Sympetrum; some ground- and tree-shells. Ordinary birds, at which I did not shoot.

November 2–5
Same district as on the 1ˢᵗ. Nothing of note except a Cyclothorax in stem of tree fern, and an Acalles from dead wood. No birds of note. I shall give up looking for Hemignathus here any longer. One is practically confined to the ridge one is on, while the bird might be quite near, yet out of sight, or inaccessible if seen or heard, where one can go neither to one side nor the other. How different from Kona! One might hunt a bird of which few individuals survive, for years on these narrow ridges without success. The chance of such a bird being on the very same ridge as is the collector and on the same part of that ridge at the same time is very small, unless the bird really exists in some numbers. The whole of the mountains here is made up of countless ridges. No doubt in former days, during winter storms &ᶜ the native birds would have habitually left the ridges for the shelter of a large, densely forested valley, as Nuuanu was. I must try some other District. Judging by my collecting in the Waianae range I do not think I shall find the old Oahu birds there, though certainly the Iiwi is more numerous than in the mountains round here, as also is the Amakihi.

[About this time wishing to get some idea of the whole island and the possibilities of the forest as a collecting ground in different parts, I walked around it with a visitor from New Zealand.[116] One day was spent in walking from Honolulu to Waimanalo round Koko Head, the manager of that plantation putting us up there. From there we walked to Kahuku, staying at the plantation, and the next day returned via Waialua to Honolulu. As we did not make an early start from Kahuku and stayed a short while at Waimea and Waialua, we did not reach Honolulu till after dark, after a tramp of 40 miles or rather more.

As a result of this survey I decided to return to Waialua with a view to working mainly in the Koolau range rather than in the Waianae Mts., where I had collected soon after my arrival in the islands. Most of the time I occupied a small mountain-house belonging to the Kawailoa ranch, but it was far too low down for any collecting of native insects in the immediate neighbourhood, though the Apapane

---

[115]   Further details of Perkins's mountain routes around Honolulu are found in correspondence: "I used to go through the planted forest to Tantalus, then on to the head of Pauoa & up Konahuanui, then from near the end of the Pauoa flat down the steep side into Manoa & thence back to town, or sometimes varied this by going by Pacific Heights on the ridge & into the head of Pauoa, or sometimes again I reversed either the routes i.e., starting from Manoa Valley. Either of these would be a long day's collecting, but when Koebele was with me we started very early, as he frequently or usually was awake at 4 a.m. & I would join him at the Govt. Nursery for a start at about 5 a.m." *(R.C.L. Perkins letter to G.C. Munro, 7 March 1949, BPBM Archives, MS SC Munro Box 13.3).*

[116]   This feat actually made the newspapers in Honolulu: "The walkists are named De Bomford and Perkins. They walked from Honolulu via Koko Head to Waimanalo on Monday Nov. 7th; on Wednesday to Kahuku, and on Thursday back to the city, a good forty miles which was done in 10.5 hours actual walking. This is good work in these degenerate days." *(The Friend, 1892, 50 (12): 93).*

came down this far in February when some Ohia trees were covered with flowers. A long tramp was necessary before one could really get amongst the native insects almost all of these for a long distance above the house having been cleaned out by the Pheidole ant. In fact in a note written on the collecting in this district I find my first written remark concerning the destruction caused by this ant, though I was aware of the fact during my collecting at Kona, Hawaii.]

The end of 1892 and early months of 1893 were not very favourable for collecting, the weather being generally wet in the mountains and there were three big spates of the mountain streams. These did very much damage to the system of flumes belonging to the Chinese of the district on more than one occasion during the winter months. At this time Waialua was much visited by sportsmen of Honolulu as great numbers of golden plover were scattered over the forehills and along the sea coast.[117] The native wild duck was common on the ponds and there were a good many pheasants amongst the Lantana on the plains, but still more on the dry forehills below the forest and within this, before the trees became continuous or dense. At intervals during the day the plover habitually resorted to the ponds near the coast, usually in small flocks at a time, and were shot from blinds near these as they flew round crude but very effective decoys — made usually from a potato on a stick which was stuck in the mud beneath the shallow water, the shadow greatly resembling a plover. Some of the men that I met at Waialua were very fine shots and on their weekend visits made large bags of duck and plover.[118] In the mountains there were a few wild chicken and here and there some wild turkeys. The pheasants when I first came to Waialua were in very fine and healthy condition, but later became much diseased, and on one occasion I found a number so nearly dead as to allow me to catch them without their attempting to fly. These sick birds were covered with lice. Below Kaala there were a few Californian Quail, but I do not think they flourished here as they did in Kona, Hawaii, and on Molokai, as I did not see any in later years. Some of the streams near the coast were full of very large mullet and having a light rod with me I made an attempt to catch these, but without success, as they refused to look at trout flies, though at last I managed to hook two small ones of about half a pound each, on a small hook with a small piece of white kid glove[119] on the point. There were however shoals of a small perch-like silver fish (called I think aholehole) which were never more than half a pound in weight, and which could be easily caught with a worm as bait. I collected over a considerable area in the Koolau range, from 'Halemano' (called

---

117   Perkins related a short passage in the Aves section of *Fauna Hawaiiensis* concerning his stay in Waialua: "On New Year's Day 1893 I flushed and shot a duck and drake near the coast at Waialua, and, when I went to gather them, I found that they had already hatched a large brood of young."

118   Perkins gives further details in later correspondence to Munro: "I was astonished about what you say about the 'swamp hen' that was so common in Waialua in 1892–93. Certainly I never heard of any of the sportsmen who used to shoot plover & ducks on week end trips out there killing any, nor as far as I knew did any one else. Being very tame & conspicuous they would never have been so common in /93 if they had been sought after. I have no idea whether they were found in Oahu localities as I did not visit any other suitable places then. There were native ducks in some numbers there in 92–93, but I was told they were much less numerous than in earlier years. It was there that Alex Cartwright, whom, I knew & who was the crack shot in the islands, on one occasion killed 102 native duck with 90 cartridges. I am not sure of the exact number of cartridges used, but it was rather less than that of the birds. I saw this record in writing that was made at the time of the shooting taking place. One or two sportsmen shooting over decoys (made of potatoes!) would take back 100 plover in a day's sport." *(R.C.L. Perkins letter to G.C. Munro, 28 January 1949, BPBM Archives, MS SC Munro Box 13.3).*

119   Kid glove leather, also known as wash leather.

Halemanu by Scott Wilson, but which, as Mr. J. Emerson[120] informed me) should probably be written Helemano, and not as I labelled my captures) to the Waimea Valley. On the Kaala side on one or two occasions I went on foot from the ranch house as far as the neighbourhood of Haleauau, though not quite reaching that stream, and it was in that neighbourhood that I first came across the little bird Oreomyza maculata. Later I found it in some numbers in the Koolau range also, but usually only far back in the forest. Apart from the wet weather, the mountains in the Kawailoa district of the Koolau range were very unsatisfactory for collecting, the ridges when one arrived at a satisfactory elevation being generally covered with masses of stag-horn fern,[121] impenetrable except at the expense of much toil and exertion. Some of the stream beds were the best paths upwards by wading up and continually crossing these one could get very far back in the forest; but this left little time for collecting and one needed a tent placed far back. I had been advised by Scott Wilson not to take out a tent with me, but here I saw camping was a necessity and I ordered one to be sent from the mainland. Before I left Waialua, Palmer and Wolstenholme,[122] Lord Rothschild's collectors, arrived there {21 March} and shared the Kawailoa mountain house[123] with me and afterwards from there camped far back in the mountains. I stayed with them some time in their tent and was present with Wolstenholme when he shot the male Loxops rufa {20 April} which had not been obtained since Lord Byron's[124] visit in 1825.

There was a second specimen in company with this, probably a female, but though we heard it, we did not get a sight of it nor of any other specimen. After I left to prepare for my visit to Molokai, Palmer and his colleague again camped for some time where the Loxops occurred, but failed to find another. Some ten years later I came across a pair far back in the forest in the Wahiawa district, but I had no gun with me at the time, as I was collecting insects with Koebele. Both here and also far back in the forest at Kawailoa Oreomyza Maculata was fairly common and from these places and near Haleauau in the Waianae range I took a good series eventually. At the time that the mountain apple, Ohia-ai, was in full flower along the stream at Kawailoa, great numbers of the Iiwi (Vestiaria) assembled therein to

[120]   Emerson, Joseph Swift (1843–1930). Born on Maui the sixth son of Hawaiian missionaries, Emerson was employed as a surveyor on the Big Island of Hawai'i but is probably better known for his research in Hawaiian history and ethnology. Fluent in Hawaiian, he interviewed native Hawaiians to learn how various artifacts were made, their history, and how they were used. His knowledge of Hawaiian folklore and history led an obituary to coin him as the "White Kuhuna."

[121]   *Uluhe*, false stag-horn fern, *Dicranopteris linearis*.

[122]   Wolstenholme, Edward "Ted" B. — A New Zealander employed by Rothschild to accompany Henry Palmer and collect birds in Hawai'i.

[123]   Palmer's notes give further details of his meeting up with Perkins:

> "March 21st.—I broke up my camp and rode to Waialua or Wailua, where I was glad to meet Mr. Perkins, the collector. He has collected for a good time and on different places on the island, but nowhere did he find any sign of *Hemignathus* or *Heterorhynchus*. He only found four species of native Passerine birds, i.e. *Vestiaria coccinea*, *Himatione sanguinea*, *Chlorodrepanis chloris* (Cab.), and *Chasiempis gayi*, Wilson. Of the white-backed and rufous-backed specimens of this Flycatcher he says he is sure, from many observations, they are young and old of the same species.
>
>   I went up with Mr. Perkins to the mountain-house he was staying in, and found it the most favourable place that could be selected. Therefore I decided to come here with my camp and did." (Rothschild, W. "*Avifauna of Laysan and the Hawaiian Islands, etc.*" p. (Di.) 18–19).

[124]   This refers to the voyage of the *Blonde*, the ship on which Lord Byron was Captain. Andrew Bloxam was the naturalist on board. Although previously described by Bloxam, Rothschild was quick to describe Wolstenholme's specimen as a new species. "On the 20th of April the only specimens {sic} of *Loxops* was shot by Palmer's assistant Wolstenholme, and therefore I named it in honour of its discoverer *Loxops wolstenholmei*, not having found out at the time that it really was *Loxops rufa* (Bloxam)." (Rothschild, W., 1900, "*Avifauna of Laysan and the Hawaiian Islands, etc.*" p. (Di.) 19).

feed on the nectar. I was much surprised to find that they out-numbered the Apapane and Amakihi together in these trees, because in my collecting throughout the Koolau range I considered the Iiwi comparatively rare and could hardly have believed that so many existed in the forests of Oahu as was evidenced by this assemblage in one small area. On Kaala at an elevation of about 3000 feet in March I saw a pair of Ou in company, but whether these were really natives of Oahu or a pair of stragglers from Kauai or Molokai on both of which islands the bird was very abundant is uncertain. Considering, the severe winter storms of this year and the fact that the Ou is in the habit of taking extended flights, often several birds together, and very high up in the air, it would be strange if individuals were not occasionally blown over to Oahu. Towards the end of my stay in the Kawailoa mountain house one day, during my absence in the higher forest this house was entered and much of the contents was carried off, including food that I had taken up. Also my notebook, paper, watch and other things disappeared with these. Fortunately my specimens were not interfered with in any way, so the loss was not serious. A brief general account of my collecting during this time contains little of interest, but I noted down the following: "Lepidoptera seem to be entirely out of season and excepting common species are scarce and this seems to be the case with Longicorns, of which, during a fine spell of weather only, I took two species, probably Clytarlus robustus [pulverulentus] and cristatus. The best insects were the Carabidae of which I got numbers under stones in gulches, under bark of Koa and some from tree-ferns and Freycinetia. There is a black, polished Anobiid, of good size under Koa bark [Holcobius glabricollis]. With the Carabids at base of Freycinetia leaves I took an Otiorhynchine beetle [Rhyncogonus freycinetiae] and with those beneath Koa bark, a large Brachypeplus [Gonioryctus sp. 7 in F.H.]. Species of Proterhinus were abundant beneath the very thick bark of dead Straussia trees, the larvae living the bark itself. In all the lower forest there is an almost total absence of native insects, though the variety of trees should, one would expect, produce many beetles. Their absence seems to be due entirely to the vast numbers of ants (Pheidole) which infest the lower mountains. The Clytarlus robustus which I found lower down than any other native beetle had Pheidole ants hanging on to its legs and antennae, in the case of several specimens. I never found any Carabidae under the bark of the Koa trees, even when these were in perfect condition for yielding beetles, where they were infested by the ants. These Carabids when a batch is disturbed emit a visible vapour of pungent or fetid odour.

Thick forest, no doubt, once came down at least to 700 feet, for there were many traces of fires, some very old and some comparatively recent. Great herds of wild pigs may sometimes be seen crossing the flats between the gulches, where they chiefly hide. I counted 42 in one lot, of different sizes, from the largest boar with great tusks to pigs only half grown. High up in the dense forest I occasionally came on a solitary old boar in the soft fern. These do not run away when one comes on them suddenly, but, if one is only a few yards distant and stands still, they will walk very slowly away, looking back at one with their small eyes, and grunt, with the bristles of the back standing erect. None of those I saw attempted to charge, but they have a formidable appearance, and I caught hold of the nearest branch of a tree on such occasions, so that I could swing myself up should they do so.

Land shells are numerous in the country between Helemano and Waimea, but I am told vast numbers of Achatinellas have been taken from the mountains here, so it is not very likely that I have obtained much of interest in this line. There is a very pretty and striking pink shell [A. rosea] in some numbers but quite local. The young occurred in much greater numbers than the adults. The young of these land shells often hide in leaves spun together by spiders, and in one or two cases I found a single beautiful little mud-cell formed by an Odynerus sticking to the leaf by the side of the spider's nest and the young shells. All these were hidden in the rolled-up leaf, the work of the spider. On the Kaala side there is one very common Achatinella of the Apex group and it varies a good deal in form and colour, but there seems to be a great lack of species, as compared with the other range. On almost my last collecting day around Kaala I found in one gulch vast numbers of elytra of a fine looking Carabid but none alive, so that either it was out of season, or else had ceased to inhabit that particular gulch [Blackburnia insignis var. Kaalensis]. On the same day, well below any continuous forest and on a bare dry ridge, I found three isolated trees standing together and in very bad condition. On these I took specimens of a Clytarlus new to me, the trees being much infested with the larvae and nearly dead [Plagithmysus cuneatus]. At the same time on some isolated Koa trees I noticed freshly emerged specimens of the two Koa Clytarli [i.e. Plagithmysus] their hind tibiae not fully hardened. The best all round season for insects is apparently beginning here, but a tent is needed as it takes far too long to go and come back over miles of unprofitable country.

In a Kukui log, so rotten and wet that the water could be squeezed out, and lying in a puddle at the bottom of a deep gulch, I found many larvae and a few adults of a species of Fornax [In F.H. described as Dromaeolus sordidus and, obscurus]. Of other beetles there were of course Proterhinus, Cis, Xyletobius &[c], but Lepidoptera were very scarce and the only thing of much interest to me was a species of Alucita [Orneodes objurgatella; later this was bred in numbers, in 1901, F.H. I, 731]. The birds around Kaala are not very numerous, especially in those parts which are nearest to Waialua. I saw there only the Iiwi, Apapane, Amakihi, Elepaio, and once the Ou; the Elepaio and Apapane a good deal more numerous than the Amakihi and Iiwi. Further away, in the direction of the Gap,[125] the Iiwi was more frequent and except the Ou, which I did not see there at all the others were quite common. There were also quite a few individuals of the straight-billed Himatione [i.e. Oreomyza maculata]. I should have liked to work this ground more often and thoroughly, but the distance was too great. There were many species of trees in this part of the Waianae range."

[The above notes scribbled in pencil were no doubt written on the conclusion of my collecting in the Waialua district, probably with the idea of using them for an article in one of the English magazines.]

---

125   No doubt referring to the large "notch" in the Waianae Range called Kolekole Pass. This is best known as the pass thought at one time to be used by the Japanese as they flew low to escape radar detection on their way toward Pearl Harbor in the surprise attack on 7 December 1941. The actual routes the Japanese pilots took were around the south of the Wai'anae Range and from the north through the central saddle area of O'ahu.

Selected Correspondence

Honolulu, Hawaiian Islands
22 October 1892
Edward Bagnall Poulton

Dear Mr Poulton,

I take this opportunity of being in town to write to you, as I thought you would like to hear how I am getting on. Very possibly however you have heard more or less from D^r. Sharp or other members of the Committee. I think I have been very successful so far, particularly of late – such doleful pictures of the scarcity of insect life has been drawn by others, I was at first quite alarmed for the results but I have found no such scarcity save naturally in species. At first I worked for some 2 months on this island (Oahu) since which time I have been all the time in the Kona district of Hawaii. I was bid thither by knowing of the existence of several desirable birds there. The best of these are a very small orange-coloured sp. of Drepanididae. <u>Loxops</u> <u>coccinea</u> of which I got 6.

A greenfinche-like bird with enormous bill & head (developed in connection with its seed-cracking habits) <u>Chloridops</u> <u>konae</u> of which I got 2 dozen & another magnificent finch lately discovered by Rothschild's collector Palmer, <u>Rhodacanthis</u> <u>Palmeri</u>.

This is a large bird – larger than any English finch & with its brilliant golden-orange head a most splendid creature. I got 16. The insects of the district were all that could be desired: about 80 sp. Coleoptera, over 100 Leps. with some fine Neuroptera, Orthopteran, Hymenoptera, Hemiptera &^c. No one who had noticed the habits of the birds, I should have thought, could possibly have supposed the scarcity of the insects to be more than apparent, yet Wilson the ornithologist told me there were really no insects & Munro one of Rothschild's collectors, & who had done a lot of entom^{cal} work in N. Zealand told me exactly the same!

I expect from 25-50 p.c. of my Kona captures will be new. I got several forms of <u>Sclerodermus</u>, <u>Sierola</u> genera of Hymenoptera, so interesting as connecting the ants & Ichneumonidae. Also many specimens & species of the endemic Coleoptera <u>Proterhinus</u> – possibly the most ancient of all existing Coleoptera. I also got some extraordinary species of thrips. Some of the spiders too are splendid. Nearly all the insects very small & very highly protected from birds.

The Cerambycid Coleoptera <u>Clytarlus</u> is the only really fine endemic genus & only some of the species of these, as they really form several genera. 10 are known so far. 3 I got on Oahu all known before as this island has 4 Maui has 4 which of course I have not yet got, & Hawaii 2. Therefore 4 of the 6 I found on Hawaii are new for certain & 2 of these probably the 2 first of the genus as at present known.

If I am able to do the group I shall probably get 230 sp. of this splendid genus. There are 4 Sphingidae in the islands all common, & 2 peculiar. Of 3 including one of the peculiar species (endemic?) I know the larvae. One is Deilephila livornica. I bred one through stages 1 & 2; are these known? It is easy enough to get larvae in stages 3, 4 & full grown. The other species Protoparce cingulata (American) & P. blackburni (peculiar). I know a full grown larvae & one of them I had described in stage 1. Its ontogeny will be very remarkable as the difference between the last 2 stages is extreme. Both these species in the larval stage "snap" like an electric spark & ♂ like Ach. atropos, but the imago does not squeak. The imago is quite like Sphinx convolvuli superficially. Just before leaving Kona I found an extraordinary larva with 2 lateral caudal horns & many other spines. It is one of the most remarkable creatures I ever saw & very interesting. I shall be on Oahu now some time in search of birds which existed 50 years ago & are very important to get if still existent. This too is a fine land-shell island so I shall be rather quiet in the insect line. I then go to Molokai, the insect fauna of which is utterly unknown & I might get a new bird.

I failed to get near the summit of the huge mountain Mauna Loa from the Kona side, the ascent being always made from the east side. Hawaii I worked pretty well throughout the forest proper, above which the fauna is very scanty. I did ascend the smaller Mt. Hualalai which is about 9000 ft. sleeping in an apology for a cave at about 7000 ft. We had no blanket & it was very cold, the ground white with frost in the morning. It half-killed my Hawaiian assistant!

The natives away from town are the best of fellows from a collector's point of view owing to their hospitality – about Honolulu they have all the natural vices with none of the kindness of the true Hawaiian, & are a miserable set.

I hope you will find time to write to me sometimes. If you can suggest any questions of wide importance that I might solve I should be glad. Nearly all the endemic creatures or rather their ancestors have arrived in driftwood – even the Lepidoptera.

Post Office Honolulu will always find me: there is no delivery of letters.

Yours very sincerely,
R.C.L. Perkins

Cambridge, England
5 November 1892
Robert Cyril Layton Perkins

Dear Mr Perkins,

Your letter of 25.9.92 is just to hand having apparently been longer on the road than usual. I also duly received yours of date 3.9.92, the former I shall answer first. I have been most pleased to find that you continue in good health and spirits, and I hope you will take care not to overwork yourself, or to risk suffering from undue exposure.

You do not say anything about the reception of the case. I despatched it to you some months since, perhaps it is waiting your arrival at Oahu, when you receive it please instruct me immediately what your requirements may be as to other things so that I may see about them as soon as possible, as it takes so very long to ask & receive at such a distance. I shall send you pins next week, 500 12 m.m. as you ask.

I am glad to hear you are now leaving Kona; the experience you have gained by your long stay there will be most valuable to you elsewhere, but I fancy it is by no means one of the richest districts in the islands, and I fancy you will do better in the western part of Oahu, and in Maui. (I return your drawings indicating briefly my opinion thereon). I quite agree with your intention to make for a period of three months or so the entomology subordinate to the ornithology and conchology, though in the latter I expect that Oahu will provide but little that is good: good series, with localities well indicated will however be very valuable, no doubt. You will always carry a tube or two & a box for dragon-flies so that you may be able to avoid yourself of a fluke in meeting with anything good.

As regards your lists of species met with at Kona, they appear to be fairly satisfactory, though I think a rather higher district of forest, where it is merging into the open grounds above will prove much richer in variety of species and in the interesting forms of Carabidae &^{c}. I am very glad to hear of the large Proterhinus though there is only one specimen. If you can give information in due course as to the habits and find the larva of this insect it would be of great interest. Your list of Lepidoptera strikes me as very good; although you think Leps. more numerous than Col. I scarcely think that is really the case. As regards your view that Hymenoptera are in diminished proportions I am inclined to agree; the parasitic Hymenoptera which make up the bulk of the lists in our country, being probably really in fewer proportion there; still they are of great interest as having an important bearing on the question of "Natural introduction." If you can make for your own use any jottings as to the thinks you may believe the parasitic Hymenoptera to infest that will be very important. With regards to Thysanura and Collembola I think them of great importance and interest: can you not turn up the genera Campodea or Japyx under good big stones at the edges of woods with a certain amount of protection by trees but so as not to be completely buried: the Mediterranean region has been recently shown to have quite a special fauna of that sort, though no entomologist suspected their existence until recently. Possibly even you might turn up Peripatus in such places!

As it takes some time to communicate, and as you are returning to Oahu, we have arranged with the Treasurer to send you another £100 by this post, it will not diminish anything for your prestige in Honolulu to have more money at your disposal than you immediately require.

I have asked Beddard[126] about doubling worms, he replies they may be doubled as M[r]. P. suggests. He sends the following recipe for Perenyi's fluid.[127] "3 parts 20 percent nitric acid, 3 parts 1 percent chromic acid, 4 parts absolute alcohol." I like your idea about putting the small beetles in tubes instead of boxes; do you not think it would be well to have some extremely small tubes, if you could then put several of them in a box with the sawdust; if you think well of this I will get you a small pocket case for holding very small tubes.

I am glad to hear Prosopis is turning up so nicely. I have been studying aculeates a little lately and have formed the idea that is likely to prove the most primitive of existing bees.

Now I want to impress on you very strongly the necessity of sending us a quantity—I think all— your results at once so that they may be overhanded and reported on in time for the application to the Royal Society. You should send off on the very first opportunity after receipt of this all you have that is available. Recollect that we have nothing at present from you except for the results of your first few weeks in Oahu, and if we have to base our application for more funds to the Royal, on that alone, I fear we shall fail to get what we require. I should like therefore for you to send all you have, now, so that I may get some reports on the material with sufficient time to do it in satisfactorily; as this lot will consist largely of insects, I should like to have a second lot with the birds, reptiles, shells, &[c] you are going to get in Oahu, sent off so that I may get it in March. You will hear from me again in a week, with pins &[c]. But the sending off at once of a very large case is an imperative necessity. Best wishes,

Yours very truly,
D. Sharp.

Magdalene College
Cambridge, England
12 November 1892
Robert Cyril Layton Perkins

My dear Perkins,

Having last week written you (4th November) in answer to your letter of 25th Sept[r] I have now to thank you for yours 16th Oct[r], to get which was an unexpected pleasure, and a still greater one has been affected by the notes of your diary (if you

---

126   Beddard, Frank Evers (1858–1925). Zoologist, one-time editor of the *Zoological Record*. Specialized in earthworms for the *Fauna Hawaiiensis*.

127   Perenyi's Fluid is a slow decalcifying solution used to soften tissues for dissection and other study that would otherwise be hardened, for example by preservation in ethanol.

send any more take the precaution of pinning them together) which I have read with interest and delight. They are capital, and I thank you heartily for them. I should like to send them straight off for publication in 'The Ibis', but I think I could hardly do this with propriety without consulting at least some members of the Committee, and since I read them I have not seen D[r]. Sharp even. But you may be sure that I shall do my best to have them so used as they may be appreciated. Wilson had nothing like them (this between ourselves) but not that he must have had good opportunities as you – if not better.

Next I must say how glad I am that you are returned to Honolulu, in order to work Oahu, and that you have got two cases of specimens off, though it is a pity they have to come by Australia. However, I don't doubt you have done your best in your power & judgment in sending them. I only wish you had put a couple of skins of Rhodacanthis into a little box & sent them by post. It is exceedingly stupid of me not having suggested this before. But I would ask you to do so with the Oahu hemignathi, should you have the luck to fall with them – you will I hope get a good many of them – but a pair of each species in a box might & ought to come through the U.S. all right, and would be something good to show. I had not before heard where M[r]. Palmer met with Drepanis pacifica. O, that you may get Acrulocercus apicalis! Or at least find out where it lives. I forget whether I told you in my last letter, that the prevalent belief among the London people is that none of the S.I. birds is extinct, but that all will be got. I may have been too despondent, and have trusted too much to Wilson's want of success – but I think the new belief is only the backward swing of the pendulum – at any rate the rediscovery of Drepanis is not enough to justify it in my opinion.

I have no doubt your observations on the plumage of Chasiempis will help to clear up some difficulties. How odd that the "Hawk" {*Buteo solitarius*} should find its chief food in house mice! How did it live before they came here? The mouse question is one you must think of – did the beast exist there before Europeans came? If so, did the first black people bring it? You know it is said that the Maoris took a rat with them to New Zealand – which rat is practically extinct nowadays. I might comment for a long while on your 'notes' – but I have not the time – for this is a busy term with me.

Your proposed movements as mentioned in your last letter to me & in greater detail in that to Sharp (which he has shown me) seem well planned – but as I have before told you, you by this time must be far the best judge, & it would be ridiculous for me or anybody here to give you advice. It was perfectly right that we should furnish you with hints at starting, according to the best information we had, for of course you then knew next to nothing, but now I have got the least wish to direct your steps – for I am sure you will do what you think right & best. It will be nearly Christmas when this reaches you – I hope you will pass a happy one & with all other good wishes believe me to be

Yours very truly
Alfred Newton

Cambridge, England
25 November 1892
Robert Cyril Layton Perkins

Dear Mr Perkins,

Your letter of 29<u>th</u> Octr is to hand, together with the fourteen boxes of pinned specimens announced in it as dispatched. The specimens have not travelled so well in this way as they do in packing cases; as the people knock the mail bags about so dreadfully, and in some of the boxes the specimens are much damaged owing to the bodies of the Lepidoptera coming off and then knocking off antennae &c; however I do not think anything is totally lost, though I am afraid the lepidopterists will look a little queer at some of the specimens. I have not had time to go through them thoroughly yet; and of course there are not many Coleops in them so I could give you little exact details. I thought however I would look at the clytarli to see about them & tell you. There are in this lot 9 or 10 species, and as you have got three other in Oahu that will make it about 13 altogether. I should think 5 or 6 of the Mauna Loa species are new, but I cannot say for certain as there are only one or two each of the little ones and these are very difficult; the only two I can identify are blackburni & filipes. The pretty Oahu one is also new. I now think you will bring the clytarli up to 30 or 40 species! It is a pity C. perkinsi is unique. {C.} filipes is the little one you send four of.

This is all I have looked at present. So I will proceed to answer your letter without saying anything more about the specimens. I think you have now got thoroughly into insect fauna & will make a revolution in it in the next 12 months if all goes well as I trust it will. The Hymenoptera certainly will be highly interesting. I have been studying Hymenoptera the last few months and find Prosopis is the primitive bee, that is very interesting, but it does not concern the question of possible introduction because it is a very widely distributed genus. It will be desirable to get plenty of males because there are fine ♂ characters in the genus though everything else is so much alike. I have no doubt the Odyneri and other things are also of great interest. The Megachile you now send is very like the one Blackburn got (I looked at that last time I was in London), so the one with tawny pubescence on the middle of the body will be new.

I shall get glass tubes boxes &^c next week but will advise you before sending them. I do not yet believe Vanessa atalanta will be ordinary atalanta, but I am willing to admit it may be an oceanic variety. I hope you will get plenty of the butterflies as they are very interesting really, & people take much more interest in them than they do sensible things like beetles & Hymenoptera. I hope you will note anything you can about habits. What you say about the dragonfly larva & so on is of great interest & don't forget to make out the metamorphoses & sexes of the Embiid which is said to abound in old roofs near Honolulu, I believe in the rotten wood of rafters or it may be thatch. I think I shall ask Mr Meyrick[128] to do the Leps. not

---

128   Meyrick, Edward (1854–1938). British-born amateur lepidopterist. Meyrick was a world-renowned specialist on microlepidoptera and published the results of his work on the Hawaiian fauna in 1899 in the *Fauna Hawaiiensis*. After his schooling at Marlborough College and Trinity College, Cambridge, Meyrick went to Australia and New Zealand for a short time where he was a school teacher. While there, he discovered a very

micros. I hope you will do the Hymenoptera yourself. The others I know I can get first rate men on the continent to do, if there is no suitable person forthcoming in this country. I do not much think we will make preliminary short papers; it makes it so much more awkward for future workers, and besides leads one into all sorts of muddles about genera; which, as well as species, is very difficult in the Hawaiian things. The locality for your Oahuan Clytarlus fragilis was "Waianae Mts beaten from dead Koa branches 2-3000 ft. April 1892"; it is much like C. filipes.

Dryophthorus runs into ridges in the rare species & is apt to look as if it has been sliced off behind; which means I believe that it lies in burrowed wood. I expect the season of the year now on is better for Carabidae than that from April to September; and I do not doubt that you will manage to find them before long.

Mr Hickson sent £100 a week or two ago, and he wishes me to say that he thinks you will have to pay 10 p. out of it for expenses of transmission. I hope you will have a good time of it in Honolulu, & that the people there will be good to you.

I am disgusted with that Parandra[129] for smashing up the Drepanepteryse (that I expect would be near the angular winged Neuroptera), but hope you meet with the species again some time.

As regards the future sending of pinned insects, I do not myself think it advisable to transmit them in that way (parcel post) wholesale; if you have any reason for wishing to transmit one or two boxes rapidly at any time there is of course no objection; but to make it the chief mode of transmission seems to me to be running an unnecessary risk, and that without any definite advantage. In any case when sending again please put plenty of pins between the pieces of cork to keep them from screwing round; and also put the small insects into distinct boxes from the large ones; those Noctuae should all go into a box by themselves for travelling in, as their big bodies coming off destroy the little things fearfully. Please also use plenty of carbolic acid in the boxes. On the whole I think for the Sandwich Islands small boxes will be better than large ones, and in future I will have small ones made for you, but that is not because I want them transmitted by post, but because you will find them more suitable for other reasons.

I enclose some pins. I shall look out & see if I can get the papers you ask for & if so will send them.

I hope now you are in Oahu you will really get some of the other things. I feel sure that you will make a success of the entomology, and I should like you very much to let the other people see that if they send entomologists to places they will

rich and unworked fauna of microlepidoptera on which he produced a great many papers and descriptions of new species. He returned to England in 1887 to take up the post as assistant master at Marlborough College in Wiltshire, England, where he taught Greek and Latin. During his life, Meyrick described more species new to science than any other entomologist (ca. 20,000), said to have been possible due to his rigor of method and habit: he worked in the evenings and stayed up until one hour after midnight each night. In 1912, irritated with having to wait long periods of time for his articles to appear in foreign journals, he started his own journal "*Exotic Microlepidoptera*" which was described by himself as "a spasmodic entomological magazine on one subject by a single contributor." It appeared, spasmodically, until 1937.

[129]   No doubt referring to the large pinned *Parandra* (a large beetle) getting loose in the insect box during shipment and causing damage to other specimens as the box was tossed around in transit.

pick up other things also. As soon as the two cases come to hand we shall have a meeting of the Committee & then we shall be able to let you know what we think of your results in other groups besides insects. With very best wishes, I am,

Yours very truly
D. Sharp.

You speak of some carded beetles from Freycintia – they are not to hand yet.

Athenaeum Club[130]
Pall Mall, England
6 January 1893
Robert Cyril Layton Perkins

My dear Perkins,

I write merely to say that the Joint Committee of the R. S. & Brit. Ass[n]. at a meeting yesterday unanimously agreed to apply for a renewal of the grants to keep you going for another year. Whether we shall get them or not is of course another matter, but we shall try our best.

Neither Sharp nor I have heard from you since I last wrote to you, which, if I remember right, was about the 9th December. Your "Collecting in Hawaii" is printed in this months 'Ibis' – I hope to be able to send you a copy very shortly. Rothschild's man has been getting some new birds on Maui—among them one, which he has called Palmeria mirabilis forming a new genus of Meliphagidae, with a crest on its head—but this is only what I read & hear, for I have not seen a specimen.

All good luck to you,

Yours very truly
Alfred Newton

---

[130]   Gentleman's club founded in 1824 by well-known rare book collector Richard Heber. Served as a gathering place for academics from Oxford and Cambridge as well as members of society in London.

Magdalene College
Cambridge, England
21 January 1893
Robert Cyril Layton Perkins

My dear Perkins,

I have no letter from you since that of the 16$\underline{th}$ Nov. to which I replied on the 8$\underline{th}$ Dec., but I wrote to you on the 6$\underline{th}$ of this month, telling you of the meeting of the Joint Committee on the preceding day, when it was agreed to apply for renewed grants from the Government Fund and from the British Association to keep you going longer.

Now I have to inform you of the safe arrival yesterday of the two cases containing your collections in Hawaii. There has only been time for me to look at some of the Bird skins, but they seem to be all right. It has been great pleasure to see Rhodacanthis for the first time—but what a rotten name it is! The bird is not rose-coloured (any part of it) or in the least like an axardis {= goldfinch}. This by the way—of course I wish there were more of them; but one must be thankful for all one gets and 5 of the 8 specimens form a beautiful series—quite young with a streaky breast, a young ♀ beginning to show the red, another further advanced, a full-plumaged ♂ & an old ♀. Nothing of the kind could be better—& I think Wilson must feel disgusted at not having discovered this fine thing! The young Acrulocerci are also very interesting. The Buzzards are of course Buteo solitarius—I wish I knew why they vary so in plumage, but they always do presenting two if not three distinct phases, quite irrespective, I believe, of age or sex—but the like is observable in some other species of buzzards or one may say of Accipters. The duck I suppose to be Anas wyvilliana but I know that species only by the figure & it is smaller than I expected to find it—in fact more of a teal than a true duck (limited). These skins are not very grand, that is to say they will want making up, but I dare say their condition is sound, so that they will turn out well enough. The other things I have really not looked at, for I did not know of the arrival till I got to the Museum yesterday afternoon & I had several other things to do while I was there. Dr. Sharp told me that the other things {illegible} all right, but I had not made special enquiries. I do not know whether he will write to you by this mail, but I do so thinking you will like to hear of their safety as soon as possible. I had hoped to have heard from you again. I only trust your silence is not caused by any ill health—and with my best wishes I remain

Yours very truly
Alfred Newton

The British Museum people have condescended to request indirectly that you should collect for them a small series of the Birds of each island you visit.

Cambridge, England
27 January 1893
Robert Cyril Layton Perkins

Dear Mr Perkins,

Your letter of Jan. 1st is to hand today. I am really glad to hear you are well and working at the Birds and Shells. If this is a good time for them it is a very fortu-nate provision of nature to have made it a good time for birds & shells when there are no insects much about.

Your remarks about finding Carabidae now in places in Oahu though you could not find them in similar spots in Hawaii raises the question about seasons in the Sandwich islands; there is little or no evidence at present about the times of appearance, and if the imago lasts but a short time & appears only in one genera-tion per annum, we must bear this is mind in considering the very important questions as to the differences in the special faunae of each of the islands; in mak-ing fair visits it will be well to give a little attention to the seasons from this point of view.

I suppose you will go to Maui insects, and if they give you free passages you might break your stay there by a short journey or two to Oahu or Hawaii so as to catch places at another season to what you have tried them at and to see actually what the differences are in this respect. Blackburn's information on this point was very vague and unsatisfactory. There are also some very important points connected with the vertical range of species in this fauna, and as to this we have no informa-tion (the insects) that can be at all depended on. Some remarks in your letter lead me to suppose that hasty generalisation on this point could be made but might be very deceptive.

I hope you will recollect to let me know plenty of time beforehand when you are going to be actually short of material; I have glass tubes, silver pins, & cork ready to send you, but I am keeping them back as there may be something else you want, and carriage of a small parcel is so expensive. I'm afraid I must however send them by the old route as the post office people wont accept glass-tubes in any quantity.

A few days ago the two cases arrived with the contents in good condition; of course the interest to me was discounted by the insects you had previously sent by post, but I was a little disappointed at not seeing more in the other departments of the fauna; I suppose however Hawaii is not rich for general collecting, and I am inclined to regret a little that you spent so long a consecutive time at Kona in 1892.

With regard to the question I put about Prosopis, you did not quite catch my meaning; I did not at all mean that I thought the numerous species would all prove to be varietal forms, but that in view of the variability of Sphecodes (which is another primitive form) somebody will probably suggest that view, so it will be as well to have as much evidence on the point as you can get. I forget whether I told you that I am now myself convinced that Sphecodes, is really – not withstanding the accumulation of negative evidence bearing the other way – parasitic.

I do not think the Committee will be anxious to get things worked out piecemeal, but on the whole will be willing to wait so as to keep the literature concentrated as much as we can. In the insects this is important because the generic question is surrounded with difficulties to would be best delayed for solution till all the species likely to be procured are before the worker. The Odyneri look to me very difficult from this point of view, & from what I hear the Tineidae are likely to prove sincerely difficult.

I do wish I could come out & see a little of the fauna myself; I am not getting sufficient outdoor work, so I will look almost with envy on your expeditions where I hear about them in your letters.

Thank you very much for your wishes for the New Year; better late than never is a well known saying; and in the matter of wishes, I daresay they are practically as effectual when given afterwards as when given beforehand, so I shall certainly value them quite as much as if you had sent them off on the first of January by the new system of air-telegraphy people are talking about.

Perhaps Professor Newton will add a few lines to this about the birds; and with the very best wishes for your health happiness & success I am,

Yours very truly
D. Sharp.

Magdalene College
Cambridge, England
28 January 1893
Robert Cyril Layton Perkins

Dear Perkins,

Sharp has sent me your letter to him of the 1st Jan. together with his reply that I may add a few lines—but there is little to say beyond expressing my regret at your not having been able to find the birds. I suppose the only inference to be drawn is that they are extinct!

It is satisfactory to have heard from {you}, as I was beginning to get a little uneasy— Your last letter having been of 16 Nov. to which I replied on the 9th Dec. writing again 6th & 21st Jan.—just a week ago, when I announced the safe arrival of your boxes sent by Australia. The birds seem all right—& as I then told you I was pleased to see Rhodacanthis & the nestling Acrulocerci. I thought before this to have had extra copies of your account of bird-collecting in Kona, which appeared in the January 'Ibis'—but they have not yet reached here. I will send you a few when I get them.

I do wish you had said more of yourself & of your doings—we ought to know what assistance you have received (if any) & who has rendered it. You have scarcely ever mentioned anybody's name. I find there is a M^r Fr. Spencer who writes to Wilson that <u>Ciridops</u> <u>anna</u> inhabits swampy <u>forests</u> above Ookala in Hawaii, & that is supposed to be the place where Mr Palmer got it as well as <u>Drepanis</u> for Rothschild. May be that <u>Chaetoptila</u> inhabits the same locality. We still know nothing about <u>Acrulocercus</u> <u>apicalis</u>. I am at a loss to add more & so with renewed good wishes I remain

Yours very truly
Alfred Newton

Cambridge, England
10 February 1893
Robert Cyril Layton Perkins

Dear Mr Perkins,

We are very sorry to hear of the political difficulties[131] that have occurred. I hope they will not seriously inconvenience you. If you should think there is any danger of a serious rising in Honolulu, I should advise you to go to one of the other islands for a time, especially if there is any spot where you know you have a friend you could rely on and stay for a little while.

If there are any people in the islands who have been kind to you & given you any actual assistance will you let us know so that the Committee may acknowledge it.

I believe Professor Newton has informed you that at the last meeting of the Committee it was resolved that Mr Perkins be instructed to obtain a small series of the birds in each island he visits when he can do so without detriment to this researches in the less known parts of the fauna. No doubt you will kindly bear this in mind; the reason for it is that the British Museum has scarcely any Sandwich Islands birds.

I do not think you have sent any ants. There is a very remarkable one described from <u>Oahu</u> by Smith, Leptogenys insularis; it appears to be known only by one specimen & is of singular interest. According to my views about ants this should have remarkable habits & there should be two forms of the workers if not more. If you can look after it & investigate it a little it will be very interesting. ... Scarcely anything is known about the <u>genus</u>; but the few species are mostly <u>insular</u>. By the time this reaches you the insect season will have set in again; & I dare say

---

131   Referring to the overthrow of Queen Lili'uokalani in January 1893.

you will be planning an expedition to Maui. I hope when there you will not omit to take things that you have already met with (or that you think you have) in Hawaii or Oahu.

Beddard reports that there are 4 species of worms, that one is certainly new, & probably all may be. Dont forget to get a little mud for D^r. Hickson when you have a chance in a land of ponds or streams. With best wishes I am,

Yours very truly
D. Sharp.

Be sure & give me plenty of notice when you <u>must</u> have things sent off for use.

University Museum of Zoology and Comparative Anatomy
Cambridge, England
18 March 1893
Robert Cyril Layton Perkins

Dear Mr Perkins,

Your last letter to me was dated the 1st Jan. 93. & here we are at the equinox, so I am a little uneasy at not hearing from you: I hope most fervently that you are well and the political upset in the islands has not interfered with your comfort or welfare in any way. I hope you will not think I have neglected you in not writing oftener, but I wished to leave you for some time without sympathy entomological, in hopes you would denounce me as a useless being and give all your attention to shells and other things. Now I think it is time for the insects to have an innings again so I mean to persecute you with letters, till I feel sure you have got another 200 new species, as I think you did in your first six months.

I am expecting daily to get a letter from you saying what things you must have sent you: and as soon as I do I shall send off what you want by the very first opportunity. I have hoped also to hear you had arranged for an expedition to Maui as I feel sure you would like that, & it would in all probability be very productive. I expect however before this reaches you that you are tired of a biological diet of snails and are now off to Maui to get some fine birds and several hundred new species of insects: as the best season will be now setting in.

With regard to the Ant, Leptogenys insularis, I mentioned in my last letter; I have recently come across some information which makes me think it will prove to be of Termitophagous habits & that the long sickle-shaped mandibles are used for carrying off its booty: does it live in the neighbourhood of Termites? and is there a second form of worker with short mandibles, as I think there ought to be? Have you in Oahu yet met with the primitive Neuroptera in its early stages? I refer to the Embiid of which you sent one specimen in your first lot.

I read with great pleasure your paper in the Ibis, and I need not say with what interest I look forward to the information you will doubtless be able to give us on a number of entomological matters.

McLachlan[132] published last winter a brief paper on Hawaiian Neuroptera, but he had only one species to add, – an antlion found by Scott Wilson in Lanai.

Prof. Newton told you I believe that we are making application for more money to the R.S. Of course we do not know whether we shall get it, and we shall have also to go to the Brit. Ass. even if we do. So I shall be glad if you can make us another parcel to reach here early in June so as to give them an account of a year's doings.

With very best wishes,

Yours very truly
D. Sharp.

Cambridge, England
22 April 1893
Robert Cyril Layton Perkins

Dear Mr Perkins,

I have been surprised at not hearing from you more than once in the last five months, especially as I sent you one or two important communications; but I now hear from your father that in all probability my letters have been lost like others sent to you by Professor Newton & himself. I have written two or three times to ask you to let me know when you should have stores sent off, and to ask you to have enough sent to last you for some time: a list of everything you require me to send you, so as to last you for some months would therefore be very desirable.

We shall also be glad to receive your acquisitions up to the end of February or March so as to enable us to publish a report to the Brit. Ass. as to total results of one year's operations, as the Committee, if it wish to keep the exploration going must get more money from the Association. I believe this could be obtained if we can shew sufficient results.

I also informed you that the Committee had resolved to ask you to procure in each island you may visit as good a series of the birds as you can, without interfering with your work on the less known branches of the Zoology. This is because the British Museum had very few Sandwich island Birds.

---

[132] McLachlan, Robert (1837–1904). Entomologist, specializing in dragonflies and damselflies, placed by some at this time in "Neuroptera"; now classified in the Odonata. McLachlan published on the Hawaiian odonates before Perkins came out to Hawai'i. However, Perkins felt there was still much more to be done after his collecting and he himself published on them for the *Fauna Hawaiiensis* in 1899.

As the communication between us has been – for some mysterious reason – interrupted, apparently for some months, I register this letter and would advise you, after making enquiries about missing letters also to register your answer to this, and make a memorandum in your note book as to the date, besides taking care of the receipt.

With best wishes, & hoping you are well, I am,

Yours very truly
D. Sharp.

Your case of specimens was received last January. Probably it contained all you put in it; but in future it would be well to send with advise note in registered letter, the number of bottles, skins &c any case you dispatch may contain.

D.S.

Charles Reed Bishop

Rev. Thomas Blackburn

William Tufts Brigham

Rev. John Thomas Gulick

Valdemar Knudsen

Alfred Koebele

George C. Munro

Alfred Newton

Henry C. Palmer

Edward Bagnall Poulton

Aubrey Robinson

Walter Rothschild

Moloka'i
11 May–29 June 1893

The following two journal transcripts and remembrances (in this and the following chapter) are the longest of all the tracts written by Perkins. Considering Perkins was an apparently reluctant journal writer, it is even all the more interesting that he goes into as much detail as he does in some of the daily entries in these journals. The East Moloka'i forest was not only in the best condition of all the places Perkins visited in his ten year's worth of collecting in the islands, but Moloka'i was the one island that had never been visited by an entomologist, thus he was more inclined to write about it.

Perkins also did some of his best bird hunting on Moloka'i; and one month after slopping through rain-soaked forests and bogs, finally collected a new bird species, the all-black Moloka'i Drepanidine (*Drepanis funerea*).

Perkins gives a summary of his Moloka'i adventures in his introduction to the *Fauna Hawaiiensis*:

"In May 1893 I crossed over to Molokai and, the west half of the island being practically forestless, camped on the southern slope of the forest-bearing end, near the middle of the island. All animal life seemed abundant after my experience on Oahu. Common species of birds were plentiful, though not in the extraordinary numbers observed on Hawaii, and of course all the Mollusca and most of the insects were new to me. This was a very wet summer in the mountains, and for the first six weeks there was hardly a day without long and heavy rains in the woods a few miles behind my camp, and when it was not actually raining, these were mostly enveloped in thick fog, through which objects were visible only for a short distance. In spite of this, collecting was good. After a time I pitched a tent in the midst of the highest boggy forest near the back ridge of the mountains. From my different camps I was able to get to Kalae on the west, where I also made a short stay, to the valley of Waikolu, and down into the deep valley of Pelekunu, where I stayed for a time in the then native village on the windward coast. It was not till autumn that I was able to leave Molokai, owing to the large amount of time spent in securing the rarer birds. And here I should state, that not only Molokai, but elsewhere the scarce birds are without doubt difficult to get even in the moderate series. I should consider that, both on Molokai and other islands, at least half of my whole collecting time was taken up in acquiring those that I obtained. For some of these birds it was necessary to be continually on the watch, and even then, and in the best localities, it was quite possible to spend weeks without seeing, or even hearing, a single individual. For this reason, until I had secured my specimens, I never dared to go about unhampered with gun and other necessaries for bird-collecting, even though I was specially in search of insects." (Perkins, R.C.L., 1913, *Fauna Hawaiiensis* 1: xxxiii.)

Further details of his Moloka'i diaries and collecting are detailed in a letter to George Munro:

"I am interested in what you say about the Molokai forests & the birds & looked up the remains of my old diaries. I still have the one scribbled in pencil in 1893, now nearly illegible. I have made a copy of the first two months (May & June) of this & sent it to Swezey with the suggestion that he turn it over to the Bishop Mus. If they care to keep it, but it would probably interest you more than any one at present, as it is so taken up with bird collecting. It is a faithful account of every bird I shot at, miss or kill & whether I lost it in the dense brush or found it. It does not go so far as the date when I took the Meyers— Henry was my special friend! But I remember Theodor & Otto very well & William less — up to my tent near the edge of Pelekunu. They were properly astonished when they found where I had been working & said they had never any of them been in that forest before & in fact it was obvious from the vegetation that no one had been so far! Although they had collected birds (as well as shells) since Scott Wilson stayed at Kalae, some years before I went out to the islands, he taught them to skins birds — they had never seen Palmeria, the Oo or Drepanis funerea until I took them to where I found them. Palmer did not get the Oo nor of course the Drepanis when he worked from Makakupaia, but I think he or rather Wolstenholme got Palmeria in about the same spot where I shot my first, rather lower down than any of the others recorded in my diary. Wolstenholme told me he shot the Palmeria, as he got them by calling & Palmer could not do this. He told me also that he killed all the few Hemignathus on Lanai, when he was alone, P. having gone down from the mountain. He killed all these either in one day or else in one bush, I forget which. P. gave me no localities as I have explained in the foreword to my diary, but I found afterwards that his Oo were all obtained further E. than mine, i.e., above Wailau. The bird was migratory & its extreme migration to the W. was even seen by me in Waikolu valley. At one time it was common in the tract called Kahanui, a fine piece of land. I got this from a native. An old woman in Pelekunu knew more about Molokai birds than any one I met on this island. She had feathers of Oo (tied in bunches using olana fibre) caught in bird-lime, with which some were stained or dirtied. There was also an old man there, a very bad leper, who knew both Palmeria & D. funerea. I was twice in Pelekunu, once over the Pali & back, when I stayed 3 or 4 days, & later by boat when I stayed over a couple of trips on the Mokolii, but the weather was impossible for collecting! I saw the Oo in the valley, though only far up & impossible to get in range of, but neither Palmeria nor Drepanis." *(R.C.L. Perkins letter to G.C. Munro, 18 May 1936, BPBM Archives, MS SC Munro Box 13.3).*

Some further details were given by Perkins in correspondence to Zimmerman in 1944:

" ... after failing to procure one in Honolulu {a tent} I got one ordered from San Francisco. This I took with me to Molokai where I began collecting in May 1893 at Makakupaia above Kuanakakai & later fixed my tent higher up, near the rather open [This spot was sometimes recorded on my labels as "boggy plateau" at almost 4000 ft.], small piece of flat swampy land, where some Loulu palms grew. From these places one could cross two or three large gulches to the parts above Kamalo in the Easterly direction or Westward to a tract called Kahanui." *(R.C.L. Perkins letter to E.C. Zimmerman, 14 February 1944, BPBM Entomology Archives).*

Although Perkins's account in his journals in this and the following chapter are primarily devoted to the birds and insects he encountered during the rain-soaked six months in the East Moloka'i mountains, he also spent a good deal of time collecting and observing snails. He had some experience with the *Achatinella* of O'ahu and was keen to note the apparent speciation that had also taken place in the Moloka'i relatives of this genus. I here reproduce the paragraphs that Perkins wrote in his *Fauna Hawaiiensis* introduction regarding shells since such detailed information is not supplied in his journals. It should be noted that the genus to which the Moloka'i species belong is not the *"Achatinella"* of Perkins (that genus is confined to O'ahu) but the related achatinellid genus *Partulina*.

"In 1893 I took the opportunity of paying a good deal of attention to the habits and distribution of some of the arboreal *Achatinella* of Molokai, the shells of that island at the time having been less collected than on Oahu. It was quite impossible not to be struck with the effect of isolation on individuals of some of those species. *Achatinella macrodon* ... was very common on a ridge close to my camp, but very local, for the next ridge to the west had none of it, nor did I see it on any ridge in that direction. After one had crossed one or two deep gulches eastward, an allied form appeared on the ridges, but with remarkable variations, tending to albinism. On the first-mentioned ridge it was comparatively constant, singularly for an *Achatinella*. Whether it had once occupied the area between these localities and subsequently died out, or whether by some such means as I have indicated above, it had passed over this area, cannot be known.

Another instance of discontinuity of distribution was examined into, over a large area, in the case of the common and widely-spread *Achatinella tesselata*. This species I found abundant over an extensive irregular plateau, where I had the occasion to collect often, at some distance N.W. of my camp. Here the shell was somewhat variable, of good size, and a striking albinoid form occurred. On this same area nine years later I found the shell much scarcer, but again the albino shells occurred. Away from this area and close to my camp on one ridge only, and only on parts of this ridge, *A. tesselata* was found in large numbers, but of smaller size than the others, and very uniform both in size and colour, excepting that here it was strictly dimorphic, with two closely similar but easily distinguished and constant varieties. I was not able to find any continuity of distribution between the two areas mentioned, in fact I am sure that such did not exist.

When we consider the sluggishness of these molluscs, it is certain that the individuals of a species on two such areas, though the distance between them in mileage is small, would, but for some chance, remain isolated for ages, if not for ever. How stationary some of these land-shells are, I had many chances of observing, for in some cases I had the same individual under observation for weeks together. A white variety of *Achatinella redfieldi*, which I had occasion to pass by almost daily for many weeks, was always seen at rest just below the fork of a large branch of a lichen-covered Ohia tree though there were many showery or wet days, it was never absent from this spot by day, though it may, of course, have moved at night and returned. This was a healthy animal, the shell not at all worn by age. A small dead lichen-covered tree, supporting individuals of *A. theodorei* in 1893, was still occupied by these or their descendants three years later, the adjoining bushes being unoccupied. These shells had the appearance of being a stunted, depauperated form of *A. proxima*, produced by isolation on a wind-swept ridge with its stunted vegetation. In 1902 I looked in vain for this particular colony." (Perkins, R.C.L., 1913, *Fauna Hawaiiensis* 1: lxvi–lxvii).

Perkins boarded the inter-island steamer *Mikahala* in Honolulu on Monday 8 May and headed for Kaunakakai, Moloka'i. After he arrived, he stayed a few days in Kaunakakai, arranging for supplies and food. After he was satisfied he had gathered together all he needed and made arrangements with the local postmaster to receive his mail, he packed his gear and headed up to Makakupa'ia.

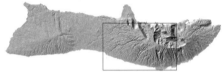

Map of Moloka'i with detail showing Perkins's collecting areas
in the highland central rainforest of East Moloka'i.

JOURNALS AND REMEMBRANCES

As mentioned in the first few sentences of the preface to these journals written by
Perkins some 40 years after he initially wrote them (see 1936 version bracketed
paragraphs below), Perkins never saw any of the typescripts of the original journal of this May-June trip to Moloka'i. He had sent them back to England in 1893,
and they were used by the Sandwich Islands Committee to help secure further
funding for additional surveying by Perkins. One of the original typescripts of
these journals was located in the Zoological Society of London and, through the
courtesy of its Archives, I reproduce here Perkins original journal entries from that
typescript. As Perkins noted, there are minor changes, mostly in grammar. In a few
cases, there is more detailed information found in the original; and in other cases,
more details are provided in the 1936 version. Those details that are added by
Perkins in his 1936 version are placed in square brackets [ ]. Any changes or additions by me are placed in curly brackets { }.

[This first portion of my Molokai notes on collecting is a copy from my diary as
it was written each day. This diary was scribbled in pencil and was very illegible.
An almost exact copy of it was sent to England at the end of June 1893, and I
believe typewritten copies were distributed, but I never saw any of them. About the

end of June 1893 I received a letter from Prof. Newton, the ornithologist, expressing dissatisfaction with the results I had obtained. He was bitterly disappointed that after months of search I failed to obtain specimens of the Oahuan Oo, its Hemignathus or its Heterorhynchus. I replied that until it was proved that these three birds were not extinct, and unless Rothschild's collectors, who were better equipped than myself found them, I could not be blamed, and that he could judge from my recent Molokai diary whether any one single-handed could do more than I was doing to get birds. Except for a few verbal alterations for the sake of clearness, a few grammatical changes or corrections in spelling, no change is made from the original diary except that Oreomyza flammea which the ornithologists had described as a Loxops is here designated flammea simply, though in the diary it was called 'Loxops' in deference to the ornithologists. Also for Chlorodrepanis, in the original diary I wrote green 'Himatione.' At that {time} the ornithologists' genus 'Himatione' included a mixture of that genus, Chlorodrepanis and Oreomyza, a very curious assembly! All the scientific names that are included in square brackets [ ] have been added by me for the sake of clearness as also are a few remarks enclosed in similar brackets. Also in the original diary Drepanis funerea, was referred to under various names 'black Drepanid,' 'black Hemignathine bird,' etc. Here I use the first name throughout for uniformity.

It can be seen from this diary that I very rarely ventured out without being hampered in my insect collecting with a gun and all the necessaries for bird-collecting, and that a huge proportion of my time was occupied by the latter. It also gives some idea of the nature of the ground over which I collected during this period and subsequently. The small wooden shack at Makakupaia had been built, I believe, from the remains of a rather large house, which had been burnt {the remains of this shack were gone when Perkins revisited Moloka'i in 1902}, and was on what might be called the lowest edge of more or less continuous forest. When I occupied it the door (which faced makai) was off, and kept inside the building which was full of mice. One night I used this as a trap, resting one end on a short peg with a string attached and scattering some rice beneath it. After a while, lying in the dark and holding the string I pulled away the support and found I had killed 18 mice in one go. Cattle[132] and deer were numerous at and above the house, but they did not enter what I called the Pritchardia bog, where were a couple of conspicuous fan-palms and generally one or more native ducks,[133] and the dense forest beyond this was quite untrodden except that there were signs of wild pigs on the bare ground beneath the densest brush, though I never actually saw one there. Achatinella was not found by me in this dense forest, except that just beyond the tract of bog above mentioned and a little way in this forest I found a single large example of A. (Partulina) proxima. On the other I hand Amastra (Laminella) depicta was abundant and generally distributed, with some other shells, up to the highest elevations. Some years later[134] I found deer had penetrated the highest forest, apparently by my old trail, and here and there they had resting places on the

---

132 Cattle — cattle were introduced to Hawai'i in 1794 by Captain George Vancouver as a gift to King Kamehameha. Kamehameha put a *kapu* on them (prohibiting anyone from harming them), Thus they roamed freely throughout the forests of the Hawaiian Islands feeding on the native understory and causing injury and often death to the trees by rubbing the bark, which was used for protection from desiccation.

133 Native ducks (*koloa*) (*Anas wyvilliana*).

134 Perkins was last in this forest in 1903, after he ceased to officially collect for the Sandwich Islands Committee.

very edge above Pelekunu. Also in places where I had proceeded for quite long distances on moss covered branches of trees without touching the ground, which lay 5–7 feet beneath the branches on which I walked, and consisted of bare, black mud, one could now walk on the ground. These were the most favorable places for shooting, as it was only necessary to mark the exact position of a bird when one shot, go straight to the spot and drop through the branches on to the knee-deep mud beneath, where the body could be seen at once on the bare ground. The dense wet forest was not very varied in its trees, nor did these attain any great height, the larger ones being Ohias and Olapas, but the most striking plants as they appeared to me were the Clermontia arborescens (from which the black Drepanis got its head smeared with pollen, while the abundant Ou was keen for its yellow berries) and the large Gunnera which grew in patches here and there, its huge leaves and erect flowering stem being very conspicuous.

During the period here dealt with, I used my tent very little while I was in the highest forest, but later much more frequently, sometimes sleeping there and often using it as a sheltering place when I was cold and soaked with rain. This diary (with its continuation) shows clearly how many of the native birds, especially the most highly specialized in habits change their localities with the seasons, a fact which later became very clear to me, and by choosing a suitable locality one could no doubt have obtained any of the rarest island birds that existed in my time, provided that one could have afforded to stay in that locality long enough. On the other hand by moving from place to place after short visits, it would have been easily possible to miss some of the rarer birds altogether, as in fact happened to all collectors in the islands.

It can be seen from my diary that already at this time, though not an ornithological specialist myself, I entirely disagreed with the classification of the Hawaiian birds as then set forth by ornithologists. I had heard from Prof. Newton before I collected it that a new Meliphagine bird called Palmeria had been described from Molokai. Hence my remarks under May 24th and June 25th. For the same reason I referred to 'Loxops' flammea, as being so called by ornithologists, though the first day I saw the bird alive (May 13th) I considered it to be an Oreomyza, since except for its red plumage it had no resemblance in structure to Loxops, nor yet in its voice nor habits. I already knew the habits and structure of these genera from having collected them together in 1892 in Kona, Hawaii. So too I had given up the idea that the Drepanididae were of different origin from the Hawaiian finches, although I had not then seen Pseudonestor of Maui.

I had met Rothschild's collector Palmer on Oahu before leaving for Molokai, but I had asked him no questions as to the localities of the birds he discovered and when we spent some time together in the mountains near Waialua where he joined me, he frankly told me that it would not be fair to his employer to give away the localities to another collector.]

Thursday May 11
[At Kaunakakai, Molokai]. In the morning, which was dull and close, I hunted on the sandy ground amongst the Kiawe trees near the beach. My captures were prac-

tically all Aculeate Hymenoptera. Specimens with one or two exceptions were scarce, but for sea-level Kaunakakai appears to be unusually rich. I got of Prosopis two species. One no doubt Blackburn's rugi-ventris of Maui and Lanai. The other species which is very distinct was in company with it. They frequented a small yellow flower growing in the sand [Noju[135]] [and Waltheria]. I also saw ♀s in the Kiawe blossoms, of Crabro I got sixteen specimens new to me with a yellow spot on the scutellum. I saw a specimen of a larger species. There were five or six specimens [species] of Odynerus. The most interesting being a very elongate faced species with extraordinarily long mandibles [Chelodynerus chelifer], and a ♂ of one of the coast species with a single yellow and white band. Two red spotted species occurred round some old native heiaus[136] a little above sea level. I saw a number of Clytus in the afternoon on recently felled Kiawe trees and got a Noctua on the trunk of a mango tree [Leucania amblycasis M.].

Friday May 12
Had things packed up to the Mountain house. Afterwards went out with gun for a short time. Shot two Himatione [Chlorodrepanis] and one Phaeornis. The latter very like the species on Hawaii in habits; frequently rising from its perch and singing in the air [on the wing]. It also shivers in the same manner as P. obscura.

Saturday May 13
Started very early in the morning with gun and went upwards. Saw plenty of Himatione [Chlorodrepanis], Phaeornis, and the [two] red birds [Himatione and Vestiaria]. A long way up I shot a fine ♂ Loxops [flammea] on a low dead branch. Its habits and voice are exactly as in Himatione [Oreomyza] (with straight bill).

Subsequently I shot one or two more both ♂ and ♀. It then came on very wet and foggy and after a vain attempt for several hours to find the way [trail] home, most of the time wading about in a bog waist deep, I endeavoured to reach the beach. While still some four or five miles above, darkness [night] came on and I lay up as best I could in sopping wet clothes for the night.

{*May 14th*}
At daybreak next morning still wet through, I started on and reached Kaunakakai [struck the coast miles east of that place] about 9.30 or 10 O'clock having been on the go, or vainly endeavouring to sleep nearly 30 hours, without food, fire or even tobacco. A pipe would have been a priceless blessing during the night.

I was excessively used up on my arrival, and worse than all, my birds were all in so decomposed a condition I was only able to skin 2♂ Loxops [flammea]. Could hardly swallow food, the roof of my mouth apparently all blistered.

P.S. Possibly from eating Nasturtium seeds the only edible things I could find, and a little warming! [I also drank salty water out of a pond at Kawela, which made me sick, and I did not properly recover for several days].

---

135   Noju — A misspelling for *nohu*.
136   *Heiau* — sacred Hawaiian ceremonial areas.

May 15
I did very little, having twinges of rheumatism and indigestion and the same condition of mouth on me, but I decided to walk up again to-morrow to the Mountain house. [Mouth still sore, but will walk up to Makakupaia to-morrow].

May 16
Was starting up towards house when I saw a small flight of Stilts on the beach.

I went after these and when about 40 yards off fired [fired at very long range]. To my utter surprise two dropped, as I never expected my old gun to touch them. I had less than one ounce of shot, but 3 1/2 drs. of powder, which may account for it.

These birds were in a filthy condition owing to their bleeding freely and falling in about an inch of water over black mud. I cleaned one well, the other I did but little to, [except to make a sound skin of it]. The skins should be quite sound, however, as I spent long time over them [as I had nothing with me], armed only with my big, hunting [sheath-]knife.

May 17
Went up to House with boy to carry pack on horseback. Still far from fit, having developed a very bad throat. Walk up fatigued me much. We had some food, after which he went home and I went upwards. Birds were hardly visible, but I got a number of Cyclothorax under and in fallen logs of Lehua [amongst dead Ohia trees], also a species of Fornax in the same situation [in a log of this]. Two species of Prosopis, one red and one black, [were] common. I only got the black one having no net with me. Two specimens of Gomphus [Sympetrum] [Nesogonia] apparently slightly different to the Oahu and Hawaii species.

May 18
Throat exceedingly painful could hardly swallow at all. Knee joints ache much and many attacks of cramp last night. Slept till late (probably 9 a.m.). Endeavoured to tidy up a bit: then went upwards. Got ♂ ♀ of little red bodied Prosopis and more of the black one. A number of land shells [Achatinella] on the Ohias in front of the house. These have a very old look about them, as if picked up empty [dead], but they were all alive.

May 19
Went a long way blazing a path up to the point reached on the day I lost myself [on the 13th]. Throat still very sore and the same touches of rheumatism. I got very little, only a couple of Carabidae. Shot ♂ ♀ Himatione [Chlorodrepanis], saw no Loxops [flammea] all day. It was a beautiful day, but the marshy upland [boggy part was] very bad to cross after the heavy rain of last night.

May 20
Woke to the sound of voices. Nailao and two boys came up after horses. Soon another man arrived. Gave them breakfast. Packed tent a little way up above the house into a Lehua grove [patch of Ohia trees]. Great difficulty in putting it up sin-

gle handed owing to high wind. If it stands to-night it will do, as it is so blowing a gale, as it has done every night I have been up here. It is placed handily for [getting] water: anything is better than the descent and ascent into the deep gulch that has to be made from this house [from the stream in the deep gulch for this purpose, when one arrives back tired at night]. I shot a ♀ or young ♂ Loxops [flammea] and also the [adult] ♂, but the latter flew [a little way] before falling and was lost. The only other things I got were a fine ♀ Prosopis (a large species) with blue wings and the little and very flat beetle (?Laemophloeus) found on Hawaii. Saw native duck and some interesting dragonflies [agrionines]. Throat somewhat better but knee joints very bad and much shivering [Mouth and throat better, but not well].

May 21
Blazed a track [trail] still deeper in [further on]. Saw several Loxops [flammea], but could only shoot 1 young ♀ [fearing that I could not gather the others]. There was very high wind very cold with rain. On a boggy ridge high up, lots of sweet[-scented] violets in bloom. Throat better, and altogether better to-day.

May 22
Packed up some food, rug &c. to the tent. Then went upwards, intending to get still further. Instead of this it poured with rain and after waiting in this for an hour or two, nearly cut in two by the high wind, I went back not having even heard a Loxops [flammea]. After getting warm in the tent went down in the gulch and collected some Cyclothorax, and some of the bronzy large species of Metromenus [Carabid] [Chalcomenus molokaiensis]. Also in tent 1 Anobiid, a pair of ? genus and near by two Brachypepli, Staphylinidae &c. Sat up nearly all night to try and get moths. Got but few specimens but one or two very nice things. One beautiful large Tortrix.

May 23
Another very wet day. Crossed gulch North of my tent and went up ridge a good way [for some distance]. Got some land-shells on the first part nearly opposite the tent. Poured with rain and was very cold. I got a second species of Tortrix — a fine thing again but smaller than yesterday's. Saw a single ♀ Loxops [flammea], which I shot and could not find. I afterwards saw 2 pairs, one pair of which I shot, badly mutilating (especially the skull) [of] the ♂. The next pair I could not shoot at, the ridge being so narrow and the sides precipices [so steep, they would probably have been lost, if killed]. I later saw a single young ♂, very prettily marked [with red], but again was unable to shoot. I shot a ♂ and ♀ Himatione [Chlorodrepanis] neither [of them] in very good plumage.

May 24
Went up gulch just below tent till I could get no further, then on to [same] ridge where I was yesterday. Followed this ridge away up over very bad boggy ground[137] till I came out in the boggy openings where the violets grew [full of violets in bloom]. On the way I picked up a couple of the bronzy Carabid and a few small striped [(Kaliko)] shells. I saw several L. sanguinea [flammea] both in the gulch

---

137 Probably Pēpē'ōpae bog, the only known open area in this vicinity (D. Polhemus, pers. comm).

and on the ridge beyond, but had only one shot, which was a bad miss. From the opening followed my old blazed trail through the wet [thick] forest. Following up a specimen of Loxops [flammea] as I was on the point of firing [and just as I was going to shoot] I saw a black looking bird in a very thick [dense] bush about 8 or 10 yards off. Saw its crest and luckily thought to put the larger charge at it [remembered to use the larger charge]. The small half [one in the right barrel] would never have penetrated the [thick] leaves. I soon handled my first Palmeria – a grand bird [a fine bird]. This specimen was a ♂. ?Why placed in the Meliphagidae. The tongue appears to me to be quite of the type found in Hemignathus &c. I went right to the end of Palmer's old trail but saw nothing [no sign] of Acrulocercus, which I fear has [if Rothschild's collectors got it here may have] moved elsewhere, now the Lehuas have no blossom here [Ohias are not in flower]. I could hardly have failed to hear its cry, which is like that of the Hawaii species [nobilis on Hawaii] — its 'booming note' as Wolstenholme called it [when I saw him on Oahu].

May 25
The birds kept me busy all the morning, three requiring a lot of cleaning. Then I had to fix my gun which had gone wrong [been damaged] and took up most of my afternoon. Towards evening I went down in the deep gulch by the house to try for Phaeornis and I managed to get a shot. This bird is somewhat shy here [in the lower forest]. It generally prefers to a [bare] dead tree to sing from, but when approached darts down into the thick scrub and is seen no more.

May 26
Started early, the morning nice and clear, but with [a very] strong wind still blowing. By the time I got well up, however, everything changed, a nasty wetting rain fell continuously. I apparently reached the end of the ridge[138] I have been following, at any rate I could see no way of getting on. There seemed to be a very deep gulch right ahead – I say seemed, as there was so dense a mist, [but the fog was so dense] I could make nothing out with certainty [only see forward a yard or two]. I shot three Loxops [flammea], all ♀. Unfortunately killed and lost about 2 ♂ adults. Got home very wet and cold about 4 or 5 o'clock. Land shells on lilies [Astelia].

May 27
Cloudy up above but tolerably light, though windy round the house. Took a beating tray and worked some little way beyond [a little higher up than] my tent. Got a few Brachypeplus, Proterhinus and Xyletobius by beating, also Eopenthes. Under bark of fallen [dead] tree a fine large Staphylinid [Leurocorynus] also Metromeni, Cyclothorax and large Oodemas. Many remains of Parandra noticed, but none living. Got a few Lepidoptera; great scarcity of Homoptera [Hemiptera] apparently but parasitic Hymenoptera mostly Chalcididae more numerous then I have seen elsewhere. I got a few shells.

May 28
Very wet morning. Went out about eleven a.m. as far as to the tent. Gathered about 30 shells. Saw no birds of note and came back very wet about 2 O'clock. After this

---

[138] The rim of Pelekunu Valley but Perkins did not realize it at the time he wrote this entry.

it brightened up and about four I went down into the [deep] gulch, [makai] with net. Got only an Odynerus, a couple of Crabros, two small bronzy Cyclothorax? [Bembidiids],[139] and two species of ants. Stream risen a couple of feet. Looks good for the boggy woods above to-morrow.

May 29

A nasty morning, with fine rain falling thickly. Higher up the mountains covered with [a dense] fog. Made an early start: got up about a mile and a half when the rain came down much more heavily and I was soon drenched. Tried a little turning over of [some] fallen trees to try and get warm. No success as far as warming was concerned, but got a fine carabid — a Blackburnia [Deropristus] — with a couple of Metromeni and Cyclothorax in fungus on a log I think — under the larger trunks. Seemingly — very rare — I found only two or three [of the Blackburnia] in a long time. Stayed a short time in tent, dried my gun as best I could, hardened my heart and went on up [again]. The bog above the tent, [where the Pritchardia are], simply beastly [was in a horrible state], the woods beyond even worse. I reached the furthest point I had previously arrived at, but again could not see ten yards beyond for the dense white fog. It seemed that each time I was on the edge of a deep gulch [pali] and could go no further [ahead]. Birds were hardly to be heard at all. I saw nothing of the least note [but the commonest kinds] except Loxops [flammea]. I pickled a ♂ adult and a ♀ (or young ♂) on my arrival home. [There were s]plendid lunar rain-bows at night.

May 30

Heavy rain last night and still raining hard this morning. Mountains above here all [hidden] in dense fog. About 9. a.m. looked little brighter. Started out with a net to catch Leps. [moths]. Got about a mile above house, then another downpour, saturating my net, self and everything else [the vegetation]. Tried log-turning for the Blackburnia [Deropristus] where I got it before. Got a couple after a lot of work. Also one Metromenus. I did not take Cyclothorax to-day. Got one Eopenthes sheltering under lichen and a few shells, mostly ground species under logs [beneath dead trees]. Returned about 1 p.m. starved with cold. About 3 p.m. it got brighter and the rain cleared off. Went down gulch to the South-east of house [east of Makakupaia] to hunt Leps. [Lepidoptera]. Got quite a number of nice micros[140] — tineids. Also a few Pyralidae. Found a large Eupethicia quite new to me on a tree trunk [collected Geometers on tree trunks] [Eucymatoge]. Also a few Larentia? species? These seemed considerably darker than ones I have seen a bit higher up in the Lehua trees. Got home just at dusk. Latter part of day highly successful. I shall have to bring the tent back towards the house [nearer to Makakupaia] as there is better moth hunting ground there. The present situation is too exposed while these trade winds rage [are so extremely strong] every night. There is fine ground higher up, but at present it is almost under water.

May 31

Pouring wet day. Saw no birds of note. Shot ♀ and two young ♂ Himatione [Chlorodrepanis], the parent feeding the young, also adult ♂ for B.M.

---

139   Bembidiids — ground beetles (Carabidae) species of the genus *Bembidion*.
140   Micros — shortened form of microlepidoptera.

[It was not till after I had been collecting for a year that a tardy request was made by the British Museum that I should get a set of birds for them and then I had already finished collecting in certain districts without taking specimens of birds they needed! The idea when I went out to the islands was that I should supplement Scott Wilson's collection of birds as far as possible by getting additional examples of such species as he collected insufficiently, and of course those which he did not get at all. Wilson's collection was in the Museum of Cambridge University].

Got a beautiful new Tineid. All the high land almost under water. Wrote to D^r. Sharp. I [must] go down to Kaunakakai [to send letters] to-morrow. Found two specimens of what looks like an Orchid on Lehua roots.

June 1

Wrote to Prof^r Newton and posted in same envelope as Dr Sharp's. Also wrote to town [Honolulu] for fresh supplies. I took it pretty easy going down and collected a good many Aculeates — the only things I saw worth collecting. The California linnet {= house finch} is very abundant on the lower part [slopes] of the mountain [here]. NOTE the long hairy palpi and having mandibles of one of the Odyneri.

June 2

The steamer did not arrive until about 4 p.m., so I stayed over night. It was annoying to see [that from here] it looked clear even higher up in the mountains. I only got an Odynerus or two.

June 3

In the afternoon went for a walk with McCartney saw many Stilts. [Introduced to McCartney the school-teacher and in the afternoon went out with him. Saw many stilts]. I picked up one just hatched. Old birds very excited flying round us and dashing down within a yard of our heads. I put it [the young one] down on a bare place to see if the old ones would take it. Hadn't gone ten yards when we looked round and it had vanished. Must really have been able to run well, though it made no effort to escape before. Old birds were very funny trying to lure us away from spot. Would pitch [on the ground] about 15 yards off and squat down on the ground. At other times would stand with the wings somewhat raised horizontally and shake them like a young bird being fed, the neck drawn in and the whole bird puffed out. Could not find the young one again after a long search. It was in the [shallow] water with its beak [buried] in the mud when I found it and [appeared] half choking. It probably ran there as we approached. I got a few Odyneri in the morning [(while waiting till school hours were over)]. A large earwig under stone by the pond on the beach [near the sea].

June 4

Started up as it looked fine above though I have to come down [again] Monday night or Tuesday morning when the steamer arrives, to pack up [my] stores. Collected Odyneri on the lower slopes, where it was very hot. Got up about 11 a.m. and started down gulch on left [W.] of house [Makakupaia] with net. Got some very nice Odyneri, two or three red spotted species. Specimens of Aculeates are very scarce except one or two very common ones, but species very well represented [the latter fairly numerous]. They cease to fly much after 3 p.m. when I came in and had a feed. Then went out beating in gulches right of the house [E.] till dark. Got some few beetles (three specimens of Oodemas and a couple of a new Xyletobius). Also a very elongate land shell new to me [Newcombia cinnamomea]. Got some very nice spiders. One green, elongate, and very curious with body much bent upwards and so humped beneath. Evidently the spiders are represented by a few main types on all the islands.

June 5

Nasty fine, wetting [thick] rain, but fortunately except at now and then, calm. I had intended to shoot, but as it was evidently pouring [raining heavily] and foggy up above I [gave up the idea] and went out to beat in spite of the rain. I again got some spiders and a few shells. Coleoptera. A large Cossonid? [Also a Rhyncogonus] (from mixed [mass of] stems of stag's horn fern and maile). The same thing superficially as a single specimen. I got in Freycinetia leaves on Oahu (Halemano) {Helemano} with somewhat of a Blaps-like look. Proterhinus two species. One minute red-headed (already faded) Oligota very minute. Two Xyletobii like yesterday's and two specimens of another species. I got some very nice micro[lepidoptera]. (N.B. bred a very fine thing from cases under bark of decayed fallen tree). It was beautifully bright at 2 p.m. round the house, so I took net and went after Aculeates, got the same things as yesterday. The ♀ of Mimesa is most extraordinary with a huge dependent cheek spine like our Andrena spinigera &c but very large. I wonder whether the Oahu and Hawaii species have this and if the specimens are the same on each island? Unfortunately I did not examine the others, though I believe I came to the conclusion that the Hawaii and Oahu species were different (from memory, for I had no chance to compare them [specimens with one another]).

I got a new (single specimen) of Cyclothorax (slightly bronzy) by sifting dead leaves at the base of what is at times a waterfall — at present only very wet not running. It is blowing a gale to-night with rain. I go down again to-morrow. I have no food left and have had no light up here [at night] since my return [I last came up].

June 6

Got down to Kaunakakai about mid-day. Steamer had not put ashore all the freight, but I got provisions [food] and lamp, but no oil. I saw very few insects on the way down.

June 7

Started up early with Pali and pack. Got to the house [Makakupaia] probably about 10 a.m. as we came very quickly. Raining fast up here. Cooked some food [rice] after which Pali returned. I went out for [land] shells — the only thing possible to do in such a wind and rain. Got but little. The strong wind made searching very difficult.

In the afternoon it cleared, but the wind continued and was even stronger than before.

June 8

Wet windy morning. Started out with gun upwards about 1 – 1 1/2 miles, then worked towards East across a deep gulch. I hoped by this means to get on the top without having to wade through so much bog. Proved much the same as my old track [trail] in this respect. Forest very nice, but birds remarkably scarce or [at least] silent, though by mid-day [at noon] it was bright and sunny [sunny and clear]. Blazed a trail cutting down ferns, [I judged to] getting about 6 miles[141] from house [Makakupaia]. Picked a few nice land shells before crossing the [big] gulch [and higher up I] heard a few Loxops [flammea] in the distance but did not leave my trail to go after them.

From the point reached ought easily to be able to get to the top in one more go. Got two small Brachypepli in the higher forest and five or six specimens of Carabidae (two or three new to me). One is in general appearance like the bronzy species of the gulches, but black and more plainly punctured. The others (Metromeni?) one has a strongly transverse thorax and is also certainly new to me.

All these were found under the dense coat of wet moss that clothes every tree in these wet forests.

June 9

Stormy below and evidently very wet in the highest forest. Consequently I made no attempt to continue the trail begun yesterday. Went up with net, beating tray, etc., to pack down tent nearer to house so that I could try the effects of light in a sheltered gulch, and afterwards returned to the house the same night. Twenty-four hours of rain up here warps wooden boxes all out of shape, utterly destroys card boxes, while you can wring the water out of tobacco[142] after a day or two.

[Before moving tent] I worked mainly around the tent, getting some nice Micros, especially a Tortrix new to me here (and probably altogether) but not a good specimen; also the long antennaed Lehua Tinaeid, with transverse pale blue fasciae and eye like apical spot, very like or identical with my Oahuan species. When getting warm inside the tent I was looking for any chance Diptera or spiders sheltering therein, when behold on the side a Clytarlus! A red species with thin legs, one of the smaller kinds [Plagithmysus aestivus]. Whether I had carried it in after beating or it had crept out of the Lehua poles of the tent, I do not know. I beat and searched every possible tree around but go no other. It was minus one leg. I got several more specimens of the Eopenthes, one with the base of the elytra pale and possibly a distinct species, a couple of Anobiids (Xyletobius), Oodemas, a few Metromenus (or allied genus) under bark, with a few Proterhinus and Brachypeplus. I got quite a number of bugs [Hemiptera], three species of Ophion, and a testaceous apterous ant-like parasitic Hymenoptera [Sclerodermus].

Returned with tent about 4, house about 4:30. After feeding, hurried back to tent to try and get it fixed up. Managed this without poles temporarily. Then back to

---

[141]   The mileage estimates in the entry for this date are most likely double the actual distances. Six miles east of Makakupaia would put Perkins too far east from where he claims to have been. His distance estimates made on Molokaʻi may have been made by judging time (and travel on Molokaʻi would have been slower and rougher than his previous fieldwork on Oʻahu and the Kona area of the Big Island).

[142] Referring to the pipe tobacco Perkins carried with him at all times.

house and got back to tent with lamp by dark. Stayed a long time, but got very little, a good sized Pyralid? and a couple of Pterophori the best. Found it very difficult to get back out of gulch and down the ridge home. It blew a gale as usual, luckily the lamp kept alight. [Got back with difficulty to Makakupaia, in the dark after midnight].

June 10
Up at daybreak and got an early start for the highest woods, though I could see what would be my fate. As soon as I reached the boggy ground it began to pour with rain and the state of this part of the woods above is even worse than ever. Again I reached the end of the ridge and again could make out nothing beyond the dense fog. I hunted around for Loxops [flammea] and got several shots (I saw two lovely [beautiful] males to-day) but was so cold I positively could not hold the gun steady and missed each time. I tried tearing off the wet moss and got a couple of Metromeni, and a single specimen of Heteramphus. Then I had to give this up as an even colder job than loitering round for birds. I picked up a Brachypeplus (one of the species with uneven depressed surface) [new to me] and a small almost black beast new to me and a single Proterhinus. Also from a leaf a Cyclothorax, quite new to me, with the elytral striae all irregular and broken up [Thriscothorax perkinsi].

Just on leaving their haunts I got a female Loxops [flammea] and a young male, the latter still being fed by the parent. I also shot a female Phaeornis [P. lanaiensis]. To-night it rains hard and blows as hard as it can.

June 11
Did not get out till 10 or 11 o'clock. Then went upwards intending to collect dragonflies in a gulch about a mile and a half above the house. A heavy rain came on before I had gone half a mile and continued all the time. I only got four ♂ dragonflies [in consequence], each a different species. Being hopelessly wet, I thought I might as well walk up the bed of the stream and hunt up a series of the large bronzy Carabids [Chalcomenus]. This, like the similar beast on Oahu, appears to be about the only carabid that is a true day walker – (except very minute bronzy species [bembidiids] here). I always find it in gulches or channels down which water (at any rate at times) flows. I got a nice little series. Some are nearly black (or quite) and, I take it, are ♀♀, as I got two pair in cop: the ♀ in one apparently quite, in the other nearly black, and hardly showing any bronze tint.

The species has the same foul scent as ordinary Metromeni. It runs on rocks especially when mossy and full of holes. Turning over stones in this gulch I got a few Metromeni and Cyclothorax, also a single minute Staph: like a pair (or ? more) sent from gulches of Kaala, on Oahu, and taken under precisely similar circumstances [Myllaena sp.]. I also picked up a couple of the short active (jumping) Hemipteron [Salda] in such situations. Under bark I got the large Oodemas, which, as usual, are inclined to run on being exposed, and a couple of the large black bigheaded Staph: previously noted.

Also a small elongate species [Lispinodes] with shining elytra, which I spotted amongst a host of Glyptoma, the latter being much commoner here than on Oahu or Hawaii; at least to me. I had my gun with me as I saw a fine ♂ <u>Loxops</u> [<u>flammea</u>] on Friday and once before, but to-day he naturally failed to show himself. It was raining fast even down at the house [Makakupaia] tonight. I hear the pleasing drip, drip from the roof into my 'billies' which means I shan't have to go down for water into the deep gulch before breakfast.

The stream was high and discolored. I saw a pair of native ducks.

June 12
Fine round the house, but raining fast a mile or two above [tent]. I concluded to go <u>below</u> the house for insects. Went down in deep gulch [at Makakupaia] on left, and worked downwards. Stream very high and discolored from last night's rain. I got by beating three or four species of Anobiids, one at any rate new to me. Only two <u>Brachypeplus</u> but several species of <u>Proterhinus</u>, two specimens above the usual size [larger than usual]. A single small <u>Acalles</u>, probably different to the species obtained before. A somewhat Anobiid shaped species (genus?) with yellowish and black-marked elytra [<u>Labrocerus</u>]. Also <u>Cis.</u> Two minute Homalotae [<u>Oligota</u>]. A few parasitic Hymenoptera (chiefly the black apterous species) [black <u>Sclero-dermus</u>] and a new species of the mantis-like bug [an Emesiid bug]. I further got a number of <u>Odynerus</u>, a single ♂ of the new [large] blue winged <u>Prosopis.</u> <u>Mimesa</u> ♂ and ♀ and <u>Crabro</u> as before. Two or three dragonflies [Agrions], some Hemerobiids (beaten) and some Micro Lepidoptera. The best of these a very minute species (perhaps of the same genus as the eyed Lehua [Ohia] species mentioned on the 9th) [<u>Philodoria</u> <u>splendida</u>]. This species has three silver spots on the fore wings and some markings at the apex [<u>Gracilaria</u> <u>epibathra</u>].

June 13
Got off about 8 o'clock [a.m.] in fine weather and made for the highest forest. Did no collecting on the way as I wanted to take advantage of the fine {weather further up}. To my disgust after crossing the [<u>Pritchardia</u>] bog, the rain began though the sun still shone, but above everything [was] wrapped in fog. Soon after entering the thick [densest] forest I saw a <u>Loxops</u> [<u>flammea</u>] (♀ or young ♂). Got a fair shot, but instead of dropping straight the wretched creature came down at an angle and was hopelessly lost in the thick bush. Soon after I saw a pair ♂ and ♀. The former was very scared [timid] and at last disappeared altogether. Got a shot at the ♀ which dropped straight and in no very thick brush yet I could not find it. I was now disgusted with the birds, and took a spell at tearing off the dense wet moss from the tree trunks for beetles [beetle collecting]. Kept at this for some hours and got a number of species of Carabidae, some clearly new to me. The most noteworthy three specimens of <u>Cyclothorax</u>, each a distinct species, one very small brownish, a second larger with the elytra very clearly pale-bordered: the third the largest of all, black with a bronzy tint and an obscure depression towards the base of either elytron.

Then there were a pair of large sized stout black species (? whether the same species) with particularly strong heads. While the rest were [taken with a number of] <u>Metromenus</u>-like creatures, big and small, some of the larger [slender and] with long antennae. All these were under moss except three or four specimens of the largest size on the blossom of a lily [frequenting the flowers of Astelia]. I also got a fine species of Heteropteron [Hemiptera] under the moss of a type I have found on Hawaii and Oahu [this must have been a Metrarga, but was not recorded by Kirkaldy in Fauna Hawaiiensis]. I had now reached the limit [end] of my previous journeys and had just been getting a small Brachypeplus from obscure [small] green flowers of a tree unknown to me [bushy tree] and from the leaves of other trees and climbed an Ohia to get at a lily blossom [Astelia flowers] on which were three specimens of a large Brachypeplus [Gonioryctus], when the mist [fog] suddenly cleared off as if by magic and the sun shone out brightly. As I had guessed must be the case I was on the edge of the cliff [pali] at the head of one of the two landlocked [deep windward] valleys, either Pelekunu or Wailau [Waikolu] [of course it was the former]. The cliffs bounding the valley are stupendous [very deep and steep], the scenery far surpassing anything I have ever come across before, the steep sides covered with dark Ohias and far below there are masses of silvery[-leafed] kukui trees, the opening [mouth] of the valley also visible and showing a stretch of the sea beyond. I fancy by working round to the East it would be possible to climb down a ridge into this valley; and I have resolved to carry my tent to a spot I have selected in this direction [near here], as soon as there is an appearance of [another] fine day. I managed to practically take in the whole geography of the Island on this occasion. I now began to hunt around for birds again, and again came across Loxops [flammea] — a small company together. I got four shots at these, and secured ♂ and 2 ♀ in fine condition. By this time I had to think about getting home — a distance of some six or seven miles, and not too soon as the sun was nearly going down on my arrival [arrived back just at sunset]. When nearly at the spot where my tent used to be, I came across a fine ♂ Loxops [flammea] very wild, no doubt the specimen I had seen on former occasions (vide note Sunday 11th).

I bagged him after quite a long chase. Besides the beetles mentioned, in the highest forest I got a beautiful little Hypaenid or Pyralid, black and grey (with [iridescent or] many colored reflections in different lights) [Promylaea pyropa], and a pretty and quite new Hemerobiid [Nesomicromus molokaiensis]. I got the pupa [took a nymph][143] and bred a lily-frequenting dragon fly [Astelia-frequenting Agrion]. It hatched [The adult emerged] on the way [back] and was consequently a good deal crumpled and distorted in developing, [the box being too small]. It is marked 13.6.93.

Reached home [Makakupaia] quite tired, but much better after supper and started up to tent with lantern. Very dark night and some rain. I got quite a number of Micros but nothing very special. The best things I got were a pretty reddish Hypaenid [Pyralid reddish] with white V mark [on forewing] [Phlyctaenia ommatias] a Tineid with white head and a couple of white spots on each fore wing [Hyposmocoma niveiceps] and another (? also on Oahu) with a dense tuft of hairs under each fore wing on basal half. Curiously enough also one of the large feathery Antennaed dark moths like one sent from Hawaii with a dense felt of hairs under basal half of front wings. ?Is the occurrence and position of these pads

---

[143] A naiad of the various *Astelia*-breeding species of *Megalagrion* damselflies.

unusual? If not, it is curious that two moths, so unlike, should have them similarly placed. (Cf. smell of Drepanididae and Fringillidae the humpbacked spiders and wasps). Got back [to Makakupaia] probably after mid-night.

June 14
Late this morning: must have been after 9 o'clock when I finished breakfast. Then I skinned birds and fixed up yesterday's captures. Fine below, but foggy and rainy higher up. Went down in deep gulch by the house with a net. Saw a number of the Vanessa [P. tammeamea numerous] on the tree trunks, but could only catch one. Also saw the little green hairstreak [Lycaenid],[144] but very worn. Got one or two Pyralids, one glorious big silvery green thing with narrow brown costal margin of fore wings. (Mem. Had seen this here before looking white on the wing, but couldn't catch it. It is a very wild flyer when disturbed by day. There is the same thing, or something like it on Oahu which I saw I several times flying but couldn't catch). Got a couple of dragon flies [Agrions] and a number of Aculeates, one small Crabro all black, new to me. Only got one ♂ of it. Most of the Odyneri rare here [at this season]. One or two are common. Got ♂ and ♀ female Mimesa.

Wrote colour descriptions of several dragon-flies which I put up in papers.[145]

June 15
Dull morning with fine rain: raining heavily above. Still in hope of its clearing up, I started about half past seven to pack up tent to the place I had fixed upon [in the highest forest]. I expected this to be a two day's job [to do this in two goes], but despite the fact that I had a considerable addition of water to carry from last night's rain [though the load was heavy from the tent being soaked by last night's rain] I made the whole distance without even a rest. The upper forest was terribly wet, quite under water, and I was soon soaked in going through in trailing through the [dense] bushes, crawling under trees, etc. [and occasionally crawling on the mud, under fallen trees along my trail]. However, it was fine enough and towards midday became quite bright and warm. I got the tent fixed up without difficulty finding good poles handy, but the ground was very wet [saturated with water]. I dug a trench round the tent to the depth of a foot or so [in the mud] which at once filled with water. This should carry off the water of any ordinary storm, and the ground inside [the tent] may dry up a bit now, being on a slope.

[For collecting] I took nothing but a killing bottle[146] with me and started to cut a trail still higher up, the forest here very thick as cattle had not penetrated it. After about a couple of hours had to leave off and return home, when nearly on the edge of a valley again. I collected a few things not far from the house, a couple of small dragon-flies and a few moths.

---

[144] This most likely refers to the only native lycaenid in Hawai'i, *Udara blackburni*, which is characterized by the striking green undersides of its wings.

[145] Referring to the field-method of placing dragonflies into papers and folding the paper closed over each specimen, thus keeping them safe until properly pinned in the laboratory.

[146] A killing bottle for insects in the 19th and early 20th centuries usually consisted of a wide-mouthed glass bottle or jar with a cloth top secured by string or elastic or a screw-top lid and contained a poisonous gas (usually ammonia or cyanide) to kill the insect after it was placed in the bottle.

In the highest forest I got some Carabidae all under moss, two or three Cyclothorax? with the broken striae on elytra [as on the 10th]: one of the large-headed black creatures genus? [Disenochus] and Metromeni [some Metromenus]. Under bark of a tree [olapa] I got a large Brachypeplus with two anterior small, and two posterior large depressions on thorax: elytra not depressed: thorax [prono-tum] very long, much narrowed anteriorly [Goniothorax conicicollis]. Several specimens, two being in cop. A brown beetle [Scolytid] was burrowing in the wood of this tree (? genus) and I got a minute Ichneumon with these and a couple of small Staphs. with depression on thorax and elytra. A single large Brachypeplus came and pitched on my tent, and I got a couple of another small species with uneven surface from a leaf.

June 16
Went down to Kaunakakai to catch mail. Sent letter to Dr Sharp. Received letters from both Professor Newton and Dr Sharp. Two from the former, all registered. The dates were 29th {March}, 15th, and 22nd April, and I had letters from home of about that time or even earlier. The stupid post office people had sent them out into the country [my last address] on Oahu: and this in spite of the fact that I had twice seen them [Honolulu G.P.O.] personally and twice written to tell them to send all on here until further orders.

It was fine when I started down, but on the latter part of the journey it deluged with rain even at Kaunakakai, an almost unheard of event in the summer.

June 17
Started up about 10 a.m. with small but heavy pack tinned meat, [shot for reload-ing cartridges], oil [for lamp] etc. Got up [to Makakupaia] about one o'clock. Started straight down into gulch on South East side of house [towards E.] after Pyralids with net. Not very successful: got one of the large silvery green species [Margaronia exaula] [as on the 14th], a pretty Eudorea [Scoparia] and specimens of one of the Pyralid-Crambid looking [Crambus-like] creatures [Talis]. The best catch three Tortrices each a different species. Two are very large and fine [insects], but one which is green is worn. It may be identical with a smaller species previ-ously taken. The other is a splendid thing.

I also got a single specimen of the uncleft-winged Pterophorid [Pterophorus-like species], very like or identical with the one on Hawaii. Note that it does not rest like a Pterophorid T-shaped, but with wings only at about 45° [with the body] /|\ in fact like a Pyralid, but its [narrow folded] wings are not broad enough to form a [complete] triangle (i.e. do not touch the abdomen) [Lineodes subextincta]. I also got a few Aculeates, a fine black Ichneumon, a large Ophion (??), one or two Cyclothorax (got before), and a couple of specimens of Staphs, one larger and one smaller, by sifting dead leaves under what are at times waterfalls. Also a couple of dragon-flies [Agrions].

Returned home about 4:30 to feed and took out gun as I had seen a very young Phaeornis being fed by the parents. Could not find them, however. Returned at dark went down in gulch for moths with lantern—absolutely nothing came, though this is the first calm night I have seen. I returned [gave up] after about one and one-half hours.

June 18

Fine calm hot morning, with the tops of the mountains clear [entirely free from mist]. Started about 8 a.m. with gun for highest forest carrying rice and tinned meat to leave in the tent. First part of ascent nice and dry, but the [highest] forest as wet or wetter than ever from the heavy rain of the 16th.

Made quick time: at the top of the first peak overlooking [up to Pelekunu] heard a strange sound: a sort of gurgling row from the top of a rather tall Ohia. Looked up I saw a fine ♂ Palmeria, the red feathers glistening in the sun. He showed evident signs of flying [alarm], so I shot quickly: a rather long, but very open shot. Instead of falling straight he came down at an angle of about 45° and was as I at once knew hopelessly lost. I spent about one hour looking for him. The ♀ was with him and I might easily have shot her but could never have picked her up in the dense brush [where she would have dropped]. Felt very sick about this after so many journeys. With a [good] dog I could have obtained both these birds easily. Went on up from the tent without stopping, improving the trail I had opened and continuing it. After a time I again heard the most peculiar indescribable gurgling noise followed immediately by an evident alarm whistle. I stood still and whistled back. The bird, a fine ♂, approached to within ten yards when I shot [with a very small charge]. It dropped [quite] straight, but again I was disappointed in finding it, owing to the dense growth of brush, [mixed up with masses of] dead leaves, and the ground full of holes. Again too I refrained from shooting at the ♀, knowing without a dog I should never gather it. There is no doubt that a [bird collector] should bring out couple of good dogs (one in case of accident) at any cost. At least 25 per cent of the birds I see I cannot shoot at [((for fear of not being able to gather them)] and the same percentage I lose, although I never shoot at any bird, rare or common, unless I think I have a really good chance of picking it up. Here every bird that does not fall absolutely straight must be lost. It was now about 3 p.m. and I was feeling pretty miserable, for although hot enough I had been wading all day in knee deep mud and working hard all the time with an axe clearing a path [for some hours], when I suddenly heard a very different sound, a note as clear as a bell, with just the least resemblance to that of the Oo. I was sure I had come across Palmer's new bird [[a short while before I visited the islands Rothschild's collector had discovered a new species of Acrulocercus on Molokai]] and practically certain of this when I saw fly onward a good sized black bird. It pitched [settled] about 25 yards ahead, but I could not see it for the density of the brush. Every four or five seconds it uttered its remarkable call. I forced through about ten yards, and then I saw the bird clearly perched across a bough straight in front of me and obviously very uneasy. I fired instantly and the bird dropped straight in thick brush, but I marked a low twig it shook in its fall and gathered it at once. To my surprise as I picked it up I saw no sign of yellow ear feathers or any yellow ones at all, but before I had time to fully realise this I heard just ahead the same [clear] cry. Throwing down my axe and hat, and the bird into the latter, I pushed on and saw another similar bird, no doubt the mate of the one just shot. It was restless, and I got a view [only] of its head and a part of its body. However it dropped as straight as the first one and in a clearer place, so I easily found it. Then I saw at once that I had no Oo but a Hemignathus-like creature with shorter lower mandible and excessively strong smell characteristic of the Drepanidae and of the Hawaiian finches. All the feathers on the top of the skull of each one were covered with a white sticky substance, apparently pollen of some flower, and they are, no doubt, honey-sucking birds. The cry is not of the loud character of the Oo but is startlingly clear and could be heard at a considerable distance for this reason. I kept on some little way but saw no other bird of note, just managing to reach the house by dark, probably a little after 7 p.m. Very tired. I got a few Carabidae under moss in the highest forest and some more of the large Brachypeplus [Goniothorax] under bark of the same tree as on the 15th. I shot several Loxops [flammea].

June 19
Later than usual this morning. Nasty day with return of the strong trades and accompanying rain. [Heavy] rain and foggy above and drizzled round the house at times [at Makakupaia] and cold.

Skinned birds in the morning, pickling the carcasses of the new ones. Did not go out except [down] into the deep gulch for water. Repaired gun in the afternoon [again, as it has been very much knocked about in the rough work here], and then was busy with the insects until the time of writing this. (late at night). There is at present a raging wind and I fear for the weather to-morrow.

June 20
A dull, heavy morning even at this house with fine rain. Hoping it would improve, I started at about 8 a.m. with rather heavy pack, containing changes of clothes, rug [a blanket, a cooking tin etc.] etc. intending to stay in tent for a night or two. I had a terrible journey through soaking rain and the [deep] mud awful. At times I had to put down my gun and clutch hold of a tree in order to pull my legs out of this. I had wrapped the pack in the remains of what was once a water proof: it proved so no longer for when I got to the tent, I found the contents of pack all more or less wet — mostly more. Tent half down, the pegs not holding in the boggy ground, although driven in [to a depth of] two or three feet, ground inside a pool in spite of my trench [around]. Re-pegged all around [the tent] and dug a new trench some two feet deep [in the soft mud], then gathered ferns [to lie on], but to stay [on today] was out of the question as the chance of a fire (and therefore anything to eat) [being able to cook my rice] being highly problematical in such a [heavy] downpour. I waited [stayed sheltering in the tent] till about 4 o'clock and there being no signs of clearing, repacked rug etc., and returned home [to Makakupaia] arriving a little before [at] dark. It had rained considerably at the house, my [other] tin, [left here] which was empty, was now full of water.

I did next to nothing in collecting a couple of Carabidae (one a bronzy Cyclo-thorax) and a black ['pug' moth] Eupethecia [Eucymatoge] (not a good specimen), quite new to me, being all. A day of misery from cold and wet.

June 21
Up at day-light, and started with gun at about 6:30. A bright here at starting, but cloudy high up, though with promise of fine—not however fulfilled. I made as great

haste as the state of the ground would allow and reached the tent without rain. Then I went still up with the intention of pushing on beyond the furthest I had reached. It soon began to rain, and continued off and on, at times looking like clearing up, but not doing so. As I was already soaked from the dripping brush, as far as comfort was concerned, it made little difference. After some time I heard a whistle, which I knew to be Palmeria's call or? alarm. I whistled in return and waited. Gradually the sound [answering call] came nearer and nearer, but owing to extremely dense brush I could not see the bird. At last it appeared only about three yards off! [peering at me from a screen of leaves] too near of course for me to shoot at. Thence it flew to the top of a neighboring Lehua, where I could have killed it with ease, but it would have been pure murder, as there could be no hope of finding it without a dog. It was now joined by a second (no doubt ♀) and I watched them feeding on the dead moss-covered boughs, seeking no doubt, spiders, and lepidopterous larvae and possibly beetles. After a time they flew off together and I went on. It was [very] difficult to hear [birds on the edge of the pali] owing to the roar of the strong wind and nothing exciting turned up on the way. After a while I came to the Pali leading down into the deep valley below.[147] This I descended for three or four hundred feet (almost sheer) but owing to rain, fog and wind [wind and rain] birds did not appear, and after a time I began to climb up — no easy matter and a good deal of it I had to do on my hands and knees, [in places] pushing my gun up in front [of me]. I now thought of returning, being unable to fix the position of the sun from the fog and clouds [as I could get no bearings owing to the mountain being wrapped in fog and heavy rain clouds]. on the way home — and it must have been within a hundred yards or so of where I shot the other two [on the 18th] — I saw another specimen of the black Drepanid. Its gave a cry, not nearly so clear as those others, probably an alarm note, and I got a quick shot. It started forward falling some ten yards from where it was pitched [settled] and was hopelessly lost. I got no more than a few of its back feathers which came [were blown] back to me by the wind. This delayed me, so I hurried homewards, hearing one more Palmeria, and by whistling I brought it near but never saw it. Of course I saw Loxops [flammea], but did not try to shoot any. I got a few Carabidae under moss and a Eudorea [Scoparia] new to me. Also a Tinaeid. Got home rather before 6: after a tiring day. It had not rained much round the house [at Makakupaia], but is inclined to to-night and just before dark I could see that it was terribly wet up above.

[Mem. I have always forgotten to note the scent given off by Hawaiian Carabidae. I fancy Cyclothorax is free from it. Sometimes when I have disturbed 'a batch' under bark [of a tree] on Oahu I was able to distinguish a vapour given off (you see a misty kind of atmosphere round the spot). When you put one of these beetles in an ammonia bottle, dense white fumes are formed. In some species I have noticed a brown fluid ejected from the mouth. The vapour given off is also sometimes shown up in a cyanide bottle, but in this case it is much less plainly seen than in ammonia.]

June 22
Thick rain round the house [Heavy rain below] and still heavier higher up [in the higher forest]. Went out after [land]shells as the only thing possible to do — about

---

147   The only place this can be is the ridgeline descending from Kaunuohua peak.

500 ft. above the house. Not very successful, owing to the heavy [rain] dropping from the trees making it difficult to look up. However, got six specimens of the species I went for. Came home about 2 p.m. and then started down to Kaunakakai to write letters for to-morrow's steamer. Got letter from home and one from Professor Newton, dated 20th May.

June 23

Had heard there were registered letters at Kalae for me which M^r. Meyer's[149] sons brought these down in the evening. These were (1) from D^r. Hickson notifying me of money, sent date May 19 (2) Box of cork, pins etc., from D^r. Sharp, May 19th. I wrote to Professor Newton in reply, but of course was too late by this time to write to the others, the mail being closed. Wrote to M^r. Damon[150] about letter received from M^r. Bishop (which I sent on to Prof. Newton, also sketch of bird's head [of the black drepanid]) asking for specimens of insects and I suppose of other animals for the Bishop Museum. Also to Fred Whitney[151] about sending case to England [for the collection I have here], to Mr Krouse[152] and others. In evening fixed up a number of [cork] tablets of the insects caught below [down here] previously and [pinned up] others caught at different times [on my various journeys] on the way down [to Kaunakakai].

June 24

Started up about 7 a.m. for house with [carrying a load of fine (or dust)] shot, caps [for reloading cartridges], tinned meat [canned beef] &^{c}.

Got up [to Makakupaia] about 10 [a.m.] excessively hot with little wind and apparently clear in the highest forest, but of course was too late to start up so far.

Worked upwards in gulches and ridges with beating tray, but insects not nearly so abundant as they should have been [for] so fine a day. The rain yesterday which I could see from below must have washed them out. I got one very fine buff-colored and very large Tinaeid, one specimen of two or three species of Anobiids, some Proterini [Proterhinus], but only one Brachypeplus one ♀ large blue-winged Prosopis. Came home about 2 p.m. and then went out with a net about one and a half miles above the house [and then] down in gulch, one large black Gnophos? [geometer] as before [Progonostola]. Several specimens of Larentia [small ones] from tree trunks, a few Micros netted, one Tortrix (not a good specimen). In decaying leaves almost covered with water a very active running Metromenus exceedingly difficult to catch, [but I took] several specimens. Also two or three dragonflies, one ♂ I think new to me.

149   Meyer, Rudolph Wilhelm (1826–1897). Manager of the Molokai Ranch and, during the time Perkins was on Moloka'i, postmaster at Kala'e. Perkins enjoyed the company of Meyers and his family immensely during his almost six months on Moloka'i in 1893. "Meyer was a well read man & quite able to discuss the Darwinian theory with me & I much enjoyed my stay of about 10 days at Kalae with him." (*R.C.L. Perkins letter to E.C. Zimmerman, 22 May 1947, BPBM Entomology Archives*).

150   Damon, Samuel Mills (1845–1924). Born in Hawai'i, the son of the Reverend Samuel Chenery Damon, he was educated at Punahou School and became Charles Reed Bishop's banking partner in 1881. He was a Trustee of the Bishop Museum and the Bishop Estate from 1884–1909.

151   Whitney, Fred (1845–1926). Whitney was a clerk for William G. Irwin & Company in Honolulu, who were shipping merchants in the 1890s, as well as bankers and sugar agents.

152   Krouse, Thomas E. (–1902). Proprietor of Hotels in Honolulu including the Eagle House and Arlington, both of which were establishments visited by Perkins during his stays in Honolulu.

[Mem. Mice or rats, or both, must have existed for an immense time on these Islands, or the land shells wouldn't have come to conceal themselves so carefully. A bunch of dead leaves especially when drawn close together by a spider for its nest generally has one or more shells inside the nest, the same with leaves which happen to press close against the stem. scraggy bushes with few leaves best for shells, probably because less blown about by winds than very leafy ones. Pink Achatinella of Halemano, Oahu when young very fond of hiding in the fresh young leaves of Freycinetia].

June 25

Up at day break and got breakfast over soon after six. A lovely morning round house, with cloud over the back ridge but promise of a fine day. Hastened over the first part as quickly as the nature of the ground would allow, hoping to reach the mountain top. As usual struck rain when I reached the first thick [dense] forest and heavy mist, everything dripping wet. Following [my] trail down from the first peak of the back ridge, saw a Phaeornis, which started the usual shivering. It was a young bird, nicely spotted, and I used one of the larger charges at it. It was some distance off, but dropped straight, peppered all over. It proved a ♂ on skinning. Went some way till [I had] passed the point where my two cut trails met without seeing anything of note. I had been pausing every 100 yards or so and whistling the call-note of Palmeria to no effect.

At last my call was answered. Two birds appeared on the top of a Lehua some 40 yards off. I sat down and kept on whistling. This fetched one of them to the top of a dead tree in easy shot [range], but with very rough ground and dense brush underneath. I shot, killing the bird and scaring off the other. My bird luckily pitched in the top of a Lehua instead of dropping to the ground and on climbing I found it at once. It was a young [and quite] immature bird.

I continued on now for a long way past the Pali down into Pelekunu. I got no view owing to the dense fog and rain. Was minded to go down the Pali, but luckily determined to continue [on past it] upwards along the backbone. After some time I came on 2 Loxops ♂ [flammea], one very bright [fine] adult; one very prettily marked young [bird]. I had previously shot one nestling young and thought in absence of other birds to annex these two. This cost me dear, as I first shot the old ♂ marking where he fell, then shot at the young one [with the lightest possible charge of dust shot]. He flew to a neighbouring tree evidently hit and I followed putting a very light (O) charge at him. Instead of falling straight he fell at an angle and I lost him, nor did I get the old ♂ [nor could I now find the place I had marked where the old bird fell], though I searched long. This wasted three of the usual stock of cartridges I carried (14) [and three which contained the most useful load, some being more heavily loaded] which afterwards I sorely repented. Now I was 5,000 or more feet up and by whistling called up two fine Palmeria. One came in easy shot [range] and I bagged it at once. The other was very scary but at last I got a shot. It flew and fell at a distance and was lost. Soon I got another fine ♂, and as I thought saw another approaching [slowly]. It came nearer and nearer as I continued whistling and then I saw it was one of the black Hemignathine birds [drepanids]. I shot it and picked it up easily. It was a young bird with the yellow of the base of the beak continued a long way forward, especially laterally. Next I got another young Palmeria, which was sucking a Lehua blossom, and finally I called two young and one adult to me. The two young began to feed on the Lehua blossoms overhead, moving restlessly [with quick gliding movements] like H[imatione] sanguinea and difficult to get sight on. I shot at one but could neither see it fall nor fly for the smoke of the gun [blew back in my face]. The old bird flew to a neighbouring tree. I called it back and shot with a very small charge (O) — all [the only shot] I had left. It flew obviously wounded to a tree about twenty yards off. The last cartridge I put at the other young one. It fell into my hands. The old bird (a glorious ♂) I now went after. It lay quite dead under the tree I marked it into. My ammunition all gone and the sun setting down I started hurriedly for home a long and wet journey— and had I but had those three cartridges, wasted on Loxops [flammea], I should have bagged two more Palmeria and another of the black bird [drepanid] on the way home, which I reached before sunset (about 7 p.m.).

The latter [bird] has besides its clear call, a sort of gurgling or murmuring [guttural] song, impossible [for me] to describe. Palmeria also besides its simple whistle has what I should call a gurgling or murmuring song but the two are not the same by any means.

Palmeria also has the strong Drepanid scent and appears to me, if shorn of its crest, to be closely allied to Himatione sanguinea, but not to the green species [i.e. Chlorodrepanis, which at this time ornithologists considered congeneric with sanguinea]. The young particularly reminds me of that bird not merely in habits, but also somewhat in general appearance. And in young and old the [narrow] hackle-like feathers of the head are a noticeable feature in either genus.

The young Palmeria as stated I saw sucking at the Lehua blossoms, but the old were feeding on the branches of the trees (chiefly moss-covered ones) and each was full of Lepidopterous larvae. [This last sentence was clearly added on the next morning as a new paragraph after the birds had been dissected].

June 26
A nasty day with rain at the house at times, and much wet above. I cleaned and skinned my birds in the morning. Afterwards repaired gun which had gone wrong. Got the locks off and put it right temporarily. Then went down into deep gulch to wash clothes. Had a bathe [in the stream] — the water exceedingly cold. Got back towards sunset and loaded a number of shells [cartridges] in hope of a fine day tomorrow.

[It has been] an impossible day except for shells [collecting] and I had no time to go [out] for these.

June 27
Got off very early, certainly [before] 6 a.m. Had had a bad night, it being unusually cold, so I was glad to get up as soon as it was light. Started off in fine weather for [the] high forest with gun. Became cloudy at 4000 feet, with rain making [the] woods very wet. Afterwards cleared up pretty well.

The first noteworthy bird I saw was a Palmeria (called by whistling). I killed it but could not pick it up. Then I saw a black Hemignathine bird [drepanid]. Did not shoot for fear of losing it and after a time lost to sight of it. Found a blossoming Lehua tree still further on with a number of red birds in it [Himatione sanguinea and Vestiaria], also one Hemignathine bird [black Drepanid] and one Oo. Put beyond doubt the question of the former being a mimic of the latter. I watched them for a long time before I shot at either. The Oo was, I believe, a this year's bird. It did not give the very loud cry as usual, but was making a noise exactly like the other bird [black drepanid]. But for its [the Oo's] long tail in the thick foliage could hardly have distinguished them. The Oo many times drove the other from the tree, but it invariably returned. In its turn the latter would drive away the red birds (Himatione), and I saw either the Oo or the other [black drepanid] drive off a casual specimen of Palmeria that came.

After many minutes of watching I shot at the Oo, killing it, and then likewise at the Hemignathine bird [black drepanid]. I gathered both with little difficulty. The Palmeria I also killed: it dropped about fifteen yards off and was lost. I pushed on a long way, first descending some 1,000 feet down the Pali at Pelekunu as I heard an Oo [calling] down below. I did not stay, however, but came straight up and continued on obtaining in all three Palmeria and losing a second [losing one or two and 1 more black drepanid].

Note the shorter bills of these birds compared with my first two. Yet these are ♂ also though probably (from small size of testicles) not adult. Still that they should grow so large without the beak growing also is most curious and, moreover the proportional of upper and lower mandible is not quite the same in these specimens. Measured the finest specimen as: bill 2-1/4 inches (very nearly), base of beak to tip of tail over back 6-1/4 inches, total length 8-1/2 inches.

Note that the very long bill is doubtless to enable the bird to reach the very deep set nectary of the Lobeliad plants. It also evidently, like the other Drepanididae is partly insectivorous. The specimen measured I watched for some time before shooting. It was diving its bill under the wet moss which covered the tree trunks, in search of insects. I could tell that the long tongue was being darted in and out, and that so rapidly that it appeared like a liquid streak, the {human} eye not being able to distinguish its movements. It had not, however, such a silvery appearance as is familiar in our own green wood-pecker.

I shot also three ♂ Loxops [flammea].

Insects, a large Carabid and a Gonioryctus? from lily flowers [Astelia] very high up. Did not get back till sun down, about 7. Very wet and cold in spite of having to hurry [back].

June 28
Occupied with the birds all the morning. Washed and dried several [skins] that were [very] dirty. Then was busy cleaning up shells and insects until late.

June 29

Packing up till the afternoon. Then started down with [all my] collections [etc.] to Kaunakakai, getting there about 6 o'clock. To-morrow I leave for Honolulu. A single [winged] Embiid came to [my] light in the evening at Kuanakakai.

SELECTED CORRESPONDENCE

During this period, only one letter was found, that being a short note from Newton to Perkins regarding purchase of a gun and giving an account of correspondence received by him and Sharp.

Magdalene College
Cambridge, England
27 May 1893
Robert Cyril Layton Perkins

Dear M^r. Perkins,

At a meeting yesterday of the Executive Sub Committee it was determined that a gun should be sent to you, and D^r. Hickson who is going to London in a few days was requested to procure one & forward it to you with all speed through the United States, marked "Personal Effects" as you have instructed me. I hope it will reach you safely and be of some use—but I confess I am not sanguine as to your doing much more in the bird-collecting way—and particularly in obtaining specimens of the other species we especially wanted.

Yesterday also brought me a letter from M^r. Bishop, informing me of his having seen you and recommended you to his agent M^r. Meyer. I presume that M^r. Bishop had been until lately away from Honolulu, but so far as I remember you have never mentioned his name in any letter I have received from you. D^r. Sharp has shown me two letters which reached him yesterday from you—the first for many months—but I could only read them hurriedly & gave them back to him that he might be able to answer them by today's mail. Having written to you at some length just a week ago (the 20th) in reply to your letter of 21st April. I have nothing new to remark upon, and so, with my best wishes, I remain

Yours very truly,
Alfred Newton

Moloka‘i
9 July–October 1893

On 30 June 1893, Perkins left for Honolulu on board the steamer *Mokolii*. In Honolulu, he once again processed and mailed specimens, wrote letters, collected necessary equipment, food, and funds, and headed back for Moloka‘i on 5 July, arriving at Kaunakakai after a few hours trip.

As with his initial arrival in May, Perkins stayed on in Kaunakakai for a few days to get his things together and no doubt catch up with acquaintances and make sure his mail would be received at either the Kaunakakai post office or possibly up at Kala‘e at the Meyer's home.

His journal entries stop at 25 September but Perkins stated that he returned then to Honolulu to pack up collections to be sent back to England and then returned to Pelekunu in October to collect further. From correspondence records we can deduce that he was in Honolulu as late as 9 October. He thus must have returned to Moloka‘i after that date. His collection numbers indicate that he collected at sea level on the leeward side of the island and at Pelekunu in October. The sea level collections may have been at the Kahanui fishpond on his way back to Kaunakakai to catch a steamer for the return trip back to Honolulu.

The next part of his transcripts was not done with the same format as the previous ones. Instead of indicating passages added since his original diary in square brackets, he placed these and those from his original diary in parentheses. Because of this, it is not always possible to discern which of his ancillary notes were written at the time of his diaries or were written afterwards when he transcribed his diaries in 1936. I have marked those passages in square brackets where it is clear that they were after 1893.

[Continuation of Molokai diary from June 29th. On the 30th I took things, so far collected, to Honolulu and began new entries on July 9th].

July 9
Started early to the highest forest for birds. Very foggy but the birds unusually active. Shot a few Palmeria, the female I think for the first time. Heard one or two of the black drepanid. After a long time I called one up to the top and watched it for some time and then shot. It fluttered only a yard or so, but fell over the edge of the pali and was hopelessly lost. The female Palmeria had conspicuously white-tipped tail feathers. Palmeria has four different calls and songs. (1) A clear call whistle, to an imitation of which it responds very easily. (2) A song, which I have called a gurgling noise, and might be imitated by vibrating a loose string. The English starling makes sounds of a somewhat similar nature. (3) A note probably of alarm or displeasure something, like the 'growl' of Phaeornis. (4) A peculiar soft call, much less loud then that of the Oo. And more like that of the black drepanid. Collected no insects.

July 10
To the same place as yesterday. I again shot Palmeria, but heard neither the Oo nor the black drepanid. It was fine until 4 p.m., and birds were very quiet. I collected a few Carabidae. Disappointing day.

July 11
Started very early to the highest forest. Shot Palmeria. This bird has become more numerous of late as many young are now about. These are very tame and like the young Kakawahie will come almost within reach of the hand. I saw one black drepanid, which I watched, but did not shoot at on account of its position. I found a few Carabidae. It rained heavily, the woods in dense cloud in the afternoon. No Oo heard and it looks as if my first one was a straggler.

July 12
Skinned birds and then went up for insects, beginning to collect at 4000 ft. Best thing was a specimen of the Rhyncogonus, but I also got some Hemiptera and parasitic Hymenoptera, a small Staphylinid under bark, a number of Eopenthes (?2 or 3 species) differing much in colour. I shall go down into Pelekunu to-morrow.

July 13
Started about 6.30 a.m. with gun and about 30 cartridges in case I should see any good birds. Got to the pali fairly dry, only one heavy shower. I found sheath-axe a nuisance, as the handle kept catching as I went down the steepest places. It began to rain, then I had gone some way down and the ridge was running with wet and slippery. I heard the Oo, but could not get to them it being impossible to move right or left from the ridge. I got down to the stream without misadventure except the loss of my axe which I had to carry in my free hand. About one-third of the way down I was walking along an apparently good piece, not steep, with bushes on my left

and a pali (or nearly) on the right. My gun was in my left hand, the axe in my right. The ridge here was overgrown with fern and I suddenly stepped on nothing, where a landslide had taken place on the right side, unnoticed by me. I naturally dropped both gun and axe and the former rested in the bushes, but the latter fell over the edge I heard it, or stones that it dislodged, striking the bed of the steam below. The ferns I grabbed hold of were stag-horn and tough and I pulled myself up carefully till my chest was well on top and all was well, except for my axe, which I made no attempt to recover. I went slower and carefully after this. Viewed from beneath, it looks like a steep climb up. On reaching the stream I waded down for some distance and then came to a small waterfall and did not know whether to drop down this on spec., to reach the coast. As the fall was smooth and perpendicular I went back, and found I could get further on by going quite high up another ridge and striking the stream lower down. From this point I waded straight down the stream till I came on some kanakas. For a long time I could not convince these that I was alone and when I told them was from Kaunakakai, they, said, no malahini could find his way from there and kept looking back to see if others were coming behind me! One of the natives, a boy of about 18, took me off to his house in the village about a mile or two from where I met them. There are only about twenty houses on the beach where we arrived in the afternoon. I was very stiff, in spite of my daily exercise, no doubt other muscles, ordinarily unused, being exerted in the steep climb down. They got me a change of clothes and washed and dried mine, for I was wet through and plastered with mud, and fed me on fish and taro. On the way down I collected only a few land shells.

The next two days were stormy with drenching rain. I was out three times but had to return after a short time. I saw the winding-up exercises at the school. The children's performances were creditable, but their number was small. I had expected to find grass houses in this valley and even possibly see tapa-making, but there was nothing of the kind. The natives are a sturdy and energetic lot as they had no horses, which would be of little use there. The boy who took me to his home was carrying a heavy sack of mangoes on his back. I was very well fed on chickens and taro. Owing to the rainfall the trees grow right down to sea level so that insects that arrived on this side would be much more likely to survive than those which reached the leeward side with its dried up coast and parched lower slopes of the mountains. I took some fresh water shells here from a heap left by the natives, I suppose. Some of them started back with me, intending to go to Kamalo, an easier journey than to Kaunakakai. We left about 7 a.m. At the head of the valley there was a fine awa plant, from which they filled a sack to take with them. I had no idea it reached such a size. I gathered some land shells on the way. High up I heard the Oo, but none on my ridge, and they were quite unapproachable. The Ou was extremely abundant, cleaning out the guavas and still more greedy for the Ohia ai, so that I could not get a single entire 'apple'. I saw flammea at only a few hundred feet above the sea in this valley, but I made no attempt to shoot the ordinary birds. I got ahead of the natives and could not hear them when I reached the top. The ascent, presented no difficulties, but it was very wet and in parts slippery. I waited for more than half an hour, but being at first hot with the climb, though soaked with rain, and then shivering in the cold fog and strong wind on top, I left for my camp, since they were bound for Kamalo. Shot one Palmeria on the way up the pali, but it was rotten when I got back, and its feathers all sloughed off over the intestines.

July 17

Out for a short time in the morning with net and caught aculeates. Bathed in the stream and started for Kaunakakai. Got down at 4 p.m. but found no foreign mail. McCartney's vacation begins in a few days, then I shall be alone down here.

July 18

Along the shore to Kawela with gun. Saw lots of Auku on the black mud. Also golden plover[153] and ahekeke. There were many coots on the pond, but this being large they kept out of range. I took one long shot and winged the bird, but it could swim faster than I could wade on the muddy bottom and I had to give it up. I found a nest with 8 eggs, but on trying one I found it hard set, so I left the nest alone.

July 19

Again went after coot and started in at the end of the pond wading down the middle. A good plan, as when I had driven the flock to the far end they had to take flight. I killed several as they crossed flying out to sea, where they settled. I sat under the wall for a long time, but they did not return. It was extremely hot and when I got back I found the birds already going rotten, and when I had skinned two the rest were quite so. I wrote to D[r]. Sharp.

July 20

Walked along the coast to Kaluaaha supposed to be about 16 miles E. of Kaunakakai. It was a very hot day and plodding through the loose sand was hard work. I stayed some time at Kawela talking to Trimble. He offered to put {me} up if I wanted to work the mountains behind, but I can easily work that country from my present camps. At Kamalo there was a heavy shower and I stayed in a native house for about an hour. The mountains behind are steep and grand waterfalls were streaming down the palis, the rain there being heavy. Got to Kaluaaha at 4 p.m. just as they were finishing the school term. I did not think it worth while to arrange to stay over here as the mountains looked less favorable than my own position. Above here I am told Palmer got his Oo, but it cannot have been common, as with his colleagues and native help, he is said to have got only 16 in about 2 months of special hunting, and eight of these on one very lucky day. There were celebrations here at the end of school term and the Mokolii was in, as there was a large gathering.

July 21

I was told the Mokolii would be at Kaunakakai at 12 noon, so having several letters to write I started back early. Got to Kaunakakai at 10 a.m. having taken exactly 4 hrs on the way. I wrote to Prof. Newton and saw McCartney off to Honolulu.

July 22

I was late this morning, feeling indisposed with a slight sore throat, perhaps from the change from the cool of the mountains to the heat of the coast and I hardly went out.

---

[153]   Golden plover (*kolea*) — *Pluvialis fulva.*

July 23
Throat still sore and I feel horribly lazy and slept most of the afternoon.

July 24
Roused myself and started up for the mountains, but reluctantly, only I thought I should be better for the change. It was a very hot day and to show my unfitness, I had to rest once or twice between the coast and 3000 ft. I have little doubt I have got the 'grippe' or influenza, which is prevalent, and with which all the officers of the *Mokolii*, who were with me at Kaluaaha, had been laid up, as they told me.[154]

July 25
Slept nearly all day and am rather better tonight. I have no food here except a little rice and a lump of bacon fat, which, at present I do not fancy. Luckily I found 3 limes at Makakupaia, left there by the Meyer's when after cattle and I made some lemonade — very useful.

July 26
Took out my gun to try and shoot a bird, as I had not eaten for two days, but I could not flush a single pheasant. Below I put up a few quail, but was too shaky to kill any. Returned after two hours, very tired. Got one red-tailed Crabro and had a fine Tineid from cases found under bark of a dead tree. Managed to eat some of the rice and fat bacon.

July 27
Started down, making a slow journey. Just on reaching Kaunakakai I came on a covey of quail and killed four, one old and 3 full-grown young with one shot. I bought some sweet potatoes and had a good meal.

July 28
Took it easy, wishing to eat entirely rid of my sore throat and cough. Examined a number of Eopenthes of different colours, but the species seem difficult.

July 29
Went over to the pond and with a right and left killed one coot and winged another, which I could not get near enough to shoot at again.

July 30
Went along coast for a long way toward Mauna Loa in search of curlew. I am told it is only here and on Lanai, but I very much doubt this. I saw none today, but there were many stilt, plover and ahekeke and one ulili. Having only a few cartridges loaded full for curlew I did not shoot any of these.

---

154   Perkins gives further details of his sickness in later correspondence to Zimmerman: "The worst attack I ever had was on Molokai. I was asked to attend the exercises at the end of summer term of a large school at Kaluaaha, I think the place was called. I came down from my tent about 3000 ft. above Kaunakakai & along the coast to the place named — a pretty long tramp. I spent the night there & shared a room with the engineer of the little str. 'Mokolii'. He told me the next day he had nearly died of 'flu' of which there was an epidemic. After the show I walked back to Kaunakakai & up to my tent. The following night I had a strong fever, which continued for 3 days & nights during which I lay there without eating at all. Then I crawled down to Kaunakakai & shot several quail & had these & poi at a native house. The next day I walked up to Kalae & stayed with the Meyers there for a week & got well fed! This was the only illness I had during my collecting for S.I.C." *(R.C.L. Perkins letter to E.C. Zimmerman, 6 November 1949, BPBM Entomology Archives).*

July 31

I put together a pack of apparatus, etc., and started up to Kalae to visit M^r. Meyer, who has invited me several times. It was a very hot walk and except a few aculeates and common Lepidoptera there was nothing of note to be seen on the way up.

August 1

Went up mauka on the Kalamaula land and looked chiefly for Carabidae. I found one or two Cyclothorax at the head of Kalawao and a largish Metromenus. The latter was very active on being disturbed and difficult to seize, being a very quick runner. I got several specimens. A few Proterhinus from the gulches near Kalae. The large blue-winged Prosopis on top of the pali. Several landshells, all of them new to me, but not many specimens.

August 2

Went up to the same part and got a number of shells in a gulch near the head of Kalawao. Had a gun, and pushed on to the head of Waikolu, then crossed over to Makakupaia for apparatus left there. Returning late, I got lost in a heavy rain-cloud it being impossible to see a yard or two ahead near the head of Waikolu. When it was nearly dark I hurriedly gathered a lot of dead wood and cut some shavings from the inside of a dry hollow, tree trunk, the only dry wood I could find, and with this started a fire in front of a great fallen tree against which I sheltered on the lee side. I kept up this fire all night and dozed at times, but was very wet and cold in my scanty and thin clothes. While the stars were still shining several Phaeornis began to sing in different directions near by, answering one another, as if in rivalry. Their songs were very welcome, as I knew the long night was almost over.

August 3

Got back to M^r. Meyer's at 9 a.m. or before. He was very worried, as he was waiting to start down to Kaunakakai having to catch the steamer for Honolulu, but did not like to do so in my absence. He had a big bonfire lit last night, thinking it might guide me back, but in the fog it would have been impossible for me to see this had it been near, much more so when miles away. It did not occur to me that he might be nervous, as I never felt so about being lost for a time. I lay down for an hour after changing my wet clothes and then went up to the pond, where I took a pair of Clytarlus [Plagithmysus aestivus] in cop. I searched hundreds of trees for others in vain. This pair was on the ground, but the trees round were nearly all Ohia.

August 4

Went to the same parts as on the 2nd, but only to the far side of Kalamaula, in search of shells. This is a curious tract of land. I got a fine bronzy Eopenthes and a variety of the large Prosopis having the base of the abdomen red.

August 5

Went to Makakupaia with Henry Meyer and slept there. Collected shells on the way and near by. In a gulch close to the big hill[155] near the head of Waikolu, while

---

155   Although this hill is not named, it is undoubtedly the general area of Hanalilolilo.

he was getting water in a demijohn, I collected several Carabids; 1 Metromenus; 2 Cyclothorax and 1 dull-pitted species, different from that found in the highest forest. A few aculeates and ichneumonids and a very large tortricid near Waikolu. [Archips subsenescens Wals.].

August 6
Went across to Puukolekole and collected a number of shells. It rained and I returned at nightfall to Kalae.

August 7
Collected from Kalae upwards and got a few shells. My captures were mostly Proterhinus the highest species having a conspicuous patch of pale clothing on the sides of the pronotum (I pickled 4 for dissection). It is attached to the poisonous tree called Akia [Wikstroemia] [P. dispar Sh.]. Collected right up to Kalamaula and returned at sunset. I also got 1 Eopenthes, 1 Rhyncogonus, Oodemas and small parasitic Hymenoptera and some thrips.

August 8
Heard from Dr. Sharp and Prof. Newton. Went up into gulch near head of Kalawao for dragonflies I had noticed there. I got several species and then it rained. Also Eopenthes, some Staphylinids etc. I looked for shells during the rain.

August 9
Went up the shortest way to Waikolu. Got a few shells, one Achatinella being new to me, but very scarce, on the marshy ground. It rained very heavily, so I went no further. I saw few insects, except some of the commoner aculeates.

August 10
Wrote to Prof. Newton, then started out with Mr. Castle's son for shells to Waikolu. There is fine 'Kaliko' shell said there [probably large Partulina proxima]. I took a gun, as the Oo was once common on this ground, and Mr. Meyer told me that when he came to Molokai, the natives spoke of the "moho" [rail] as being found. In fact those were apparently of two kinds a redder and a grayer species quite likely, but I had no use for my gun. We got back about sunset.

August 11
I went alone to the same place and got a nice lot of shells. Also a solitary one new to me. Took a gun but saw no birds of note. I shot two turkeys that I put up in the brush near Waikolu, with a right and left and carried them back to Kalae, arriving just at dark. I caught one splendid large tortricid [Capua variabilis Walsh].

August 12
I started early for Makakupaia as Henry Meyer intended to come over towards evening and join me, so that I could take him up to my highest camp tomorrow. I went straight to Waikolu collecting shells. I got a number of Brachypeplus from ieie and caught a few Aculeates.

August 13

Went up with Henry to my tent. He was surprised to find where I had got to, never having been in that forest. While inside we heard an Oo call and rushed out in the direction of the cry. After a while I spied the bird and shot it. It was in fairly good plumage. Soon he shot another but it was in miserable condition with the neck almost bare. I shot one Phaeornis also. Theodor and Penn Meyer followed us up and we heard them shoot, but it was not at Oo but Kakawahie. We returned to Kalae in the evening, the others on their horses as usual, but myself on foot.

August 14

Skinned my birds and then went to look for a special shell near the Leper Settlement[156] pali [Newcombia plicata probably]. I could not find it, though I searched for a long time but Miss Meyer kindly gave me several she had collected there.

August 15

Packed up my collections and apparatus and went down to Kaunakakai, feeling fine after the change from my monotonous diet of boiled rice; tinned salmon and corned beef day and night to the varied and well-cooked food at the Meyers. Every day a fine lunch was packed up for me to take out when I was collecting, while, when by myself, I never eat or drink from the time I start in the morning until evening.

August 16

Went back to Makakupaia, for I must get more Oo. Collected shells along the way for an hour or so, then went up one of the ridges to the W. and got a lot, the best a "Kaliko" shell and a small and very local form of {*Partulina*} tesselata.

August 17

Crossed over to the mountains above Kamalo and collected a considerable number of shells, a rather large Eucnemid [Fornax], Cyclothorax and I found the remains of a large Otiorhynchini in hundreds, but none alive, at roots of the Ohia trees, when collecting Amastra [either Rhyncogonus lanaiensis or a very closely allied species], Oodemas under dead ohia and a Ponera. Also a Hemerobiid was found at the ohia roots.

August 18

Collected a number of shells in various directions around Makakupaia.

August 19

Again collected shells on a ridge to the W. from Makakupaia, so as to complete my series of these.

August 20

Went up to the highest forest and shot some Palmeria, mostly young. Heard Palmeria utter its four different cries or sounds (1) a call note a little like an Oo,

---

156   Kalaupapa peninsula more than 1000 feet below the *pali* was where the Leper Settlement was located.

but much softer (2) a song like the vibration of a string (3) a sort of 'growl' like the Omau (4) a clear and distinct whistle (This note on Palmeria is practically a repetition of a former observation). Heard an Oo but could not get sight of it.

August 21
Skinned birds and then went out to see If I could get 2 pheasant for food, as I had seen one near by. There are a few around here, but I have not shot at any. I did not get one and thus save my tinned stuff, as I had hoped.

August 22
Very wet and I could only collect shells.

August 23
Took 3 days supply of food up to my tent. Collected a good Staph. under moss and Brachypeplus big and little from flowers of Astelia and Clermontia. It is very wet and raining hard tonight [late].

August 24
Shot a female Oo during the only hour when it did not rain hard. Raining all night again.

August 25
Could not leave my tent it rained so hard all day. I made a sketch of the Clermontia on which the black drepanid feeds.

August 26
Could only do some insect and shell hunting, as it continues very wet.

August 27
Beyond the Pelekunu pali I shot one Oo. Here I found a large species of Prosopis new to me. I got several between my fingers but only managed to hold one, being very cold and wet. It has blue wings and a red clypeus. Collected some shells and shot Palmeria. Came down from tent and at about 4000 ft. found a big Chrysopa drowned in a pool.

August 28
Went over to Waikolu for Aculeates; 3 or 4 species of Crabro, including a series of the red-tailed species, probably C. abspectans of Blackburn from Maui. A few shells. I shot a young turkey.

August 29
Collected on the way right up to my tent again in the wet woods. Several species of Brachypeplus, Thrips, Proterhinus, some parasitic Hymenoptera and Micro-lepidoptera. Also two rare Carabids in moss, but neither were new to me.

August 30
After birds. I got 2 Oo in poor plumage. Caught several Agrions and also several species of Lepidoptera. Brought down a pack to Makakupaia.

August 31
Sorting and packing up shells and insects all day.

September 1
Came down with a pack to Kaunakakai. Got letters from D^r. Sharp and Prof. Newton, dated Aug. 3, July 22 and 29.

September 2
Replied to these.

September 3
Henry Meyer brought down registered letter from Kalae for me from D^r. Sharp (July 27th) to which I replied.

September 4
Spent a whole day letter-writing. Clearing up all correspondents to both Honolulu and England.

September 5
Went along the coast specially for Aculeates, to get a proper series. It was very hot. I got a number of coastal species of Odynerus and Prosopis and Megachile, but no Crabros.

September 6
Went up with a pack and collected on the way to Makakupaia. I examined a number of Koaia trees, but they were covered with foreign ants and I got no Clytarlus, which I had hoped would occur on them. Then continued up, collecting in gulches to the East. Collected staphs, Ponera, a phytophagous beetle on Poha, a fine large Ophion, blackish Geometer [Progonostola cremnopis], Aculeates and a few Tineid moths.

September 7
In the highest forest with gun. Shot two Male Oo. Collected two species of Scoparia, the large Prosopis, as on the 27th the big black Ichneumon [Pycnophion molokaiensis] big-headed Carabid (1) [Disenochus] and a few Microlepidoptera.

September 8
Skinned several birds, then went down to look up the Acacia trees. Found numbers of Koaia and a few Mamani, but no sign of Clytarlus on these. Immature Embiids and a green Homopterous insect on the former. Higher up, the Odynerus with long mandibles [Chelodynerus]. Also Ponera, male and female together.

September 9
Went back to the highest forest. Shot a male Oo. Also Phaeornis young — a bad skin — and Chlorodrepanis. Collected Prosopis male and female, Ichneumons, Brachypeplus and one pitted Cyclothorax.

September 10
Shot an Oo and young <u>Phaeornis</u>, neither good skins, also young <u>Vestiaria</u>. I don't know what species of common birds the British Mus. may want. They have not communicated with me at all! Took one staph and one <u>Brachypeplus</u> on the wing, an unusual occurrence here. Also caught several Agrions and one Tortrix.

September 11
I would not look for birds, as it was a really fine day. I collected some Carabids (2 or 3 spp.), several Microlep., <u>Brachypeplus</u>, <u>Proterhinus</u>, <u>Cis</u>, <u>Oligota</u> — 3 genera of Staphs in all. Diptera 3 or 4 species, of which a male and female taken in cop. are unlike one another [Coenosia Dispar — In F. H. the elevation of 6,500 ft. is no doubt an error for 4,500].

September 12
Shot several <u>Palmeria</u>, black Drepanid two (but one was very bad) [possibly beak broken off, or may refer to plumage]. Collected a Tipuline and a few other Diptera, Ichneumons and Lepidoptera. One of the Dolichopodids has rudimentary wings and can jump but is unable to fly [These flightless flies[157] of which I collected 2 species are not described by Grimshaw in F.H.; possibly they looked as if the wings had been stuck together by being wet. They were quite different from the <u>Emperoptera</u> Grimsh. and both different habits]. I also collected 1 pitted <u>Cyclothorax</u> [probably <u>Thriscothorax perkinsi</u>] with <u>Brachypeplus</u>, <u>Metromenus</u> etc. as usual. I packed up my tent, etc., and brought them down from the high forest.

September 13
Nothing to note; skinned birds; fixed tent.

September 14
Was late this morning intending to collect all night with light in my tent, now near here. It turned out so very wet p.m. that I gave up the idea.

September 15
Went down to Kaunakakai taking recent collections down so that they would dry.

September 16
Returned to camp and collected <u>Lepidoptera</u>; <u>Scoparia</u>, Geometers, Crambids and Tineids.

September 17
An execrable day in the high forest. I shot, but lost, one Oo and got one <u>Phaeornis</u>. Collected slightly bronzy <u>Cyclothorax</u> 2 spp. <u>Brachypeplus</u>, two of <u>Metromenus</u>, Diptera, 3 species of <u>Scoparia</u>, one very dark one found just emerged under moss was new to me, one fine <u>Tortrix</u> just above the first station in which I had my tent.

---

157 These flightless flies refer to species of the highly speciose long-legged fly genus *Campsicnemus*, the flightless forms of which are characterized by their much narrowed wings. There is one species described from Moloka'i (*Campsicnemus bryophilus*). The second species Perkins refers to is a mystery as subsequent collecting in the area has only turned up the single species. The genus as a whole has over 150 species in the islands, only 3 of which are flightless.

September 18

A wet night and evil-looking morning, but with a chance of improving. Rained hard in high forest. Started to Waikolu, as I wanted more Crabros. Only got to the big hill when it poured with rain and a thick fog or rain cloud enveloped everything. I heard an Oo at Waikolu, across the gulch. Collected Brachypepli from two kinds of Lobeliads, a green cricket [Banza] Geometer Crabro and its prey [before the rain].

September 19

Ominous-looking morning, in heavy cloud above. I started out for Lepidoptera at 9 a.m. Had only pinned up three Micros, when there was a huge downpour. It rained for a long time but after this I went E and collected a number of Aculeates, a Proterhinus from Pteris, some minute Chalcids, and an Emesiid.

September 20

It was hot below and seemed fine above, but after 2 days and nights' rain I did not go into the highest forest. I found Aculeates are now frequenting the flowers of the Akia [Wikstroemia], Crabro, Prosopis and Odynerus. Took a few more Proterhinus from Pteris. At night a fine Tortrix. D. _____[158] is on the Ohia blossoms.

September 21

In the highest forest I collected the large Prosopis and microlepidoptera, and 8 or 9 species (in 5 genera) of staphylinids, one brown species with large subquadrate head and small narrow pronotum, new to me [Nesomedon brunnescens] Proterhinus, Brachypeplus (two fine large species) Cis, &c. Also two small pitted Carabids, 2 Metromenus and its larva [preserved in alcohol]. I shot two Palmeria. Heard the Meyer boys shoot in the distance, but I did not see them.

September 22

Highest forest. Shot three female and two male Palmeria. Two very large tineids found drowned, there being very heavy showers and dense fog. One spotted-winged Dipteran as before [Hypenomyia varipennis] one pitted Carabid (black drepanid ? 2). [Entered thus, I suppose I found I had two skins of this, not entered at the time and believed they were shot on this date, and so put a ?].

September 23

Worked up to the high forest. At 4000 ft. got 3 spp. of Tortrix, two very fine single specimens. In the wet woods higher still another species and several Pyralidina, 1 dark Scoparia as before and several nice Tineids. In a boggy opening a Bactra and two fine Ichneumons both of the high forest Prosopis, but only one male of the smaller, 1 rare Odynerus, 1 very fine Chrysopid. In the highest forest also some Metromeni, Staphs and Dryophthorus. Three small land shells, two new to me. One Palmeria shot, but not gathered. Took again the small subapterous fly.

---

[158]   The species referred to here is a mystery. Perkins transcription leaves this spot blank without a notation as to its identity.

September 24
Poured with rain without a break and the forest was in a dense rain-cloud. No birds, but about a dozen Carabids, 1 pug moth [Eucymatoge] and a very pretty pyralid. Near camp a few Aculeates, including the probable sexes of the Agilis-like Odynerus, the ♀ very different from the male [O. molokaiensis].

September 25
Started to Waikolu in rain, hoping for a clearance. Between showers I got some Crabros, which was my main object. Also shells — 3 of an Achatinella I specially wanted. Also Mimesa and Odynerus, one very fine species marked with red [O. cephalostictus]. It is a very rough night, blowing a gale and pouring with rain.

[This diary ends here; from August 1st to September 25th was written on small loose sheets of paper more or less torn and discoloured by wet. Probably I now took my collections to Honolulu and then returned to Pelekunu where I landed from the S.S. Mokolii and stayed some time in continuously wet weather. From there I returned to Kaunakakai in October, but have no diary of this period].

SELECTED CORRESPONDENCE

Magdalene College
Cambridge, England
11 July 1893
Robert Cyril Layton Perkins

Dear Mr Perkins,

I have only time for a very few lines in answer to your letter of the 1st June which Dr Sharp sent me on my return from a visit to Scotland together with your letter to him of about the same date. I very much regret to hear the losses you have suffered by the robbery of your watch and notebook—the latter perhaps the most serious since the former can be replaced & also the inconvenience if not hardship to which you have been exposed through the unfavorable weather—but I am glad to observe that this has not put you out of spirits, and that you seem to be working in earnest—on the other hand I am sorry that I must renew my complaint of your not mentioning what letters, if any, you have received from Dr Sharp or myself. I have so often before pointed out your neglect in this matter, that I am a little surprised that you should compel me to notice it again—but, I trust, for the last time.

Through the sudden death of my servant which occurred a few days ago in my absence all my Sandwich Islands papers are at this moment inaccessible to me, and therefore I am unable to reply fully to some of the questions you put—for my memory is apt to be defective. I do not recollect having heard that a new species of "Oo" had been obtained in Molokai, as I infer from your letter has been the case. If so, I certainly hope you will succeed in obtaining a specimen or more of it. It is satisfactory to find that you have procured one (& that a ♂) of Palmeria, which I hope is on its way home, as I long to see it, and you have done well to preserve its tongue, as well as to get a good series of the "Loxops" – I should think that two dozen specimens would be quite enough. There appears to be some muddle, which I have not yet fathomed, about the bird that Wilson described as Himatione aurea. I have no doubt it will be cleared up in time. You must of course not trust implicitly to the list I published in "Nature". It was drawn up according to the best information I at the time possessed & that is all I can say for it. I quite appreciate your disinclination to press enquiries in a certain quarter. It is indeed an unfortunate thing that you should not have had the field to yourself—but that is past regretting now. I only hope you may yet succeed in getting the "Mamo", Ciridops, Viridonia &c for I suppose you intend to return to Hawaii. All I know about the supposed 2d species of Rhodacanthis I wrote to you. I think it may well be that there is only one. But my greatest disappointment is that you should have failed to find either of the Oahuan Hemignathus or to ascertain the precise locality of Acrulocercus apicalis.

The collection of birds from Oahu is arrived & I was looking at it yesterday. I am glad to find one coot in it. The Duck puzzles me as yet. It seems quite different from A. wyvilliana, & ought to be (I think) new to the fauna, though I can hardly suppose it to be undescribed. The series of species did not get into a yellowish plumage as does the curved billed one. If so that will be a curious fact. The series strait-billed Himatione is small (only 4) but it would appear as if that species did not get into a yellowish plumage as does the curved billed one. If so that would be a curious fact. The series of Chasiempis skins looks as puzzling as ever, but I can't believe in there being more than one species in Oahu. I hope your observations will enable you to clear up the mystery.

You will have heard before this that we have the £200 we asked from the Royal Society, & we mean to apply for another £100 to the Brit. Assn. but I don't feel over sanguine about getting it, as it is expected not to be a good meeting, & funding will be scarce. Once more wishing you all prosperity I remain

Yours very truly
Alfred Newton

Cambridge, England
13 July 1893
Robert Cyril Layton Perkins

Dear Mr Perkins,

Your case of specimens sent through America came to hand about a fortnight back, and I have since received your letters of the 31st May and the 15th June. The specimens in the case are all right and I do not note that they have taken any harm whatever during their journey.

On May 19$\underline{\text{th}}$ sent you a registered letter containing 1800 silver pins and a little cork and about a month ago I sent off to you a case containing another gun, some collecting boxes, and a quality {sic} of tubes (glass). I did not send any of Perenyi's fluid, because there was great danger it might get out and injure the gun. In a few days from this I will send by post another gross or two of the small slices of cork, which I have ordered to be cut.

I was glad to hear from your letter of May 31$\underline{\text{st}}$ that you think Molokai a good spot. But I was very sorry to hear of your loss of your watch and journals: the last I consider a great misfortune. Do you not think you should communicate with M^{r}. Bishop or some one else in Oahu as to the advisability of offering a reward with a view to getting the journals back. I am very glad from your subsequent letter of June 15$\underline{\text{th}}$ to learn that you have found so many Carabidae and other insects on Molokai. You are quite right in supposing that those Carabids with pits or interrupted striae are specially interesting. when you go to Maui as I hope you will soon I think you will get quite a haul of them. As regards the cost of carriage: I paid £3.16.6 for the case I received last month. That is more than things cost the other way, but if you think it preferable to send again this way pray use your own judgment.

I have been sorry to hear from your accounts and from the things received that there is so little to be done in the islands during the off 6 months of the year, as this increases the length of time that must be taken to get all the things together in such a way as to make a comparison of the different islands, which is apparently going to be a matter of great importance. It appears to me now that it will take several years to do the islands. I do not know whether the Committee will like to go on, until we know fully what we are doing. And I am inclined to think that the best thing could be, instead of your passing another dead period in the islands to return to this country. This would enable the Committee to get the things completely worked out, and if it thought proper to form a definite plan for the completion of the exploration, but I think you should have a trial at Maui and also see the other islands before you come back, so as to say to the Committee from your own knowledge how much work you think there is to do there. If this suits your own views please let me know, and in that case make a rush through the other islands. Indeed I think you should do this in any case as without it you cannot tell what there is to do, and may leave some of best localities quite untouched.
I notice there is a simple immature Embiid in very nice condition in your last lot.

I am afraid there has been much miscarriage of correspondence; unfortunately you do not make it a rule to mention in your letters the dates of communication you have received, so we cannot say what may be missing in letters we have sent you. We did not send you a copy of the Ibis, but of your paper therein, of which a certain number of separate copies were printed.

If you can catch some more butterflies it will be interesting: there have been very few specimens procured, and information will consequently be rather scarce about them. Even Vanessa cardui would be acceptable, and we have not seen Atalanta yet.

By the way I forgot to mention that in the case I despatched to you there were 2 or 3 pairs of shoes and some other little things sent you by M^r. and M^rs. Perkins.

With best wishes I am

Yours very truly
D. Sharp.

The case I sent you was despatched on 21st June by S.S. Ruahine for Honolulu via Auckland. I fear it will be a long time before it reaches you. I paid carriage & insurance £2.1.8.

P.S. Superficially I doubt your Proterhinus larva. It looks like a Longicorn: say Clytenthes. Try again: also get Clytarlus larva if you can identify them.

Magdalene College
Cambridge, England
22 July 1893
Robert Cyril Layton Perkins

Dear Mr Perkins,

Having written to you on the 11th of this month in answer to your letter of 1st June it is with great pleasure that two days since I received yours of the 23^d June acknowledging mine of the 20th May, while D^r. Sharp sent me a letter he had had from you dated the 15th June in which you acknowledge mine of the 15th & 29th April. This shows a satisfactory state of things as regards our correspondence.

Now I have to congratulate you, & that most warmly, on having got what cannot fail to be a good thing in the bird-way, & I think you have very rightly assigned a plan to your discovery of the new form. Of course it would be rash for me to decide without seeing it, but from what you say it looks as if it would require {illegible} distinction & in that case how would Drepanidops do for it? Moreover it is a great triumph for you to have got this in an island that has lately been so much worked as Molokai seems to have been—and I am extremely glad that it has fallen to you.

But I had better take the subjects of your letters in order. Perhaps I took too desponding a view when I wrote to you on the 20th May, but I think my letter of the 2th {sic} bore a fairer complexion—though even the former, as far as I remember, did not say that the Committee were "not pleased" with your want of success—that they were disappointed there is no doubt; but there is much difference between the two expressions. The Committee will meet next week to prepare a Report for the Brit. Ass^n. What they will decide upon I dont know, but you may be sure that either D^r. Sharp or I will write to you as soon after as possible & acquaint you with the result. The fact that your letters have been more frequent of late, & have now become business-like in form cannot fail to produce a more favorable impression, for you must please to bear in mind that your long silence during the winter necessarily had a very bad effect—especially as many letters were written to you in the meanwhile, & I have never to this day heard whether you got them or not. I have no reason that any of your letters to D^r. Sharp or myself have failed to reach us, but of course I cannot be sure of this.

It does not surprise me that you should think of settling yourself in the islands—for I dare say there are opportunities of getting a decently good livelihood there—and there must be many chances in the place.

I have to thank you also for information as to those who have assisted you – & we must take care in our report to give credit accordingly though I rather gather from what you say that the assistance has really not amounted to much, but it is right to be thankful for small {illegible}.

Now again as to birds—Himatione chloris & H. maculata are of course rare things, but we had them already—while of the Oahu Hemignathi – one, H. lichtensteini, is known by the single specm. at British only & of H. lucidus there are but 3 or 4–& these not in the best condition. As regards Mr. Rothschild's new things, I think I have always given you all the information he vouchsafes (his object is to conceal everything that could lead others)—but I will {illegible} subjoin a list of this year's discoveries as far as announced—

> Hemignathus affinis. Maui (near to H. hanapepe)
> Loxops ochracea. Maui.
> Palmeria mirabilis. Maui.
> Pseudonestor xanthophrys. Maui (a Finch)
> Himatione wilsoni. Maui (straight bill?)
> Himatione newtoni. Maui (curved bill?)
> Hemignathus lanaiensis. Lanai (apparently like H. obscurus?)
> Acrulocerus bishopi. Molokai —

This last he only described in May & I did not see the description till this past week. It is of course the "Oo" of which you write—& pray don't neglect to get it—it is a prime rule for collecting not to waist {obscure form} the earliest chance of getting anything because you think you can easily get it later. I have known many things lost in that way. It would not in the least surprise me if your Palmeria was to prove specifically distinct from his—being from a different island. If, as you say, it is not Meliphagidae you will score off him, for he positively {illegible} it is nearest to Acrulocercus. I am so glad you have kept the tongue. That there should be a new Hemignathus in Maui & another in Lanai is only what be expected, & so with the 2 new Himatione in the former—I only wish the confounded fellow had not called one of them after me, for I have long considered that the gravest insult that can be offered to a real naturalist.

I hope the next week or two will bring me the Palmeria & "Drepanidops" – for I am of course very anxious to see them—Pseudonestor (a very absurd name) must be very close to Psittirostra—if indeed distinct. The so-called generic characters are ridiculous being the similarity of coloration between ♂ & ♀ – though the latter is much smaller, & the ♂ has the maxilla enormously prolonged—so as to resemble the beak in the <u>Nestor</u> <u>parrot</u> — I am extremely sorry to hear of your losing specimens for want of a dog. Cannot one be obtained anywhere? Dr Sharp thinks with me that you should get one at the Committee's expense if you can. It would be a most legitimate outlay—& then if you return to Hawaii & look after <u>Pennula</u> you would find him most useful then.

Your last Duck still puzzles me, but I suppose we shall make it out in time. Has anyone introduced any S. American Duck to the island? If so it would no doubt breed in captivity & the young might escape. I forgot whether in my last letter I mentioned a so-called "Gadwal" {kind of duck} described as an immature specimen from Fanning Is. —but on looking up the description I find that whatever it may be, it cannot be your bird.

I will lay M^r. Bishop's request before the Committee & have little doubt that it will be favorably considered—but it will be a long while before your insect collections are worked out, & of course until then no division can be made.

D^r. Sharp writes to me "I have been struck with the fact that there appears to be in the Sandwich Islands no endemic insect fauna of the plains or rather the lowlands. You will be able I dare say to say whether this be also the case with the living birds. But you will perhaps not know whether it was the case with the extinct birds. If not, when you are writing to Perkins, will you ask him to enquire whether the localities at which the <u>missing</u> birds are supposed to have been found were elevated or not. He will perhaps be able to gather some information on this point." I think this raises an interesting question or series of questions. I doubt not you will give the matter your best consideration.

Now I must congratulate you on your escape from the bull; but unless yours is a very sure hand, the possession of a revolver might have only made things worse! It is very well you got off. We shall soon I hope be hearing of your having the other gun. I dont know that I have anything more to add except my best wishes, & so I remain

Yours very truly
Alfred Newton

I suspect it would be safest to describe your new bird as <u>Hemignathus</u> (<u>Drepanidops</u>) ....? I can't bring myself to name a species after anybody—the practice, never a good one, has been of late so much abused that it ought to be wholly abandoned. One thinks of {illegible} but then the existence (once upon a time at any rate) of a form intermediate between <u>Drepanis</u> & <u>Hemignathus</u> might be presumed. How would you like <u>fortunatus</u> or _____?_____?

Cambridge, England
27 July 1893
Robert Cyril Layton Perkins

Dear Mr Perkins,

At a meeting of the Sandwich islands Committee yesterday, results of the first year's exploration were considered, and a letter was read from Lord Walsingham making it clear that you have done well in Lepidoptera. No definite statement was made as to the other number of species and novelties in the other orders, but it was said the latter were considered to be considerable. The shells are thought to number about 80 species and approach 1000 specimens; it is not thought there are any novelties among them, and their chief value will consist in the cases of many specimens collected in one locality, especially if the content of that locality can be accurately stated. The birds you know about. The Committee will make the effort to obtain further funds to continue the exploration, and it has authorised me to inform you that if it can get a grant from the British Association and if you wish to do so you may visit England during the coming winter.

It comes to this conclusion because it appears that you can do but little in the winter in the islands. For this purpose £100 can be placed at your disposal for travelling to and fro, and a sum of £3 (three pounds) per week while you are in England, engaged on the Committee's work. It is thought that if you decide to accept this you will not be absent from the islands for not more than five months, and that the time you will be in this country will be 12 or 13 weeks.

I think myself this will be a decidedly good arrangement from every point of view. If you fall in with it you must arrange with the Treasurer what sum you wish placed at your disposal for travelling home. I am in hope that you may be able to secure some remission of cost by arranging about return tickets, and of course if you pay for return tickets you will require more money than you would for a simple journey ticket, so that you must consider the question before you write to the Treasurer for funds. You will know when you think will be the proper time for you to leave, so on coming to a decision you must count up how much you will require to carry you on till then, and how much you require sent you to travel to this country.

If you come over you can see to the distribution of specimens to the specialists and give them information and get information yourself and perhaps work up some portion of the Aculeata. You can if you think proper make your headquarters at Cambridge, for I believe Prof. Newton would endeavour that you should have facility for operations at the Museum, he being most anxious to encourage those who are engaged in the advancement & promotion of Zoology, and I think there is room at present.

You will of course bring all your collections over with you so that altogether there will be plenty to employ you profitably for ten or twelve weeks in this country.

Hoping you are well and all prosperous with you, I am,

Yours very truly

D. Sharp.

The Treasurer I find intends to send you £100 very shortly; you will know how long that will last you, and when you wish to start for England if you decide on doing so; you should therefore as soon as you come to a decision let him know if your require a further sum, and if so the amount. In that case he will if we get a grant from the association – which we shall know by 20th Sep^r. – remit you the amount at once. Your letter to him written at once should reach him in just about the 20th September.

Magdalene College
Cambridge, England
29 July 1893
Robert Cyril Layton Perkins

My dear Mr Perkins,

In writing to you a week ago I told you you should hear from Dr Sharp or me the result at which the Joint Committee arrived on the 26th. Accordingly a letter from him goes by this mail & I have little to add to it. For some time past he has been of {the} opinion that it would be a good thing in many ways if you were to come home for this winter & return in the spring—& you will find from his letter that the Committee has come to the same conclusion—it being left however to determine whether you should or not—& further the possibility of of {sic} our application for a further grant from the British Association being refused necessarily makes things a little uncertain. We shall not know our fate in this respect till the 20th September, but I will write to you by the mail of the 23d, so that you, knowing when you may expect my letter, can make arrangements accordingly.

Individually I am not so sure the decision of the Committee is a wise one, but it is most desirable that you should stand well with its members—& I must say that all except myself took Dr Sharp's view. It seems to me that there is much to be said on both sides. & I have not been able to realize it as a necessity that you should find collecting impossible during the winter months, as seemed to have been the case last year. But I see that very great advantage will be gained by your coming home—You will be able to see your collections in mass & judge of them accordingly so that on your return you will know precisely the points to which your attention should be especially directed. Then again it can't fail to be beneficial to you to be again brought into touch with scientific workers—after so long a separation— so that I regard the conclusions of the Committee with equanimity & a good deal of hope. The Committee was of course much interested to hear of the new

Hemignathoid bird, & I can't tell you how anxious I am to see it—as well as your Palmeria.

Since writing to you last I have found that Rothschild has described another Loxops L. wolstenholmii from Oahu, which he says can be distinguished from L. coccinea & ochracea by its smaller size & dull cinnabar-red upper parts—the rump & belly are also cinnabar, but 'flushed' (whatever that means) with orange. He only got one specimen! You must look out for this bird; but I dare say it is not a new species. Rothschild refers Himatione maculata to his genus Viridonia. This makes me think that Viridonia (as I before suspected) is not a good genus. He also describes the noddy of the S. Ids. as a new species Anous hawaiiensis—on what appears to be a very insufficient ground—Try to get some specimens.

Yours very truly
Alfred Newton

I suspect the Oahu Loxops will be found to have been discriminated before as L. rufa Bloxam. But anyway it wants investigation. Sharp is to communicate a paper to the Brit. Ass^n. on the Entomology of the Sandwich Islands in the hope of exciting further interest.

The Committee came to no conclusion about M^r. Bishop's application, but I dont doubt he will get a share of the spoil when it is divided.

Magdalene College
Cambridge, England
12 August 1893
Robert Cyril Layton Perkins

Dear Mr Perkins,

Since I wrote to you on the 1st of this month in answer to yours of 3^d July I have read the pages of your Molokai journal, & hardly know how to express my admiration of your perseverance in working on under so many & great difficulties. Your narrative enables me to realize as I have never before done the vast amount of energy required for zoological exploration in such a country & in such weather— and at the same time it shows me that you have been fully equal to all the requirements. This makes me all the more glad to think that your tremendous labour especially in getting birds has been to some extent rewarded. The new Drepanis (for I think one can not take it out of that genus) is an especial triumph, & I am strongly inclined to suspect that the Palmeria may also prove to be new. The description of P. mirabilis is however so clumsily drawn up that I can not be sure. I hope it will be figured in the first part of Rothschild's book, which is to appear forth with, and then perhaps I might ask him to let me see a specimen. I certainly could not do so before that, as I should not like to risk a refusal.

When I last wrote to you I told you that I was thinking of sending a description of your new <u>Drepanis</u> to appear in the October 'Ibis'. I have since learnt that so early an announcement of your discovery might be dangerous, as I understand that M^r. Palmer & Co. are to leave the islands in November, & were it known in time that they had missed this good thing they might get orders by telegraph to delay their departure till they had been and procured it. It therefore seems to be better that the bird should be described at one of the meetings of the Zoological Society, and in this case there being no special need of haste it would be most fitting that you yourself should describe it; but this being a business at which you are new I have drawn up & herewith enclose such a paper as you can if you think fit adopt—in that paper I have also inserted a provisional notice of the <u>Palmeria</u> in case that such changes as you think fit, & send the result to me. I have left the specific names of the birds in doubt, because I think that is a matter in which you ought to please yourself—but I would suggest <u>atra</u>? For the <u>Drepanis</u> & <u>nitens</u>? or <u>fulgens</u>? (preferably the former) for the <u>Palmeria</u> if new. But I beseech you not to name either species after anybody—for the practice has been so much abused that no one who has any self respect takes it as a compliment. Individually I have long regarded it as an insult.

In the case of the <u>Palmeria</u> you must give me authority to compare the diagnosis subject to the characters of <u>P</u>. <u>mirabilis</u>—supposing that I am able to see a specimen of it—but the description you will, I think, find to be fairly accurate. You no doubt will have obtained other specimens of both species & so be able to test the truth of my words.

One thing more. Sclater[159] is very anxious that you should write for 'The <u>Ibis</u>' a paper on your collecting in Molokai such as you last year did in regard to Hawaii. This of course could not appear before January, if then, & should you come home this autumn you might manage to compose it on board ship.

Dr Sharp has shewn me a letter he is sending you by this mail. I confess I am not so sanguine as he is as to the probable advantages of your making a cursory exploration of the other islands—but you will see that he really leaves all to your own discretion, & so do I. I have before told you that by this time you must be in a far better position to judge than we can be. As regards birds you are not likely to find anything new in either Maui or Kauai & Knudsen has been collecting on the latter for years. But no doubt each island would supply plenty of insects. My suggestion, which you must take for no more than it is worth, would rather be for a return to Hawaii, & exploration in the district where Palmer is said to have got <u>Drepanis</u> <u>pacifica</u> & <u>Ciridops</u>. In that quarter also seems to lie the best chance of <u>Chaetoptila</u> – in the presumed extinction of which I cant bring myself to believe. <u>Acrulocercus</u> <u>apicalis</u> (Oahu) & the Oahuan <u>Hemignathus</u> I am afraid we must

---

159 Sclater, Philip Lutley (1829–1913). English lawyer and zoologist; educated at Christ Church College, Oxford, studying ornithology under H.E. Strickland. Sclater was one of the members of the Sandwich Islands Committee; and, as founder and editor of *The Ibis* and secretary of the Zoological Society of London, he was one of the primary publicists of Perkins's work in Hawai'i, giving reports in *The Ibis* whenever they were passed on to him by Newton or Sharp. Other than his editorship of *The Ibis* and his ornithological publications, Sclater is probably most famous for his 1858 publication setting up six zoological regions of the globe: the Palaearctic, Ethiopian (now Afrotropical), Indian (now Oriental), Australasian, Nearctic, and Neotropical.

give up, though Palmer's getting (as I wrote to you) a supposed new <u>Loxops</u> in that island shews that its ornithology was not wholly exhausted. We shall try to telegraph to you the result of our application to the British Assⁿ. & the receipt of a single word "granted" or "refused" as the case may be will help you to settle your plans. We ought to know the result on the 20<u>th</u> Sept. So with all good wishes I remain

Yours very truly
Alfred Newton

Is there a spec. of <u>A</u>. <u>apicalis</u> in the Bishop Museum. If so could you "swap" one of your new birds for it? We want it badly. Only three specimens known & all in the British Museum.

Magdalene College
Cambridge, England
19 August 1893
Robert Cyril Layton Perkins

My dear Mr Perkins,

I wrote to you on the 1st of this month in reply to your letter of the 3rd July, at the same time telling you of the safe arrival of your Molokai journal & the 3 valuable bird skins—and just a week ago I wrote again sending you draught descriptions of the new <u>Drepanis</u> & of the <u>Palmeria</u> (if that also should prove new) for communication to the Zool. Soc. I have now to thank you for your letter of the 21st July which reached me two days ago—& Dr Sharp wishes me to acknowledge also your letter to him of the 19th July which also arrived this week. Neither of them reports any great success, but that one cannot always expect, while it is always a pleasure to hear of your well being. Dr Sharp is rather alarmed at the risk you may run on account of leprosy, & is by no means assured that it can only be communicated by inoculation. He being a medical man ought to know, but for myself I have every confidence in your taking proper precautions against contact—though I think it my duty to give you his warnings. I read with great interest your account of your descent into the valley of Pelekuna {Pelekunu} (I am not sure that I have rightly deciphered its name—which is new to me) & as you accomplished it safely I shall not consider you "a fool" for making it—for I believe in the "nothing <u>venture</u> nothing <u>have</u>" principle, but I hope the spoil you get there will reward you for the danger you ran—& doubtless this was not little. What I much more regret is your losing so many of the fine birds you shoot—& more than ever wish it had been possible for you to have had a dog. Without one I fear you will not be able to ascertain truth of the report about 2 species of "moho"[160] or even about one of them. That the ♀ <u>Palmeria</u> should have its tail tipped with white may be an additional reason

---

[160] *Moho*—Hawaiian name for the flightless rail, *Porzana sandwichensis*. Hawaiian oral history mentions Moloka'i residents knowing of two different species of flightless rails but only one species has ever been located in museum collections. Not to be confused with the genus *Moho*, a genus of Hawaiian honeyeaters.

for thinking it distinct from the Maui species—but as I have said before Rothschild's description of the latter is so clumsy that one can make nothing more of it than I have already done. I hear that the first part of his book is to be out next week, & then I hope to be in a better position to judge, i.e. if he includes it, as I expect he will—since it is one of the best of his spoils. I dont know whether to be glad or sorry that M^r. P. met with so little success on Oahu—however he is said to have got a different <u>Loxops</u> there though I suspect it will prove to be the old "<u>rufa</u>" described & figured in the "Bloxam" voyage, & ever since confounded with <u>coccinea</u>. That we shall make out in time. It is entertaining to hear that we have been collecting for the B. Mus.! I expect we will not get much that is new in Niihau—but about Nihoa I know nothing, & I am sure I hope you will do well there.

I will now repeat what I mentioned in my last letter, namely that we ought to know by the 20th Septr whether our application to the Brit. Assⁿ. is "granted" or "refused"—& that Hickson will arrange to telegraph one or the other of these words to his friend in San Francisco, who will communicate the result to you by the earliest opportunity—so that you may make your arrangements accordingly. With best wish I am

> Yours very truly
> Alfred Newton

> *Kaunakakai, Molokai, Hawaiian Islands*
> *3 September 1893*
> *Charles Reed Bishop*

Dear Mr Bishop,

I have asked Mr Damon to forward this letter on to you as I do not know your address. I sent your request (respecting the insects) to Prof^r Newton as chief of the Committee & he writes to me that on the completion of the task of describing the novelties a division of the specimens will be made & that the Museum here will no doubt come in for its share. Of course I could not tell you this on my own authority when you wrote, but I really had no doubt that they would consider my opinion as to the distribution of specimens.

I think that I told I had 200 new species of insects my first year. I now find it is better than that, as Lord Walsingham who is the authority on moths reports that in my first years collection these alone amount to about 400 species. Dr Sharp (& I intend to agree with him) thinks this number may have to be reduced & that 300 is about the number "with probably 250 new species". As to the beetles, bugs, bees & wasps &^c these are not at present worked but the new things are believed to be a 'considerable number'. As to the bees & wasps (a small group), as I happen to have a special knowledge of these myself, I should say I have obtained about 65-80 species with about 50 p.c. new. The other things I cannot report on.

The Committee wish me to return to England for the winter months (leaving perhaps about Nov: 1st & returning in the Spring). I should stay about 12 weeks in England, which would enable me to see all my collections en masse while my memory is quite fresh, & I should be able to consult with all the specialists about these & discover the special points to be looked up. At the same time I should probably be able to work out & describe the new species in my own group as far as collected. I was very doubtful as to the wisdom of this expenditure (seeing how exceedingly difficult it is to raise money for this sort of work) at first, but the advantages secured will be enormous & I have decided to adopt the wish of the Committee for altho' they most kindly left it to my decision it would be impolitic of me to go against their almost universal opinion. However I am now myself convinced of the wisdom of making this journey, because I doubt whether the things can be satisfactorily worked out even by the best scientists (to whom they will go) unless I can consult with them & it will aid me greatly in my future work. I suppose I must be away 5 months in all & in a way I begrudge every day as it is pitiable to see how rapidly introduced beasts are cleaning out the native ones.

I am most pleased with my Molokai collecting. I got both birds discovered by Rothschild's collectors – the beautiful Molokai 'Oo' – a finer thing than the Hawaiian one as it has long yellow feathers about its ears as well as under the wings – Acrulocercus bishopi he has named it. Also the other fine thing, the crested bird – Palmeria mirabilis. But the best of all was a fine new all black bird, a connecting link between the old 'mamo' of Hawaii & the 'Akialoas' & therefore of particular interest. It was a great score for me to get this after Rothschild's collectors had overrun the Island for 3 months just before.

Yours very truly,
R.C.L. Perkins

I have lately spent 2 most enjoyable weeks at Kalae. I got a number of shells & some new insects. After living 3 months in absolute solitude in mountain hut or tent one appreciates the comfort all the more —indeed I never enjoyed anything more than this visit.

Magdalene College
Cambridge, England
8 September 1893
Robert Cyril Layton Perkins

My dear Mr Perkins,

I was very glad to get your letter of the 8th August which reached me two days ago, & to find that your attack of Grippe produced no lasting effect. It speaks volumes for your good constitution & healthy mode of life that you were able to throw it off under such unfavorable conditions. I am not the less concerned, however, that you should have had it at all, & suffered from it in such very uncomfortable circumstances.

As to letters, the last of mine that you acknowledged was that of 20th May since then I have written to you on the 27th May, 11th, 22th & 29th July, 1st, 12th & 19th August while I have received from you letters dated 1st & 22d June, 3 & 21st July—besides that which has just come. You also wrote on 8th July to Dr Sharp acknowledging his of the 26th May, but how many times he has since written to you I cannot say. So much for correspondence. I should have been pleased to hear that you had got some more birds, but I have always been satisfied that you were doing your best in that way, & I am content with the result. I trust that the request collections of shells will prove important & that when you again go after drepanid & the Oo you will be successful. The Rail business is curious. I wish you could get one or both but without a dog only some marvelous stroke of luck is likely to throw one in your way. In former letters I have written at some length about the Palmeria. The whole thing puzzles me much. The bird was originally described from Maui & therefore prima facie. The Molokai bird would be distinct—but I did not know till this last letter of yours that Mr P{almer}. had got the latter also. If so, I suppose he will have sent home specimens & in that case any differences between them would have been at once detected and announced. The first part of Mr Rothschild's book[161] is out, but is entirely devoted to the Birds of Laysan—but of course those which are also common in the Sandwich Islands (all waterbirds) are mentioned. I had hoped he would have included Palmeria in this part, in which case I could have asked to see a specimen—but until it has been figured & fully described I dont like making such a request—as a refusal would be unpleasant. You may be sure I shall do the best I can for your interests, & I only trust that you will get my letter with the draught description of the new species for the Zool. Society. It strikes me as being quite possible that misleading information has been purposely given to you; but of course I have no knowledge in this subject.

Immediately on getting your letter I wrote to Dr Hickson, and hear from him in reply that he wrote to you about a fortnight ago on money matters—but in case of accidents I may as well say that his last remittance (£100) was made through Messrs Baring whose agents in Honolulu are Messrs H. Hackfeld & Co. I hope however that you have already got the money. It seems that the delay has been in measure due to the recent financial disasters in Australia though the exact way in which it came about is more than I know. Dr Sharp who has seen your letter, informs me he has no other message for you just now than his best wishes & with my own, I remain

Yours very truly
Alfred Newton

---

161 The shortened title *Avifauna of Laysan* is actually misleading as the complete work includes all the birds known at the time from all of the Hawaiian Islands. It's full title is *Avifauna of Laysan and the neighbouring islands; with a complete history to date of the birds of the Hawaiian possessions*. It is primarily the results of the collecting of Rothschild's men in Hawai'i, Henry Palmer, George Munro, and E.B. Wolstenholme. The first part was published in August 1893 and continued to be published in 3 parts, the last coming out in December 1900.

I intend going to the Brit. Ass^n. meeting at Nottingham next week, & then hope to succeed in getting a renewal grant, but this will not be decided until the 19th or 20th, D^r. Hickson will also be there.

Cambridge, England
28 September 1893
Robert Cyril Layton Perkins

Dear Mr Perkins,

Prof^r Newton told me he was going to write to you last week, and would inform you of the arrival of your Molokai case. It came to hand on 15th Septr during the meeting of the British Association, contents quite safe and in accordance with your letter of advice of July 3rd. The Lepidoptera seem mostly new, and very interesting. The unpinned things I have only been able to take a very partial preliminary glance at; they appear to be very interesting; you certainly are getting at the Carabidae now!

I read a paper at the Brit. Assoc. on the subject as I was informed it was necessary to do so if we were to get another grant; and I am glad to say that was accomplished.

We have now therefore funds in hand to keep things going about another year. I judge from your last letter to Prof. Newton that you will decide on trying a winter campaign in the islands, and if so I do sincerely hope you will not have such a wretched time of villainous weather as you seem to have encountered at the beginning of the present year. I have, as I told you in my last letter, no intention of interfering with your 'plan of campaign', but I repeat that I hope you will make a try at Maui & Kauai, even if only to see how the land lies: of course you could return again after you made a preliminary inspection. I expect those islands will do great things for you. Hillebrand's <u>Flora</u> quite tallies with Blackburn's views. It seems there are on those islands at a considerable elevations a sort of boggy ground – almost peat-mosses, containing peculiar – the most peculiar – parts of the flora, and these I feel sure will have some – if only a very few of the most peculiar insects of the islands.

I appear to have puzzled you by saying in a previous letter you had not sent <u>Vanessa</u> <u>atalanta</u>: It was a slip of the pen for <u>V.</u> <u>cardui</u> which is said to occur in the islands. But <u>V.</u> <u>atalanta</u> is very interesting & if you come across it again by all means catch it as well as the native admiral, or admirable.

I am glad you got the Molokai <u>Clytarlus</u> a second time. I have not seen the species in the pinned things so do not know what it is like yet.

Your remark about the ant exterminating the insect fauna of the plains & low elevations is very interesting. I was puzzling myself about the almost complete absence of native insects there, and you have perhaps saved me from insinuating a glacial period or something of that sort to account for it. No doubt the destruction of the low forest by the old native inhabitants, as well as the ravages of this wretched introduced ant, are quite sufficient for this poverty.

Your aculeate Hymenoptera look to me very interesting and I think you are getting a very nice string of species together. How really remarkable their blackness is. {illegible} however it is almost parallel in New Zealand, where however there are no Vespidae if I recollect right. (Pompilidae are the great predators there).

Your Molokai Carabidae will I fancy involve a new genus connecting Blackburnia with the more ordinary forms, and there appear to be several species of it. I wonder whether it will prove the genus peculiar to Molokai.

I expect shortly we shall hear from you as to your decision as to your movements. I look forward to your announcement with much interest and I hope you will not forget to take as good a period of rest & refreshment from hardship as you feel to be advisable and as you can obtain.
    With best wishes,

Yours very truly,
D. Sharp.

Do you think you might find some of the natives who would look out for a clutch of the larvae of Vanessa for you & then rear them & send you the crysalids. It would be of great interest to get some idea of their range of variation in the islands. The fact of atalanta being in these islands as well as Madeira & Canaries is very interesting.

The Eagle House and Arlington Hotel
Honolulu, Oahu, Hawaiian Islands
9 October 1893
Charles Reed Bishop

Dear M^r. Bishop,

I have to thank you for your letter of Septr 1st lately received, just before I came to Town on a flying trip. I think it quite probable that after all I may not visit England this winter, for from letters written since I informed you of my intention to do so, I fancy members of the Committee are not quite so certain of the advisability of my doing so, as they were some time back. If the next mail says nothing definite on the subject I certainly shall not go home. Unfortunately they talk somewhat vaguely about the matter, although Prof^r. Newton the ornithologist who is at the head of the Committee seems personally to have always wished me to stay here, but to have given in to the opinion of others.

I have seen Mr Brigham, but he had not the list of birds at his home which you speak of. He tells me they are mostly water-birds & from the outlying Is. – Laysan – I do not know whether Mr Rothschild prefers to send you similar samples from all the Islands or whether that is to be all, but if you yourself are aware of his intentions I should much like to know, as I hope my people will be able to supply you with some birds & of course I have to regulate the number of species I get according to the species existing in the Museums I have to supply. I have so much to do I cannot afford the time to get more specimens than are requisite. I have little doubt that if I am asked to do the islands thoroughly I shall obtain nearly if not all the things Rothschild's collectors have got & of course there is still (after my getting the Drepanis on Molokai) the chance of something new.

You will find it necessary to have at least 6 specimens or so of birds on account of their difference between male female & young & these again in some cases have different plumage in summer & winter & then there is always the fear of an accident to some specimens at some subsequent time, when these species may no longer be procurable. From what has happened to the birds on Oahu, it is only too clear what will also happen on the other Islands especially on the smaller ones like Molokai, Lanai &^c.

I have just heard that the Committee have obtained the British Association grant of £100 again. They were doubtful whether they would do so, so it is the more gratifying. Fortunately I mentioned how an introduced ant, was destroying the native insects wholesale, & this seems to have largely contributed to garnering this result.

I have to thank you very much for the offer of dog & gun. The former I must have later on, but I dont think I shall want one on Lanai. A gun I believe has just arrived from England for me though I have not yet seen it. Were it not for the present uncertainty as to my movements, I should like to get a couple of puppies in preference to a full grown dog & break them in myself for myself. Should I return here, I hope I shall be able to see you on the way as you wish.

Yours very truly,
R.C.L. Perkins

PS I find I shall have to return again very shortly to town as I have not been able to get all that I want.

Magdalene College
Cambridge, England
21 October 1893
Robert Cyril Layton Perkins

My dear Mr Perkins,

I wrote you last on the 7th of this month in answer to yours of the 2nd & 4th Sept. now I have to thank you for yours of the 15th Septr. which reached me two days ago, & first I may remark that it does not allude to money matters, whence I hope that you have at least got the £100 sent to you a long while ago by D[r]. Hickson through Mess[rs] Barings' agents, whose name I find I sent you on the 8th Sept.—Hackfeld & Co. of Honolulu.

I am sorry you are disinclined to describe the new <u>Drepanis</u>—I hold strongly to the belief that whewn & where possible every discoverer ought to describe his own discoveries, & I trust that you will think better of your determination. At any rate I hope your next letter will contain an intimation of the specific name you prefer for, in that case, I shall give you credit for the same if I have to send a description of the bird to the Proc. Zool. Soc. I quite forget what name I suggested, but know there were several. I now feel inclined to call it <u>D</u>. <u>funerea</u>, not only from its sombre colouring, but in allusion to the sad fate that probably awaits it. In my last letter (7 Oct[r].) I told you that I had found no difference between <u>Palmeria</u> of Maui & that which you have got. It is a nice series you have sent us, & better I suspect than that which Rothschild has. My correspondence with him has been going on in a friendly fashion. Perhaps after all he was not so hostile as I had imagined, but only did not know how to behave. At any rate since the return of his men, & in the end (as I suppose) of his operations in the Islands he is most amicable, but he writes "Perkins was taken up the hill country in Oahu by Palmer & Palmer <u>gave</u> him a certain number of birds." I should like to know <u>from</u> <u>you</u> more about this. in his last letter to me, 2 or 3 days ago, he tells me that his example of <u>Drepanis pacifica</u> was got at Hilo & Hartert (the Curator of his museum) writes by his <u>desire</u> to say that the <u>Ciridops</u> was shot at Awini which I take to be the same part of Hawai. I asked for the name of the native who got it, but that they have not told me & perhaps they do no know. By the way they say that <u>Ciridops</u> is a Finch, but a {sic} is nearest to <u>Loxops</u>, 7 this I can hardly credit—at any rate if you should have the luck to get it, please make a point of keeping the tongue at least, the whole carcass would be be better still. I have got Gadow to make an examination (preliminary) of <u>Palmeria</u> & he wholly agrees with you as to its being essentially an <u>Himatione</u> (very ner <u>H</u>. <u>sanguinea</u>) & certainly not a Meliphagidae as Rothschild announced. The latter tells me that a new <u>Phaeornis</u> which he is going to describe was got on Knudsen's Estate in Kauai. It is smaller than <u>P</u>. <u>myadestina</u>. The two <u>Hemignathus</u> which Palmer saw but could not get on Lanai were on Hayselden's land, & in Maui in all parts of the bush. You ought to be able to get them—but it is not clear to me from what R. writes whether both are on both islands, or only one on each. I daresay I may get more details of other things as time goes on, & of course will let you know accordingly. It will be very well to get the Curlew, I daresay it would give "sport"—but is not worth wasting much time over—as it is not a <u>peculiar</u> species. Let me remind you that you only sent one Coot, & we ought to have some more if possible. Cant the Kanakas kill some for you? I am glad you approve the notion of collecting in Molokai— & with kindest regards in which D[r]. Sharp (to whom I shewed your last letter) also joins believe me.

Very truly yours
Alfred Newton

I hope you may be going to winter in Hilo country or some better place if you know of one.

Lāna'i
11 December 1893–22 February 1894

Perkins spent a short period in Honolulu packing up collected Moloka'i insects for the post, arranging for more collecting supplies, and getting a fly made for his tent. After having spent such a horrid wet winter the previous year, he decided to look for dryer climes, but also remembered Newton's 21 October letter about the Lāna'i *Hemignathus* Palmer failed to get. He thus headed off for Lāna'i on 11 December 1893 where he enjoyed the hospitality of the Hayseldens during his collecting on that island. Fred Hayselden[162] had, a few years previously (1888), inherited the Lāna'i Ranch from his father-in-law Walter Gibson[163] and was to manage it for only a short few years before it was purchased by Francis Gay (1902) and eventually put under the management of Perkins's longtime friend, George Munro. Perkins met Hayselden in Honolulu who invited him to visit his home in Kō'ele.

> After my experience of the previous winter I concluded that it would be better to spend this season on the small and comparatively dry island of Lanai, the forest area being very small. Nearly all my extensive series of Lanai birds, shells and insects were obtained during these months." (Perkins, R.C.L., 1913, *Fauna Hawaiiensis* 1: xxxiv.)

Although arriving in mid-December 1893 and conducting fieldwork almost immediately (Lāna'i Gulch and Halepa'akai as well as the Hayselden house in Kō'ele), Perkins's entries for this trip do not start until 5 January 1894, possibly due to an illness he contracted, which was alluded to in a 27 March 1894 letter from Sharp to Perkins, or because he was at the Hayselden house during December and did not pack up his tent and move out to other collecting areas until January.

> "I did some collecting from his {Hayselden's} house & in Jany packed my tent to the head of a valley or gulch near by as there was some water to be got in some places, though no permanent stream. Here the sides were steep, but one climbed out onto an area covered with dense brush, & beyond this could proceed to the highest point of the main ridge, though there were no trails other than the runs made by wild pigs, which were very numer-

---

[162] Hayselden, Frederick Howard (1879–1924). British-born manager of the Lāna'i Ranch during the time Perkins visited. He also was the postmaster on Lāna'i.

[163] Gibson, Walter Murray (1822–1888). Initially, a self-declared leader of the Mormon Colony on Lāna'i when he arrived in Hawai'i in 1861. A land squabble led to his excommunication from the Church and the Mormon's abandoned the island for Lā'ie on O'ahu, leaving the island to Gibson, who for many years operated a sheep and cattle ranch there. In 1879, he left its operation to his daughter Talula and son-in-law, Frederick Hayselden and opted for politics, leaving Lāna'i for O'ahu. Gibson occupied a number of positions in government including being prime minister of Hawai'i two times during the reign of Kalākaua. Political scandals led to his expulsion from Hawai'i in 1887. He died in San Diego, California in 1888.

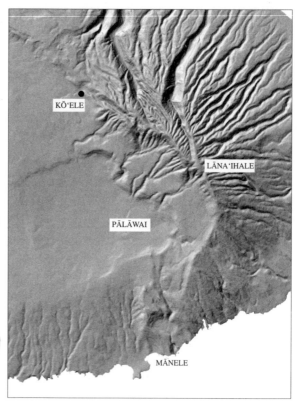

Map of Lāna'i with detail showing Perkins's collecting areas.

ous. I collected on one or two occasions on the coast at two places, Manele & Awalua, where some bees & wasps were numerous. At one of these I stayed for a day or two in one of the empty native houses, which had been deserted by the inhabitants after a murder by a kahuna had taken place there. The only water procurable was brackish & disagreed with me, so that I was glad to leave when the steamer called there." *(R.C.L. Perkins letter to E.C. Zimmerman, 14 February 1944, BPBM Entomology Archives).*

Journals and Remembrances

January 5
Went up a gulch behind Koele for Coleoptera. Took Brachypeplus and the staphylinids (N° 2 and 3) {= No. 223?} in mush under the bark of a decayed tree. One Carabid under a stone and others under bark of a wet, rotten tree. An introduced Staph. [Homalota] in hundreds on a window in Hayselden's house. I shot both Oreomyza and Chlorodrepanis. Wrote to Prof. Newton.

January 6
Same gulch as yesterday. Collected minute parasitic Hymenoptera, Cis, Brachypeplus &c. A very small Oligota and a dubious genus of Staphylinidae from

dead wood. I shot nothing and returned wet through at 3 p.m. The afternoon was very wet.

January 7
Went down to Palawai with Macfarlane. I shot a large wild cat. No insects of note. I had a big feed at Henry's.

January 8
Made a pack of my tent and took it up the gulch and collected from the point where I left off yesterday — Proterhinus, Cis, Brachypeplus, Oligota &c. Shot a ♀ wild cat, these animals being very numerous. Returned to Koele at 4 p.m. and carried up cooking tins, oilskin to lie on, blanket &c., &c., and did not get back till dark, after fixing my tent.

January 9[164]
Packed up food, then went out from the head of gulch on to the flat. I saw a very fine long-billed Hemignathus, a ♂ of bright yellow colour. It was on a tree overhanging a perpendicular side, practically a Pali, so I could not shoot, nor could I entice it on to the top. It was feeding along large moss covered limbs and dead branches and was not five yards from me. Beetles as usual. Collected 3 species of Prosopis.

January 10
Packed and carried up the fly of my tent with more food, powder and shot &c. Collected Carabidae and have now made my tent all comfortable for to-night.

January 11
Went out with gun and collected almost to the highest peak, but I saw no birds of note. Took Aculeate Hymenoptera including 2 large and 2 medium-sized Prosopis and two species of Odynerus. Also the common Metromenus.

January 12
Up the same ridge as yesterday, with gun. No birds of note seen. Odynerus as previously. Two spp. of Crabro new to me; Prosopis and Proterhinus, Cis, Brachypeplus as before, also Xyletobius. Large Oodemas under bark, perhaps the same species as on Molokai.

---

[164] Some further details from this date are found in later correspondence:

"Did you get the 'Akialoa' — the one I did not shoot at when I saw it, because it would have fallen far down a gulch & probably been lost. It was on a tree overhanging one of the gulches that run up to the flat I spoke about between the summit ridge & Koele & the date was Tuesday Jany. 9th 1894. I had a tent near there, & had packed up a supply of food that morning from Koele." *(R.C.L. Perkins letter to G.C. Munro, 17 February 1918, BPBM Archives, MS SC Munro Box 13.4)*

"That one Akialoa I saw on Lanai & did not shoot at, was a male in full plumage & much lighter than the specimens that Wolstenholme shot, so the fully adult male has never been described." *(R.C.L. Perkins letter to G.C. Munro, 22 April 1924, BPBM Archives, MS SC Munro Box 13.4).*

"I saw one fine adult male of the rare Hemignathus, evidently in full plumage & unlike the figure in Rothschild's work. It was in an unusually large, very old & partly dead Ohia, extending over a nearly perpendicular cliff & I watched it feeding for several minutes, at times not five yards distant from me, but I could not induce it to come on to the flat area where I stood & had I shot it, it would have fallen many feet below into exceedingly dense brush. Though I spent much time afterwards about this spot I never saw the bird again, nor any of the other species." *(R.C.L. Perkins letter to E.C. Zimmerman, 14 February 1944, BPBM Entomology Archives).*

January 13
Went out of gulch and upwards; then down a ridge above Palawai and through several gulches, but no Hemignathus was seen. Thence up a very steep and difficult ridge considerably this side of the waterholes and on to the backbone of the mountains. I got back to my tent after dark very much torn about in the climbing and having seen nothing good except a female Crabro, with spotted scutellum. [Nesocrabro compactus var. lanaiensis].

January 14
Worked down to Koele and stayed the night at the Hayselden's.

January 15
Returned to tent, carrying a pack. A nasty drizzling cold day. I worked all up the gulch for small landshells of the more obscure genera. I got 4 spp. of the Helix lot [Endodontidae] other than the transparent-shelled species. Succineas seem quite rare here. Collected a few Carabidae under stones.

January 16
Upwards very early with gun. I got a Cyclothorax on the leaves of a bush — the genus was not collected by Blackburn on this Island. I saw only the usual birds, but I collected some Achatinellas. Male and female of a very small Prosopis, a new species. Also collected Mimesa and saw but did not catch Sympetrum.

January 17
Went down a deep gulch on the other side of the plateau. I saw a very small Phaeornis, but did not shoot it. It was in adult coloration — not spotted — and in fact in company with a similar adult bird, which was of the usual size. There are some fine trees here, but I saw not a sign of Hemignathus. I shot Phaeornis and Oreomyza. Got a nice Cis of the ephistemoides shape (black with much pale marking, thorax densely punctured) [Apterocis ornatipennis] a red Agrion and the usual Salda, running on wet rocks.

January 18
Wrote to Sharp and a number of other letters, skinned the birds and then to Hayselden's with the letters and I stayed the night there.

January 19
Up very early at my tent; a dull, threatening day with the wind blowing hard from Maui. Spread the fly of my tent, which I had put up separately, over the tent itself, in anticipation of heavy storm. I then went on to the top of the mountains. No birds of note, but the beetles quite good. Brontolaemus on dead Myrsine [now Suttonia] several Proterhini, Cis, brownish with dense even covering of fine, erect hairs [Apterocis hystrix], dark-legged Carabid from Freycinetia [Atelothrus depressus] Cyclothorax as before. Also gathered a number of landshells. Last night, when I was at Koele a cat got in my tent and tore in pieces about a dozen of my bird skins, which were drying.

January 20

Woke up to find it pouring with rain and so it kept on till nearly evening. It was quite dry in the tent with the fly covering it. I only got one large 'Helix' species new to me, an Oodemas in bark, and the common Metromenus.

January 21

Went some way down the gulch to a small pool of water in order to wash the mud out of my clothes. Then up a ridge with gun and then down another to Koele and thence back to tent. Collected a few Aculeates, Dryophthorus, and the large Staph. under Olapa bark as on Molokai.

January 22

Started upwards at daylight. It was very cold, the vegetation being all soaked with the heavy dew. I went along the top ridge and collected a number of shells, but no bird of note, only Oreomyza and Chlorodrepanis. Got a few Anobiids and Brontolaemus. I found Walter Hayselden and Gus in my tent on my return.

January 23

Hunted round and round the spot where I saw the Hemignathus on the 9th for three or four hours but it was no go. Then I collected insects on the flat: Proterhinus and the large Staph. and shot a ♂ Oreomyza. I took a fine specimen of Rhyncogonus, but subsequently lost it in my tent, dropping it from my cold hands, when it fell amongst the brush and ferns collected to form my bed.

January 24

Spent the day in the same way as yesterday. I could not find a Rhyncogonus on the flat, but near my tent, just as I was giving up, I got a specimen and also found elytra of dead ones. It must be rare at this season. Shot Phaeornis.

January 25

Skinned a few birds and did some insect collecting as the weather was fine. Result much as usual, Xyletobius, Proterhinus, Oodemas Staphs &c. I was burdened with a gun but did not attempt to shoot the ordinary birds.

January 26

Collected in the gulch Brontolaemus, Oodemas, Proterhinus (1 or 2 large species) a yellow-headed Liophaema and 2 species of Xyletobius, then went on top with gun but saw only the usual birds. I caught a very fine dark-coloured Tortrix at night.

January 27

Upwards with gun. Shot Phaeornis. A very windy day. Crabro with yellow spotted scutellum and black abdomen [C. mandibularis] an uncommon Carabid and an Anobiid &c. I heard the Oreomyza sing. It rose straight up from, a bush singing in the air like Phaeornis. A short vigorous little song and rather pretty, not like that of [Chlorodrepanis] the Amakihi. I have heard it sing two or three times before this, when it is much excited. I am rather stiff to-day, having slept in damp or wet clothes most nights since I camped here.

January 28
Packed up my collection, apparatus, clothes &ᶜ, and took them down to Koele, where I slept.

January 29
Went up the gulch and brought down tent and fly to Hayselden's.

January 30
Macfarlane took my tent and other things over by pack mule to Waipaa in the morning while I walked over carrying my gun and collecting apparatus. Fixed up my tent here, where I believe Rothschild's collectors camped, but I do not much fancy the locality. No doubt it was on the top above this that the Hemignathus was got. Wolstenholme told me that he shot all the few they got when Palmer was away and I believe all on the same day and practically in the same tree or bush. They were feeding at the flowers of Clermontia.

[I kept no daily notes of captures while in this camp, where I stayed for about three weeks, spending much of my time on the main ridge of the mountains in search of Hemignathus, but I saw no sign of this bird. Once or twice when the weather was very bad above I went down to the coast at Manele returning towards evening. I made the following brief note written crosswise in the pages of my diary.]¹⁶⁵

"During the time spent at Waipaa I worked the top of the mountains and to some extent over the windward side. It was not a pleasant camp being very cold and damp and the steep climb up to the top. Before one can hope to do much good with birds was a tax on ones energy at the start. One gets very hot with the steep and hurried climb to the top and then one gets into the cold wind and pouring rain on most days. However, I worked a good deal of the ground, but not thoroughly, as I wished to leave in good time for Maui. I collected some of the ordinary birds, Lepidoptera, Aculeate Hymenoptera, Hemiptera &ᶜ, and in beetles a considerable number of Anobiids, some a little over the windward side and some not far above my camp near the waterholes. Perhaps the best thing I got was the red Achatinella which I found on the top on Suttonia but only in a very limited area. There were a good many young ones of this, the shells of which indicate that it is an extreme modification of variabilis [This red shell is A. hayseldeni] I saw no Hemignathus, the Lobelias which it would be likely to visit were not in flower. I shall have to return here in the Summer as I have not taken a single Elaterid nor any Plagithmysus, although I have found two or three different native trees affected by them."

February 21
Went down to Awalua to await the steamer due on the 23ʳᵈ. There are no inhabitants here and the water brackish. The natives left the houses after the murders that took place there some time ago.

---

¹⁶⁵   Further details from this three-week camp are found in correspondence from Perkins to Munro: "... & the third was on Halepaakai, to which I had to pack water. I was in the latter three weeks, & could not even spare water to was the arsenical soap off my hands, nor wash the rice before cooking it!" *(R.C.L. Perkins letter to G.C. Munro, 22 April 1924, BPBM Archives, MS SC Munro Box 13.4)*

February 22
Collected a number of Aculeates, which were abundant on the usual coast flowers and a few beetles from drift.

February 23
Left Awalua for Honolulu.

[No doubt when I was in Honolulu I packed and shipped my collection to England, after I had examined, as was my custom, such specimens as were available for examination — i.e. insects pinned or carded and not packed up unmounted in sawdust — so as to get some idea of what I had been getting in the way of species. I did not reach Maui till March 6th.]

SELECTED CORRESPONDENCE

Cambridge, England
12 December 1893
Robert Cyril Layton Perkins

Dear Mr Perkins,

In a letter Professor Newton received from you about a fortnight or three weeks ago, dated I think 23rd Octr, you mentioned that you had written to me some days previously. I have not however received any such letter, my last communication to hand from you being dated Sep. 16th.

In that you spoke of being about to send off case with your Molokai things, and I have consequently been hoping to hear of its despatch: everyday I expect to hear of this, as we shall have to make a report to the Royal Society in February, and at present all I have to report to them since November 1892 is your two months work on Molokai during May & June of this year.

I have not sent you particulars as to contents of the last case I despatched as I had no doubt from the postscript to Professor Newton's letter that you would succeed in getting possession of it all right. We are also expecting to hear that you are in possession of the £100 we wired you at Bishop's bank in October last.

Those of the Molokai insects you sent I have looked at are nearly all different from what I have seen before, which is very interesting: you should have done the Fauna of that island pretty thoroughly a whole season devoted to it.
In case you should not have sent off a parcel yet, please advise me by letter what results I shall mention in the report to Royal Society; and also say something to me about your plans for the future so that this may be discussed at a meeting of the Committee.

Please also to let us know your probable requirements in small stores plenty of time beforehand.

I sent on the Molokai Lepidoptera to Lord Walsingham, but the several {sic} illness of Lady W. has prevented him paying much attention to them. I am glad to say she is now better, but his Lordship is going abroad for a little – indeed gone I think – so I shall not have any report about them just at present.

I had the pleasure of meeting your uncle at Entomological Society on Wednesday last, he had just come from a visit to your father and reported all well.

With best wishes to yourself

I am,
Yours very truly,
D. Sharp.

Cambridge, England
1 March 1894
Robert Cyril Layton Perkins

Dear Mr Perkins,

Your letter of January 18th from Lanai reached me Feb. 27th, I was glad to get it & find you are well. It enclosed list of shells referring to a pencil map also enclosed & which I should think will be very important to the Conchologists. Your second case of Molokai things I am expecting daily as they have reached Liverpool, but for some piece of stupidity or other do not come on here.

Thanks for particulars as to your Lanai captures; I expect the season of the year may have something to do with the things you have not found as well as with what you did find.

I see Blackburn got his 35 species of Coleoptera in a week there. From what you say I shall not be surprised if between you the list of Lanai beetles runs up to about 100 species, as he was there in September.

I had the first part of the Molokai journal which you sent some months ago, typewritten & distributed to the members of the Committee.

I suggested to you in one of my last letters, that before coming back in September, you should make one or two short trips to some of the other islands. I see you in the letter I have just received, express your objection to such excursions as useless; yet I cannot help thinking them advisable. Blackburn used to do a great deal in insects by having only a few days in an island. I do not think you could expect to do very good in birds in a short trip, but I fancy if you were to confine yourself to insects you would find it very productive; Blackburn got 50 spp. of Coleops. in his four days in Kauai; and I feel convinced that if you were to give a fortnight to each of Kauai Maui & the other side of Hawaii, you would bring your list of insect captures up to 500 or so species more than it would be without.

Dr. Hickson wrote you some time ago to Eagle house telling you that he was sending you £100 and the manner of his doing so. He wishes me now to say that he changed his ideas as to this latter point, and sent you in a registered letter of date Feb. 7th, a letter of credit for £100: the letter was addressed post office Honolulu.

Professor Newton is intending to write you by this post, and I shall send you a few lines as soon as the Molokai case comes to hand.

I sent you pins in registered letter as soon as I received your request for them.

With best wishes I am,

Yours very truly
D. Sharp.

Magdalene College
Cambridge, England
3 March 1894
Robert Cyril Layton Perkins

My dear Mr Perkins,

I wrote to you on the 3rd Feby & by the same mail I believe that the silver pins you wanted were sent to you by Dr Sharp's orders. This week he has your letter from Lanai of 18th Jany., in the postscript of which you acknowledge the receipt of mine of 28th Novr. & as you beside send some information for me, I at once write to thank you. It appears that you have been working hard in Lanai of which I am very glad, & only wish you had had better luck among the birds; but as usual you say little about your movements or plans—& your silence in regard to the latter is again a great disappointment to us, & positively a detriment—because when one is asked respecting them by members of the Committee or others who are concerned in the Government Grant Fund one has no answer to make!

In my last letter I told you we were going to apply for another £100—whether we get it or not will depend much on what we may hear from you in the course of the next 2 or 3 weeks, & also on the contents of the 2d Molokai box about which there is some hitch. It has not turned up here yet, though Dr Sharp was advised of its arrival at Liverpool more than a week ago. It seems to have been addressed only 'Dr Sharp, Cambridge' which is thought to be insufficient.

I have written to Wilson asking him to let you have a copy of the plate of Drepanis funerea, which I dare say he will do. Do you want to have it sent to you? Or shall I keep it for you against your return? Being of 4to size it might be damaged in the post. I dont quite understand whether you think that all the straight-billed species of Himatione have the tongue simply split & not with frayed edges— but if you are sending specimens in spirit that will be all made out in good time.

I trust you are not going to be troubled again by a rival. Mr Rothschild certainly wrote that his man was only returning to get some sea-bird or other. What you say about the abundance of cats in the forest is very sad & at the same time suggestive—They may have had more to do with the extinction of the birds than I had given them credit for. I forget what I wrote about a short-billed Hemignathus on Lanai, and my copy of Rothschild's last part (in which I think he said something about it) has been borrowed so I can not now turn to it.

I do not know that I have any news for you & with my best wishes, I remain

Yours very truly,
Alfred Newton

Maui
6 March–12 May 1894

After a short break in Honolulu packing and shipping his Lānaʻi collections, Perkins headed off to Maui, his first experience on that island, but not an entirely successful one. This was to be his first attempt at collecting in the West Maui mountains and he had bad luck. The mountains there are almost constantly shrouded in clouds and fog, the weather is only sporadically conducive to good collecting, and the topography of the land is treacherous afoot with narrow, almost impenetrable valleys and steep sides. However, his experience on East Maui, especially Haleakalā, was especially gratifying and he returned a number of times, once with Koebele, to collect on that mountain.

"In March 1894 I proceeded to Maui, working with not too much success in the broken West Maui mountains, where I have invariably had back luck from weather and other causes, with satisfactory results on Haleakala. As I was returning to England for the winter I was unable to make a stay of more than two months ..." (Perkins, R.C.L., 1913, *Fauna Hawaiiensis* 1: xxxiv.)

Perkins gave a summary of his Maui collecting in 1944 correspondence to Zimmerman:

"In March and April 1894 I was on Maui collecting partly in Iao Valley & on ridges of W. Maui mts, & partly on Haleakala. In the former localities I was occasionally accompanied by Bro. Matthias Newell & on the latter mountain I at first joined two men,[166] Weiske[167] & Hamilton, who were collecting birds from a ranch house above Olinda, but for the most part of the time I was alone. Birds in the W. Maui mts. Were not very numerous, being represent-

---

[166] Perkins wrote briefly about these two collectors in later correspondence: "Nothing was written about the collecting of Weiske & Hamilton who were with me on Haleakala about 1895 {error for 1894}. I know they collected all the known Maui species there except Palmeria & I gave them one or two of these, as I had plenty from Molokai & found it numerous on Haleakala, though they missed it. They were young men touring the world & taking temporary jobs to pay their expenses. They were for a time P.G. {Provisional Government} soldiers in Honolulu, but collected birds before they left for Fiji. They sent me a few bees from Fiji but I heard no more of them. I presume they sold their birds." *(R.C.L. Perkins letter to G.C. Munro, 8 August 1951, BPBM Archives, MS SC Munro Box 13.3).*

[167] Weiske, Friedrich Emil (1867–1950). Born in Germany, Weiske toured the world, taking temporary jobs to pay for lodging and food wherever he went (e.g., in California, he was a cowboy on a ranch; in Hawaiʻi he became a soldier of the Provisional Government; in Fiji he worked on a sugar plantation and lived with native Fijian families). He traveled also to New Zealand, Australia, and New Guinea. In New Guinea, a premature explosion of dynamite used for fishing caused the eventual amputation of his right hand. He then returned to Germany, but made subsequent expeditions to Siberia and South America. His natural history collections are housed in the Stadtsmuseum der Stadt in Saalfeld, Germany. The Hawaiian birds Perkins gave him may be there.

ed only by the common species, but on Haleakala all the Maui species were represented, mostly close to & almost about the camp, but <u>Palmeria</u> only in the very boggy forest some way to the East. My collecting was done almost always at too great an elevation for land shells of the genus Achatinella, which I saw only at Olinda, where A. (P.) perdix was found on the Koolea {= Kolea} trees, almost all being very immature shells. Insects were numerous & most species collected by Blackburn were found, & many others." *(R.C.L. Perkins letter to E.C. Zimmerman, 14 February 1944, BPBM Entomology Archives).*

In a later letter to Zimmerman in 1950 Perkins related some further collecting experiences on Haleakalā:

"The first time I was collecting on Haleakala at 5000 ft. <u>Dasyuris</u> <u>holombra</u> {= *Megalotica holombra*} flew in hundreds or probably thousands in the mornings, but I took only one or two specimens, being so much occupied with birds. I think I saw only a single example in my subsequent visits." *(R.C.L. Perkins letter to E.C. Zimmerman, 14 June 1950, BPBM Entomology Archives).*

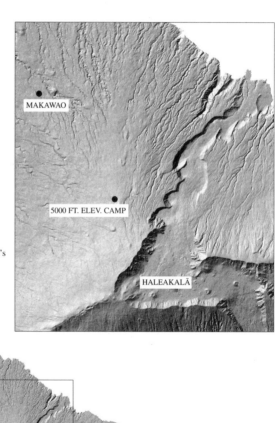

Map of Maui with detail showing Perkins's collecting areas.

JOURNALS AND REMEMBRANCES

This diary refers to my first visit to Maui from March 6th, 1894 to May 12th. Half of the time was spent on Haleakala and half on the West Maui side. I had very poor luck comparatively on the West Maui Mountains, since the very wet weather, which was comparatively of little account on Haleakala were several birds which were especially wanted, was disastrous on the other range, rendering it often impossible to reach good collecting ground, and spoiling the insect collecting. Although there is no mention of bird collecting in West Maui, I took specimens from the Iao Valley; and also some land-shells both there and on Haleakala, but made no reference to these in my diary, considering them probably unimportant. On many of my collecting days in West Maui I was accompanied by Brother Matthias Newell,[168] who also carried a gun and shot a few birds for his collection, while at other times he assisted me in collecting insects on the sandy isthmus between the mountains. I also spent some very wet days looking through his insects, much of his collection having been spoilt by mould and thrown away (as he told me) at various times, so that he had given up the idea of keeping a collection of these permanently. He very kindly gave me the two finest beetles he had obtained a Nesotocus that he found on his coat after he had been collecting up the Iao Valley and a Plagithmysus (P. newelli) which was round in Wailuku, having no doubt been brought down from the mountains by accident. These had both been obtained some years before my visit. We searched in vain for these in the Valley under very unfavorable conditions, and with no definite knowledge of their habits. Compared with the Haleakala entries which often filled up the small space in the diary I carried, those for West Maui collecting were very brief and on a good many days, I made no entry or merely 'same as yesterday', 'Iao V. as before', 'Sandhills as before'. Before leaving for Maui I had entered at the end of the diary a list of species of beetles previously collected on this Island, which I found useful, but I mistook some of the genera of Carabidae (as these genera were in 1894, before their later division) and a little later corrected these in the diary, when I had access to a copy of Blackburn and Sharp's paper, left in Honolulu.

Having spent the winter months in Lanai I had a good view of Haleakala from that island on many occasions. The upper part was for a time well covered by snow not long before I visited Maui, the snow coming down the mountain side to an unusually low elevation. When I visited the summit, there was still a good deal of snow in some of the gulches considerably below the summit and near the so-called Ukulele cave. This cave and the mountain around were on this occasion, as many others had found them before hence the name of the cave — prolific in fleas. Inside

---

[168] Newell, Brother Matthias (1854–1939). Born in Bavaria in 1854, Matthias Newell immigrated to America in boyhood and entered the Marianist brotherhood in 1868, moving from Maryland to Louisiana to Texas and California before arriving in Hawai'i. He became one of Perkins's favorite collecting partners whenever Perkins visited Maui, where Newell was at St. Anthony's in Wailuku, Maui. Before coming to Hawai'i in 1884, Newell was in San Antonio, Texas, where he had garnered the local nickname of "Rattlesnake-catcher," owing to his passion for the natural history of the area. His fervor of local natural history extended to Hawai'i and he gave Perkins many specimens of insects and birds he collected throughout the islands. In 1908 he became an agricultural inspector at Hilo, Hawai'i. In 1923, he resigned from the Hawaiian Board of Agriculture and moved to Dayton, Ohio (the headquarters of the Marianist Church) where he lived in retirement. He is buried in the Marianist cemetery there.

the cave the Carabid Barypristus and the Cossonid Oodemas were quite numerous.[169]

The bird Heterorhynchus in this diary was variously styled 'short-billed Hemignathus' or 'nukupu' or simply 'Hemignathus'. The list of birds which Professor Newton had given me, when I left England did not recognise the genus Heterorhynchus, and similarly the genus Himatione, was a mixture of species of Himatione, Oreomyza and Chlorodrepanis in that list. When the Heterorhynchus of Maui was called simply 'Hemignathus' in my diary, I have changed this to nukupu or Heterorhynchus as Maui has no true Hemignathus, as restricted. Chlorodrepanis = green Himatione of my diary.

It will be noticed that in the case of a number of particularly interesting species as I considered them, I have been able now to add the specific names given to them later in F.H. Many of these were then unique or very rare specimens, of which the actual day of capture was given by the describer. Such additions are in square brackets. On Haleakala I first stayed in a mountain or ranch house, considerably higher up than Olinda, by the kind permission of the owner*. For a few days two young collectors** who were travelling round the world. And paying their way by collecting birds or taking temporary jobs in various places occupied this house with me. Later, when the owner and his family came up to stay, I moved into my tent, a short distance away in the forest. Rather curiously one of the features of the insect life on Haleakala I remember most clearly is not even mentioned in my diary. On most mornings, even though cold and foggy, the rather large black-looking geometer, Dasyuris holombra, flew around my camp in almost incredible numbers, but supposing it would be some well known species I made no attempt to collect a series. Later (in 1895) when I knew the Lepidoptera better, and wished to get specimens I saw but a single individual! Exactly the same was the case with the smaller but rather similar-looking moth Hydriomene aphoristis, which I saw on one occasion in numbers at Kilauea, flying by day over the Vaccinium growing in open forest, when I had no means of catching specimens. In other years I saw only a few single individuals. All words in square brackets [ ] are additions, not in the original, but this does not apply to those in simple brackets ( ).

{Perkins's footnotes}:
*   Mr. Pogue.[170]
** Their names are Hamilton and Weiske and I heard from one or the other later from Fiji. They had collected Pseudonestor or Heterorhynchus (also the common birds of course) but not Palmeria, before I met them. I think I gave them the first Palmeria shot on Maui.

---

[169] In an interview with E.C. Zimmerman in August 1949, Perkins goes into a bit more detail (as related by Zimmerman): "There is a cave high on Haleakala where Blackburn stayed, & when Perk stayed there he was greatly annoyed by fleas. Perkins had a sack made with a drawstring at the top & he would wear it at night to keep away from fleas. He found Mauna frigida very common under stones in the cave." (E.C. Zimmerman, *in litt.*)

[170] Pogue, William Fawcett (1856–1932). Manager of the Haleakalā Ranch on Maui (the ranch that Perkins refers to above). Pogue was the son of Hawaiian missionary John Fawcett Pogue in Lahainaluna. His mother (Maria Kapule Whitney) was the first white girl born in Hawai'i. Pogue was educated at Oahu College on O'ahu and Marietta College in Ohio and became an irrigation expert and at various times managed the Rose and Haleakalā ranches and the Kīhei Plantation on Maui. In 1888 he was a member of the Territorial Legislature.

March 6
Left for Maui by S.S. Claudine.

March 7
Went some way up the Iao Valley in stormy, windy weather. Saw nothing of note except some small Agrions, but my baggage not yet having reached Wailuku, I had no net. I got one toe crushed and damaged by rocks in fording the stream and was lame in consequence.

March 8
On the sandhills[171] near Kahului. Three species of Odynerus, two being yellow-banded and one red-spotted, also one yellow-spotted Crabro, and five species of Prosopis. Gathered a long series of Rhyncogonus vestitus from Vitex. No other beetles except the normal Scymnus &c; Larvae of D. livornica very common. I called at the Catholic school to see the Brothers. Brother Matthias showed me a Pseudo-nestor, Heterorhynchus and an orange coloured male Loxops. He had one of each. I also saw his beetles, but nothing much of note except a very large example of the big Cossonid Munro found in the Kohala Mountains, Hawaii [Nesotocus].

March 9
Weather fair and I worked right up to the head of the Iao Valley and got a good number of beetles — Proterhinus (3 or 4 species), three species of Brachypeplus, a Cyclothorax and a species of Pentarthrum. A fine red-marked Odynerus and also several species of Agrions were taken. I saw both Chlorodrepanis and Oreomyza and some other birds, so must now carry gun etc.

March 10
A wet day, so I went up one of the ridges, Brother Matthias, who accompanied me, saying it would be impossible to get far up the valley. Collected only Agrion and some spiders, when the downpour caused our return.

March 11
On the sandhills between Wailuku and Waikapu, mainly for Aculeates, of which I got a number.

March 12
Got my baggage taken to Makawao, then walked up Haleakala, with apparatus &c, to 5000 feet. There are two naturalists up here, a German and an Englishman. One of them had shot a nukupu [Heterorhynchus] and I took an Oodemas from its stomach. They are collecting birds for sale.

March 13
Went out to shoot and got 1 Palmeria, 1 Pseudonestor and Loxops. Saw plenty of Chlorodrepanis and Oreomyza. Under bark I collected one Heteramphus. Also collected several species of Carabids, especially one strongly punctured species with the thorax angulated in front and sharply behind [Atrachycnemis].

---

171 These are the sand dunes between Kahului and Wailuku, Maui, today mostly removed (along the coast by Kahului) or (on the western portion of the dune system) are covered either with vegetation or houses.

March 14

Went out with gun, but only shot male and female Loxops, the latter green. Again got several Carabidae one more of yesterday's punctured species and one Blackburnia [Deropristus] 2 near the upper edge of forest, where highest. One yellow-banded Odynerus at 6000 ft. outside the forest, is a distinct new species, as shown by the 2nd ventral segment.

March 15

Went up to about 7000 feet, then worked over to the east and into the wet forest. Shot a Palmeria there, but could not gather it. Got Loxops, male and female. Carabidae as before, and also a fine Metromenoid species much larger than any I have found elsewhere [Barypristus rupicola]. It is found under stones, above the forest. A good sized punctured species was with it and more numerous, also an Oodemas, with the elytra posteriorly abrupt [Mauna frigida and O. nivicola]. Got a nice little series of the Blackburnia, also Metromeni, Cyclothorax &c. Two Proterhini beneath dead wood, above the present forest. [I have no idea what these were, and suspect they were lost when the insects were mounted in Cambridge].

March 16

To the same place as yesterday in search of short-billed Hemignathus [Heterorhynchus i.e.]. I shot a Palmeria in a wet boggy place, and on the way back Loxops male. Near this I saw a male Nukupu fly on, and watching this while following fast after it, I fell into a deep fern covered crack with a stream or water at the bottom. Got out of this rather shaky, but took a quick shot and killed the bird, a beautiful male. I also shot a young male of Pseudonestor. Under bark at 5000 ft., I got a large dark Brachypeplus with narrow elongate thorax [Goniothorax cuneatus]; also Proterhinus and two species of Cis of the ephistemoides group. A few Carabids were casually collected.

March 17

Went some way upwards and about 2 p.m. Bagged a male Nukupu, badly shot in head. It rained very hard from about noon and being very cold I returned at 3, having also shot 1 Palmeria. Gathered a few beetles, Proterhinus, Brachypeplus, Cis and Carabids; an Oodemas under bark. Found a very fine Totrix drowned in a puddle, a large species dark brown, with orange, red and white markings [Panaphelix marmorata]. Also a Pterophorid new to me.

March 18

I went out rather late with my gun not feeling very fit, having trouble with the toe which I had squashed and cut on the 7th in the Iao Valley. Wading about in the mud of the boggy parts of the forest to the east, where Palmeria and some good beetles occur, has not improved matters. I shot only one Loxops, but I did some fair beetle-collecting getting two or three species of large Proterhinus, one red-marked under bark of dead Straussia, the other with strongly ridged elytra from another small tree [P. lecontei]. A series of Cyclothorax from twigs of various trees. Several species of Brachypeplus, one pair with very shining, and smooth and of rather large size [Eunitidula sublaevis], Oodemas, Cis several species, one good one with very dull surface, several minute parasitic Hymenoptera. Also a Hemerobiid with aborted hind wings and the front ones somewhat abbreviated, two specimens of Brontolaemus and some minute Staphylinids; one fine, large, drab Tortrix with a few small dark spots [Archips punctiferanus].

March 19
I was up before daylight, having been bothered all night by the fleas, which swarm here, and we started out early. Went out above the forest, then across to the East and into the wet woods, but I only heard Palmeria and birds were not abundant. I may lug my tent over here; though there are signs of a big fire on the upper edge of the forest, it is wet enough inside. Probably chiefly Koa trees were destroyed. Collected about 50 Carabids, Barypristus, Mauna and Blackburnia chiefly. One male and one female of the small new Prosopis one Heteramphus in dead wood. On the way back to camp being tired and not collecting any more, I thought I caught the sound of a Nukupu in the distance so went down about 50 yards into the forest and sat down to listen. I heard nothing for 10 minutes so went a little further down and saw the bird running up a dead tree-trunk. I got a good shot and killed it, but it took me half an hour to gather it.

March 20
Started out very lame from my sore toe, hurt on 7th. Collected from tree branches two very brightly shining, slightly bronzy Cyclothorax. Also females of a new Prosopis. I did not shoot any birds and came back at 1 o'clock. Made a poultice from hard-tack soaked in boiling water for foot.

March 21
Poured with rain all day. Poulticed toe several times in the morning and opened the sore at midday. After this felt much better. Wrote letters to Newton and Sharp.

March 22
Another very wet morning, but somewhat better at 9 a.m. When I started in a fine drifting rain and fog. Saw a female Nukupu and was just going to shoot when a red Himatione flew at it and drove it to another tree. I got a poor shot and wounded it, when it flew to another tree a few yards further off, but only its tail was visible to me. When I moved it flew again about 15 yards to another tree and lay close on the bark. I was going after it, when I heard another bird behind me and turning saw it on the topmost branch of a tall tree some way off. I shot and it dropped straight about 15 yards from me. When I had picked it up (a male in non-breeding plumage) the female had disappeared, having probably fallen to the ground, but I could not find it. Afterwards I got another male in the same condition of plumage. Came back to camp at 2 p.m. and went out again at 3, shooting a ♂ Pseudonestor on a Koa tree. This bird did not utter the excited squeaks of the others, but a 'chick, chick' more like an Oreomyza. It was full of Clytarlus larvae and pupae, one of the latter near-ly mature also contained a moth caterpillar. The Hemignathus [Heterorhynchus] chiefly filled with Oodemas and caterpillars, with some spiders. Collected 1 Brontolaemus, a number of a largish Oodemas from Koa and another tree, and large Proterhinus from the same, two more Cyclothorax, as on the 20th, under bark, Metromenus in moss and one of the large Carabids of another species under bark down below my camp [Baryneus sharpi]. Also beneath bark of Koa an Emesiid bug, some Staphs and a black Brachypeplus.

March 23
Went out after the Nukupu, but neither heard nor saw one all day. Shot only one male Loxops and one female Chlorodrepanis. Collected one very large brown Holcobius and two small Xyletobius only of note in beetles, but I got several nice Microlepidoptera, Tortrices and Tineae. One large Prosopis female, like the one with red clypeus [P. satelles] on Lanai and Molokai. It was a very foggy damp afternoon and cold. There was a large black slug, which I have not seen before in the islands, under stones.

March 24
Rained hard till 10 a.m. Then I started for Makawao hoping for mail, as I badly need silver pins. No letters, except from my people at home. I was lame on reaching Makawao, but there I got a large pair of light canvas rubber-soled shoes and hurried on to Paia, catching the train to Wailuku.

March 25
Visited Brother Matthias and went for a walk in the afternoon.

March 26
Started back for Haleakala at 8 a.m. It was extremely hot and dusty walking up from Paia to Makawao where I stayed a while talking to Anderson at the store. There I took on a load of supplies and made good time up to my camp, but I was tired as it kept hot to near the end, when I reached the clouds.

March 27
Dull, with fog and drizzle this morning. Went after Nukupu, but saw none. Shot 1 male Loxops and two male Chlorodrepanis. Returned at 2 p.m., but went out again immediately and collected some nice Microlepidoptera. Also a single black Disenochus above the forest together with Mauna, [I should think this was D. agilis, but it is not recorded in F.H.] and the two big Carabids in and above the forest [Barypristus and Baryneus.].

March 28
Cold morning with drizzling rain. I intended to collect insects, but had to go out with gun instead. Shot only one male Loxops and two Oreomyza. Back at 12 and skinned the birds, then downwards in improved weather, but everything wet. Did well with Coleoptera: Cyclothorax with a few shallow pits on elytra [M. multipunctatus] another with these covered with apparently a fine pile and with large pits, the most remarkable of these Carabids yet found by me [M. sobrinus] as well as Barypristus, Metromeni and ordinary Cyclothorax. I found one very small Carabid and a Heteramphus under a stone) the others were from varied situations. Oodemas and Proterhinus under Koa bark as before and with these a pair of large flat Brachypeplus quite new to me and a single Anobiid. A small parasite was wandering amongst larvae of Brachypeplus and a Sclerodermus found entering a burrow in dead wood. Ponera and a Myriapod new to me, with long pointed jaws, under large rocks. Returning I flushed a native duck, for which I was unprepared, but I loosed my gun cocked it and brought the bird down quite dead. Its plumage was poor, but it was very fat, so I plucked it and found it excellent to eat. In addition to the beetles above mentioned I took an Anotheorus under bark of Koa.

March 29
A fine morning, so I went downwards wishing to collect some insects on what was probably the ground where Blackburn made most of his Maui captures. The part I tried was very unproductive. I got one Clytarlus (of the fragilis group) and little else in a long time, when I returned up to camp and went up still further. Collected a Proterhinus with strong carinae on the elytra from the leaf stalks of a fern (not tree-ferns) [P. sharpi]. This was new to me. Took Cyclothorax spp. as before, a single Heteramphus, a small Oodemas and a Brontolaemus, and some very nice Microlepidoptera. Several of the remarkable flightless Hemerobiids. At 4,500 ft. one fine red Chrysopid. I saw no birds that I cared to shoot.

March 30
Went out to try for Nukupu. Saw one after walking about a mile and followed it through dense ferns and akala brush, when I repeated my accident of the 16th. and walked into a deep hole. I could not see the bird on scrambling out — I had discharged one barrel of my gun when I fell and probably scared it away. Afterwards I sighted a pair, male and female, but by a piece of cursed foolishness I took a very difficult shot at the female instead of an easy one at the male. I had not yet got a female, nor did I get this one and both disappeared. Finally at the place where I saw the first this morning, I shot a male (non-breeding) no doubt the one I had seen earlier. I shot a male Loxops and one of Oreomyza. Collected a few beetles, especially a minute Staph. with closely punctured bronzy elytra, under bark and new to me, ? Oligota; also small Cyclothorax under bark and Glyptoma. A fine large gray Geometer, resting with outspread wings, and a black and white Pyralid. Male of blue-winged Prosopis, but mutilated in catching.

March 31
Wretchedly cold, drizzling morning. Went out for about 1 1/2 miles to shoot. I saw very few birds and none of note. The Ou, however, was singing much more than usual, otherwise I should not have supposed it was so abundant here, or has there been a sudden incursion? Other birds were notably silent to-day. I returned after three hours and went down to Olinda in similar weather. Here were Koa trees of huge size, but all dead, from which no doubt Blackburn had collected. Under the bark of some of these were the remains of many fine beetles, but nothing living: Eopenthes and (probably) Itodacnus, Parandra, Aegosoma, a giant Holcobius, 2 species of Fornax and an Otiorhynchid. In the living forest I took a live Fornax under a stone and a Cyclothorax with irregular striae and pits on the elytra and outside the forest under a dead Koa limb a Disenochus different from former specimens [D. anomalus probably.].

April 1
A lovely morning but I was not very early. Went first upwards and then down into the forest. Shot a male Pseudonestor (not breeding) in a Koa tree. At noon misty and cold and the birds ceased to be active, so I returned to camp and then went down past many Koa trees, if haply I might get another Pseudonestor. I saw only one and that on the wing, so I got no shot. I did some quite successful beetle-collecting. Of Carabids I got a fine Metromenoid metallic species [Anchonymus agonoides] together with Cyclothorax and one or two species of Metromenus under the bark of smooth-barked Koa. Under a stone a black Disenochus [D.

agilis] and under dead wood a single specimen of a form new to me having short antennae, subquadrate, sharp hind-angled pronotum, resting on base of elytra — a very curious species [Mecostomus perkinsi]. Two specimens of Anotheorus under bark and one Heteramphus under a stone. In the morning I had collected Blackburnia, Cyclothorax with dull surface and a few shallow pits, one Fornax in dead log and a minute Oodemas.

April 2
A lovely morning. Went out about two miles, but saw nothing worth shooting — i.e. no rare species. Returned disgusted at 2. Then worked down through the forest in the direction of Olinda. Collected comparatively few insects; a fine new Tortrix on a tree trunk, 2 or 3 species of Clytarlus on a big smooth-barked Koa [Plag. finischi and Neoclyt. pennatus vars.], a Laemophloeus, 3 Acalles (♂ and ♀ apparently very unlike), large dark brown Holcobius, giant Staph. allied to, but different from the Lanai form and even larger. [All the specimens of this insect (Leurocorynus cephalotes) which with the weevils of the genus Nesotocus frequent the Olapa (Cheirodendron) trees on the various islands as its most striking inhabitants were considered to belong to one variable species by Dr Sharp].

April 3
Rather fine till noon. Searched for the Nukupu but saw none, so I shot one Loxops and 3 Oreomyza. Went out again about 3 p.m. but had no luck. Returned at dark with one more Loxops and two more Oreomyza. All the museums want these birds which are abundant here. Cold, foggy and wet afternoon. I did no insect collecting, but picked up a fine big Tortrix, orange-coloured, with dark markings and a beautiful new black and green Geometer [Eucymatoge prasinombra]. Skinned my seven birds.

April 4
Went for about 2 miles for birds, but neither heard nor saw any Nukupu. Shot ♂ & ♀ Loxops and 1 Oreomyza. Female Loxops ready to lay. I saw a pair on the ground getting material for their nest, the ♀ also pulling off the soft down covering the just springing fronds of fern. The birds rather rarely sing, but are incessantly calling to one another 'kee-weet, kee-weet'. They feed mostly on small caterpillars, spiders etc., and search the buds and flowers of Ohia, probably for insects. Rained after 10 a.m. so I returned and skinned my birds at 1, and started again at 3 p.m., when I shot a female Pseudonestor, which, as usual, was packed full of Clytarlus larvae. The male was with her, but I did not get another shot. Both sing, the song only a simple, but very distinctly whistled note, repeated several times in quick succession. They would stay their feeding every half minute or so to sing thus. When alarmed the bird frequently utters a 'chip chip' like Oreomyza, only more squeaky. This bird is very parrot-like, hanging in all sorts of queer positions. It searches smaller twigs the mandible and maxilla grasping opposite surfaces, and it gets a grip necessary to split or break very tough wood. I shot one male and one female Nukupu also. Collected casually Blackburnia and one Heteramphus — the latter in dead log.

April 5

Was late, as I had to wash and dry my good birds shot, during yesterday's rain; they were wet and dirty. Took out gun again and shot 1 ♀ and 1 ♂ Nukupu, but the latter, though winged, escaped in the thick brush. Found Brontolaemus on Koa and also on Okala (Rubus) and from the latter I also collected Oodemas and Proterhini. One good Carabid as before, Metromenus-like elytra, but short antennae, subquadrate sharp-angled thorax, as on April 1st [Meconemus]. Also two rather light brown Metromenus under logs. I cut a pair of a minute Prosopis out of a burrow in a hard dry trunk of a dead Ohia. New species, but allied to the smallest one on Lanai probably [Nesoprosopis mauiensis.]

April 6

Went out for birds. Fine morning. Heard the Nukupu and Pseudonestor, but could not get a sight of the former nor a shot at the latter. Heard Pseudonestor in full song, very much like that of Chlorodrepanis. The Amakihi here when at its best often sings much more loudly than at other times and the song of Pseudonestor is like this, but fuller. Rained fast at 4 p.m. when I returned. Collected some Carabids, dull Cyclothorax with broken striae, small bronzy Bembidiids like those on Molokai, also a very dull Cyclothorax with black head and thorax, brown elytra and four large shallow punctures and impressions on these [Mecyclothorax longulus]. I also got Disenochus and under a stone 1 Fornax. Also the forest Barypristus [i.e. Baryneus] and Mauna outside the forest.

April 7

Went down to Olinda woods for Anobiids and hoped to find Elateridae. Could find no living sign of the latter, but got the former all right. They hardly seem to occur so high as this [as my camp]. I got several species, but only one large one and only one specimen. I got it from Kolea [Suttonia]. It is one of the much hooded forms, possibly capucinus of Karsch. It hardly seems to be Xyletobius intermediate. I also got two of a large or Holcobius but black, punctured species under bark of Acacia, very like those I got back of Waialua Oahu [Holcobius Glabricollis]. The others were ordinary Xyletobii and Mirosternus, the former very close to or identical with Lanai species. Under a log I got what seems to me to be true Disenochus, quite different from species previously guessed at as that genus. This specimen has a shining unpunctured thorax. Can the others be Atrachycnemis? [Yes: the wrong genera were corrected in the diary after I came down from the mountains, as mentioned in the foreword] [The specimen referred here as 'true Disenochus' was D. terebratus afterwards separated generically by Sharp as Prodisenochus]. I also got the large Carabid [Baryneus] from under Acacia bark and in the dead boughs of smaller trees appears quite different from the higher elevation species being deep black with different sculpture to the apical (visible) segment beneath; never disgorges brown fluid. Also got Cyclothorax, Metromenus &c. Found elytra, and legs of fine Plagithmysus, but none alive. Fine, rough Proterhinus from Maile. [P. epitrachys] and a pair of large very finely punctured Brachypepli taken from different species of tree (Kolea and Pua), 1 Fornax under log. I also got some magnificent Tineids. A lovely day till 4 p.m. Then foggy and cold with drizzling rain. One or two Odyneri. Big Carabid [Baryneus] seen ovipositing in chunks of Acacia bark.

April 8
Went down into forest. Heard the Nukupu twice, but got no shot. Sunless and cold day and the underbrush dripping wet. Grubbed about for beetles while listening for birds and got a number of small Carabids, spp. already obtained. A single new and very distinct species with pale elytra, black spotted, and 4 shallow large punctures thereon [Bembidium advena]. Found 3 specimens of Metromenus with long antennae in lilies (Astelia). Only shot one Amakihi [Chlorodrepanis]. The voice of the Maui Nukupu is much weaker than that of the Hawaii species and it sings less often. Here I never hear those woodpecker-like taps. It feeds quite silently. Saw Loxops ♂ and ♀ sporting on the wing, rising up till they appeared mere specks in the sky. They did not descend for several minutes.

April 9
Started with rug, food and gun &^c for Blackburn's cave {= Ukulele cave} at about 9000 feet. I got there about 10 a.m. although I went down nearly to Olinda before ascending, as I wished to go on the usual trail. Worked from 9000 ft. to the summit. Got 3 or 4 species of Cyclothorax, the large punctured species as below, [i.e., Mecyclothorax montivagus, common from 4000–10000 ft.] the small ones all new to me apparently. Also Mauna and the big Carabid [Barypristus rupicola] one or two species of Oodemas. I brought down 80 beetles from the top 1000 ft. Packed my things down again, as I think one more visit will be enough. Got home long before dark!

April 10
Shot a fine male Nukupu. It has two distinct songs, one much like the 'California linnet' and I suspect it has learnt from this introduced bird, which is very abundant throughout the forest here. Picked up a good number of Carabids, two of the small bronzy Bembidiids as on Molokai. Also got a considerable number of Lepidoptera. Toward evening I went out for earthworms and pickled these (in alcohol only). I took one or two species of Brachypeplus in flowers of tree Lobelias and another of the brilliant golden brown Oodemas from Akala stem, with Proterhinus.

April 11
Started up for the summit early, but from 7000–9000 ft went slowly for Aculeates. Then I began to work for Coleoptera, which I found most plentiful from 9,500 to the top, or to within 100 or 200 ft. short of the top. The soil perhaps too much like ashes on the top. Got the giant Carabid and Oodemas actually in the Ukulele cave, where Blackburn stayed. Above this, Cyclothorax as before, but more numerously, and Mauna. Also other specimens apparently between this and Blackburnia one being redder than the others [Pseudobroscus lentus] very rare to me. Near the summit two Myllanea under stones and at 9000 ft. 1 Proterhinus from a stunted bush. Several species of Noctuid moths near the summit and at 9000 ft. 1 fine Tineid and a Pterophorid. [The 'Tineid' was Heterocrossa atronatata] Prosopis and Odyneri all the way up to 9500 ft. and about there and up to the top 2 (or ?3) species of Oodemas.

April 12
Packed all my insects and carried them down to Makawao, then returned back to camp to bring down the rest to-morrow.

April 13

A very wet morning, so I came down without most of the stuff to Makawao and arranged for a man to go up with a horse for my wet tent &c, and that these should be forwarded to me at Wailuku. I then walked on to Paia and caught train to Wailuku.

April 14

Wrote to Dr Sharp, home and many other letters to England and Honolulu, also to V.R.P.[172] [an uncle and keen collector of birds and insects in England]. In all day.

April 15

Did no collecting. [On this and other Sundays I generally visited Bro. Matthias at the Catholic Mission, when he told me all about his experiences of collecting in Texas and of his first attempts at this in Hawaii.]

April 16

Went up ridge S. side of Iao Valley, but I had not got far when a very heavy rain began. I did not get into any good forest and the only thing of interest was a single Hypaenid, the same as occurred high up in the Waianae Mts. [Nesamiptis plagiota {= *Hypena plagiota*}. This locality was not recorded in Fauna H.]

April 17

Same ridge as yesterday. Very wet and in heavy rain cloud, but I got up a fair way. Collected a few Carabids and found plenty of dragon-fly {= damselfly} larvae in the lilies, but it was too cold and wet for adults.

April 18

Went up the valley but the water was so high I could only reach the 2nd crossing. Everything native was practically exterminated by Pheidole, of which there were nests under every log and stone. There were, however, some Odynerus to collect.

April 19

Wet in the mountains so I kept to the sandhills, collecting Odyneri and Prosopis. The little red-bodied species are parasitic on the others. One may notice that the females of these, when handled, never — (or hardly ever?) disgorge the mixture of pollen and honey, as is the almost invariable habit of the black species, nor are they keen on flowers, which are freely visited by the others.

April 20

Was able to get up the valley, the water being lower, and the weather fine. Went up the left branch crossing about 7 times. There were practically no Lepidoptera to be seen, a strange contrast with Haleakala. I noticed the cane-borer in the banana stems here and also a small Calandra.

---

172   Perkins, Vincent Robert (1831–1922). Vincent Perkins (VRP) was the son of R.C.L. Perkins's grandfather, the Rev. Benjamin Perkins, vicar at Wotton-under-Edge. Aside from his job as banker, VRP was a keen local naturalist and member and officer of various natural history societies in England while also devoting time to community service in Wotton including being its mayor and alderman. He collected all orders of insects but was apparently partial to the aculeates, perhaps having an influence on the young R.C.L. Perkins when the two were together on collecting trips and attending meetings of natural history societies.

April 21
Collected as yesterday, with nothing special to record.

April 22
Wrote letters and went down to see Bro. Matthias p.m.

April 23
Went up south of Iao. Cold, foggy and wet, but I got higher up than previously. Found a large-headed Carabid in moss [Disenochus cephalotes], Metromeni at base of leaves of Freycinetia [Atelothrus gracilis, probably] and a Brachypeplus on Astelia.

April 24
A very wet day in the mountains, so I had to go on the sandhills. There were only Aculeates and the Rhyncogonus of native insects. Deilephila livornica caterpillars were in thousands.

April 25
Got up the valley again. Spent hours examining Pandanus trees in search of the Cossonid [Nesotocus] that Bro. Matthias took. I have no clue to this except that when I casually met Munro in Honolulu he told me the species he got in Kohala, was running on a "tree that sent down roots to the ground". I do not know whether it was Pandanus. The Ohia and other trees do so under some conditions. Anyhow the Pandanus neither produced this, nor any native beetle. I got some good Aculeates to-day and some Agrions after this waste of time. [The tree indicated by Munro was, of course, Cheirodendron].

April 26
Wet cold and foggy up the valley, the head part in heavy cloud. I wanted more Aculeates and Agrions, but I did not get up far enough, nor collect anything of much account.

April 27
River very high, so had to go up a ridge. A few more Carabids and a small Staph. from Freycinetia and also Brachypeplus. It was so cold and wet I could not stick it out after 2 p.m. I see no hope of getting up to the top of the valley for some days.

April 28
Same as yesterday, with similar fog and rain. Nothing new to me except a new Anobiid not very far up.

April 29[173]
Did not collect. Visited the Brothers.

---

[173]   This was a Sunday and Perkins usually took Sundays off.

April 30
Tried Waihee, but could do no good, the stream much swollen and unfordable. Saw nothing except a few dragon flies.

May 1
Tried the Valley[174] again, but I did not dare try the first crossing. It was raining fast even here and above this the valley was invisible.

* * * * *

[After this I ceased to record daily my attempts at collecting in W. Maui, as the weather continued very unfavorable. Only on one occasion did I reach the cave far up the valley, and on that day I collected a few, and saw many, of a small land-shell which was, without doubt, Perdicella minuscula, and shot a few birds. By some error, in F.H. this shell is recorded from Molokai by myself and from W. Maui by Baldwin, and there is, no doubt, that from a misplaced or incorrect label the locality of mine was the wrong one. As a very bad storm was threatening (which a little later developed into a thunderstorm with very heavy rainfall) I hurried down the valley, but at the final crossing was unable to ford the river, which had risen high and was rolling down loose rocks, until fortunately a native came along on horseback and pulled me through holding on to his stirrup-leather. On May 5th I recorded that Bro. Matthias helped me to collect Aculeates on the sandhills, where D. livornica {= *lineata*} was common on the Lantana flowers in the hot sunshine and that P. cardui caterpillars were feeding on an unusual plant, the 'Kikania' (Datura stramonium), in great numbers, instead of on the normal Malvaceous weeds.]

* * * * *

May 11
"Got ready to leave here with joy and thankfulness. The weather all along has been vile and the difficulties of collecting in the mountains very great in consequence".

May 12
I left for Honolulu arriving the next day. "A very rough night, the sea breaking continually over the upper deck".

---

174 'Iao Valley.

SELECTED CORRESPONDENCE

Cambridge, England
7 March 1894
Robert Cyril Layton Perkins

Dear Mr Perkins,

Your second case of Molokai things has arrived, contents undamaged, though one of the boxes of pinned things had just begun to show signs of mould on the cork.

The shells seem to be a fine lot; I think they are not the worse for their journey though I fancy it was rather risky trusting them merely wrapped in papers in such a big box.

Your Embia seems to me to shew that the female is probably really apterous & larva-like as has been suggested. I think if I were you I would try to get a few males gummed on card, as these pinned specimens dont seem up to much: it is apparently one of the most fragile of insects.

I hope you will get a good lot of insects this summer. I expect when results come to be totaled up it will be found that you have done best in this class of animals. still there will not be so many species as I expected from the time. You have lately given so much time to the birds that it has evidently put you somewhat off the insects, and the supply of butterflies, Orthopteran, & especially dragon-flies is much smaller than I hoped. Couldn't you employ a boy now & again to go about with you & catch butterflies, dragon-flies & these things that want chasing but that any body can see on the wing. I do not think you have got all the dragon-flies that were previously known.

I took a few beetles out of one of the tubes to mount & see that they were in good order: there {sic} were quite all right, a very fine new Brachypeplus was among them. The aculeates look very nice too. I hope you are getting a supply of the ants: I see a Ponera, looking like one of the lot that have apterous males. I hope you have got some of the sexes of these: also the sexes of the termitophagous species of ant of which the ♀ is quite unknown & has for years been a riddle (Leptogenys).

The Lepidoptera & Aculeate Hymenoptera are evidently the pick of your Molokai things. I expect the island is as you say not really so good for Coleoptera as Hawaii is. I am quite surprised at the extraordinary number of species of Lepidoptera in proportion to the specimens. I fancy the Aculeates too will turn out a good many species, though they are so much alike superficially that it is difficult to say until they are worked out.

The Orthopteran are clearly very interesting, but of these you seem to me to have got specially few. The Diptera look the most uninteresting but I hope even they may turn out well. I see one specimen of Dolichopus amongst them; I had been surprised previously at that genus not having been represented.

I suppose by the time this reaches you you will be just getting into the best season of the year & I wish you all success. I wish I could come out & have two or three months with you myself, but I am afraid the friends of the Committee would not permit it.

With best wishes I am,

Yours very truly,
D. Sharp.

Magdalene College
Cambridge, England
10 March 1894
Robert Cyril Layton Perkins

My dear Mr Perkins

I wrote to you this day week (the 3^d) in answer to that part of your letter of 18 Jan. to Dr Sharp which concerned me, and he tells me he has written to you this week in answer to the other part also informing you of the safe arrival (after much delay at Liverpool) of your 2^d Molokai consignment. Yesterday he got your letter from Lanai of 29 Jan. acknowledging his of 12 Dec. & mine of 30 Dec. to which & to mine of 28 Nov. it is in part a reply. The amount of your doings is satisfactory to both of us, & we only wish we had had such a report before.

The miscarriage of your letter of 17th Oct. to Dr S. was indeed most unfortunate – no doubt had it arrived, we should have been in possession of all the information we so earnestly desired—but there is no use in now lamenting its loss, I am only glad we have it at last, & am thankful to you for giving some indication as to your future movements. Here let me say once more that Dr S. & I place all confidence in your doing that you consider the best under the circumstances. It would the height of folly for us to direct you to go in this that or the other place. We can tell you, & have told you, of such or such objects which seem especially deserving of attention, but the advisability of your attempting to get them is a question entirely for your own discretion. For instance Ciridops, Chaetoptila & Pennula are things I should greatly like you to procure, but it would be absurd for me to desire you to go in search of them—you must know far better than I as to the chance of success. In the same way you are a far better judge than the whole Committee put together whether it would be worth your while to return to Lanai to get the Hemignathus supposing you dont get it now. I am strongly against the making of hard & fast rules—I always like to look out the best man I can for a job, & give him a free hand to do it the way he thinks best. Even if the result should show that he had made a mistake or two, be sure that I should not blame him—unless some piece of downright carelessness were to be manifest, but that I dont expect. All the same it is quite right that I should from time to time make suggestions to you—just like that in my letter of 28 Nov. (to which you refer in your last) as to work on the lower levels—I am quite content with your rejoinder that you have tried it & it does not answer.

As to Committee meetings—there is no stated time. We have as few as possible (Dr Hickson, Dr S. & I being constituted an Executive Sub Committee & all living here we can act on an emergency) & the last one had to be called about a month earlier than was expected, as the R.S. anticipated by that time the day by which all reports & applications were to be sent in. Had this not been the case & had not the last lot of things been delayed at Liverpool they would have arrived in time. There was a proposal that the Committee should meet again in May, but I see no necessity for it, though we may have to do so about the middle of June, by which time the Lanai collections ought to have arrived.

The 2^d Molokai coll^n, in regard to birds is rich, but I can't compliment you on the conditions of the skins—they are recoverable however, but you should take care if possible not to pack them up damp. The worst part is that so many beaks have received irreparable injury & this in all cases is seen not to be due to shot, but looks like crushing afterwards—say by the lid of a box. It is very much to be regretted. There are 3 more specimens of Palmeria than the no. given in your list—so much the better & 3 Numenius & 3 Fulica not included in it at all. The last are the first I have seen of the species—unfortunately they are all female.

I shall get Dr Gadow so soon as he has time to investigate the Himatione tongue business properly. The absence of odour in the straight-billed species may not mean much—though it is curious & worth noting. Here in Europe Totemus? Ochupus has a strong scent of musk (almost like a Petue ? But I know no other Totemus that has it. Anomalies, for which we can't account, are by no means rare in nature. I have never noticed that the mandibles of Loxops are crossed as you mention, but I will take an opportunity of looking. The L. coccinea is a very scarce thing—Wilson got, I think, only 3—one of which he trod upon & spoilt it—I forget how many you have sent.

If you can conveniently separate the entomological from the ornithological portions of your letters it would be a good thing. I have been obliged to copy the greater part of the latter from your 2 last letters—as being addressed to Dr S. he naturally keeps them, which I need to have the information at hand—& copying takes me a long time which I can ill spare.

I thank you for explaining the mystery of being so well acquainted with the sayings & doings of Mr R. {Rothschild} & his man, who I most sincerely trust has not been bothering you again.

With best wishes I am
Yrs very truly
Alfred Newton

Have you heard anything more of your lost notebook? Very glad you are well.

Mr R. puts the Lanai <u>Himatione</u> <u>montana</u> in <u>Oreomyza</u>, as he does the Maui bird which he calls <u>O</u>. <u>newtoni</u> & says the latter was only found on one side of Haleakala, district of Makawao where it was rare & extremely local.

Magdalene College
Cambridge, England
24 May 1894
Robert Cyril Layton Perkins

My dear M^r. Perkins,

Your letter of the 21$^{\underline{st}}$ April reached me 3 days ago and was very welcome. Dr. Sharp has since shewn me your letters to him of the 16$^{\underline{th}}$ & 21$^{\underline{st}}$ April which arrived at the same time. I am very glad to learn that though you are but "skin & bone" you have been keeping well, and I am duly sensible of your continued zeal and perseverance in collecting. I am afraid, however, that you have been somewhat disappointed as to Wailuku as a locality. In a former letter you seem to think it would turn out better than Haleakala, and that does not seem to have been the case—which is a pity, but can't be helped, for I am sure not only that you have been doing your best, but that no one could do more. If the things are not there you cant make them! The D^r seems greatly pleased with your entomological feats.

With regard to your future movements, I can't write any positive instructions. I quite see & appreciate your point about the <u>Hala</u>[175] blossoming in Sept. & that being the time to secure the Lanai <u>Hemignathus</u> but I cannot take upon myself to alter the decisions of the Committee, so as to empower you to stay longer—yet I very much wish you could—& I will see what can be done in that direction. The Gov^t Grant Committee of the R. S. yesterday agreed to our application for another £100, but in asking for it we had chiefly in view the working out of your collections after your return. Let me, or D^r. Sharp, know what money you have, & what you will want before you come away, & please to do this as soon as possible, that there may be no inconvenience to you or anyone else in the matter. I see in one of your letters to him you say you think nothing I sent you has been lost except 'The Ibis' paper. Of this I am glad because I am sure I must have got another copy or two of it—but really you never before acknowledged, in any letter that I have seen, the two packets of 'Nature' sent to you 2 years ago + more. I have written to Wilson asking him to send at least one copy of the <u>Drepanis</u> plate to your Father, & now to return to your letter to me—

As to your doings in Hawaii, "luck" assisted by such experience as you have now must naturally be of great importance. It is getting on for two years since I heard anything of that M^r. Vrydenburgh {= Vredenburg} of Waimea who said he thought

---

175   Hawaiian word for Pandanus.

he could procure both Ciridops & Chaetoptila—but it is obvious that he has not met with either, or he would have written to me. I gave you his address, but you have never mentioned whether you have been in communication with him. Neither of those birds ought to be affected by mongoose which, by the way, I now learn for the first time has been introduced into the island. Wilson only complained of cats—but I can well understand the mongoose being fatal to Pennula as also Rallus sandwichensis—a larger? species, of which there is no specimen in England. I still hope you will in the end secure the Lanai Hemignathus & trust you may have got a few more of the Maui one. I know well how hard it often is to get skins dry before packing them, & I have seen many arrive in a worse condition than your last Molokai consignment, but still I thought it as well to let you know that they were not in a good state. You may be sure that I am careful to unwind the paper [cover or cones] whenever it is needed. I know also the difficulty of shooting birds at a very short distance without damaging them—but the proportion of broken bills seemed rather out of the way in that lot. The question of generic distinction between the straight & curve billed species hitherto ascribed to Himatione is out for future consideration aided by your own observations. It is gratifying to learn that M^r. Palmer had not put in an appearance up to the time of your writing.

Now I have to report the safe arrival of the Lanai collection. The bird skins (48 in all) are in a far better condition, & no one could be reasonably dissatisfied with them. I observe that you did not inscribe the locality otherwise than "Lanai" on the labels, but I suppose that this will be shewn by your journal. They otherwise call for no further remark—except it be that the series of Himatione (both species) is a fine one.

26th Since I wrote the above I have had another talk with D^r. Sharp. You must please let us know as soon as possible whether you think the chance of procuring the Lanai Hemignathus in Septr. is reasonably good. I suppose you have given up all hope of either of the Oahu species? But remember that Palmer's man got a Loxops on that island – only a single specimen! I have just heard from Wilson that he has ordered two copies of the plate of your Drepanis to be sent to your Father.

With very best wishes I am yours most truly

Alfred Newton

Cambridge, England
27 March 1894
Robert Cyril Layton Perkins

Dear Mr Perkins,

Your letter of Feby 28th from Honolulu is duly to hand. I am so sorry to hear of your attack of illness in Lanai: it must have been very trying for you in a tent like that in the winter. But I am glad to learn, at the same time, that you are feeling pretty well again.

I think your idea of giving much time for Maui and Kauai before you return is very good: according to the resolution of the Committee you are quite at liberty to dispense with looking after birds for a time, if you find you can be better occupied with insects and other things. So you need not fear any reproaches on the score of undue neglect of that branch and I feel you have done a good deal at it. By the way Rothschild has offered to buy our duplicate insects, but I think there will really be few duplicates after two good sets have been made.

I hope if an opportunity offers you will have a try at "Olinda" & "Grove Ranch" the two places where Dr Finsch[176] got his things. Several of these have not been correctly worked out: I think his Anisodactylus cuneatus from the former locality is a second species of Atrachycnemis. Mind you try & bring back a good supply of Orthopteran & Neuroptera. M^acLachlan who loves to pooh-pooh everything he has not the chief hand in will be sure to say you have not done well, if you give him a chance. I think as I mentioned in my last, that it would be quite worth while to get a boy or native to run after the dragon-flies for you. The Orthopteran – of which you have sent very few specimens – are excessively interesting.

When you have made your arrangements about coming back, you must let us know as we shall have to see about getting a grant to enable us to get the things properly worked out.

As soon as the Lanai things come to hand I will overhaul the insects as you wish to see that they will not be here till the end of May.

My idea for working out the things is to get the whole published in one large volume: I think we may manage that; if there are enough species to run to two volumes I think we may possibly even contrive that: it will be much better than separate papers.

My object in coming out was to see for myself the conditions of life in the island; but I have abandoned the idea for the present, and we shall have to look to you for a general account, that will enable us to make our theories not quite ridicu-

---

176 Finsch, Otto (1839–1917). German naturalist, specializing in ornithology. From 1864–1878, director of the Naturhistorisch-ethnologisches Museums in Bremen. With support from the Humboldt Museum in Berlin, traveled throughout the Pacific (including Hawai'i) from 1879–1882 while curator at the Natuurhistorisch Museum in Leiden.

lous. Such observations as those you make about the things being on the leeward side of the islands are very valuable. I hope you will jot down plenty of them.

This being Easter Prof. Newton is away from Cambridge, but I shall send your letter for him to read. I have heard nothing about a second batch of your diary for me to take care, as you suggested in a former letter.

With best wishes, you will have a successful time this next six months, and not overtax your strength, I am

Yours very truly
D. Sharp.

Cambridge, England
14 April 1894
Robert Cyril Layton Perkins

Dear Mr Perkins,

Your letter of March 8th 1894, from Wailuku is to hand & I write to express my satisfaction at your being in good health & spirits. I have heard nothing of the Lanai things yet, indeed I am not sure when they were sent off so I do not know where to expect them – but whenever they come to hand I will take the precaution you suggest, of opening and carbolising all the tubes & little boxes.

I have just been shewing your fine lot of Molokai shells to Mr Cooke[177] our best Malacologist at Cambridge, & who may possibly be the man who will work them out. He says that from the point of view of making out what are really species it is necessary to have some specimens with the animals in them collected into spirit. He also says that the littoral shells will be of considerable importance. I expect you have had but little opportunity with your multifarious occupations, in looking after these, but perhaps you may get the chance on the lower region of Maui or elsewhere. D^r. Blanford[178] – a good malacologist & member of the Committee makes the same remark about the shells in spirit – a few in spirit of each kind is very desirable.

I expect the discrepancy between yourself & M^r. Blackburn as to the Lepidoptera on the isthmus part of Maui is largely due to your collecting them at a different season; at any rate I have formed the opinion from your letters that the Leps. are largely dependent on season. I should think Blackburn's Maui isthmus collections were made chiefly in October, from what he says.

---

[177] Cooke, [Reverend] Alfred Hands (1854–1954). Malacologist. Zoologist at the Zoological Museum at Cambridge from 1880–1890. In fact, it was Ernest Ruthven Sykes (1867–1954) who eventually worked up the shells Perkins collected and not A.H. Cooke (no relation to famous Hawaiian malacologist, Charles Montague Cooke or his son of the same name).

[178] Blanford, William Thomas (1832–1905). British zoologist, paleontologist, and geologist. Served for 30 years on the Geological Survey of India, but also had a strong interest in land shells. Retired to England in 1882. A member of the Sandwich Islands Committee from 1890–1905.

I have been thinking over sending you some shot; but as it appears to take quite 3 months – usually more – for a parcel to go by any other way than the mail, it is clearly not worth while, as we could not expect it to reach you before the middle or end of July. It will be quicker & cheaper if you really want it – which now that you are coming away in the autumn seems rather doubtful – for you to write to Prof. C.V. Riley, Division of Entomology Department of Agriculture, Washington, and ask him to send you a small quantity. No doubt he can do it without any difficulty and I am sure he would be very pleased indeed to do so.

I do trust you will take a little care of yourself while in Maui. I thought you said you were going to have a man with you in one of your previous letters, but hear nothing of it in this last one. I do not think it advisable to do much camping out by yourself at an elevation in such lonely places, there is always the risk of an accident that might lame you or something of that sort, & I think you should make arrangements to be within reach of assistance if you require it. With very kind regards,

Yours very truly
D. Sharp.

Kaua'i
15 May–16 June 1894

Perkins returned from his Maui trip to Honolulu on the S.S. *Kinau* on 12 May. While in Honolulu, he quickly packed up his Maui collections for shipment to England, then made arrangements for his next trip, only a few days after his return from the Maui trip.

Perkins embarked on this overnight trip from Honolulu to Kaua'i on 15 May in company with George Munro aboard the Inter-Island Steam Navigation Company's *Ke-au-hou* and arrived at the docks at 'Ele'ele on 16 May. Perkins stayed at the Munro home in Makaweli soon after his arrival. He briefly summarized his Kaua'i trip in correspondence to Zimmerman:

> "On my return to Honolulu I shipped this collection & in May & June was collecting on Kauai, where I stayed at Makaweli with Mr G.C. Munro. After some preliminary collecting in the mountains there by the kindness of Mr Francis Gay I went up to his mountain house on the plateau above Waimea, where nearly all the Kauai birds were known to occur. The insect collecting was very good & interesting, the more so as Blackburn had done very little collecting on this island &, as on Lanai, had found none of the important family Carabidae, nor was it known whether the native Longicorns occurred there. After leaving the plateau I stayed for some time in the Hanapepe valley not far below the falls & collected on the land between this & the Olokele gulch. Birds were numerous on the ridges in Hanapepe, the long-beaked Akialoa being common, but some of the species of the plateau were absent or few, & so far as I remember did no shooting here." (*R.C.L. Perkins letter to E.C. Zimmerman, 14 February 1944, BPBM Entomology Archives*).

Munro wrote little of Perkins in his diaries but apparently found Perkins's habit of walking everywhere (rather than taking a horse or carriage) noteworthy enough to have made it as an entry:

> "Took Perkins up to Kaholuamano. He walked the whole way up to the new small establishment of the cabins, he has been in the habit of doing so all over the islands." (*Munro diary entry 1894, BPBM Archives, MS SC Munro Box 13.2*).

Perkins's transcribed copies of his journals for this particular trip vary slightly in substance. He transcribed this diary more than once. One holograph version (with associated typescript, both in BPBM Archives) gives details as they were written in his original notes (the version given here). Another typescript held in the BPBM Archives was written for G.C. Munro, who was an ornithologist, rather than writing for entomologists or general naturalists as it only gives details concerning bird catches and observations, while parenthetically abbreviating the entomological observations. For example, compare the "original" entry for May 20 (see p. 225 below) with the following abbreviated version written for ornithologists:

> "Went back in forest for some miles with Munro. Shot 1 male H. hanapepe which was full of small lava fragments and no food. (Various insects enumerated). This is a difficult country in which to find the way about, i.e. to go back home from a long distance."

In places where the abbreviated version has more detailed or additional information than in the original, I have distinguished those words from those the full version by placing them in double square brackets [[ ]].

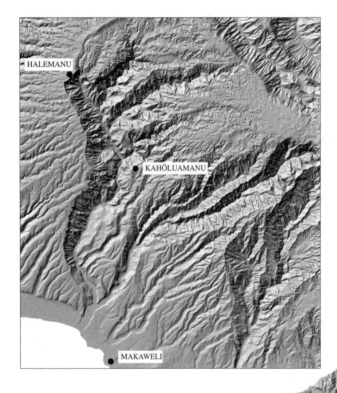

Map of Kaua'i with detail showing Perkins's collecting areas.

JOURNALS AND REMEMBRANCES

May 15
Left for Kauai. A very calm night.

May 16
Got off at Eleele & walked on to Makaweli, staying with Munro.

May 17
I walked up the mountains for a long way [[about 6 miles]]. It was very hot for the first part, where I saw only some Odyneri. Unfortunately I did not get beyond the range of Pheidole before the rain came down heavily. I collected a new Rhyncogonus, Oodemas & a few other things. Amongst the birds I saw for the first time the Kauai Oo & the long-billed Hemignathus, the finest species of the genus.

May 18
Walked to Waimea to get food for the mountains. I collected ♂ and ♀ of Prosopis. The commonest & largest of the Hawaiian Odynerus, O. nigripenne, is here replaced by a closely allied yellow-banded species. The other is on all the islands except this. A red-spotted species with peculiar iridescence of wings is very common.

May 19
Went up to the mountain house[179] with Munro & a native who packed up the food &ᶜ &ᶜ. I carried my insect-collecting apparatus. As Munro has only to-day & to–morrow at his disposal, we started out at once [[collecting]] on arrival up. Got several spp. Carabidae. A ribbed Metromenoid form looks like a new genus. Also a species with rugosely punctured prothorax. Shot [[Chlorodrepanis]] Amakihi & Oreomyza. The forest is mostly Ohia. There is a lot of Straussia & Elaeocarpus &ᶜ the undergrowth largely ferns and open. Collected 2 living & two dead Apterocyclus & an ovate Longicorn on a dead log. [I have no idea what this last refers to]. Also Brontolaemus.

May 20
Went a long way back [[in forest for some miles]] with Munro. Shot one male H. hanapepe in full plumage. The song is exactly the same as that of the Maui species. Its stomach was full of small grit [[lava fragments]] (pieces not more than 2–3 mm long) & no food. Collected Carabids as yesterday, also two minute species (Bembidium?) & a single specimen like the big-headed ones of Molokai & Maui [i.e. Disenochus]. Also 2 or 3 species of Oodemas. This country looks as if it would de difficult to find the way about or rather to get back home from a distance.

---

[179] This refers to the house known as Kaholuamano, located on the east side of Waimea Canyon at about 3500 ft elevation. At the time, this was the mountain house of the Sinclair family of Kaua'i. Scott Wilson gives a fair description of the territory surrounding the house: "... the cottage is some five hours' ride from any other habitation, and is completely surrounded by forest on three sides — the fourth having a fine outlook onto the sea, across a stupendous and thickly wooded ravine, which separates it from the next plateau—one could not imagine a better camping-ground." (Wilson, S.B. & Evans, A.H., 1892, *Aves Hawaiiensis*, p. [113]).

Valdemar Knudsen's mountain cabin Halemanu near Koke'e on Kaua'i (ca. 4,000 ft.) in the 1890s.

May 21

Went the same way as yesterday alone. Collected a Brachypeplus n. sp., Proterhinus, several species, Cis, Oodemas & Carabidae. Hemiptera are scarce here now. The Oo is not a great honey-sucker here, but eats caterpillars & other insects largely. I saw it catch an insect on the wing. They are mostly in pairs now & probably have young.

May 22

Went further up than I had been with Munro on the 20th. Collected a few beetles Cis, Proterhinus & a short roundish Brachypeplus (new) but was a little disappointed. Carabidae in some numbers, including one of the stouter black species [Disenochus] from a tangled mass of vegetation. A beautiful day, but birds quite scarce. I shot a Hemignathus [[Akialoa]] — not in good plumage. It was full of larvae & fragments of Brachypeplus.

May 23

Mr Gay[180] kindly sent up a man with my mail — letters from Sharp, Newton & Hickson — also a parcel containing cork tablets & 400 more silver pins. Found Munro's Cossonid [Nesotocus] here; no doubt, on the same tree as he did on Hawaii, viz. Cheirodendron, which in wet woods often starts well up some other tree & sends down roots to the ground. Microlepidoptera are numerous here & I made a good bag with some Tortrices. Collected one Rhyncogonus. [[Sat up nearly all night collecting moths.]]

---

[180]　Gay, Francis (1852–1928). Francis Gay was a businessman and in 1880, co-founded Gay and Robinson, a company with sugar and ranching interests on Kaua'i and Ni'ihau. Gay was born in New Zealand, the son of Jean Sinclair and Thomas Gay. The family arrived in Hawai'i in 1863 and settled on Kaua'i and Ni'ihau.

May 24

Shot a few common birds. Picked up odd specimens of Carabids & Brachypeplus from the very fine tree Lobeliads here. Collected a number of Microlepidoptera & a large yellow cricket [Prognathogryllus alatus]. Two Carabids came to the light in the house.

May 25

Went up as before with gun, but I heard no sound of the Nukupu. Collected Munro's Cossonid with Oodemas & Brachypeplus [Gonioryctus kauaiensis]. Coming back I shot a fine male Hemignathus procerus, but it hitched high up an unclimbable tree & I had to leave it, also Oreomyza, Loxops, Phaeornis & Acrulocercus. On some boggy or peat-like soil I found a small new Carabid with somewhat parallel-sided elytra, unlike any I have seen previously [Gnatholymnaeum blackburni]. A minute Oligota on Olapa.

May 26

Shot a few common birds & returned at 1 p.m. expecting Munro for the week end. He did not arrive till evening, so I collected a good many beetles, & while I caught Lepidoptera in the evening he skinned my birds for me.

May 27

I went across the stream & up the ridge, but saw no birds of note. Collected the large Staph [Leurocorynus] & a smaller species of somewhat similar form under bark [Xanthocorynus deceptor]. Also took Oodemas, Carabidae, Munro's Cossonid & Microlepidoptera (in numbers); 1 female Rhyncogonus.

May 28

Went across stream & up ridge with Munro. Shot 1 ♀ Hemignathus, birds being scarce. Collected some beetles Carabids, one Apterocyclus & Parandra. I picked up the Hemignathus I shot on the 25th. It had fallen from the tree & was full of maggots, but I made a fair skin of it. Collected many moths — some at light the night being calm & very dark.

May 29

Went across gulches to numerous Koa trees to look for Clytarlus & birds. No bird of any importance seen or heard. A few Carabidae & 1 ♂ Clytarlus only. The trees showed little or no trace of their borings. Mr Francis Gay & a Mr Bull came up in the evening to stay overnight. Windy night & few moths about. I saw the Oo sucking at the flowers of the tall palm-like Lobeliads. On the margin of a stream in a deep gulch I found 3 or 4 of a Carabid new to me under stones [Bembidium pacificum].

May 30

I started out early & Munro & Mr Gay left me. I thought birds might show up more earlier in the morning but it certainly was not so. No doubt I have struck a slightly off season in this locality & the birds are just now elsewhere. Collected a few Carabidae & returned at 2 p.m. & rested for a couple of hours, intending to go out at night with a light. At 4 I did some more collecting, getting a few Oodemas,

Proterhinus &ᶜ. The night was not very favorable, as there was a rather strong wind. Still I collected a fair number of specimens & only gave up at daybreak.[181]

May 31
Heard from Bro. Matthias & wrote to Sharp & Newton. Was late this morning & then killed & pinned yesterdays insects. After midday went out with gun but did not shoot anything & then went down to probably about 3000 ft. to collect Anobiids & did fairly well, 2 or 3 spp. of Xyletobius & a good number of specimens. Also Proterhinus, Cis &ᶜ & one of Munro's Cossonid down here. Above a few Lepidoptera, & there is a fine elongate Oodemas with the elytra very coarsely sculptured.

June 1
Killed & pinned up Lepidoptera & cleaned up things generally in the morning. Afternoon: went out with net & collected 2 ♂ of a Prosopis allied to facialis, but with much short, wider face. Also, a red-bodied ♀ (probably parasitic), 2 or 3 species of Agrions & Lepidoptera in considerable number.

June 2
Went upwards with gun & actually saw a Nukupu but could not get at it. Shot one Hemignathus in indifferent plumage. On black, peat-like soil got a couple of small Carabids with less rounded elytra & longer antennae than is usual in Cyclothorax [Gnatholymnaeum blackburni]. Collected some (not large) Tortrices & many Tineids &ᶜ.

June 3
Went downwards & did not take a gun, so I saw a very fine ♂ Hemignathus! Collected 4 Plagithmysus* & 3 little Clytarli from Acacia koa. A single Eopenthes, some nice Lepidoptera, 2 specimens of an Emesiid & a few spiders. A very small Oodemas occurs in the dead stems of the climbing Smilax [O. apionoides]. I notice that up here in the shade the temp. varies from 58°–70° F.

{Perkins's 1936 footnote}:
*[This seems to be the first use in diary of this name, probably given me by Sharp (in litt.).]

June 4
Went out for birds, but saw nothing rare. Shot some of the common Kauai species. Collected a few Carabidae. I saw a large beetle on the wing & suspect it was Clytarlus [Plagithmysus] so hunted over all the neighbouring trees & at last found a specimen still in the burrow. Subsequently got 2 more on the same tree (Ohia-ha). Its colour is like that of my unique Oahu species, but it is larger [The Oahu sp. was P. solitarius, afterwards found in plenty on Ohia-ha & Ohia lehua]. Collected many Lepidoptera.

---

[181] Munro in his diary stated further: "{Perkins} is getting a fine collection of moths of the small family, his greatest hauls are made at night by putting a lamp in the window to attract them. He works at them until the small hours." (*Munro diary entry, 30 May 1894, BPBM Archives, MS SC Munro Box 13.2*).

June 5
Pinned up the small Leps. & put the larger in papers. Then went down for Clytarli.
Took a number of small ones off Koa — apparently 3 species. Came up to look for
the red-bodied Prosopis, but I only got 1♂ & 1♀. Then I went out with gun & shot
2 Chasiempis & 1 ♂ H. parva. Birds are quite scarce.

June 6
Crossed gulches to left (looking mauka) & went upwards with gun [[to edge of big
gulch]]. I saw one Hemignathus on the wing & shot some commoner Kauai birds.
I dont know what species the Brit. Mus. may want. Got 5 or 6 of the big Staph.,
Brachypeplus, Anotheorus &ᶜ. I came back about 3 p.m. to pack everything up, as
I am intending to carry them down to Munros to-morrow.

June 7
Got down to Munro's at 2 p.m., red all over from the clouds of red dust, stirred up
by the strong wind on the last part of the walk.[182]

June 8
Got some Aculeates & at light one male Embiid. The foreign Megachile here [M.
schauinslandi] is brighter or in better condition than those I took on other islands.
I saw no males.

June 9
Went to Waimea to get some things [[tinned food]] from the store & picked up
Aculeates [[bees & wasps]] going & coming back.

June 10
[Sunday, no entry. I think I drove with the Gays to church in the morning & spent
the day with them afterwards. Francis Gay had much information about plants &
birds & all other Hawaiian matters & I learnt much from him in the small time we
were together. He gave me much help, in the use of his mountain house & men.]

June 11
Munro took me up to a house in Hanapepe Valley for a few day's stay. It was a hot
& tiring walk up & quite a few miles. In the afternoon I went up a dividing ridge
of the valley & shot a nice male Hemignathus & collected some other things.

June 12–15
The few days spent up here were for the purpose of getting a few more Clytarli if
possible & of the gray Otiorhynchid, of which my single specimen had got lost or
mislaid. I only got 9 specimens of Clytarlus [= Plagithmysus + Clytarlus of Sharp]
but 4 species, all from Koa, & the species the same as above Waimea, but a useful
addition. I took one Aegosoma & one dead Apterocyclus. I collected several of the
Rhyncogonus [R. vittatus] from Koa & Straussia at about 3000 ft. The yellow,
immigrant dragonfly [P. flavescens] was swarming & the Chinaman's native wife
caught a number with my net round the house, where also Pison & the largest

---

182   Munro stated further in his diary: "Went down to pond with P. and saw an old stilt & two young, the latter
were not really grown but would fly well." (*Munro diary entry, 7 June 1894, BPBM Archives, MS SC Munro Box
13.2*).

Odynerus occurred, the latter also high up the mountains with the white-spotted Crabro. I also collected some Cis, Proterhinus &^{c}. I also shot some nice Hemignathus male female & young of both sexes. Three tied together & put in alcohol are from the same nest, the one young & male & female parent. The female Oo makes a peculiar squeaking noise when disturbed. This species & the Elepaio keep in pairs after breeding. I shot two male white-spotted Elepaio paired with rufous females. Many birds are very bare of feathers, being in the moulting stage. Song of the Hemignathus is a pleasing trill, its comparatively loud call or alarm note is easily recognised. The Oo feeds a good deal on larvae found under the bark of trees, which it rattles with its beak, when hunting for these. The Hemignathus eats the same, & both are fond of the small native cockroach & spiders. At times the Akialoa probes into holes in the trunk of the trees with its long beak, even to the base of this, but generally it seeks for food beneath the loose bark.

June 15
Took my things down to Makaweli.

June 16
Left for Honolulu & arrived at 4 a.m. after a very smooth passage.

SELECTED CORRESPONDENCE

Cambridge, England
25 May 1894
Robert Cyril Layton Perkins

Dear M^r. Perkins,

Your letters of April 14th and 21st came to hand on the 20th inst. and on same day I received the case of Lanai specimens of whose despatch from Honolulu you advised me about three months ago. The specimens are all right; in quite as good condition as when you despatched them; they are in fact the best lot as to condition we have received I think – certainly better than the Molokai lot – I have opened several of the sawdust tubes & boxes & find them as clean as possible not a trace of mould; neither will there be any as your careful carbolising has evidently killed any germs that might have been present. The pinned things are just as fresh as when you put them in.

Your news from Maui is very good indeed & I must congratulate you heartily on having accomplished so much in so short a time, even if you have not got Artachycnemis it may still turn up, and I anticipate its being almost unobtainable. your account of 1.500 Carabids strikes me with astonishment as it is not so very long since you could not find Carabidae at all!! I am very sorry that I cannot send you the diagnoses of Mauia & Atrachycnemis as our house is at present being papered & painted and for a few days I cannot get at my books. I should not be surprised if you have found Mauia as I believe it has little resemblance to the true Blackburnia. Blackburn did the Carabidae himself out in the islands a few at a time so that his first attempts were necessarily not very successful.

I have sent a copy of your Molokai journal to your father, and he will also receive a copy of the Drepanis picture from Scott-Wilson.

With regard to the date of your return – If you refer to my letter of the end of January last, you will find the exact words of the Committee's resolution. If you think it desirable to stop a little longer in order to get something specially desirable please let us know, and we will send you instructions on the point: but you must accompany the intimation with a statement as to funds: So that we may be able to take that into consideration in deciding. Write to the treasurer & give him formal intimation of what funds you require to bring you back, in conformity with the decision of the Committee; and at the same time say to him, if I am desired permitted to stay so many weeks longer I shall require x in addition to the sum I have mentioned.

Please let him know plenty of time beforehand, that is in fact <u>at once</u>: this letter will not get to you till the end of June, your letter in reply will not reach home till end of July, & funds or answer sent in reply cannot reach you <u>till the end of August</u>. So please attend to this at once in order to prevent any muddle. At the same time you must instruct him what is the quickest & best way for the remission of money, as it wont do to have money arriving for you after you have left the islands, or for you to be delayed in so doing because you have to wait for funds.

We cannot tell here how that may be, and must leave it entirely to you to arrange details as regards the disposal of the remainder of your time in the islands, you will recollect that we leave it entirely to you to do as you think will be most profitable, we shall none of us be discontented if you think you can do on the whole best by confining yourself to one or two things. It seems pretty clear that some one will have to go again to complete Hawaii, which cannot at present be considered above a quarter done; and which in fact requires about two years to itself.

As regards the dragon-flies you certainly have not got all, there being two <u>gigantic</u> species known that you have not found; one of the two N. America, the other the biggest endemic, & known I believe by only a single or possibly two – individuals. With very kind regards,

Yours very truly
D. Sharp.

Honolulu
17 June–24 June 1894

During this short period back in Honolulu, Perkins packed up his collections, wrote letters to colleagues, and arranged for his upcoming trip to Lāna'i. This was to be his second trip to Lāna'i and he was hoping to capture the rare and elusive *Hemignathus lanaiensis* but, as is apparent from his letter to Bishop, his mind was also on his impending return home to England after being away from his family and friends for over two years.

SELECTED CORRESPONDENCE

Honolulu, Oahu, Hawaiian Islands
23 June 1894
Charles Reed Bishop

Dear Mr Bishop,

I thought it as well to inform you that I leave the Islands for home on Septr 1st. I fear I shall not see you before I go unless you happen to be coming back to Honolulu, as I am going by the Canadian Pacific route which is in many ways the best for me. I am probably going to superintend the mounting &^c of the collections when I get home & I anticipate it will be fully a year or probably a year & a half before the insects can be described & the book published. I got a glimpse at Rothschild's book at your museum the other day; as much I see he has made some very bad blunders & I dont think the illustrations are equal to Wilson's, though larger. The taxidermist at the {Bishop} Museum has made a wonderful job of some of the birds considering their age and the very different state of their preservation.

I hope the new insects obtained may amount up to 1000 species or thereabouts. It appears that the Islands are about half done now & some one should come out again for another 2 1/2 years. I believe an effort will be made to send someone when these things are completely worked out but I have doubts whether they will be enabled to raise further funds, & for myself I dont know that I should care to spend another long period on a labour of love – or rather I couldn't well afford to do so. I am off on Monday to Lanai, there is an all but extinct bird there I have not got & I much want it. After that I shall take a hurried trip to Hawaii and Maui before leaving.

Yours very truly,
R.C.L. Perkins

Lāna'i
25 June–13 July 1894

Perkins decided to return to Lāna'i to once again try for the rare *Hemignathus lanaiensis* (the Lāna'i Akialoa), possibly at the urging of Munro and other birders he met on his recent trip to Kaua'i. However, after only three weeks on Lāna'i he returned empty-handed with regard to the *Hemignathus*, but made fairly significant strides in his collections of Lāna'i insects.

It is not known what happened the first two weeks he was on the island as his journal entries do not start until 4 July and then are sporadic and only written down if he felt there was something significant to discuss with regards to his collecting efforts.

A brief notice in the *Ibis* for 1894 gives a distilled version of the problems Perkins faced while collecting on that small island, much of which had been cleared and converted to ranching years before.

> "Mr. Perkins is at present working in the island of Lanai, the fauna of which, already greatly depauperate, is at present in process of rapid extermination, owing to an abundance of goats" (1894, *Ibis* (6) 23: 328).

The damage to vegetation by goats is further corroborated by Perkins in a letter to Zimmerman in 1944:

> " ... when I returned in July, the bushes were in very bad condition, the bark having been gnawed off all around the main stems, probably by goats, which were in vast numbers." *(R.C.L. Perkins letter to E.C. Zimmerman, 14 February 1944, BPBM Entomology Archives).*

JOURNALS AND REMEMBRANCES

[Near the end of June I was again in Lanai, the Hemignathus being my chief object — which was not attained. I did not keep a daily account in my diary, but only a brief general account of my collecting which was done from two camps — one my original station near Koele, the other on the top of the ridge near the highest point in the mountains {Lanaihale}.]

July 4

I intend to leave for the top of the mountains tomorrow after a week's vain search for the Hemignathus in the neighbourhood of the place where I saw one about 6 months ago. I begin to think it may have been the sole survivor of the brood found by Rothschild's collector.[183] It is curious that it was all alone, although in full male plumage, at a time when nearly all the birds were in pairs. Now birds are in very poor plumage — at least the old ones — with the tail feathers wanting or young ones sprouting. I shot a few young of Amakihi and Oreomyza, which are abundant and very tame and also one spotted young of Kamau (Phaeornis). The Ou — very abundant — was feeding on the base of the Ohia blooms; at first I thought on nectar, but on killing and dissecting one so feeding I found it was not so. The Clermontia has flowered in my absence and has now an abundance of unripe fruit. I find almost no Lepidoptera which is extraordinary, but I have collected a good many beetles, a number of Proterhini which I have carded in excellent condition. I also got some rather good Brachypepli of large size, the best in decaying lobelia wood together with the big black Staph., Glyptoma and an Oodemas. There are also one or two other Staphs from the same tree. Also I collected a few Anobiids, a solitary Anotheorus, 2 spp. Acalles, 4 Carabidae (one a Cyclothorax), a Brontolaemus, a few small Oodemas, Mimesa ♀ and some Hemiptera.

One day I went to the coast at Manele and caught aculeates; the foreign Polistes stylopised[184] there.

In the mountains I also collected a single ♂ green Locustid [Banza] and the small brown gryllids, 2 spp. of large Prosopis, as previously and some Agrions &c. A solitary 'pug' moth [Eucymatoge] was the only moth I took, at least of the larger Lepidoptera.

July 13

On July 5th I moved camp to Halepaakai, it had taken up for me on a mule by Macfarlane, as far as the animal could go, about 6 or 8 gallons of water, there being no standing water on the top except in some pig wallows. I took only the fly of my tent and as little food and apparatus as I could do with. I found the clump of Clermontia bushes, on which I strongly suspected the Hemignathus had been got, had been gnawed by goats since my last visit and were dead or dying. Here too except for a few species of Geometers well-known to me Lepidoptera were

---

[183]   Henry C. Palmer.

[184]   Stylopised = being parasitized by members of the order Strepsiptera. Strepsipterans (including the genus *Stylops*) are parasitic insects. They are found internally in the abdomens of wasps and bees.

almost absent. I did better with beetles, as I got some Elateridae as I had expected, a single Clytarlus [Plagithmysus lanaiensis] on a Straussia, surrounded by Ohia a series of Cyclothorax, Rhyncogonus and some Anobiids. I was unable to find any of the two or three species of Clytarlus on other trees, which I had previously noticed, though on this occasion also I noticed the trees attacked, in places quite out of the way of the foreign Longicorns. The only birds I took were young Phaeornis and young Oreomyza.

July 14
Arrived in Honolulu.

SELECTED CORRESPONDENCE

Magdalene College
Cambridge, England
17 July 1894
Robert Cyril Layton Perkins

My dear Mr Perkins,

When I last wrote to you (which I think was the 24th May in reply to your letter of 21st April) I mentioned that I was starting towards the end of June for a cruise on the Scotch Coast, which might last some 3 weeks. You will therefore have been prepared for some little delay in my answer to your letter of the 31st May—which did not come into my hands till the 13th of this month, and today is the first opportunity I have of writing to you since I got it—for it so happened that you enclosed it in the envelope addressed to Dr. Sharp, & sent me the one you had intended for him. However this does not seem to have signified very much. We are glad to hear that you are flourishing and anxiously expect news in a few days as to the amount of money you will want.

I may take this opportunity of saying that if you desire to prolong your stay in the islands for a few weeks—in order to return to get that Hemignathus when the proper flower is in bloom, or for any other similar & sufficient purpose—Dr. Sharp, Hickson & myself, who constitute the Executive Committee, are not likely to raise any objection—& indeed I myself, having perfect faith in your discretion, should counsel you to do so should you think fit, but of course I should expect you to furnish us with information that will justify us in countenancing such a proceeding to the eyes of the rest of the Joint Committee—

I have as usual with your letters read this last with much interest, but there is not a great deal for me to say about it.

I am sorry you expect to do so badly in birds on Kauai—but I was never very anxious that you should go there, for Knudson & Wilson must have pretty well done what there was in that line there—I am in no hurry to declare myself one way or another in regard to the genera of Drepanids—whether the straight billed <u>Himatione</u> should be put under a different name, is a question that can be well deferred till you come home & guide Gadow or some other anatomist (yourself, perhaps) with your notes. I am confident it will all come out at last when the proper materials are to the fore but it is a nuisance that so much of them are practically inaccessible to us. I am told that D[r] R. B. Sharpe[185] makes <u>Acrulocercus</u> a Drepanid, & that rather amuses me. That there should be two species of <u>Rhodacanthis</u> frequenting the same haunts always seemed to me doubtful, & I am glad that from what you now say my doubt seems well founded. I do hope you may get <u>Viridonia</u> which I have never seen. I fear we must abandon hope of the other Hawaiian rarities—<u>Ciridops</u>, <u>Chaetoptila</u>, & <u>D</u>. <u>pacifica</u> as well as the Rails—

I expect to be away from Cambridge during most of Sept[r] but am not going far, & shall be sure of returning about the very beginning of October, when you will find me here. I also go to Oxford next month for the Brit. Ass[n] meeting. I enclose a draught of our Report, which you may like to read. It has not yet been adopted by the Committee, & perhaps some verbal changes may be made, but I expect it will not be much altered, and with my best wishes

I remain
Yours very truly
Alfred Newton

I am glad you are satisfied that there is only one <u>Chasiempis</u> in Kauai. It would have been absurd for there to be a second.

Honolulu, Oahu, Hawaiian Islands
18 July 1894
Charles Reed Bishop

Dear M[r] Bishop,

I have received your letter of July 4th & I thought I had better write to you as I hear M[r] Damon is away. I have not seen Wilson's 5th part yet & I suppose it will be some time before the 6th is published. I presume he means to make it up from the 6 birds he failed to get on Maui, the beautiful Kona finch &c. I am thinking of publishing a paper on the habits of some of the birds — neither Palmer's nor Wilson's notes seem to have amounted to much — but as this would not be more than a small pamphlet I may offer to do this for Wilson's 6th part if he likes. I have no doubt you will receive the copy of his book promised you sooner or later.

---

[185] Sharpe, Richard Bowdler (1847–1909). Sharpe was the British precocious zoologist who would become librarian to the Zoological Society at age 20 and Senior Assistant in zoology at the British Museum (Natural History) five years later. He eventually became Assistant Keeper after twenty-three years of employment there. He specialized in ornithology and helped author the *Birds of Europe* and wrote the twenty-seven-volumed *Catalogue of the Birds in the British Museum.*

You have no Oahuan Hemignathus in the Museum nor did Palmer or myself find either of them, though I believe with unlimited time one could still get the long billed species. Only one specimen is known it was got about 40-50 years ago by Deppe & is now in the Vienna museum. They have very old specimens of the short-billed one at Cambridge & elsewhere. I have never had any loss of specimens sent the way your Chaetoptila was so I daresay it has got there all right. I am a little alarmed for a very valuable case of about 3 or 4000 specimens that are now in the States.

As to the birds I collect, 2 sets of each species must be left at any rate in England as the whole collection I believe will be kept at Cambridge, but the B. Museum asked for a complete set of the birds only & as 2/3 of my money is from Government funds their demand must be complied with as it is the Government museum.

With regard to the insects – of some considerable number, there were plenty of specimens more than I ever could have hoped after M[r] Blackburn who was here 6 years & a great specialist at the things stated "One remarkable factor in Hawaiian entomology is the extreme rarity of specimens in comparison with the number of species the very common insects being very few indeed, & the rather common ones almost none at all." I should certainly advise the authorities here to make some arrangements with my own people of a definite nature in case of a renewal of this expedition – there is at least 2 1/2 years more work to be done. This would enable you to get practically every bird in the group, for a collector coming out for that period would be able (on my instructions if I didn't return myself) to easily procure extra specimens of those birds I got but a short series of, & the same with the insects. I reckon there are at least 4 or 5 birds yet to be discovered in the Islands & a considerable number of insects & shells.

With regard to the insects I may tell you that they are probably disappearing even quicker than the birds indeed the whole native insect fauna of the lower forests has entirely finished through an introduced ant. Just so far as that extends up you find anything native now & it is obviously still working upwards until the forest gets dried up from the incursion & destruction of cattle goats sheep &[c].

If I should return again myself, I should probably know all the insects obtained & could keep back specimens of everything obtained & of duplicate new species, then when the collection of that was over, could stay on for a bit & mount & name them for the {Bishop} Museum here, but should a stranger come he would of course have to send all specimens to England. I am convinced if you dont get those things from this expedition then the Museum will never get them, for it will not be worth anyone's while to send a man out here after the completion of this exploration (say after 2 1/2 yrs more work), & the native creatures are going to the well wholesale before introductions. By the way, Rothschild offered to buy up all the duplicate insects I send, but I didn't think they will sell any to him.

At the same time, should they be unable to make any arrangement as to expenses with those interested in your museum I think it not improbable that they may be forced to get him to join in the continuation of the expedition, because the amount of money shunted to scientific exploration is so utterly inadequate to the explorations that are being carried on. I am perfectly astonished, that with all the demands on them, the Royal Soc. should have been able to keep it up for so long (3 years, for they have been obliged to day of a same for the expenses entailed in working out & mounting specimens &^{c}). Rothschild is evidently very keen after Hawaiian things & I could probably arrange to come out & get him certain birds & all the insects with advantage to myself, but could not do it, after the utterly mean way he behaved on my coming out, in regard to the instructions given Palmer to get in my way as much as possible &^{c}. Had I known this at the time I would never have had anything to do with Palmer here. I feel a sort of satisfaction now in seeing some of the idiotic scientific mistakes that Mr R. has made in his book, which otherwise might have been deplored.

I am sorry I shall have no opportunity to talk with you again, but I will see some of the trustees before I leave the Islands as I must have some time to fix up for leaving. To morrow I go to Hawaii & Maui on a last trip so thanking you for your good wishes I remain

Yours very truly
R.C.L. Perkins

Hawai'i Island
20 July–22 August 1894

This was the last collecting trip for Perkins before his return to England to help with unpacking and sorting of the things he had collected the first few years in the Hawaiian Islands. He decided to try the windward side of Hawai'i island, having had such great success on the leeward (Kona) side two years before. He followed in the footsteps of Scott Wilson and decided to base his exploits at Volcano House near the rim of the active volcano, Kīlauea. He boarded the *W.G. Hall* on 20 July in Honolulu and arrived (after numerous stops along the way) on 22 July at Punalu'u where he made his way to Kīlauea and the Volcano House hotel.

Perkins summarized his visit to the Big Island in correspondence to Zimmerman:

> "In August {= July} I paid a brief visit to several islands & spent a few days at Kilauea, the volcano being active. Insects were numerous here & it was evidently as easy collecting ground. For the first time I found the small bird, <u>Loxops</u>, in some numbers & on the last day of my stay. I started out before daylight & shot several specimens before I had to hurry back to the coach to the steamer. All the ordinary birds were seen, most of them very abundant, while <u>Rodacanthis</u> {= *Rhodacanthis*} was present in the Koa trees some miles from the Volcano House. This was the last trip I made before I left for the coast (Vancouver) where I did a little collecting & then left Montreal on a boat carrying sheep to England." *(R.C.L. Perkins letter to E.C. Zimmerman, 14 February 1944, BPBM Entomology Archives).*

JOURNALS AND REMEMBRANCES

July 20

Left for Hawaii on the W.G. Hall. The steamer was crowded and I could not get a mattress to lie on, nor even a pillow. The school-children were all returning to the various islands for their summer holidays and practically all of them were very sea sick, lying on mattresses on the deck, so that one could not walk about.

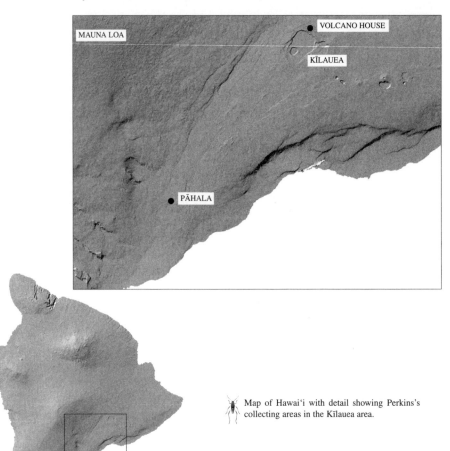

Map of Hawai'i with detail showing Perkins's collecting areas in the Kīlauea area.

July 22[186]

Landed at Punaluu at 5 a.m. Thence by rail to Pahala and by stage to Kilauea. The drive was too much for my fellow passengers — several of them — the rough road over rocky places causing them to bounce up and down like India-rubber balls. They stayed in bed the next day.

July 23

Went up the mountain,[187] but I only saw the following birds in a very long day's tramp. Iiwi, Apapane, Amakiki, <u>Oreomyza</u>, Akialoa, Olomao, Elepaio. I collected <u>Clytarlus</u> [<u>Plagithmysus</u>] from Koa and also <u>Eopenthes</u>. It was wet and very foggy in the afternoon.

---

[186]   Perkins signed in at the Punaluu Hotel on the Sunday the 22nd writing the following: "R.C.L. Perkins (Naturalist appointed by the Royal Soc. & British Association, England for the study of the land fauna of the Hawaiian group.). Enroute to Kilauea." (*Register of the Punaluu Hotel, Hawaii Volcanoes National Park, Library and Archives*). Curiously, he did not sign the register for the Volcano Hotel upon arriving, but penned a brief report of his activities in the Volcano Hotel guest book (see entry for 25 July 1894 below).

[187]   This no doubt refers to Mauna Loa along the road now called the Mauna Loa Strip Road.

July 24

Same route as yesterday. I got plenty of the Clytarlus and a number of Aculeates. Also a Metromenus from tree-fern,[188] a Cyclothorax, and from under Koa bark two Barypristus. I shot two ♀ and one young ♂ Loxops coccinea, which I wanted badly, but the latter was very badly shot in the head. The crater is very active, but the floor is low. There were about half a dozen fine fire-fountains playing. I went down with a small party, some tourists and a Miss Severance of Hilo, who was more interesting. Came back at 10 p.m. Skinned birds and packed up insects, then after two hours sleep, I started at 4 a.m. to the place where I had got the Loxops.

July 25[189]

I shot 1 male and 2 young Loxops, but I also killed 1 male and one female which I could not gather, having no time to search properly. I then rushed back to the Volcano House[190] and just caught the stage as it was leaving for Pahala. I sleep at Punaluu[191] to-night. {The next morning he caught the steamer to Kealakekua.}

July 26

Got off at Kealakekua and walked up from the landing calling on Mrs. Greenwell for permission to shoot. When was here in 1892, the Oo was abundant, breeding at 3000 ft; but I did not then particularly want it, as Cambridge Museum had Wilson's specimens. I know nothing about the British Museum. [i.e. what species of birds they wanted.]

July 28

Shot a single Oo male near Holokalele. The bird is no longer here, at any rate at this season. The general conditions are much as in 1892, but I notice that cattle have now made tracks on the Aa flow where the Oo was abundant and where I caught young ones. There were none of these tracks two years ago. [In several days I saw no other Oo.]

August 2

Went up to Pulehua; having started very early I was there at 9:30 a.m. Shot Nukupu, 1 male Loxops and 2 or 3 Oreomyza.

[No daily account kept after this {from 3–14 August}, as the fauna in this locality was already familiar to me.]

August 15

Left Kona. One cloudy and foggy day in the high forest I heard a number of the whistling 'finch' [Rhodacanthis but could get no sight of them. Their calls were very infrequent and insufficient for locating the birds. I saw the male Loxops feed-

---

188   Tree fern (*Cybotium* spp.).

189   See p. 34 for Perkins's entry in the Volcano House memoirs book for this date.

190   The Volcano House near the Kilauea caldera rim. This hotel is the oldest hostelry in the Hawaiian Islands, starting business in 1866 and served many visitors coming to see the active Kilauea volcano. The original Volcano hotel burned and was rebuilt by the time Perkins arrived in Hawai'i. The rebuilt hotel was restored in the 1970s and is currently the gallery for the Volcano Art Center in the Hawaii Volcanoes National Park.

191   This refers to Volcano House's proprietor, Peter Lee's, Punaluu Hotel, built solely for the purpose of housing the tourists who would be taking the Punalu'u route to and from the Kīlauea volcano.

ing a young one in the top of a tall Koa and the female was also there. I killed the male, but the others disappeared. It was in good plumage. The beak is yellow, like a dried pea, and more or legs darkened at the tip, brightest at the sides along the cutting edge, so that it differs greatly in this respect from the Maui and Kauai Loxops. One can tell the young and the female from either Oreomyza or the Amakiki even in the tallest trees by its longish forked tail. The bird is no doubt fairly common here, only a fraction of those seen being in the red adult ♂ plumage, and the others are easily overlooked. In winter I am told the Alala (Corvus) comes right down to the road at Kaawaloa. The Palila (Loxioides) is now almost totally absent, though at this season in 1892 it could be seen in numbers here every day and in all conditions of plumage. I have seen but two males on this occasion and I particularly wanted some. I shot one only. It was feeding on the Sophora beans in the usual manner, holding down the bean on a branch with its foot, while it worked at it with its beak. The Oreomyza has practically the same voice and habits as the Kauai species and somewhat different from those on the intermediate islands. I shot very few on account of their poor plumage, but enough for my purpose. It is a thoroughly typical Oreomyza in my opinion. Insects were not at all abundant and I could not find any Clytarli. A Metromenus [probably Colpocaccus] was numerous and I took a single specimen each of three species of Fornax, the smallest of these running very quickly on the leaf of an arborescent Lobeliad. I did not take a single Xyletobius, the wet weather being bad for these. Since I was here last, both the mongoose and the mynah bird have appeared and are becoming numerous. Coffee is being planted everywhere by Japs and kanakas as well as by whites.

[This note, so far as concerns birds, is of some interest when considered in conjunction with my brief experience during a visit in 1896 and that of Prof. H.W. Henshaw[192] some years later. In 1892 I sent to Prof. Newton some notes on the birds of Kona, describing the locality above Kaawaloa as an Ornithologist's paradise. These notes — unfortunately without my having proofs sent to me for correction — were published in 'The Ibis'.

In 1896 I again visited the locality having arranged to meet Scott Wilson, who was revisiting the islands for the purpose of collecting some eggs and nests of native birds. As he was delayed in Honolulu, I had time to look around for the places where birds were most numerous. At 4000 ft. they were generally scarce, the Koa trees at the time being stripped by swarms of caterpillars of Scotorythra and the fine bird Rhodacanthis, which Wilson wished to collect, had moved down 1000 ft. below its habitat of 1892. The month being March, many birds were nesting and on one occasion I came across a pair of Phaeornis at their nest-building. As I had arranged to leave for Maui, I directed Wilson to this nest, but unfortunately after my departure he was unable to find the place again. Birds were definitely less numerous than in 1894.

---

[192] Henshaw, Henry Wetherbee (1850–1930). Ethnologist and ornithologist who accompanied the Wheeler Expedition in the Rocky mountains in the 1870s collecting insects, birds, and made ethnological observations on Indian tribes. Best known as an ethnologist and photographer of native Americans, he came to Hawai'i because of health problems. From 1893 to 1903 he resided in Hilo and published the first comprehensive catalog of birds known from Hawai'i. In 1905 he joined the Bureau of Biological Survey in Washington, D.C. He kept up with his photographic skills and took photos of native Hawaiians and landscapes for postcards while living in Hawai'i.

Some years later (probably about 1902) I advised my friend Prof. H.W. Henshaw, a most clever collector and student of birds, subsequently Chief of the Biological Survey at Washington, to visit my Kona localities, as he was very anxious to collect the local birds <u>Chloridops</u> and <u>Rhodacanthis</u> and others. I think he failed to find any of these and he wrote to me that my bird paradise was the poorest place he had ever collected in during his stay of years in the islands.]

{In fact, Henshaw wrote elsewhere that he was concerned about more than just the reduction in numbers from the Kona area and was instrumental in helping legislation get passed to protect birds in the State}:

> "When I first reached the islands there were practically no laws affording any real measure of protection to Hawaiian birds. Subsequently I drew up a law which was introduced into the Legislature ... the same law with modifications was enacted, and at present {1920} the island birds appear to enjoy adequate protection so far as the law can afford it. They appear to stand in greater need of protection than the birds of mainland countries, possibly because, owing to their sedentary habits and the lack of competition during their many centuries of occupancy, they have become unable to cope with changed conditions, as the partial clearing of their native forests and the introduction of foreign species such as the mynah and others. Be the cause what it may, not a few of the island birds have become extinct within the memory of man, and others appear to be on their rapid way to the same sad fate. As bearing upon this point I may quote a letter of January 1, 1919, from Brother Matthias, referring more particularly to my old collecting grounds in the districts of Hilo and Puna, Hawaii. In these, where, during the decade from 1894 to 1904, I found certain species numerous, he states that of late years the island birds have greatly diminished in numbers for no obvious reasons, and he expresses the opinion that 'Hawaiian birds are doomed and fifty years hence most species will be extinct'" (Henshaw, H.W., 1920, *The Condor* 22: 96–97).

Selected Correspondence

Magdalene College
Cambridge, England
27 July 1894
Robert Cyril Layton Perkins

My dear M^r. Perkins,

I was much pleased last night to get your letter of 15 & 19 June, & I hope this may reach you before you depart from the Islands—but apparently it is the last I shall address to you there. I wrote to you 10 days ago, on my return from the North, in answer to yours of 31 May—the chief point of my letter being to say that if you had sufficient reason to delay your departure for a few days you were at liberty to do so, provided that you enabled Drs Sharp, Hickson & myself (who form the Executive of the Joint Committee) to justify ourselves for making the resolution 'elastic'. However from your last letter there seems little chance, for your face is obviously set homeward & I have heartily to wish you a good voyage as well as to assure you of a welcome on your arrival. You must contrive to come & stay here for some time—as there will be a great deal to arrange about the working out of your collections, & your assistance will be almost indispensable. I need hardly do more than hint to you that reticence as to the number of specimens of any kind is desirable. You will find people wanting to "pump" you as soon as you arrive.

I have to apologize to you for wrongly charging you with not acknowledging the first copies of 'Nature' I sent you nearly 2 years & a half ago. How I came to forget that you had done so, I do not know.

I have read your last letters with the greatest interest—O, if you could but get that big <u>Hemignathus</u> of Oahu! Unless there should chance to be one in the Bishop Collection, it would seem to be only in Berlin, & I think they have but one there. Your hints as to what may be expected in future are of great value, & I do hope some one will be found to act upon them. There is evidently work for another committee, before the islands can be regarded as exhausted. I am surprised however at your not being more sanguine as to the results of further exploration in Hawaii proper. But I have no wish to set up my opinion against yours, & I look forward to discussing that & many other questions with you in the course of the autumn. You will naturally let us know of your arrival as soon as may be. We are about to lose Hickson who has been appointed poor Marshall's successor at Manchester, but you will find D^r. Sharp here. He has shown me your last letter to him received yesterday & I am glad to see from that that you do not need any money to be sent to you.

28 July—I have just got a postcard from Hickson, who is away from Cambridge, saying that he had heard from you acknowledging the last £100 & confirming my inference as above.

I am very glad you were going back to Lanai & hope you have prospered there. With best wishes I am

Yours very truly
Alfred Newton

Cambridge, England
26 July 1894
Robert Cyril Layton Perkins

Dear M^r. Perkins,

Your letters of June 8$^{\underline{th}}$ from Kauai, & June 17$^{\underline{th}}$ from Honolulu are to hand today by same post together with the box of beetles announced therein. The latter much broken, about half of them having come off the cards. Still there is sufficient for me to judge about them. The 17 Carabi seem as you suppose to represent 16 species. I should say all unknown to me, except the A. mysticus one, which looks like an old friend. The ribbed ones will I think be a new genus. The small ones are Bembiids more or less aberrant, the one a size larger – 2 specimens – is a new genus, an abnormal Bemibiid, allied, I should say to the St. Helena ones Wollaston[193] got.

The 11 Clytarli represent 7 species; all new except that one may be the Palolo Valley species (a single specimen in bad condition). Rhyncogoni both new. Brachypeplus new.; Cistelas new to me, one probably? Waterhouse's[194] Labetis. The big Staph. a quite new {one}, by which I mean nov descriptet, genus. The smaller one I should think a new Pachycornus. The bug a Scutellerid no doubt introduced.

I dont think you could nearly expect much more "newness" than that (N.B.) I am pretty sure the mysticus is not mysticus. I doubt the big Cossinid being the same species as Munro's Hawaiian one. The Clytarli are astonishing: with seven species in Kauai, one would suppose 40 should occur in the archipelago, as they appear to be all confined, or nearly all, to single islands. The large Cistela you say you lost was probably Waterhouse's species, which is that size if I recollect right.

We shall be very pleased to see you and I hope that after you have seen your friends & had a little time with them we shall have the pleasure of welcoming you at Cambridge.

As you say you do not wish more money sent, we shall of course not remit, I hope you have enough to get back comfortably; better than find yourself short would be to go to Bishop's bank and ask them to advance you a small sum.

I expect you will be back some time before the case you sent off arrives, and will be able to open it yourself.

With very best wishes,

Yours very truly
D. Sharp.

It is no good my sending pins as they would be too late.

Prof. Riley is in England I believe.

---

[193] Wollaston, Thomas Vernon (1822–1878). The English-born Wollaston specialized in beetles and is best known for his works on the faunas of Madeira, Cape Verde, St. Helena, and the Canaries, Atlantic islands on which he resided during his many months of study. He initially went to Madeira for his health after contracting tuberculosis. Constant illness left him incapacitated much of his last 30 years before he finally died of a massive pulmonary hemorrhage.

[194] Waterhouse, Charles Owen (1843–1917). Born and died in London. Godson of Charles Darwin and Sir Richard Owen, he specialized in Coleoptera, and joined the Entomology Department at the British Museum of Natural History in 1866 and rose to the position of Assistant Keeper, which he retained until he retired in 1910.

David Sharp

Lord Walsingham

E.B. Wolstenhome

E.C. Zimmerman

Hualālai summit in the 1890s.

Bishop Museum Archives

Rainforest above Makakupaʻia, Molokaʻi.

Photo: Clyde Imada. Hawaii Biological Survey

Palmer's Campsite on Moloka'i; typical of what Perkins's would look like at Makakupa'ia.

Volcano House Hotel, Volcano, Hawai'i Island, 1891.

Return to England
September 1894–24 March 1895

Upon his return to Honolulu from the Big Island, Perkins packed his things and made arrangements to return to England to work on the insects he had collected the past two years. On 1 September he boarded the New Zealand and Australia Steam Ship company's S.S. *Warrimoo*, a relatively new passenger vessel built only three years earlier, and sailed for Vancouver. After a nine-day sea voyage on board the *Warrimoo*, Perkins arrived at Port Moody, collected some insects in the Vancouver area, and then traveled by rail to Montreal. He soon realized that he may have made the wrong decision in telling Sharp months earlier that he did not need funds wired to him for his voyage home. Apparently, he was running out of money by the time he reached Montreal. Searching options for a cheap passage home, he opted for boarding a slow-going cattle-boat that was taking on a few passengers, and sailed for eleven days surrounded by the discomforting combination of the overpowering smell of diesel oil and bovines across the Atlantic Ocean to Liverpool, England.

After arriving in England, Perkins spent some time visiting family and friends in Raglan, Wales before heading to Cambridge to work on the sorting and processing of specimens he had collected. Despite his efforts at working up his collections to get them ready for specialists, Perkins had no idea what his future would hold and surely not that it would include his return to Hawai'i to continue collecting for the Committee.

> "... when I came back in 1894 there was no talk of my being sent out again to the islands, in fact Walsingham asked me if I should like to go as naturalist to a proposed expedition to S. America of some sportsmen who were after big game [It never came off]. Then suddenly I was asked by Newton if I would go back to Hawaii & I got ready at a moment's notice!" *(R.C.L. Perkins letter to E.C. Zimmerman, 1 November 1948, BPBM Entomology Archives).*

The report of the Committee to the British Association for the Advancement of Science detailed the activities of Perkins during his stay in England:

> "He {Perkins} accordingly arrived in England last autumn, and for the last four months was engaged in overhauling the very large collections he had previously made. These proved to be of great importance, and the Committee has gratefully to acknowledge the zeal and perseverance displayed by Mr. Perkins in carrying out its wishes. As was to be expected, close examination made it evident that much still remained to be done to com-

plete the Committee's work of exploration. From information given by Mr. Perkins, it was clear that, unless the deficiencies be made good without loss of time, this will never be done, the extinction of many members of the existing Fauna not only being inevitable, but immediate. The Committee, believing that it would be a matter for serious regret if the task of which so much labour and money have already been expended, were left unfinished, resolved to send Mr. Perkins out again." (*Rep. Br. Assoc. Adv. Sci.* 1895: 467–468).

The short note below is transferred to here from Perkins's remembrances of "Hawaii Island 20 July–22 August 1894."

JOURNALS AND REMEMBRANCES

The entry August 15th (above) was the last one made by me during my first period of collecting. It had been arranged that I should return to England in the autumn of '94, and there was no definite prospect of my return to the islands. On September 9th, I was at Vancouver; on the 19th I left Montreal in a cattle boat, taking a few passengers, and arrived in England on Sept. 30th. I now spent about 3 1/2 months in Cambridge, mounting specimens of insects, distributing these to specialists and describing bees and wasps. About 6 weeks in all I spent with my parents. It was then suddenly decided by the Committee to send me out again for further collecting, so I got the necessary apparatus together and started immediately, and began a new diary on Kauai in April 1895.

SELECTED CORRESPONDENCE

Magdalene College
Cambridge, England
5 October 1894
Robert Cyril Layton Perkins

Dear M[r]. Perkins

I thank you for your note just received. I returned yesterday afternoon but as yet I have not seen the College tutor, and therefore cannot say whether it will be possible to find rooms for you next week—for the men will then be coming up, but I know that there is generally somebody who (perhaps at the last moment) fails to put in an appearance, so I hope to find you accommodations. Unfortunately I have no spare room & I hear from D[r]. Sharp that his home happens just now to be full.

Professor Hickson (as he now is) is gone to Owens College, Manchester and it would be as well that you should write him a few lines there.

Scott Wilson is abroad somewhere, and I quite forget what was done about the figures of your <u>Drepanis</u>; but I only know that I followed your instructions regarding them, and I certainly understood that at least one copy had been sent to your father. I had even taken it into my head that Wilson had one framed and glazed for him.

I am sure I sent you some copies of your 'Notes' as printed in 'The Ibis', and I think I must have two or three still at your service but at this moment I cant lay my hand upon them. However to satisfy your natural wish I send herewith the copy I had kept for myself. I believe I was guilty of the unfortunate interchange of the name of the two Hemignathei—a mistake which M^r. Rothschild (or M^r. Hartert[195] who 'devils' for him) was not slow to notice—but the Editor of '<u>The Ibis</u>' is not free from blame as he never let me see the revised proof for which I had stipulated. Had he done so I should no doubt have detected my error.

I am sorry the end of your campaign was not signalized by any great victory & especially that the Maui <u>Hemignathus</u> did not again appear—If you could but have got 2 or 3 specimens of that & also of <u>Viridonia</u> (which I have never seen) you would have little cause to complain—

I am extremely busy & you must excuse this hasty reply—

Yours very truly
Alfred Newton

I open this to ask if you can give any information about ducks. Salvadori who is cataloguing Anatidae for the Brit. Mus. imagines that <u>A</u>. <u>wyvilliana</u> interbreeds with <u>A</u>. <u>booces</u> (Ex. <u>domestica</u>?) & that one of your specimens is a hybrid. This does not seem to me likely—are there 2 species wild?

25 Chesterton Road
Cambridge, England
8 February 1895
Edward Bagnall Poulton

Dear Prof. Poulton,

I received your letter on my return from a 22 mile skate up the river which I took today as I do not get a great deal of exercise. I was very pleased to hear from you after so long a time. I think 'offended' is rather too strong a term for my feelings, though I certainly was disappointed not hearing from you when I was away. Of course I only heard of your Professorship only after my return last October, & I fully

---

195   Hartert, Ernst Johann Otto (1859–1933). German born and educated, Hartert was employed by Lord Walter Rothschild as his ornithological curator at Rothschild's private museum in Tring, England from 1892 to 1929, after which he retired to Berlin. While employed at Tring, he published the journal *Novitates Zoologicae*, which was essentially a "house" journal publishing the results of research at the museum. During his employment, he traveled to India, Africa, and South America to collect birds for the museum.

understand how busy you must have been. It is somewhat late in the day to congrat-ulate you now, but I take the opportunity of doing so. About the time I wrote you I also wrote to Garstang[196] but to this day I have heard nothing of him. I think he can hardly have got my letter (many of mine miscarried as also those written to me). Since I got back I have been too busy to write any letter not absolutely necessary, & moreover I never for a moment expected till a few days ago to go back again, at any rate till after a considerable stay at home, so I have been content not to open any correspondence with old friends & now my sudden departure makes it impossible for me to do so.

I always intended to come down to Oxford about Easter time, had I not suddenly decided to go back to the Islands immediately.

If I can get a day to visit Oxford immediately before my departure I should much like to do so, though I fear the chances are not very great. I have after 3 years away only had 10 days at home and my people are grumbling at me not unnaturally & owing to serious disturbances in Hawaii[197] my mother is much concerned about my going back now. In reality I think there is not the least cause for any alarm & as I was present at the last revolution there, I know something about it.

You will perhaps be surprised that your former pupil who was always ill off & on has never had a days illness since except a few trifling accidents. It is of course very rough country & very rough life, but neither the changes from the great heat of the coast to the cold of the high mountains, the sleeping on the bogs, or the everlasting wet affected me in the least.

Still when I return this time I think I shall not be inclined to do similar work again, as I think I shall have done my share. I look upon the work as most impor-tant & I think it must have been about the most complete as yet accomplished in the oceanic islands & in some respects will widely change people's views as to the life in such places. Apart from this the creatures themselves, if small & mostly inconspicuous are most of them of the most interesting kind.

I saw Prof. Hickson a short while ago, for a little while I was very pleased to meet him again after so long a time. Next week I have to go to Merton to see Lord Walsingham again & probably once or twice to London & I have very much to do here before I can get away here. My father now lives at Raglan Vicarage nr. Newport Monmouthshire, a most lovely place.

With kind regards,

Yours very sincerely,
R.C.L. Perkins

---

[196] Garstang, Walter (1868–1949). British marine biologist, paleobiologist, embryologist, and amateur poet. Garstang was an undergraduate at Oxford (from 1884–1888) when he met Perkins and was the one who encour-aged him to apply for the position with the Sandwich Islands Committee to collect in Hawai'i. Garstang was a mem-ber of the faculty at Oxford from 1894–1897 and became chair of Zoology at the University of Leeds (1907–1933) before returning to Oxford in retirement. He is most famous for being the primary proponent of the theory that larval forms adapt to their environment as needed; contrary to the one by Haeckel, which said that ontogeny reca-pitulates phylogeny. Garstang's poetry remains popular among many biologists to this day as it often satirizes Haeckel and his other opponents.

[197] No doubt referring to the failed attempt at restoring Queen Lili'uokalani to the throne and resulting arrest and trial of those involved.

PART THREE

Second Expedition (1895–1897)

Kaua'i
9 April–22 May 1895

With fresh funding in hand from the Sandwich Islands Committee, Perkins left Liverpool on 28 February on board the White Star Line's steamship *Teutonic*. He arrived at Ellis Island, New York on 7 March, traveled from there to Montreal, boarded a Canadian Pacific Railway coach and traveled across the North American continent to Port Moody, British Columbia, and then sailed on 16 March from Vancouver to Honolulu via the Canadian Australian steamship *Miowera*.

> "CASS Miowera, Scott commander, arrived Sunday at 4p.m., eight days from Vancouver, having left that port on the 16th. Favorable weather was experienced throughout the entire voyage. The Miowera brought seven passengers and a considerable quantity of freight." (*Pacific Commercial Advertiser* 1895 (25 Mar)).

Perkins's arrival in Honolulu Harbor on 24 March 1895 was accompanied by a very brief notice in the local papers:

> "R.C.L. Perkins, entomologist from London, arrived by the Miowera." (*Hawaiian Gazette* 1895 (26 March): 5).

In the five days he was in Honolulu in March he had enough time to make his way up the mountains behind Honolulu to collect at the head of Pauoa Valley [collecting the wasp *Ectemnius stygius* (Kirby)], wrote Sharp two letters (26 and 27 March 1895), and made the necessary arrangements for travel to the other islands. The first island on the agenda was Kaua'i and a return to the home of his good friend, George Munro. He boarded the inter-island steamer *Mikahala* on 1 April and made the overnight trip to the port of 'Ele'ele arriving the morning of 2 April.

Perkins gave a brief summary of this trip in correspondence to Zimmerman:

> "In April & May I was on Kauai, first on the plateau above Waimea & then I visited Mr Knudsen & went up to his mountain house at Halemanu — now, I suppose, at or near the place called Kokee. The former locality was already known to me, & I needed specimens of one or two of the birds found there as now it had been arranged that some of the specimens collected by me were to be shared with the B.P. Bishop Museum. The rarer birds, however, were scarce at this season, no doubt being occupied elsewhere. At Halemanu birds were more numerous, but two of those which occurred at Kaholuamano seemed to

be absent, though the locality appeared admirably suited for them. The small species of Phaeornis, at this time imperfectly known, was particularly interesting, its food consisting largely of species of the big weevils, Rhyncogonus. Insects were numerous, but I hardly did justice to them. I collected in various directions, so far as somewhat beyond the way down at Kalalau, but I only went down a short way on the steep descent, as it was unsuitable for any collecting. On Kauai at this time were (with the exception of Bro. Matthias of Wailuku) the only three people really interested in my collecting, namely Mess[rs]. Francis Gay, V. Knudsen, & my friend Munro & this made my work there particularly pleasant. So far I had not met Koebele." *(R.C.L. Perkins letter to E.C. Zimmerman, 14 February 1944, BPBM Entomology Archives).*

After spending a week catching up with Munro at his home in Makaweli as well as his other friends and acquaintances on Kaua'i, he got his collecting gear together and began work on his second expedition upslope. His journals start on the first day out hunting.

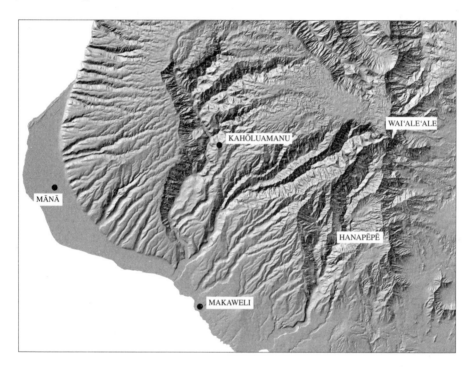

 Map of Kaua'i with detail showing Perkins's collecting areas.

Journals and Remembrances

April 9

Went up the valley at Makaweli, as I wanted to get a native duck 'Auku' for skinning. Went up ridge to first branch, then up the right branch of stream. I first flushed a pair of duck, then a batch of three, but a long way off. I took a shot at these and hit one hard, but it managed to top the gulch, though with difficulty, and was lost to me. I saw the giant Anax[198] and caught one worn female after a long hunt. It is much less plentiful than the smaller and very similar immigrant American species. Took a pair of Agrion in cop., the male one of the thin-bodied bright red species, the female also red, but duller. Noticed Holochila (Lycaena) blackburni. Took male Odyneri with white clypeus. I brought down some nice maidenhair fern plants from the left branch of the stream by which branch I returned. Munro brought in 2 Auku, a fine adult crested male the other also a male with smaller testes, spotted plumage and no crest. The former had the beak black, the legs behind and the feet beneath yellowish. The latter's beak had pale greenish markings. Munro, however, has previously shot both male and female crested, the male with longer plumes, female with shorter and the beak of the fully developed male may be partly pale.

April 10[199]

Skinned the Auku, a nasty job, as they smelt strongly, and the fat was running with the heat.

April 11

Went to Waimea, after seeing the bullock drivers come down from the mountains. Ordered my stores which were delivered in the evening and packed up for to-morrow.

April 12

Started on foot for Kaholuamano and waited for the kanaka and pack animal beyond the 2nd crossing of the river. Water was high and I misjudged the depth; thinking it about knee deep I went in well over the waist and the current was strong. I waited for about 2 hours drying in the sun and then I heard shouting from the top of the ridge and natives down below yelling out that my man was on top and calling. Although it was hot & sunny and windless for a wonder, I made fast time to the first house in the valley, where I bathed to cool off. There is very fine scenery along the gulch before one makes the last steep ascent to the plateau. The cliffs are mostly bare and sheer and of great height. I was on top about 2.30, but could not get at any cooking utensils, the key having been left behind. The kanaka left me at 4 and I went out and collected beetles and a good set of the apterous

---

198   *Anax* – this refers to the giant *Anax strenuus*.

199   Munro stated further in his diary on this date: "Mr. Perkins naturalist arrived here again last week, having come back to finish his investigation on the islands, after almost 6 months work on his former collection in England. Saw the other day at the head of the Mikikona Valley the larva of the ladybirds, released a few months ago at the Makaweli home feeding on the scale. Mr. P. is trying to find out about the Auku whether they are one or two species." (*Munro diary, 10 April 1895, BPBM Archives, MS SC Munro Box 13.2*).

earwigs (Anisolabis) that occur here. The larvae of Apterocyclus are common under dead wood, but I saw no adult beetle. There were few moths about. Beetles collected mostly Metromenoid Carabids, including the ribbed species (?n.g.[200]) with setae near middle of lateral margin of pronotum and one of the more solid black species with setae at the hind angle [Disenochus aterrimus]. I caught a few Noctuids at dusk and a nice dark Pyralid [probably Pyrausta dracontias]. At 9 p.m. the temperature was 54°F.

April 13
Temp. at 6 a.m. 52°. Went up with gun and took also a net. The birds are all far back. I saw plenty of Loxops and Oreomyza. The Ohia is in full flower and consequently the two red birds swarm everywhere, whereas in June last year there were, comparatively, few of these. I could hear no sound of the song or call of the Nukupu (Heterorhynchus) but I caught a glimpse of what may have been a female on the wing. The fine Lobelias are not in flower and I have not seen any Agrions about yet. Collected a lot of Carabids, but not many species. In addition to some numbers of the black one obtained yesterday, I got another, less elongate and more shining beneath, with it under bark of a dead tree. Also with these five of an apterous Gryllid, male and female [Leptogryllus kauaiensis] a yellowish brown species with dark markings, the legs pale and translucent with similar marking. I preserved 1 male and 1 female of this in alcohol. On very damp soil beneath dead wood I found what may be Itodacnus Sharp, to my surprise, not expecting Elaters at this season and temperature [Dacnotus currax]. I came back about 4.30 p.m. to collect nearer home. Result Lepidoptera (not very numerous species) small brown Gryllids, some Proterhinus, one nice species like hystrix, but looks different; four Rhyncogonus. I collected about 200 specimens of insects to-day.

April 14
Skinned 3 birds shot yesterday Hemignathus male, Oreomyza male, and one poor specimen of Loxops (sex?). To-day I have seen none of the scarcer birds. Collected some beetles, Carabids &c, including 2 small bronzy Bembidiids and some Trichopterygidae, from under dead bark, these put in alcohol tube. Got one more of the apterous cricket of yesterday and a second very distinct species, very pale yellow, rather immature-looking, and translucent, the head, apices of femora and tibiae pale brown, each abd. segment with a black diamond-shaped spot on each side, ovipositor long, narrow, dark at extreme tip — found under bark of Ohia-ha. Saw P. tammeamea and caught an Odynerus, while moths were rather more numerous than yesterday. A very windy night.

April 15
Same way as yesterday and went quickly for about 3 miles, not staying to collect on this part, as I was after birds. I saw a pair of Hemignathus and killed one cleanly, yet I could not find it. Afterwards, I shot one as it sucked the Lehua flowers. Also shot one Loxops. I saw Oreomyza twice visit the Lehua flowers and apparently for the nectar. As usual most of them were on the trunks, hunting very methodically for insects, crossing constantly from one side to the other as they climbed up. I neither saw nor heard Heterorhynchus and it must be largely else-

---
[200] Abbreviation for "new genus".

where at this season unless it has got scarce. Cattle are plentiful up here — wild of course — and the underbrush seems to have been much killed. President Dole[201] and a party were up here just before me and I heard that they shot 18 animals — ? in one day. I collected also Brachypeplus (already known to me) and several Proterhini. From tree-fern Pentarthrum, a Bembidiid, and Proterhinus. Three or four spp. of Oodemas under bark, mostly single ones, one a large species, vertical behind, like nivicola. Large Staph. with these and several Lispinodes and a solitary Diestota. I took a solitary non-metallic Bembidium — these and the little metallic species have a median prothoracic seta on each side and one at each hind angle. Collected also some Microlepidoptera. I worked for more wingless crickets and got a good series of both sexes. They are found both under bark and amongst dead fern leaves. Most are losing their mottled appearance and turning black from decomposition. This is the case with the other species, and most of to-day's specimens I therefore put into alcohol. The long, thin antennae are often broken. Under a log I found a single rather large 'Helix' which I have not got before, under bark a large Succinea and a number of the minute hairy 'Helices'. Under bark and in dead fern leaves a Machilis is common and I took some spiders. The large Isopod, Ligia, was with these and also the land shrimps, some carrying young, which become detached in alcohol. A good day's collecting except for birds. The flycatcher, thrush and perhaps the Oo seem less numerous than they were last June, but owing to the Ohias being in flower, the Iiwi and Apapane are in thousands. I also hear the Amakihi every where, though it was scarce last June. The Ou is very numerous in the flowering trees. I strongly suspect it may be eating nectar at times, though it may be only the bases of the flowers that it is feeding on as I found on Lanai.

April 16

A cloudless morning and very little wind. I crossed gulches to left and though the sun was hot there was nothing stirring; except an occasional small moth and a solitary Odynerus, not a sign of insect life was observed in a long stretch of forest. I crossed the near branch of the Waimea river and went up a ridge. Took a single fresh Apterocyclus and a number of the mysticus-like Metromenus [Apteromesus maculatus] and the wingless cricket (under bark). Under dead wood, quite rotten, a single specimen of a white earwiglike creature [Iapyx]. At about one o'clock, after wandering around collecting I found myself uncertain as to the homeward direction so I came down into the gulch and struck a rather curious part of the stream bed, as 3 parts of the stream flowed almost alongside, two in one direction and one in the other. By this time it was raining hard, the water already becoming thick, and I was cold in my very light clothing, so I left the valley by no means sure of the way back and not recognising my exact position until I was only a mile from the house. At one time I doubted whether I should get back that night unless the weather cleared up. On the way back under stones on border of stream I got

---

201 Dole, Sanford Ballard (1844-1926). Honolulu-born, bird-collector Sanford Dole was probably better known in political circles as Hawaii's first president and also first governor. He studied at Oahu College in Honolulu and Williams College in Massachusetts. He entered the bar in Massachusetts and, when returning to Hawai'i, practiced law in Honolulu and was president of the Bar Association. He was a member of the legislature during the Kingdom of Hawaii from 1884–1886 and an associate justice of the Supreme Court from 1887–1893 before being placed as the head of government in 1893. He was interested in ornithology and published a list of Hawaiian birds in 1869 and an updated version in 1878 in Thrum's *Hawaiian Annual*.

the Metromenus with pale apices to the elytra, which does not seem common here [not Metromenus but Colpocaccus posticatus]. Many of the Carabids found here have fungi growing on them, especially on the pronotum and apices of the elytra, so that those which I observed, when mounting Hawaiian beetles in England last winter and especially on the common pale lily-frequenting species were evidently present in life and not a post-mortem growth. I note that 2 of the mysticus-like species collected now show setae at the hind angles of the pronotum, the first I have seen so in fully 30 examined [Sharp gives this genus Apteromesus as having no pronotal setae in his description in 'F.H.']. I made up the skins of a couple of birds shot yesterday, a female Hemignathus male Loxops. The pink Begonia (Hillebrandia) which I saw on Maui and Molokai is in full flower here in many places, and masses of a yellow Composite, probably a Campylotheca.

April 17

Went downwards to look for Clytarlus on the Koa trees. A hot bright morning without wind, like yesterday a.m., and rather close. About half-way down the steep hill I found a recently fallen Koa, from which I got several specimens of the larger Clytarlus [i.e. Plagithmysus aequalis] and one of the minute species., Afterwards got 2 or 3 more specimens of the latter, which is very like the Oahuan C. fragilis. A few Anobiids, 2 or 3 spp, of Mirosternus and a few Xyletobius. It was now cloudy and when I reached the bottom of the steep {cliff} it began to rain heavily (at noon) & I started up again in a break and was back in an hour. Collected male (and ? female) of a thin-bodied red Agrion. Caterpillars of the foreign plexippus swarmed on their food plant, eating the blossoms for choice, leaves when the flowers were finished. As it continued to rain heavily I carded most of the beetles captured. At 5 p.m. it cleared somewhat and I went out and collected ground shells. Also some beetles, Dryophthorus, Oodemas, Glyptoma and Munro's Cossonid and a large number of moths towards and at evening.

April 18

A fine bright morning, but likely to turn out wet later. By 11 a.m. I had not finished pinning and packing away yesterday's captures, when a kanaka came up. Wrote a letter for him to give Munro. At noon it poured and was stormy all the afternoon. Could only go out for moths a little before dark. At 7 p.m. the wind got up and it became a bright starlit night. Collected some nice species of the broad-winged Micros with raised scale-tufts, some fine Pyralids &c.

April 19

Fine hot morning, clear sky, no wind. Went out to collect beetles chiefly and came back at noon with Cis, Proterhinus, Anobiids, Rhyncogonus &c got my gun and started upwards. Had only gone a mile when there was an extremely heavy downpour and I was drenched in a minute. Returned again with a Crabro, a Prosopis male (which I dissected) and a fine male Hemignathus, shot as I hurried back. It continued raining during the afternoon and I carded about two dozen of the Anobiids. Stopped raining at 5.30 and at 8 p.m. was very bright and starry. At dusk I caught a fine large black and white Scoparia, a Parandra and some Metromeni. One species of these will come to light on dark nights, but only early in the evening and often 2 or 3 together, after which no more are seen. The other

Carabids never come. [Those coming to light were not Metromenus but Colpocaccus (formerly Colpodiscus part.). It was not known to me at this time that the other. Metromeni s. l. were flightless species].

April 20
Hot, still, bright morning. Went up the usual way with gun. Saw nothing special in the bird line, only 2 female Akialoa, one of which I shot, but it pitched high up in an unclimbable tree. I brought back 1 Loxops female, 1 Amakiki and 1 Oreomyza. I lost several Loxops. Came back by the ridge, making a circle round the nearer forest. Collected a number of Carabids and there were some Odynerus about to-day. Bright, starry night, temp. 58° at 8 p.m. no wind and warm.

April 21
Fine and hot. Went up with gun on the way by which I returned yesterday. Saw Mimesa and Odynerus, but only caught one of the latter. Holochila blackburni was flying high up the trees. I shot a female Hemignathus, which was no doubt nesting, as it contained a large egg, just ready for extrusion. Later on I shot another, a male in non-breeding plumage and dull and I saw another. Shot male Loxops and Amakiki. I saw a fine male Heterorhynchus, which I killed, but unfortunately could not find. So far I must have lost half the number of birds shot. Last year with Nixie I never lost one, either killed or wounded, though I shot at them then in any situation without considering where they might fall. [Nixie was the survivor of the two dogs sent out from England for Lord Rothschild's collectors, and at this time was being kept by Munro and later, I think, was turned over to Fred Whitney]. Rained hard at 2 p.m. but on getting back at 4.30 I found it had not rained in this part of the forest. I collected a nice new Xyletobius, but only one specimen, also a number of Mirosternus, including a pair in cop. It poured with rain from 7 p.m. till 8.30 and then became clear and starry. Temp. at 8 p.m. 60°, at 10.30 52°.

April 22
Skinned birds killed yesterday and on the 20th. Collected near home the usual things, Proterhinus, Anotheorus, Rhyncogonus, big Staph. and Lepidoptera. I took a splendid specimen of perhaps the most beautiful of all the Scopariae, white with a single large black spot on the middle of the costa. [I do not think this species was ever described. I saw at Lord Walsingham's, a number of smaller Lepidoptera, including Scoparia, which were picked out by him with the true micros in the collection on a casual selection and I doubt whether these were ever sent to Meyrick, who described all the other groups — i.e. other than Tortricina, Tineina and Pterophorina. Neither S. rhombias nor S. amphicypella answer to the definite description of this specimen]. I watched one of the minute Gryllids [Paratrigonidium] stridulating at night. The tegmina are raised perpendicularly to the body and moved outwards through an angle of 30° then closed together again, being kept upright all the time. I never saw those on Oahu stridulate in this way, though superficially the species appears to be the same. Pinned the specimen in stridulating position.

April 23
Went straight mauka. Saw several Hemignathus and one male Nukupu, which flut-

tered a little as it fell and was lost in the brush. I had my net with me and caught Lepidoptera. Shot Oreomyza female and two male Hemignathus procerus. Caught some moths later at night with light. The species (i.e. some of them) come to this only during a brief period, as in England. At 8 p.m. 4 of the white spotted black-winged Pyralid came together then no more [Phlyctaenia calliastra], about 9 o'clock 3 of a conspicuous Scoparia not seen again, at 12 several of a large dark broad-winged Micro with the raised tufts of scales [Heterocrossa sp.]. I stayed up till daylight but there was no repetition of these flights. Took out the bodies from birds.

April 24
Went across to the river keeping along the ridge amongst Koa trees. Collected Anobiids and Dermestids, the latter only found where the former occur in company, also small scarce Cossonid (? genus) apparently similar to those found on Oahu and in Kona Hawaii [Deinocossonus] clothed with bright golden pubescence. Shot Amakiki, but did not shoot at two Hemignathus seen, because they were in trees on a very steep side. Caught P. tammeamea and several H. blackburni, all females. A fine hot day, though cloudy after 2 p.m.

April 25
Started early into the forest intending to go further in than on any pervious occasion. I wanted birds, but saw nothing better than a few Akialoa. I shot, but lost, a fine male, and bagged two females of this. Birds are already beginning to deteriorate in their plumage. Penetrated a good deal further back than before. I caught Lepidoptera, the best thing a yellow and black Geometer quite new and a pretty species [Xanthorhoe epixantha]. Also with other moths later a large yellowish Pyralid (with long palpi) which had considerable resemblance to the geometer in life. [Loxostege helioxantha]. I also collected a brown Holcobius, a new Xyletobius larger than my other Kauai species of this genus, large Brachypeplus &c. It is warm to-night; temp. at 10 p.m. 58°.

April 26
Pinned insects and skinned yesterday's birds and made up the skins of some previously obtained and left unfinished. Went a long way back, keeping out till dark thinking that the Nukupu might be less silent towards evening, but it was no go. I shot a couple of Loxops. I saw three Oo near together, singing each in turn and very sweetly. They uttered the usual squeaks when I disturbed them. Bright starry night.

April 27
Collected near home, but nothing special. However, I obtained a good many Lepidopterous larvae, hoping to rear some, also some beetles.

April 28
Went far out with gun, but the result was mainly Lepidoptera and a few Odynerus. However, I shot 4 Loxops, 1 Hemignathus and 1 Oreomyza. I suppose I shall have to leave here in a day or two.

April 29
Sunday. Did not go out, but skinned birds, washed clothes &c.

April 30
Cleaned up generally, then went out specially to collect Microlep. larvae with fair success.

May 1
Started to come down from the mountains, but as it looked fine and was very warm — the thermometer had registered 72° this morning — I changed my mind, hurried back and went in search of Aculeates. Collected the ordinary things 2 or 3 <u>Prosopis</u> (both sexes) <u>Mimesa</u>, the carinated form only [<u>Deinomimesa</u>] some <u>Odyneri</u> and two or more spp. of <u>Crabro</u>. Also the two native butterflies.

May 2
Came down early and at half way down met native bringing up letters — Prof. Newton April 1st, C.R. Bishop March 5th [had probably been directed to England] and others.

May 3
With Munro and cleaning up correspondence all day.

May 3–7[202]
[Did some collecting on the coast and spent one day going to Mana with Munro where the mirage was perfect, but the sands would not bark.[203] On the 7th I went to call on Mr. V. Knudsen and get permission to stay in his mountain house[204] and having obtained this, carried up my collecting material, while a native rode beside me and took up my food etc. It took me 3 3/4 hours to walk up from Mr. Knudsen's by the side of the native's mule. It was a very hot day.]

{Perkins's prefatory note to the following diary entries:}

[I had 2 copies of this diary, differing slightly both verbally & in particulars. This is an exact copy of the original, the other was one sent to England to some of my family interested in Natural History.]

May 3rd and following days
On coming down to Munro's I did no collecting in the mountains, as I had many Microlepidoptera &c to fix up on {cork} tablets and label before sending them home. I collected some Aculeates, including two species of <u>Prosopis</u>, both new to me, in Munro's yard at Makaweli.

---

[202] There are apparently two Kaua'i typescripts. A second typescript of Perkins's collecting trip starts with a 3 May entry, gives more detail for the entries above dated 3–7 May, and continues until Perkins left Kaua'i for Honolulu on 22 May. It is reproduced below.

[203] This refers to the famous barking sands of the west coast of Kaua'i, which consist of cupped grains of sand and small broken and eroded sea shells. When crushed under foot they make a barking sound as the air in between the grains escapes.

[204] Valdemar Knudsen's mountain house, Halemanu, was located at the 4,000-foot level on the way up to the Koke'e area of Kaua'i. Knudsen built this house around 1870 for his family when they outgrew the original grass one. The lumber was shipped from New Zealand and hauled up the mountain by oxcart as far as possible, then by horse and on foot. Halemanu served as a "mountain home" not only for the Knudsen family, but also many birders who were guests of Knudsen or the Gay and Robinson families.

May 4

Went to Mana with Munro. Killed one duck, a quite typical wyvilliana, female, and I did not skin it. The 'barking sands' would not bark at all, and I could see no difference between this sand and any other. Not a single Aculeate was seen on these lovely sandhills nor any other insects of note. The mirage was very fine and it, was curious to look back over ground we had just before traversed and see the apparent reflection of the cattle in large sheets of water. Munro found four stilt's eggs, but hard set. I found only broken shells and a dead, freshly-hatched chick, already rotten. The bird usually nests on little mounds, a mere depression on the top forming the nest.

May 7

Drove to Waiawa and thence walked up from M^r. Knudsen's house to Halemanu. M^r. K. says the measured distance is 18 miles, but I hardly think it can be as great, elevation about 4,000 ft. It was a very hot cloudless day and for once I suffered for want of water, drinking a vast quantity when I reached the mountain house, and to-night I have a headache and slight sore throat. I left M^r. K's house at 10.15 a.m. and reached the mountain house at 2 p.m. nearly, though Munro told me he thought it would take six hours. I went quickly, keeping up with the native's mule all the way. The lower slopes have considerable stunted Alii{= *'a'ali'i*} bushes almost to the foot of the hills in some places and Koa at no great elevation — a good deal of young growth of the latter and lots of Holochila blackburni in the lowest real forest. Fine tufts of tall grass. I found there were no blankets at the house so sent the boy down to buy some and to get some beef. [Knudsen told me afterwards that he had told the kanaka to let me know that there were no blankets, but no doubt he failed to do this, in order to have an excuse for not staying up in the mountains alone.]

At 5 p.m. I went out and collected 80 Anobiids and a fine Cistelid, ? Waterhouse's Labetis tibialis, with the elytra entirely pale. Also one small Clytarlus, some Proterhinus and Microlepidoptera. A beautiful little bronzy species of a n.g. with turned back tips to the wing, apparently ovipositing, in a broad leaved species of Pelea, like the one called 'mokehana' {= *mokihana*} in Makua valley, Waianae.

[This moth was Opostega dives. The Pelea leaves were much mined and probably by larvae of this species.]

May 8

Went back behind the house, A dull cheerless morning with very fine rain and the undergrowth dripping wet. Very few birds of any kind and those of the commonest, so I returned about 1 p.m. Then went back on another trail mauka amongst fine Koa trees. Got 2 Clytarli (? 2 species) the one specimen apparently closely allied to an Oahu one (? C. cristatus) and a few Anobiids. [The specimen alluded to was probably a female of P. arachnipes]. Saw a dilapidated specimen of male Hemignathus, which I did not shoot at. The kanaka has not returned. I found the white ear-wig-like insect again, and took some worms of a species new to me in the islands and resembling the [English] 'Brandling' [Allobophora foetida].

May 9

Started at 7.30 on same way as yesterday afternoon. A fine day, but too early for Aculeates when I was in the best part for these and only a few Mimesa, Odynerus and Crabro were on the wing. I saw the giant Anax, but too wary to be caught. Pushed on past the Koa trees when the country becomes something like that behind Kaholuamano, but much drier. I got a lovely view of the Kalalau valley and was just returning thence when I heard shouting, so I fired a cartridge and soon the kanaka appeared. He seemed surprised to find that I, being a stranger, had got so far from the house, but this is an easy country after parts of Hawaii, Maui and Molokai. He said his brother's wife had died and that was why he did not come back last night, also that it was 'too bad' as she was only 16 and had a two year old child. I sent him down after we returned, as he wanted to 'put her in the dirt'. Said he would return on Monday and bring his wife and child up with him. I got a few Aculeates and Microlepidoptera and a lot of Anobiids, which are more abundant here than in any other locality so far visited by me. Also one small Clytarlus as before, several Labetis and a single Cistela, ? n.sp. Also both species of Rhyncogonus as yesterday, Proterhinus &c. Birds were hardly to be seen all day, but I saw Loxops [caeruleirostris] near Kalalau pali. It appears to be a steep climb down there. In the evening I collected larvae of P. cardui on mallow.

May 10

Went mauka towards Kalalau, then downwards at right angles to this course. Saw nothing of note in the bird line. I did some insect collecting, taking about a score of Holochila blackburni. Many were worn but it was abundant. I took in more Anobiids and a couple of brown Holcobius these on Opiko (Straussia).

May 11

Same way as on the 10th, but entered forest on left, looking towards Kalalau, at a different point. Got two large and several smaller Clytarlus, Anobiids, and Microlepidoptera. The latter from Koa. About 2 p.m. heard the 'squeak' of a bird—sound new to me. Saw the bird looking like a diminutive 'Kamau' (Phaeornis). Took a very long shot and only feathered it. About an hour afterwards heard it again, either the same bird or its mate, for probably there were two at first, but it was so scary I could not get a shot. Left at 4 p.m. but returned to the place at 6 p.m. after getting some food. Again heard the bird, but failed to get a shot. The ground covered with leaves and dead brush made it impossible to approach without much noise.

May 12

Started at 7 a.m. for the same spot. Heard the bird but could not see it. Heard it again at 1 p.m. but could not get near. At 2 p.m. went home and skinned a young Oo (? sex) shot yesterday. Its parents were feeding it at the top of a very tall Koa tree. It has no sign of the yellow breeches of the adult. Also skinned a very fine male Himatione parva shot at the same time. Returned for the Phaeornis at 5 p.m. Heard it at 6.30 and got a glimpse of it, but out of shot and very wild. Picked up Labetis, a Carabid and a few Psyllids the latter on large and thick-leaved species of Pelea. They rest on the upper surface and jump like leaf-hoppers.

May 13

Went after the Phaeornis with nothing to carry but my gun. Tramped around from 7 a.m. to 5 p.m. I heard it once or twice but got no shot. Once I saw two birds fly across a gulch and they were probably this species. At 5 p.m. I heard them not very far off, so sat down in the fork of a Koa branch which touched the ground. Soon after I heard the ♂ sing, about forty yards away. It has a short but loud song like the Nukupuu almost exactly, but it seemed a little louder and shorter. It repeated this about six times and then began its squeak of alarm. The ♀ was evidently with it. I left when it was nearly dark without a shot though the ♂ once flew over my head.

May 14

Up at 5 and at 7 was in position to wait for the Phaeornis. I was very cold and dripping wet to above the waist with the dew, which was very heavy on the rank herbage. By 1 p.m. I had only once heard a sound of the bird in the distance and even that doubtful. At 3 p.m. cramped and disgusted, though now dry, I again heard the male sing just like the Nukupuu (Heterorhynchus). At 5 o'clock one flew over my head and pitched in the brush in front of me, but out of shot. This was clearly the ♀, the ♂ being somewhere behind me. Soon he followed and settled overhead and I could nearly touch him with the gun. I had put on a short yellow oil-skin coat, nearly the colour of the fallen Koa phyllodes and evidently he did not see me. He then flew behind me and settled on a dead limb almost 20 yards off. I screwed round and got a shot and saw the bird fall a little way, when it got in the full glare of the sun and I lost sight of everything, being quite dazed. I could not when I got up be certain of the exact direction nor of the tree in which the bird had settled. I searched for nearly two hours and was just starting home in the dusk when I picked it up. The white line round the eye did not seem so plain as in life. The beak longer in proportion to its breadth than in other Phaeornis and the long pearly white legs are its chief characteristics. It is a very distinct species, mine no doubt a male. The voice of the ♀ is decidedly less loud. It was quite stiff when I gathered it and held tightly in its beak a large green Geometer caterpillar, which was still alive.

May 15

Went into the forest further down than before and then worked upwards. Heard the Phaeornis [palmeri] and shot it. It was quite tame, a ♂ with the testes very large. I found in the stomach little except beetles, mostly Oodemas and Rhyncogonus, apparently nothing of a vegetable nature; some spider remains possibly present. I could see no great difference between its anatomy and that of the common Phaeornis [myiadestina] of which I shot a ♂ for comparison. Both have the same large orbits and eyes, only in myiadestina the skull is depressed or grooved between the orbits considerably more than in palmeri — in the latter hardly at all. Legs of palmeri pearly white, almost colourless, the feet yellow beneath. Collected a few beetles near house.

May 16

Same locality as yesterday. Collected some beetles. I had made three trips by breaking branches of trees to attract Clytarlus and these produced 7, 5, 1 specimens representing 3 species. I caught 3 species of Prosopis, but could not get a female of the smaller black one. Also <u>Proterhinus</u>, <u>Brachypeplus</u>, <u>Cis</u>, Anobiids and a fine large <u>Rhyncogonus</u>, grey-pubescent all over, which looks as if it will be another new species; <u>Sierola</u>, <u>Sclerodermus</u> (1) and a minute Chalcid, bronzy-green, which I extracted from a long mine, probably Lepidopterous, in a leaf. Shot a ♂ <u>P. palmeri</u> in the spotted, juvenile plumage, but on dissection I found the <u>testes</u> much enlarged, as if it were breeding. The stomach contained broken up <u>Rhyncogoni</u>, and <u>Carabidae</u>. It was on the ground when I first saw it, but flew from this into a dead bush 15–20 paces away. It was mostly shot in the head.

May 17
Shot another male <u>P. palmeri</u> like yesterday's specimen with the testes enlarged in spite of the immature plumage. Natural size of testis.   Collected some Aculeates, beetles and got female <u>Prosopis</u> with yellow   pronotal tubercles.

May 18
Went out for Aculeates and Lepidoptera, but did not do very well as it poured with rain about 2 p.m. and continued for the rest of the day. Before the rain there was but little sunshine. I heard a <u>P. palmeri</u> once, but got no sight of it.

May 19
Exactly the same thing happened as yesterday, except that the downpour was heavier. However, before it began, I caught about a score of <u>Holochila</u> and some <u>Aculeates</u>. Again I heard the same <u>P. palmeri</u> but got no shot at it. Shot a ♂ <u>Hemignathus</u> when singing. Song most like that of Nukupuu, or between that and the green <u>Himatione</u> [C. stejnegeri]. I have several times seen the birds in this spot sucking the Lehua flowers but have not shot at them before not wishing to disturb the <u>Phaeornis</u>. At this season the <u>Hemignathus</u> is not common just here, and the <u>total</u> absence of <u>Heterorhynchus</u> from forest which appears most suitable is highly remarkable.

May 20
Went out with net and gun &c early. Got Aculeates and a number of <u>Holochila</u>. At 10 a.m. began to rain and poured at intervals till 3 p.m. when I returned. Got a shot at a <u>P. palmeri</u>, but probably owing to being so wet and cold I failed to get it. This was close to the spot where I got the first one. I took <u>Clytarlus</u> from my traps. Got a rather large yellow <u>Eopenthes</u> from my firewood.

May 21
Started at 9 a.m. everything dripping with wet and I was soon wet through. A very hot and close day. At 10 it poured with rain which came down in a deluge at intervals till near evening. Took two or three <u>Clytarlus</u> from my traps. Shot ♂ and ♀ <u>P. palmeri</u> in spotted plumage the one with diseased feet, the ♂ with large testes and the ♀ with the ovaries considerably enlarged. These birds were in company and evidently paired; at one time they were sitting on a horizontal bough side by side and actually touching one another. They were full of caterpillars, fragments of beetles and in one there was a land shell such as one finds under logs and beneath bark. Soon I heard another singing high up in a Koa tree, not so loudly as on a for-

mer occasion. It repeated this song which was very short dozens of times, but I could not get a sight of the singer. First it seemed in front, then behind me or to one side or the other, yet the bird could not possibly have moved without my seeing it. Finally I called it down by imitating the grating call or alarm note. It was in unspotted plumage. The song is much more like that of Heterorhynchus than of the other Phaeornis. Like the others it contained many Lepidopterous larvae. These birds frequent the thickest brush on the sides of hills or slopes where it is more or less open on top with Koa trees around. They fly low as a rule and their flight is sometimes very rapid and straight like that of our {English} kingfisher. Sometimes they come down to the ground, and generally keep low down. I heard one sing when on the wing, but more often when perched high up in a Koa tree. The white of the tail feathers shows very plainly in their flight, but the spots on the breast were not noticeable in the thick brush, where the light is not good. Finally I got another ♂ (spotted). It was comparatively tame and I easily got a shot at it when it had flown up from the ground and perched on a dead branch a foot or two above. Generally I have found this bird rather difficult to get a shot at, except when one first comes on one. I found no vegetable matter in the stomachs of any of my specimens, but spiders, caterpillars and beetles and, as mentioned above, once a land shell swallowed whole. During the heavy storms to-day it thundered very loudly many times. I hope to go down to-morrow as the weather has been bad and my last day after palmeri has been the most successful.

May 22
Came down to M^r. K's in 3 hrs.10 mins. Had lunch with him and his son gave me a dead specimen of his new shell H. knudseni Baldw. He had three, found alive, and had given six away. M^r. K told me a great fire had destroyed the forest down from Halemanu, in 1864, I think he said. It burnt for a fortnight or more. He also told me of a bird said by the old natives to be brown and called "The Akua of the uninhabited parts of the mountain" supposed to be around Waialeale.[205] It was brown like a mynah and the size of the Ou.

The plants around Halemanu are very fine, the district being very rich in species of trees of smaller size, most of the genera seen elsewhere seem to be represented. The 'Mokihana' is plentiful and looks like the Alani that was numerous at Waianae, which natives there called 'Mokihana'. Probably the Halemanu fire {of 1864} exterminated many landshells which do not occur much at high elevation. There is nice young forest of Koa now growing on part of the burnt area.

M^r. Knudsen pressed me to stay for a while at his house in the kindest manner, being very much interested in what I told him about the various insects in his forest and the differences between this and the fauna of Kaholuamano. I should have, been glad to stay on for a while, but had already arranged for my next collecting trip, so left for Makaweli in the afternoon.[206]

---

[205]   Waialeale — the highest point of Kaua'i, this mountain is claimed by some to be the wettest spot on earth.
[206]   An entry for 25 May in Munro's diary mentions the following: "Mr. Perkins left for Honolulu today. He was successful in getting insects at Halemanu, he also got the small species of thrush getting several specimens. Some being adults, he found them hard to shoot, feeding on a peculiar species of beetle on the dead koa branches where the scrub is thick." (*Munro diary, 25 May 1895, BPBM Archives, MS SC Munro Box 13.2*).

Selected Correspondence

University Museum of Zoology
Cambridge, England
19 April 1895
Robert Cyril Layton Perkins

Dear M^r. Perkins,

I was very pleased to hear of your safe arrival in Vancouver: and I hope you are now at work in the islands.

I have been in correspondence with the Hon. W. Rothschild about some insects. He is anxious to have parasites collected: & is specially anxious for those on the Hawaiian bat. I enclose some hints he has drawn up.

I should also mention that he is anxious you go to Laysan, that you should get a series of specimens of birds in some number, as he wishes to be a purchaser of duplicates.

We got the Lepidoptera quite safely into Meyrick's hands, but he has not reported on them yet.

We have had most detestable weather since you went away, but at last we have had two or three days of nice spring weather.

Gray turned out of one of the Mauna Loa boxes a specimen of a quite new genus of Eucnemidae, at which I am much surprised: it is more like some of the New Zealand things than Fornax.

With best wishes,

Yours very truly
D. Sharp.

University Museum of Zoology
Cambridge, England
31 May 1895
Robert Cyril Layton Perkins

Dear M^r. Perkins,

Your letters written to me up to date of April 28<u>th</u> have all I believe duly arrived. Thank you very much for sending me M^r. Bishop's letter which I now return. We here had a grant of £200 made us by the Royal Society. I can draw it after the 15th June, and I shall then ask the Treasurer to <u>wire</u> you a credit of £100 if it will get to you much sooner, about which I am not clear: it will take some days to arrange about this so telegram be sent off about 22nd June, & then arrive at Frisco' same date; enquire therefore, after the date it should be in Honolulu, which you will know, & you should find a credit to you of £100 somewhere: should you not find it, do not think anything has gone wrong, as I am not yet quite sure the Treasurer will agree to wiring.

We are going to have a meeting of the Committee on the 6th and I shall thereafter write you again. I fully expect to arrange with the Bishop Museum on the terms you have suggested. I am very much obliged to you for the trouble you have taken in discussing it with them which will save me a great deal of correspondence.

The moths went to Meyrick very shortly after you left, & travelled quite safely. He is one of the men who will not answer letters, and I can at present get no further information from him than that they are a very interesting lot. I told him to write to you, quite a month ago, so possibly he may have done so: we have also got all the dragon-flies mounted & taken back to London, but I do not suppose McLachlan will touch them at present!

In reference to the dragon-flies sent by the Catholic brothers from Maui I am truly sorry I cannot name them at present. After labelling them with localities Gray destroyed the numbers that they were sent under, so that the clue is quite lost. They will be specially mentioned by means of locality when the paper is published about them. Blackburn has replied offering to sell all his Hawaiian Coll. that he has left, and I have asked him to have a price & will then see whether the Brit. Mus. will take them.

Thanks for your news as to your doings in Kauai: it is certainly remarkable that the Lepidoptera are in such force; from which you say I judge that at time of writing you were quite too early for Insects generally.

Immediately on receiving your letter I ordered the pins you wish: if they come in time I shall put them in this letter: if not they will come in another next week. I shall also send by post a new substance for mounting small things on.

We have completed the mounting of your things; one or two new genera have turned up among them. Gray is now cutting up & labelling.

Prof Newton is writing you by this post and he will say anything that he thinks proper in the way of influencing your movements. So far as I am concerned I recognize that you now know so much more about what is wanted than I do, that I had better not express an opinion — for fear you might attend to it.

By the way those Heteramphus never turned up. Among your Maui things there is a single specimens of a highly interesting thing appearing to connect

Heteramphus with Oodemas: it is bright green & has a much larger rostrum than any other Oodemas.

Thanks for your kind enquiries about myself. I am longing for a little outdoor work which I think would make me all right; unfortunately I cannot get it at present as Macmillan's are insisting on the vol. of Insects coming out. With very best wishes

Yours very truly
D.Sharp.

Wiawa, Kaua'i, Hawaiian Islands
6 June 1895
Robert Cyril Layton Perkins

Dear M^r. Perkins,

Your letter of May 31 reached me this weeks mail and is quite interesting. Thank you for writing it.

As you say it would not be likely to find much difference in the insects that inhabit Halemanu & Kalalau heights from those of Makaweli. Still a difference is found in plants, in shells and as you have a new bright, metallic moth also partly in insects. I am much pleased that you made this find and congratulate you.

On the lower lands along the coast north-west from my house, Mana, Milolii and Nualolo seems to me to be a field quite new and also larger. When you some time have nothing better to do, it might pay you to go and visit those high valleys and also Kalalau. I shall be delighted to assist you, if you should come. We have a large new boat for use. I am my dear sir very sincerely,

Yours,
V. Knudsen

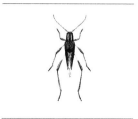

Ka'ū and Puna, Hawai'i Island
12 June–19 September 1895

Perkins arrived in Honolulu from Kaua'i on 25 May, blocked up the microlepidopterans and other delicate pinned insects, packed his Kaua'i collections, and shipped everything off to England.

While in Honolulu the first part of June, he met Albert Koebele for the first time and the two had what may have been the first ever discussion of impacts of bio-control agents in Hawai'i on non-target native insects:

> "Owing to my own occupation in the forests of different Islands and to Koebele's infrequent visits to Honolulu, we did not happen to meet during the earliest years of my work, but on returning from a considerable stay in the Kauai forests in 1895, I found him in Honolulu. Among other matters, we discussed the possibility of his economic introductions proving antagonistic to my own work on the native fauna, especially as some of the rarer Hemerobiids, which had been unusually numerous on the *Aphis*-infested *Pelea* trees at Kilauea, had disappeared after the introduced *Coleophora* had eaten up the *Aphis*." (Perkins, R.C.L., 1925, *The Hawaii Planters' Record* 29(4): 361).

There are few records of Perkins's activities in the field in late May and early June, but his insect labels state that he had done collecting on O'ahu around Honolulu and up to Kōnāhuanui.

After finishing letters to Sharp and Newton, Perkins again started up on his next trip; this one to the Big Island. He left for Hawai'i on 12 June and arrived at Punalu'u on 14 June (signing in at the Punalu'u Hotel) to begin his journey from Punalu'u to Volcano via Pāhala. Perkins signed in at the Volcano House hotel on 14 June,[208] but one of his first letters (to Newton) after arriving on the Big Island is dated 15 June 1895 and the place of origin as "Kau," which is the region in which Punalu'u in located. This may have been written while Perkins was at the Punalu'u Hotel and left it to be posted the next day; or, more likely, Perkins wrote

---

[208] The register of the Volcano Hotel has Perkins signed in on 14 June and listed his intended time of departure as "19 June" heading for 'Ōla'a. This was changed to 17 September. It is possible that he changed his intended departure date to 17 September to match up with the departure date of Zoë Atkinson and her entourage. The fact that Perkins and Miss Atkinson left the island of Hawai'i together is supported by the two names being signed in together (both in Perkins hand) at the Punalu'u Hotel on 17 September as they awaited the *W.G. Hall* to leave for Honolulu. The person signing below them, a Thomas Wall, states "...been liaising from Hilo to this place for two weeks trying to catch a steamer for Honolulu at last got the W.G. Hall." (*Hawaii Volcanoes National Park Archives*). Zoë's sisters and Mr. Brown instead returned to Honolulu the way they had arrived — via Hilo.

the letter on the 14th while at the Punaluʻu Hotel, but got the date incorrect. Another letter (dated 6 August 1895) has him in Kīlauea, where he lodged at the Volcano House hotel (*R.C.L. Perkins letter to C.M. Hyde, 6 August 1895, BPBM Archives, BPBM Letters*). Perkins, in fact, used the Volcano House as a center of operations for three months and collected at many different sites in the area including some ventures down to Hilo and others up the slopes of Mauna Loa. He finally left on 17 September with Zoë Atkinson, who had arrived at Volcano with her sisters Lani and Mollie and A.M. Brown on 7 July.

JOURNALS AND REMEMBRANCES

During this period I collected insects in large numbers from about 1200 ft. in Puna district to about 6 or 7 miles up Mauna Loa above Kilauea, and as far down from the crater as the halfway house[209] between Pahala and the volcano.

I also collected birds in some numbers though most of these I left alone although they were extremely numerous. Loxops coccinea was fairly common Heterorhynchus abundant, and Hemignathus in considerable numbers. Rhodacanthis occurred far back in the forest from Kilauea but not in the Koa forest within several miles from the crater. I only visited its locality once or twice and did not shoot at this bird. During my stay at Kilauea H.W. Henshaw the ornithologist and skilled collector of birds was staying at the hotel[210] being in poor health and at that time not himself doing any collecting. At times I brought him some birds to skin, and learnt a great deal from him. He used dry arsenic entirely on his skins instead of the messy arsenical soap I had been using, and nothing but a pair of rather blunt-pointed scissors. He prepared excellent skins very rapidly. At the time he was collecting in America — I think with the geological survey — he told me that he had to make 40 skins each day and took 3 1/2 minutes a skin. Those he made in my presence took him a minute to a minute and a half more, but he said he was much out of practice, not having done any such work recently. He also told me that he used a short tube in one barrel of his gun, which would take a .22 shot cartridge, with which he could kill small birds at close quarters without injury to their skins. At this time I was using a 20 gauge gun with a light charge of dust shot in one and a heavier one in the other barrel, but on returning to Honolulu I had a solid steel cartridge made to fit my own gun and bored eccentrically so as to fire the small .22 cartridge. I found this of greatest value in collecting, as it killed birds with certainty at short distances and also saved a considerable weight to be carried, with many other advantages. Up to this time I had lost many rare birds in the dense

---

[209] This was the halfway house built by Peter Lee, who was also the manager of the Volcano House hotel. It was built primarily as a lunch stopover for visitors to the Volcano House who traveled to and from the steamer port at Punaluʻu along the southwest coast of the island of Hawaiʻi. The port was originally created for transporting sugar, but Lee, being the enterprising hotel manager he was, built a road from the Punaluʻu port to the volcano and thus made the port available to vacationers to the region. Lee also built the Punaluʻu Hotel near the dock for visitors to stay overnight while awaiting steamers going to Honolulu or to rest after arriving in Punaluʻu before taking the carriage trip up to the volcano.

[210] The Volcano House hotel.

brush, since they were too close to be shot even with ordinary cartridge, and if a very light charge in my they flew on they were lost to sight. It was a great surprise to me to find that the tiny .22 shot cartridges fired from a 20 gauge gun killed so far as I could judge, just as well as if fired from the rifle of their own calibre. Up to this time I had shot only a few specimens of the pretty little bird Loxops coccinea, which was fairly common in the Koa forest, as I supposed it would be, from the results of my hurried visit to Kilauea for a few days in 1894.

I spent many days in the now well-known "Kipuka"[211] near Kilauea in and around which I found a number of Plagithmysus mostly new to me, P. bishopi on Pelea (later also bred from Xanthoxylum) and the curious var. gracilis, P. vitticollis on Rubus, but not in the great numbers in which the var. longulus occurred in Puna, P. perkinsi on Myoporum, the larvae much more frequent than the beetle, and varians and darwinianus very abundant on Koa and Mamani. Most of the few original specimens of sulphurescens occurred in the Kipuka on Wauke, but a few which were of the form I afterwards named giffardi, perhaps only a variety of the other, were taken on the wing. This giffardi I afterwards found abundantly near the volcano on Suttonia where bilineatus was abundant on the Ohia.

Neoclytarlus filipes was frequently seen on the same trees as P. darwinianus, but N. claviger on the Koa was much rarer and occurred on this tree about a mile from the volcano house on the Hilo road, where it was again noticed 10 years later. In the Olaa district at 1500 or 1600 ft. birds were less numerous both in species and individuals than round Kilauea and the almost constant heavy rains and extreme density of the pathless forest made collecting very difficult.

The ordinary, common birds including the Phaeornis and Psittacirostra, were very numerous, but I saw nothing I cared to shoot. The Phaeornis which at one part of the season I did not see at all at Kilauea appeared in numbers there at another time, and I presumed they worked up from the Olaa district at certain times of year. In spite of the continual rains Lepidoptera were very numerous in Olaa.

During my stay at the Volcano House the crater was visited by Signor d'Albertis,[212] the brother, I believe, of the traveller who in 1874 collected the otherwise unknown Plagithmysus albertisi, the locality for which remains doubtful, but one would suspect that it is attached to Ohia, possibly on West Maui.

---

[211] *Kīpuka* — Hawaiian term referring to an island of vegetation formed by lava flowing around and through patches of forest. Some of these *kīpuka* are home to some isolated and endangered native flightless insects that do not venture across the hot open country to other forested areas. This particular *kīpuka* is no doubt Kipuka Pua'ulu, more commonly known as "Bird Park." Around the late 1890s and early 1900s, efforts were made to restore the area from the devastation it had suffered at the expense of grazing cattle in the area.

[212] d'Albertis, Enrico Alberto (1846–1932). Sea captain, explorer, shipowner, and cousin of Luigi Maria d'Albertis, the latter who made significant cultural and natural history collections in New Guinea and Australia for the Genoa Museum. In writing these remembrances 40 years later, Perkins was mistaken in his remembering the year of d'Albertis's visit to the Volcano. Records have him visiting there in 1896 (arriving 21 August and leaving 8 September), not 1895.

SELECTED CORRESPONDENCE

Cambridge, England
24 June 1895
Robert Cyril Layton Perkins

Dear M[r]. Perkins,

Your two letters, one from Kauai 25.V. the other from Honolulu 29.V. are both to hand together. In them you mention having written to Prof. Newton with tube enclosed for me. This is not accessible as Newton has gone away yachting, & I do not suppose I shall be able to answer anything therein for about three weeks: and I anticipate that you also cannot hear from him till then. I am so pleased to hear you were successful with the thrush. Fifty Clytarli sounds very nice. I wonder what the trap is, and whether it will be successful in the case of C. perkinsi. Meyrick answered me at last saying he could not tell how many species of Leps. there are, as the species appear to be both very closely allied and extremely variable. That would be about the same as what is probably the case in the shells. I am quite astonished at the absence of Cyclothorax from Kauai.

I wrote you last week that I had received £200 from R.S. and had instructed the Treasurer to remit as soon as possible. I will set to work to get a dozen suitable wooden boxes &c. & send them out as soon as possible.

I am sorry to say we have had a very disreputable affair with Farren.[213] He disappeared from Cambridge some weeks ago, & is said to have gone off with a young woman leaving his wife and children in Cambridge. I only know what rumour says about it, & this is very unfavourable to F.

I am very sorry not to be able to answer your communication made through Professor Newton. I thought I had better write & tell you how it is I am not able to do so.

We have had scarcely any rain here for about two months, 7 things are very much dried up: it will again be very bad for the farmer. We are to have a general election in a few weeks & till then no one will talk much about anything else. With very best wishes

I am,

Yours very truly
D. Sharp.

---

[213]   Farren, William (1865–1952). Cambridge naturalist, taxidermist, furrier, and picture framer. His father, William Farren, Jr. was one of the original members of the Cambridge Natural History Society and he himself was its Secretary in 1909.

Hilo, Hawaii, Hawaiian Islands
18 July 1895
Charles McEwen Hyde

Dear Dʳ. Hyde,

I have today received your letter, & as a steamer {the Likelike} leaves this afternoon I take the opportunity to answer it. Please excuse the pencil as the writing place is fully occupied by others so I am writing in my room. I shall be going back in a few days to the Volcano which is good both for birds & other things.

The {steamer} Kinau also brought me the terms of the division of the spoil as drawn up by the Committee. These seem to me both simple & reasonable. For instance there is not a single species of bird so far collected, of which at least one & generally several specimens would not come to you by this arrangement. I expect to be in Honolulu in about 3 or 4 weeks when I can talk to you & Profʳ Brigham fully about the matter. I am very sorry I was not in the Necker expedition but I waited so long in Town I could not afford to do so any longer as the expedition was still uncertain. It was a thousand pities no scientific naturalist went. I believe Hall went but I hardly look at him in that light as the birds would be much less important than the other things.

If you can arrange to find me a good dog by the time I reach Town it would be most useful.

Mʳ Dowsett or Fred Whitney would probably know just what I would want is a thoroughly well broken dog – a good retriever, very tender committed {sic}, or a pup still young but partly broken would do as well as I could finish training him myself.

Yours very truly,
R.C.L. Perkins

I shall probably receive money from England in a week or two if indeed it has not already come, as supplies were to be sent me about June 22ⁿᵈ by wire addressed as Frisco. Probably there is already money to my credit at one of the banks or at Hackfelds in any case I am in no hurry.

Kilauea, Hawaii, Hawaiian Islands
6 August 1895
Charles McEwen Hyde

Dear Dʳ Hyde,

Your letter of Aug 1ˢᵗ with copies of letters is at hand. I have not received a copy of the agreement from you, but I have one from Dʳ Sharp so do not require another. I wrote to you about 2 weeks since from Hilo saying that I thought the arrangement both simple & fair. I am obliged for the copies of letters. I can see about a dog when I return to Town which will probably be soon. This is a splendid locality for certain species & I have got some very nice new things.

When you have definitely settled matters I should like to hear on account of writing Dr Hickson respecting money matters.

Yours very sincerely,
R.C.L. Perkins

Cambridge, England
15 August 1895
Robert Cyril Layton Perkins

Dear M^r. Perkins,

I have received three letters from you since I wrote you last on the 24$\underline{th}$ June: viz. 22.VI.95, 5.7.95, 16.VII.95. At Puna you have been much annoyed by heavy rain & no doubt the difficulty on the wet sides of the islands must be to find fine weather to collect in. Blackburn I think tried evening sweeping, about sundown with more success than other methods in these localities, but of course doing that depends on getting some fine weather.

Your last letter from Kau records brilliant success in the matter of Clytarlus & is of course very pleasing. It is now clear that your exploration of the islands was only just in time to permit us to see the really rich nature of the endemic fauna of the islands, which I am pretty sure ran formerly upwards of a hundred species. I think if you come across any of the larger species in considerable numbers I should like some specimens in alcohol to examine the condition of ovaries &c.

With regard to Scott Wilson, he is independent, going as he does on his own account. But you are of course master of the situation. If the arrangement with the Honolulu Museum people is ratified you had better tell Wilson this & suggest to him that he should present specimens of what he may shoot to the Honol. Mus. or to our Committee for it. On the other hand our Committee will no doubt have duplicates which we can place at his disposal of he wishes. If he takes this view of the matter at all, you should of course do all you can to help him as it will be of considerable assistance in getting the work of the Committee done: if however he does not seem to mean helping the Committee in its work, there can be no reason why you should assist him, with either information or in any other way. I think with a little talk with him, & your telling him you have to get specimens for Brit. {sic} Mus. Honolulu, & that it will be a great advantage to you to be relieved of particular bits of ornithological work, you will get him to arrange with you sufficiently to relive you to some extent. If he wont cooperate it will at worst leave you in the position you are in at present, & in such case you need not, as the Scotch say, fash, with him at all. I have not seen or heard anything about him, more than Prof. Newton told me he is going. No doubt he will be very anxious to get information from you, & this you can withold if he is not inclined to help forward the public work. Of course if any of us were making a profit there might be delicacy in getting assistance from him, but as we are all making sacrifices for the public benefit, there is no reason we should not expect him to do the same.

I hope you have improved weather; for permanent rain must be as injurious to health & temper as it is to entomological operations out of doors. We have had wet weather here now for two or three weeks past, & the harvest has suffered considerably.

Nothing has been heard here of W. Farren since his mysterious disappearance three or four months ago. His friends think the he may possibly communicate with you if he is alive, and if he does so they would be very much obliged if you would send them his address.

I have heard nothing of the case yet. I sent off a case to you a few weeks ago, containing two dozen boxes, &c.

Cost of carriage seems to have increased as this little lot come to £3.10.0.

I am very anxious to have an answer as to the negotiation, for the Honolulu Museum to share with us, as till I get that I cannot decide as to what steps to take with regard to money. I have asked them if they agree to place funds at your disposal immediately, should they not do so you must be so kind as to let me know at once, so that I may call an immediate meeting of the Committee. With best wishes

Yours very truly
D. Sharp.

Cambridge, England
4 September 1895
Robert Cyril Layton Perkins

Dear Mr. Perkins,

I have received your case of Kauai things, and your letters of 22.VII. and 4.VIII.95, from Puna and Kauai. The specimens have arrived in the best possible condition, and those you have taken so much trouble to mount, especially the

Tipulidae and fragile things will be very valuable on account of their fine state of preservation. I have written to Lord Walsingham & Meyrick to tell them of arrival and offered to send off at once. The Leps. are extremely nice as well as all the other things. I think there is a new genus of Elateridae, two specimens, much shorter in the body than Eopenthes, but with longer legs; this is extremely like a New Zealand thing. The case only arrived two days ago, and I have not disturbed any of the sawdust things, except to open a box or two and notice that nothing has gone wrong. The Kauai fauna is certainly very remarkable: indeed the diversity in the fauna of the different islands you are brining to light is altogether very surprising.

Gray will take these Kauai things in hand in a few days, and I'm sure he will do them in improved fashion. Mr. Haviland[215] is here working at Termitidae, he inclines to the opinion I suspected that the island ones are distinct, so please look out for them a little.

The news you give about your Hawaii things is very interesting. The Clytarli lot are turning out more and more surprising. I will superintend the mounting of the Anobii and see that they are done justice to.

To turn to other matters. I think you have done quite right about the Farren matter. Of course though we are very sorry for Mrs. F. We really cannot have anything to do with it. We do not know the rights and wrongs of the matter at all, and clearly Mrs. F. has been very deceived about her ideas of her husband going out to the islands. I took quite the line with her that you have done in your letter: and I should not be surprised if Mrs. F. were not very far off after all. Probably London would be the place to find him. No entomologist has heard of him as far as I can learn.

The British Association meets next week; I have no doubt we shall have our arrangement with the Honolulu Museum sanctioned, and as soon as that is done, I will write to Mr. Hyde and ask them to supply you with funds. Perhaps you will let me or the Treasurer, know your views and theirs on this point.

The case came by the Agency of Mess.rs Wheatley: they have charged a guinea on account of a "Landing certificate" due to the things being "shipped in bond". I presume it is a swindle, but please bear it in mind and if there is any way of avoiding our being done in this way, adopt it.

Re pins. I will forward your complaint about the softness to Watkins & Doncaster.[216] You said you would send samples of another size, but have not done so. I shall wait a little to see if it turns up before taking any steps about a fresh supply.

---

[215] Haviland, George Darby (1857–1901). Haviland was a surgeon and naturalist. As an entomologist, he specialized in termites. However, as the second director of the Sarawak Museum in Borneo (1891–1893), he specialized in flowering plants.

[216] Watkins & Doncaster were the standard suppliers of equipment and supplies for natural history collectors in England.

I am interested in what you say about the Japyx, because your words are almost exactly the same as those I have used in the book about the European species, which I found under a stone in company with newly hatched earwigs which it greatly resembled.

A single one of your tubes of Kauai things got broken. It contained a very few small Machilis or young Crustacea & some minute Coleopterous larvae, I am afraid they are about spoiled.

I have heard nothing fresh about Scott Wilson: he ought to be starting now I should think: but I see very little of Professor Newton in this vacation time.

Typical advertisement of Watkins & Doncaster in a British entomological journal.

The first set of birds hitherto received have been sent to the Brit. Mus. and we have received a special letter of thanks: the lot contained 27 species & 5 genera new to the Museum collection!

I expect the Vol. of Insects (1st part) of the Cambridge Natural History[217] will be published next month, and I hope to send you a copy. The Brenthidae of the Biologia are printed and published, and the Insecta of Record for 1894 also printed; this last is bigger than ever, there being 100 titles more than there has ever been before.

I must now conclude as I have to go to the University Library to look up a passage from S^{t}. Augustine for a motto for the book, so with best wishes, I am,

Yours very truly
D. Sharp.

Many Oodemas have appeared since I wrote last, but not many Heteramphus. I think however there are more species of these latter than supposed.

---

217   The *Cambridge Natural History* (1895–1902) was a 10-volume "encyclopedia" of natural history edited by S.F. Harmer & A.E. Shipley. The insects by Sharp appeared in two volumes (pp. 83–565 of volume 5 [1895]; all of volume 6[1899] totalling 626 pp.). The set of volumes remained a standard reference of natural history for over half a century.

Kaua'i
15 October–10 November 1895

Soon after arriving in Honolulu from Hawai'i Island in September, Perkins packed up his collections and had them sent off to England. He then sat down and wrote to Hyde on letterhead of the Honolulu Hotel that he had just returned from Ka'ū, Puna and expected to go on to Kaua'i before Mauna Kea, but was concerned about the "cholera scare."

His intended departure for Kaua'i was briefly mentioned in the local Honolulu newspaper:

> " R.C.L. Perkins, naturalist for the Royal Society and British association of England, will leave on the next island boat for Kauai." (*Hawaiian Gazette*, 1895 (4 October): 5).

However, Perkins's concerns to Hyde were well founded. As soon as he made arrangements to leave Honolulu to go to another island, he was put into quarantine due to the cholera outbreak in Honolulu (which lasted from 20 August to 18 October 1895). Being confined for weeks to the Honolulu quarantine facilities, on what was called Mauliola or "Quarantine Island" outside of Honolulu harbor (filled over in 1940 and subsumed into what is now Sand Island), was obviously an unfortunate inconvenience for the oft-traveling Perkins. Perkins wrote at least two letters to Sharp from there (labeled as "quarant." or "qu.") in early October, near the end of his quarantine, and expressed his concerns to Sharp and Newton about having his movements restricted for a period of time. At that time he was quarantined with some Kaua'i residents waiting to return home from Honolulu. One of them wrote a parody of the stay at the quarantine station in one of the local newspapers:

> "Immediately upon our arrival here, the fumigation commenced, and oh, how shall I describe the most delightful process? Those who have experienced the delights of Russian or Turkish baths can form but a faint idea of the blissful effects produced. The Volcano House sulphur baths are considered a luxury and a delight, for which we are eager to squander our ducats, but there is little or no comparison between any of these and the Mauliola fumigation baths. Suffice to say that every mother's son of us, and daughter too, including the baby, enjoyed this rare treat, gratis. So thoroughly and well done was it, that we have not yet lost the delightfully exhilarating effects, but go capering about like a lot of juveniles just freed from school.
>   The surroundings of Mauliola are all that go to delight the heart of an artist, lying opposite the beautiful Nuuanu Valley; the majestic hills with their varying lights and shadows

on either side, and the broad expanse of the "grand, old ocean" to the south and west, afford scenic effects that must be seen to be appreciated.

The accommodations are all and more than could be expected, and surpass those offered guests at many of the hotels in Honolulu. The service is good, and the kindness of the officials in charge is a most remarkable feature of the place. We have enjoyed our stay upon this lovely spot so fully and pleasantly that we cannot realize that our time is up and we must bid farewell to our pleasant surroundings and go, and are exceedingly loath to do so.

Our days were passed in rambles about the island, novel reading, cribbage, whist, etc. Our evenings, glorious moonlight evenings, never to be forgotten, in song and dance — as we have a number of accomplished musicians and several very sweet and well cultivated voices among our number." (*Hawaiian Gazette*, 1895 (4 October): 5).

Perkins finally left the quarantine facility after his prescribed stay and on 15 October, he boarded the inter-island steamship *Mikahala* and made his way to the island of Kaua'i, visited his friend Munro, and did further collecting upslope at Kahōluamanu and Halemanu. Ironically, a few days after he left (18 October 1895), the quarantine on all travelers from Honolulu was lifted by the Board of Health.

JOURNALS AND REMEMBRANCES

In October 1895 I revisited the high plateau above Waimea. This visit was necessitated by the fact that previously I had seen few specimens of the bird Heterorhynchus hanapepe, of which there were no specimens either in the British Museum or the Bishop Museum. When I first went to the Islands it was presumed that all birds collected by me would be added to the Scott Wilson collection in the Museum of Cambridge University. Since this Museum already possessed the original specimens collected by Wilson, the Heterorhynchus was not specially marked in the lists of birds with which Prof. Newton furnished me when I went out to the islands, as one that he particularly wanted me to obtain. In consequence of the British Museum request for a set of birds I now concentrated on obtaining this species and making some further study of its habits.

At the time of this visit birds were very abundant and in very fine plumage, the adults having fully recovered from the moult following the nesting season.

Both the parents and young of Heterorhynchus together with the various other species were keeping together in mixed companies at this season. In some of these assemblies all the known forest birds of Kauai excepting only Phaeornis palmeri were present. The Heterorhynchus, Hemignathus, Oreomyza, Chasiempis, and the two species of Chlorodrepanis were mostly in the smaller trees, e.g. Elaeocarpus, while Vestiaria, Himatione, Loxops and Psittacirostra were generally overhead in the larger Ohia trees, though at the time these also came low down and associated with the others, as also did the Oo-aa. Heterorhynchus was definitely the rarest of these species, then came Hemignathus about three to one of the former. All the other species were common, most of them very common. In all I saw many more specimens of the Heterorhynchus than I cared to shoot at.

Insects I noticed were much less abundant than in the earlier months of the year, and I seem to have collected comparatively few species new to me, though this would have been partly due to the special attention I gave to the birds. Lepidoptera were particularly scarce as compared with their numbers on my earlier visits.[218]

SELECTED CORRESPONDENCE

Honolulu, Hawaiian Hotel
Oahu, Hawaiian Islands
Monday {23 September 1895}
Charles McEwen Hyde

Dear D[r] Hyde,

In case you have not seen that I have returned to Town with my Kau; Puna, collections I send this note & enclose the latest from D[r] Sharp. You will probably wish to see me & I can do so at any time. The only engagement I have is to night after dinner so far as I know. I expect to go to Kauai before beginning Mauna Kea, but my plans have been rather upset by the cholera scare & I am not yet sure.

With kind regards

Yours very truly,
R.C.L. Perkins

Cambridge, England
1 October 1895
Robert Cyril Layton Perkins

Dear M[r]. Perkins,

I enclose copy of our report to the Brit. Ass. The £100 been granted to us. I have written to M[r]. Hyde pressing him to arrange that you shall be supplied with funds during the next twelve months, and I hope this will be acceded to by them.

Please let me know if you think this will be done all right, for it is necessary for us to make our plans long beforehand.

---

218 A brief entry in Munro's diary supplements this small narrative as follows: "Mr. Perkins was with us for a short while last month. He spent about 2 weeks at Kaholuamano getting birds of which he got a good series including 3 series of Nukupuu. He kindly left a few birds in spirits." (*G.C. Munro diary, 28 November 1895, BPBM Archives, MS SC Munro Box 13.2*).

Meyrick is very pleased with the last lot of Macro-lepidoptera. The Micros I gave to Lord Walsingham tomorrow.

The sample of pins has never arrived so please recollect that I have done nothing whatsoever about pins: and let me have instructions as soon as possible.

A set of the first lot of birds has been selected for the Bishop Museum and a list of the specimens sent to the Trustees.

Hoping you are well, I am with best wishes,

Yours very truly,
D. Sharp.

Magdalene College,
Cambridge, England
26 October 1895
Robert Cyril Layton Perkins

My dear Perkins,

Your letters to Sharp & myself of 26 August, 20-22 Sept. & 27 Sept. have reached us this week, & as he is not writing to you by this mail I take it on me to thank you for all of them. It is of course with much concern that we hear of the cholera outbreak, not that either of us have any fear for you, but we know how much inconvenience it is certain to cause you – as indeed it has already begun to do. It does not surprise me to read that people had lost their heads in consequence, because that nearly always happens in communities not superior to belief in quarantine & fumigations – I only trust that there may be enough sensible men to see that the precautions that are really effectual are taken & then the disease will have no great run. I have never been exposed to the risk, & you may say that it is very easy for me sitting here to despise it, but that it is quite otherwise if you are brought face to face with cases, of which a large percentage are fatal. However, I do implicitly believe that with care to avoid swallowing anything that can contain the bacillus there is no danger at all. In some cases I admit it may not be easy to do that, but I think that generally a prudent man can manage it – & of course water that has not been sterilized by boiling is especially to be shunned. We heard by telegraph some weeks ago of the outbreak, & directly afterwards Wilson wrote to Evans to say that he should not go out this year. I can't blame him for that. I think I should not go out myself if I were he, because I know of the extraordinary inconvenience to which one would be subject – & I pity you uncommonly for your bad luck in such an affliction falling on the islands while you are there. I saw Evans 2 days ago who said he had heard from you & also that Wilson is expected here next week. I dare say I could get him to reconsider his determination not to go out, but I will not do so. If he went & took the disease, which from his careless way of going on he might easily do, I should be held responsible. This being so I think you need not disturb yourself as to his arrival & its consequences, & to dispose of that matter at once I may say that what you now tell me is the first positive information I had on the subject. I know that something went wrong with him at Kona, to which he would not return (& hence got only the first Chloridops & never a Rhodacanthis), but I had always suspected that the young gentleman had got into some scrape with a man there. I am sorry that you have not got on well with everybody – but with the best intentions misconstructions of conduct will arise – & it could not be expected that you should be so long in the islands without some people not liking you as well as others do, so I think none the worse on that account. Wilson, it is true, brought back a good many red birds, but I feel sure that he has never sold any to "clothing shops" by which I suppose "plumassier" are intended. You can safely contradict such a report. I dont in the least mind asking him however, though I shall be careful not to compromise you in any way, & I regret you have had so much bother about the Farren business, but I can't see how it concerns you. I believe nothing has been heard of him, but I really dont know, and am careful not to enquire. I see a notice in the shop that everything in it is to be sold by auction before long. Of course I pity his wife for I have not heard that she was in any way to blame.

Sharp has read your letter to me & bids me to say that your wishes about recarbolizing the insects, when they arrive, shall be duly attended to. We are much obliged to you for cautioning him.

It is gratifying to hear that you have got £200 from D^r. Hyde & I hear from Hickson that he has your letter announcing the fact – but it seems to me strange that D^r. Hyde (or M^r. Bishop either) has not written to either Sharp or myself on the subject. I shall be very glad to get the bird skins off to him; but I dont like sending them without definite instructions.

We shall of course continue to be in some degree anxious about you, & I hope you will be keeping us informed of your movements & welfare. The irregularity of the post is shewn by the long time your letter of 26 August took to reach Sharp – & here I may maintain that beside my letters the receipt of which you acknowledge I wrote you on the 7th Sept. (my last) announcing the arrival of the Kauai colln, but that letter could not of course have reached you by the 27th though I hope it would a few days later.

I observe what you say as to young Chasiempis & the genus Himatione. If that has to be still further broken up it is the group of curve-billed green species that must be newly named – so you had better invent one. H. sanguinea must remain as it is without a doubt. I always thought "Poacheria"[219] was very near it, & indeed suggested to Wilson to call his specimen saturata in reference to sanguinea, for it looked very much as if it would prove to be (with other differences – though of course one never dreamt of the crest)[220] a very deeply coloured form of the com-

---

219 Poacheria = *Palmeria*, referring to Rothschild renaming it, i.e., poaching it.
220 Wilson only collected the young without a crest. Perkins got the adult.

mon species. The Laysan one I have not seen – I wish I could get it! By the way I may tell you confidentially that the Golden Walter wrote me about a month ago, offering all sorts of rarities for a specimen of your <u>Drepanis</u>, but I declined recommending our museum authorities to accept the exchange. I told him that I should even hesitate about doing so if he offered us the <u>Ciridops</u> which, but for him, we should have had! Please dont let this go further.

Though this is a rather poor answer to your long letter, which greatly interested me, I think I have touched on every subject you mention & I am really much put to it for time. I am not even able to read over what I have written being very busy today & the post is now going.

So with my best wishes – all the more fervent seeing the inconvenience to which you are exposed – I remain

Yours very truly
Alfred Newton

Cambridge, England
11 November 1895
Robert Cyril Layton Perkins

Dear M^r. Perkins,

I have now received Brunner von Wattenwyl's paper on the first lot of Orthopteran, & at once communicate its contents to you.

The genus Brachymetopa, (the green & brown short-winged Locustids) peculiar to the islands is brought by you from one species to three. The genus of small crickets with remarkable wing-cases, Paratrigonidium, has two new species. And the long wingless crickets form a new genus, Prognathogryllus, with two species. You have also one new Blattid. Quite a number of species mentioned in de Bormans list were not in your lot, including one endemic earwig found in all the islands by de Bormans. You had four species of earwig against de Borman's 7.

One or two of the introduced species you found were not known from the Archipelago previously.

The total number of Orthops. now known is 29. I expect you will bring it up to 40, with new indigenous crickets & Brachymetopa, & perhaps one or two new Phyllodromia and earwigs & another or two of Paratrigonidium.

I trust all the quarantine & cholera difficulties are over by this time.

I think it improbable Scott Wilson will come out: you understand I am sure that you will do just as you like about him. He has nothing to do with the Committee, goes on his own account, if he is inclined to help you well & good, if not you can't help it, & must do just as you like about giving yourself any trouble for his sake, or giving him information.

With best wishes, I am,

Yours very truly,
D. Sharp.

Your letter of 10th Oct^r. (written in quarantine) duly arrived. I sent a little cork & a few long pins in registered letter last week.

'Īao Valley, Maui in the 1890s.

Wailuku River, Hawai'i Island in the 1890s.

Slopes of Mauna Kea, Hawai'i Island
Early December 1895–28 January 1896

Perkins this time wanted to collect birds on the slopes of Mauna Kea above Hilo and had hopes of finding *mamo*, *'ō'ō*, and the "Green Viridonia." Having spent a good deal of time on the relatively drier west side of the Big Island, Perkins this time wished to check on the more moist and thickly forested areas in the windward side. There was only one steamer that went on this route: the Wilder Steamship Company's S.S. *Kinau*. Perkins booked passage on the 29 November trip, leaving Honolulu Harbor at 10 a.m. and scheduled to arrive in Hilo the next day at noon.

On the overnight voyage, which took many visitors to the Kīlauea volcano on a packaged round trip from Honolulu to Hilo and back for only $50 (including lodging at the Volcano House), Perkins took the opportunity of getting off the boat at the various stops along the windward (Hāmākua) coast of the Big Island that it made along the way the next morning. These brief stops were merely to "spy out" the land for potential collecting areas, after which he would get back on board and resume the voyage to the port of Hilo. Upon arrival, no doubt Perkins made his way to the home of H.W. Henshaw to gather information on bird collecting in that vicinity, and to make arrangements for a number of local assistants to help him in the field.

Perkins's trip up the slopes of Mauna Kea was one of the few times that he took Hawaiians with him to help him in his hunting—one of them, a bird catcher. Although he preferred not to do this during his Hawaiian fieldwork, the dense forest cover of the Hāmākua slopes of Mauna Kea, especially around the Wailuku River necessitated assistance in clearing to allow him to spot and collect the rare birds he was after.

> "In the winter months several camping expeditions were made on Mauna Kea, birds being the chief object. On one of these two expeditions there was not a single day without heavy rain and the collecting was very trying. On account of the density of the forest, had a gang of natives with me, in order to cut trails through the forest. They all suffered much from the wet and cold, it being impossible for dry clothes for sleeping in, and one of them met with a bad accident. On my last attempt, however, I had exceptional weather for two weeks and secured the bird I chiefly wanted, and some rather nice insects." (Perkins, R.C.L., 1913, *Fauna Hawaiiensis* 1: xxxiv).

This area of the Big Island is still one of the wildest of forest areas, with no easy access into the deeper forest and remains to this day largely unexplored.

"On the Hilo side of the island, the perpetually wet windward flanks of Mauna Kea remain an entomologically unexplored wilderness above 700 m elevation where the cane fields end." (Liebherr, J.K. & Polhemus, D.A., 1997, *Pacific Science* 51(4): 351).

Perkins gave a long account of this trip in correspondence to Zimmerman:

"After leaving Kauai I proceeded to Hilo in which district except for some brief trips to other parts I remained until the end of Jan.y 1896. During this period I made four or five camps, one at Kaumana close to the 1880 lava flow, on both sides of which I collected, another somewhat further North (the name of the place I have forgotten, but I think it was Kaiwiki) & on two or three occasions I camped near the edge of the Wailuku river. Here the forest was very dense & I had natives with me to more or less clear a path upwards, so that I could traverse this fine forest belt. I collected on both sides of the river, but mostly on the left side (looking downstream). In this area the Mamo was once common & the old native who was with me showed me the exact spot when a number were shot in 1880, the year when the great lava flow nearly reached the town of Hilo.[221] He himself was there when these birds were shot. As he accompanied me he would at short intervals imitate the cry of the Mamo by which it could be attracted, the cry being slightly less loud, but otherwise exactly like that of the black Mamo of Molokai with which I was well acquainted. To his surprise we neither heard nor saw any of this bird, but I was pleased to meet with Viridonia for the first time. This bird was unknown to him, though he knew all the others that were found here. I have no doubt that had I stayed for a long period the Mamo would have occurred, as these birds like others move their quarters according to the flowering times of various trees. The Oo was common in this, but exceedingly wild & many other birds were abundant, notably Loxops & Heterorhynchus. In two of my visits it hardly ceased raining day or night & the water streaming down from the tall trees made it hard to look up & keep birds in sight, their being mostly high up.

About the 1880 flow were many fine Loulu palms & there I spent much time in hope of finding Ciridops, which one might have expected to occur, but no doubt it was the wrong season. Nothing very special occurred in the way of insects during these two months, but as will be seen the weather was very unfavorable for the most part & I was largely occupied otherwise. In the forest about the 1800 flow the mongoose was in extraordinary numbers, as were the rats, but the former retired entirely at sundown & the latter in the day time." *(R.C.L. Perkins letter to E.C. Zimmerman, 14 February 1944, BPBM Entomology Archives).*

Regarding the Hawai'i 'ō'ō, Perkins related the following little-known note in later correspondence to his friend Munro:

"I suppose that you know that either in Kalakaua's later years or in Liliuokalani's reign a number of Oo were captured & brought from Hawaii & turned out on the windward side of Haleakala. I was told that individuals of these still existed for several years on Maui, but I neither heard nor saw any in 94, 95, or 96." *(R.C.L. Perkins letter to G.C. Munro, 28 November 1945, BPBM Archives, MS SC Munro Box 13.3).*

The tract below Perkins entitled "Collecting on the Slopes of Mauna Kea from Hilo."

---

[221] This lava flow, the first in over 1,000 years to come as close to Hilo Bay as it did, actually started in November 1880 and continued into June of 1881 before it came to a stop just outside the current city limits.

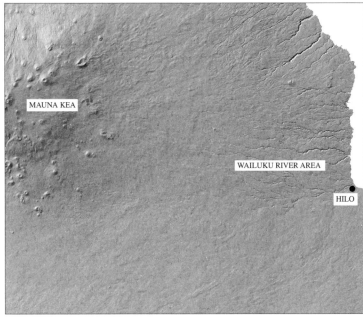

Map of Hawai'i with detail showing Perkins's collecting areas on the slopes of Mauna Kea.

JOURNALS AND REMEMBRANCES

[About the middle of January {= December} 1895 I made my first attempt for birds on Mauna Kea. I took a supply of food up on a pack animal to the native houses which were highest above the canefields in Amaula. The forest above being very dense I engaged several natives (at one time 4–5) to make trails where this was densest. Many of the trees were very fine and tall and were thickly covered with masses of the climbing Ieie. From the houses above mentioned we packed my tent, the fly, food, and cooking tins &c well into the forest, I myself being comparatively lightly burdened, carrying only a gun, ammunition, and collecting apparatus wrapped up in oilskin. Fortunately the morning was fine and at 1 p.m. we halted, and built a rough house about 20 ft. by 10 ft. roofing it first with banana leaves and above this with the fly of my tent. The latter was erected separately and the other house was mainly used as a shelter when eating, and sometimes for the purpose of trying to dry our clothes. On the way up through the forest I made a note that I saw several specimens of "Deilephila calida" [should have been pyrrhias] {= pyrias} hovering over Lehua flowers, and that "I had no net available to catch specimens". Owing to the excessively heavy rainstorms, a fire was kept up continually in the open during my stay, great logs, practically dead tree-trunks, being supplied to this, so that by removing the upper ones, one could always cook rice or boil water for coffee in spite of the rain. It was not until December 19th that I made some continuous notes of the collecting.]

December 19
It poured with rain in the afternoon. I saw 3 Oo, very wild and unapproachable, and all far out of shot.

December 20
Made trail still further in, from 8 a.m. till 4 p.m. There was very heavy rain. I saw Heterorhynchus, and Loxops and I shot a Hemignathus but unfortunately a shot carried away its beak, so I did not skin it. The natives' dogs caught {cornered} a very large sow, which I shot. They {natives} cut up and took this down {to their houses below}, but the old man stayed with me. About 3 p.m. I heard a strange sound from a bird, but could get no sight of it. It was not much unlike the softest cry of Drepanis and I was very excited. I kept on calling the attention of the old native to this sound, but either he could not or would not hear. He looked very fagged out, and I myself was extremely tired at this time, as we had had a very hard tramp clearing or forcing through the brush.

December 21
I sent the kanakas down for more food. They use up a great deal and this is rather a disadvantage in taking natives with one. On their departure I left the old man to keep the fire going and went out alone. I saw great numbers of Heterorhynchus not only old, but also young ones being fed by their parents. Very remarkable at this season, but here nothing could be more unlike the conditions than those where the bird is plentiful in the dry, upper forest of Kona. I shot 3 Hemignathus and 3 male and one female Loxops. I saw no other birds, except common species. It rained early, but cleared up at noon and was very wet by 4 p.m. again. The old man with me here tells me that the Mamo was common at the time the 1880 flow came down nearly to Hilo, and the Oo very abundant. He seems to know nothing of Rhodacanthis and Chloridops nor of some of the obscure birds, whose feathers would not have been considered valuable. The Amakihi and Akialoa and the Akialoa nukupuu he knew at once, the two former visiting flowers for the nectar with the Mamo and Oo, as he said.

December 22
Went up by yesterday's trail, but birds were comparatively scarce; shot one female Loxops. I took a series of wingless crickets [Leptogryllus] from tree ferns and a few of the small Gryllids [Paratrigonidium]. Some beetles: Cyclothorax, Oligota and Brachypeplus. Some of the giant Anax were flying up and down a branch of the river, over the water. I killed one as it flew, missing it or failing to kill it with the first shot, but the left barrel brought it down and I recovered it by wading.

[Later I shot several more as they flew over the water, without spoiling them as specimens]. It rained as usual.

December 23
Went up the same way as before and shot one fine ♀ and one young ♂ Loxops. The latter was badly diseased round the eye. It rained all the morning, but cleared in the afternoon. A green Locustid [Banza] I picked off a Lobeliad leaf, and from a rotting stem a long series of 2 or 3 Staphylinids, a probably new Brachypeplus and a single Cis. The small earwig is abundant here. The Kanakas came back with more food.

December 24
Crossed to the other side of a branch of the Wailuku river I saw a ♂ and ♀ Oo on the top of a very high tree, but could not get near them. Later another pair, of which I killed the ♀, a very fine bird and bursting with fat. I also shot 2 ♂ and one ♀ Loxops. It never ceased to pour with rain all day.

December 25
The same way as on 24th. Shot a fine ♂ Oo in the same tree as yesterday's female. I heard a strange bird. Can it possibly be the Mamo?

December 26
It has poured with rain and I have sent down the natives, all of them have the worst kinds of colds. I myself am free though I have slept wet and cold each night. I went by myself up the same track. I shot two young ♂ Loxops and one old one. I heard the strange bird in exactly the same spot as on the 25th. Soon I saw a bird, very indistinctly, amongst a dense mass of Ieie enveloping a large half-fallen Koa tree and killed it. It was an adult ♀ Viridonia, rather, badly hit about the head. Stomach &c nearly full of the little native Gryllid crickets, which the natives sometimes call 'Kopena' [Paratrigonidium] but small caterpillars (e.g. Tineids) from dead Ieie stems were also present. The song of this bird is Drepanine, but distinct from others. The male bird was evidently or audibly there, but I could get no sight of it. I returned to camp for awhile to wring out my clothes, but hurried back to the spot where I had shot the female at 3 p.m. I heard no sound from the male, nor could I see it. The deluge of rain on the foliage made it almost impossible to hear any bird. The presence of this bird is a surprise to me, as I had certainly inferred from Palmer's conversation, that he had obtained it when his headquarters were at Waimea and in quite a different part of Mauna Kea. He did not, however, definitely say that it was from that neighbourhood. I note that the maxilla is dark above and pale bluish white along the lower margin on the basal half, the legs and feet are slate colour, the iris brown. There is a distinct crop or dilatation of the oesophagus and the tongue is typically Drepanine as in the Amakihi. This bird is not known to my old native, who examined it with great interest.

December 27
I started at daybreak for the Viridonia locality, but I saw no sign of it. I shot at one Akialoa, but unfortunately could not gather it, as it was not killed clean. I took one fine male Loxops and one male Heterorhynchus, the latter for the sake of the local-

ity I took two Uhini males [Banza] one green, the other the brown variety. There were only one or two showers, it being the first really fine day up here. Very disappointing, as to-morrow I must go down to Hilo to refit.

* * * * * *

[I made two other camping trips to this forest. Of one which was short I have no note. It never ceased to rain and the results were of no importance. There were many Loxops feeding high up in the Koa trees, but the water streaming down from the foliage of the trees made it difficult to look up or to shoot. As I had still only obtained the one specimen of Viridonia, as recorded above, I again returned to my first locality and fortunately obtained some quite good weather. On this last occasion I worked more to the south of my former trails. I made the following brief note on the results of this trip after I left the forest.]

I have now obtained 6 Viridonia. Its song is very like that of the Amakihi, but it is louder and sometimes at the end there are one or two very powerful notes. Its call note is low and rather plaintive, but can be heard from a long way off, somewhat resembling the old native's imitation of the Mamo's call. There are always crickets in the food contents, and occasionally the larva of a Scotorhythra. [Scotorythra].

On this occasion I have seen Oreomyza and have shot 1 Loxops and two male Hemignathus. Except for a few beetles and a green cricket [Banza] collected casually, I left the insects alone. The Oo was not at all rare. I did not shoot at any, when after Viridonia, but the natives were always excited at the sight of an Oo and finally I shot at one on the top of a very lofty tree some way from me. The bird was winged, but fell down on to a lower thick branch and ran along this. I could easily have shot it again, but one of the younger natives climbed up amongst the Ieie on the trunk (wishing to catch it alive) until he reached the branch, about 30 feet from the ground. He then fell head first, being dizzy, and cut the top of his head, right across, on a fallen trunk. Owing to the difficulty of getting him down through the forest I returned with him to Hilo, instead of staying a few days more in camp. I am quite sure that by staying in the woods for a longer period one could still get the Mamo. Where I have been was a definite locality for the bird, and the old man showed me the very tree in which it had been shot at the time when the 1880 flow was approaching Hilo. He was in the forest then, and a dozen were killed at that time. Whenever he has been with me, all the time as we go along he gives what is no doubt an exact imitation of the Mamo's call. It is similar to that which I have so often heard from the Molokai Drepanis, but probably less loud. Though he tried hard, he never succeeded in getting any response to his call. Moving about as birds do, one might have to stay here months before coming across a rare bird like the Mamo and if after all one failed, one would probably have but a poor show of insects as a reward for much time, labour and discomfort. Yet I am sure the Mamo is still here at certain seasons and it would be interesting if one could stay in this forest for a year and settle the matter.

[At the beginning of January I was camping alone in the forest at Kaumana, but only for a short time. I have the following brief note on collecting there.]

The only bird's I have shot are the Elepaio, the Io and the <u>Oreomyza</u>. I have collected some rather nice <u>Lepidoptera</u> here, but not much else in insects. Birds are abundant, most of the ordinary species being common. I spent a great deal of time around the <u>Pritchardia</u> palms in the hope of coming across the Ula-ai-hawane, but I had no luck. Though the palms are numerous they were not in good condition for attracting birds. Rats and Mongoose are in extraordinary numbers here. The latter are very active all day, but the rats only come out towards evening and they do not interfere with one another, as the mongoose have then retired.

One wet morning I killed eight or nine mongoose in a short time. Each time I shot one, another would quickly appear and begin dragging off the dead one. The forest here is a very likely place for <u>Ciridops</u> when conditions are favourable.

SELECTED CORRESPONDENCE

Hilo, Hawaii, Hawaiian Islands
3 January 1896
Charles McEwen Hyde

Dear Dr Hyde,

Although I expect to come back to Honolulu on the Kinau which will take this, I thought it better to write you in case I am not able. I particularly want to get to Waianae by February to get some insects as the windward sides of the islands are no good so I have done little here. My main object was to get the bird called 'Viridonia' by Rothschild perhaps the best known of all the Hawaiian birds & known only by the four specimens got by his collectors. It is quite unknown to the natives: old bird catchers here who have taken the 'Mamo' by scores & who accompanied me here had never seen it. I must say I have been successful in getting about half a dozen specimens altogether. Rothschild with his usual sagacity had assigned it to an utterly wrong family of birds by putting it with the 'Oo' &^c while really it belongs to the 'Amakihi' 'Iiwi '&c group of Hawaiian species. It is no beauty but a great rarity. I should have got more but one of my kanakas yesterday very nearly killed himself with a bad fall away up in the forest. I hope he will recover all right in time, but at first I thought it was certainly all over with him. The woods here are absolutely impenetrable, so I have to take groups of natives along to cut trails which is of course very exhaustive work, & collecting here is no light undertaking owing to the roughness & the living for days together up in the wet woods. Generally we built huts of banana leaves which saved carrying tents.

By the way all the natives here now know Viridonia by the native name I gave it 'Nukupololei' which is very suitable as there is a 'Nukupu' here too to which it is rather closely allied. It is rather curious that an outsider should create a native name for a bird in a spot where several real old Mamo & Oo hunters still remain, though the finer bird is gone from its old haunts. Some time I shall have to get more Viridonia as all but one are females. Another remarkable fact, as that sex is usually much more difficult to get than the male.

I got a beautiful series of skins of the 'Akakani' a bird generally confused with the 'Apapani' but utterly different & much less common. Commoner birds I could not waste time over in such a difficult hunting ground.

Yours very sincerely
R.C.L. Perkins

Magdalene College
Cambridge, England
3 January 1896
Robert Cyril Layton Perkins

My dear Perkins,

Your letters of 26 Nov^r. (Honolulu) & 2 Dec^r. (Hilo) have reached me this week, & for each of them, I thank you. The "dead failure" reported in the former has been of course a great disappointment to me as it must have been to you & I condole with you accordingly. The objection of the people to cooking for you I dont understand, but it could not be expected that you should stay to be starved. I note what you say as to the collection from Kauai you were sending off – the small Petrel, I presume, will have to go back to the Museum when it has been determined? A good thing that there is no more Cholera. I should say that <u>we</u> do not want any more of the Molokai <u>Drepanis</u>, but I dare say the Bishop Museum people would like another specimen or two & if so their wish is reasonable – otherwise I would rather the poor birds were let alone. So much for your first letter – the second is hopeful, & I am sure I trust all will turn out well in regard to <u>Viridonia</u>, <u>Ciridops</u>, & the rest. There are very few places in the world that are really inaccessible, & it will not surprise me to find that you make your way up to the forest between Waipio & Waimanu (I am not sure I have read the names right – & being away from home I have no map to consult) at any rate I dont doubt you will have a good try for it – if only to get away from the hateful <u>cane</u> <u>pieces</u>, for which when I was in the West Indies I had just as strong a loathing as you have, & for the same reason.

Being away from home I can not say when I wrote to you last – but it was not so very long ago & I then disquisiterized (to your edification I hope) on the difficulty of establishing "Families" in the Order <u>Passeres</u>. I believe that if I had then had more time I could easily have made the case stronger but I will not bore you further on the subject.

The chief if not the only important news I have to tell you is that Wilson was here today to luncheon. He has positively taken passage for himself & his Spaniel on the N. German boat from Southampton on the 22^d last for New York. He will then go by easy stages to San Francisco, to see Bishop among others & expects to embark on the 7th March & to reach Honolulu on the 12th of the same. He will then take an early steamer to Hawaii & thinks of going <u>first</u> to the Greenwell country —but will immediately put himself in communication with you. At the present moment he proposes to care only about getting the tailless Rail but I shall be much surprised if his ardour does not recur to him & knowing him as I do I believe you will be able to use him as wax. I have today been especially dwelling to him on the need of getting the other Rail – <u>Crex</u> or <u>Rallus</u> <u>sandvicensis</u> of which the unique specimen he lists at Leyden. Being one of the species obtained by Cook's people it must have been either from Kauai or Hawaii. Now we know that <u>R.</u> <u>ecaudatus</u> was the bird in the latter, & therefore the presumption is that it came from the former, while what you wrote some time since of the upland bog, which no one of late seems to have tried seems to hold out hope of that being the locality where it may yet be found. At any rate it is worth looking after <u>with a dog</u>, & Wilson says he means to go, to Kauai before he has done, in order to visit Gay & some other people there. Pray then second my efforts in this respect. One thing more – please endeavor to make out the Petrels that breed in the islands, & get some specimens if you can. You have not mentioned the Ducks lately – but I hope you will succeed in solving that mystery – for it is a very curious one.

4th Jany. Nothing to add this morning except my best wishes for the New Year.

Yours very truly
Alfred Newton

Dont forget birds eggs if you can get any.

University Museum of Zoology
Cambridge, England
10 January 1896
Robert Cyril Layton Perkins

Dear M^r. Perkins,

Professor Newton has written you telling you we received the case you sent last Sepr. The contents were all right though a little mouldy in the small box of pinned things; a few more pins between the squares of corks would have been a little better. The spirit all came out of the two bottles of shells you put on top of the butterflies in paper, & produced a sort of solution of <u>Vanessa</u>. The Clytarli are very nice, and there seems to be a fair supply of novelties in the Lepidoptera. You have not many Orthopteran. Some of the roaches that are introduced are scarcely known to entomologists so dont neglect them altogether, though you need not give yourself much trouble about them.

I have also received your descriptions of Vanessa larva; I suppose you do not know anyone who would & could make a drawing of it & the chrysalis. If so we would probably be able to get them published with your descriptions. You have a beautiful series of the Vanessa now. An American has just published a description of one of the large sphinx larvae from Honolulu. I suppose there is no one in the islands who could blow larvae? If you thought there was we might send some apparatus: after we have got the things described there ought to be some persons in the islands to go on with working out the metamorphoses.

I sent you a copy of the Volume of the Cambridge Natural History. It has been received quite as well as it deserves here; you will please forgive the blunder in the explanation of the figure of Sphex Chrysis: where "f" is called a division of the mesonotum. I am now writing up Lepidoptera.

I asked Prof MacAlister a little since if he would like more shells. He replies yes a lot, & would be pleased to bear the expense.

You have just told me about how you are &c. So I can only give you good wishes. I shall be most pleased if you get some more Drepanis funerea for the Honolulu Museum.

Although we have got so far on with the winter we have had neither frost nor snow! Friday was the warmest day in January for 25 years. It has been miserable dark black weather like November. We have been kept in excitement by the prospect of having little wars with America & Germany however!

The last case came at a reasonable price, & it would be well to adopt the same route if you should have occasion to send again. you have never informed me of the arrival of the case we sent you in July last. So I have taken it for granted you did get it and have paid the account.

If you want more material recollect to let me know plenty of time beforehand, though I think now we might manage to get a little to you more quickly by simple post.

With best wishes,

Yours very truly,
D. Sharp.

Magdalene College
Cambridge, England
4 February 1896
Robert Cyril Layton Perkins

My dear Perkins,

Your letter of 29 Dec[r] duly reached me on the 30th Jan[y]. & Sharp had another from you of the same date. Most provoking that the package he sent off to you months ago had been so much delayed! But he will if possible prevent such a thing from occurring again.

Perhaps the most important thing I have to tell you is that 3 days since (i.e. on the 1st) I had a telegram from Wilson "Just off", which I was heartily glad to get – as he ought to have gone back months, not to say years, ago, and I have been ever at him about it – but he never wrote me a word since I saw him in London just after Xmas, which I think he might have done. When he will turn up in the islands I don't pretend to say – or what course he will take.

Now let me congratulate you on having got Viridonia – (but I trust more specimens will fall in your way) – & this I do cordially, as it cost you so much trouble. As to the publication of the note you have sent, I have not yet quite made up my mind, because Evans has borrowed that part of R's book which contains his account of this species, & I do not remember sufficiently what he says of it, so that I cannot say offhand whether to insert it in 'The Ibis' would be expedient. But I shall have the book back in a few days & will then go into the matter. As I wrote to you some time since the whole question of S.I. genera has to be considered, not only as a whole but in connexion with those of other "Families" or so-called Families. That Viridonia was not one of the Meliphagidae seemed to me pretty plain a long while ago – if not from the first, and hence it is reasonable to suppose it is a Drepanid – as indeed you seem to prove.

I dont know that I have much else to remark on. I am afraid you have had a trying time of it through bad weather & the nature of the country, & nothing but your indefatigable pluck seems to have pulled you through. It is bad to hear of the coffee-planting in the Ciridops district. Strange that Acrulocercus should get so fat! That proves at any rate that the species ought not to be starved out just yet. I am very glad you have been able to employ natives to some extent & hope they will lessen your labours.

> I may just mention that my later letters to you have been
> 17 Jan[y]. in answer to yours of 14 Dec[r].
> 3 Jan[y]   "   "   "   "   2 Dec[r]. & 26 Nov[r].
> 14 Dec[r]. "   "   "   "   15 Nov[r].
> 7 Dec[r].   "   "   "   "   1–5 Nov[r].

Salvin has determined the little Petrel to be Oceanodroma cryptoleucura as might have been expected. I understood you to mean that it is to be returned to the

Bishop Museum – if so how had it better be sent? Try to get some more – also some <u>Corvus</u> <u>tropicus</u> of which you have obtained none, & <u>we</u> have here only a wretched specimen. <u>Viridonia</u> of course we shall want – as if you get no more, this first specimen will have to go to London. Your 'note' on this genus will scarcely require touching if printed. There is nothing "offensive" in it. My only hesitation is as to the expediency of publishing it at present, & no one is likely to anticipate your determination if R. has not done so already.

We are having a mild winter, but it has been disagreeable enough at times. Sharp was here last Sunday night, & does not seem to have much the matter with him. The Report to the Royal Soc^y. has gone in.

Some people here are working themselves into an excitement on the question of giving degrees to women, but it does not much concern me as I am I not likely to marry one because she is a B.A.ess. Poor Gadow has been suffering very much (he calls it rheumatism in the nerve-<u>sheaths</u> – the very name of which strikes terror) & is hardly up to much work. I have no other news & so with continued good wishes I am

Yours very truly
Alfred Newton

The sooner you can <u>see</u> Wilson the better – he is very easily influenced by the last person that talks to him.

Honolulu, Oahu, Hawaiian Islands
4 February 1896
Charles Reed Bishop

Dear Mr Bishop,

I have been in Honolulu a few days, after a fairly long trip over Hilo way & so take the opportunity to write to you, before I leave again. First I must tell you Wilson is returning here, & is to arrive on March 5th I think & he will I believe call on you on the way. His coming is of some importance to me as there are one or two birds which will probably take months to get & which occur in places where there are practically no insects. Now if I can make some arrangement with him to work these localities it will give me months in other places to get both birds & insects & will enormously increase my collections. He comes quite on his own account & therefore can do as he pleases about collecting but I hope he will fall with my plans.

A lot of my first birds have arrived here & I think they are all right. Mr Hall has already mounted some; they will increase your collection by many new species & several new genera.

Since I returned to the islands I have obtained two of the rarest birds here – one the little Kauai thrush <u>Phaeornis</u> <u>Palmeri</u>, apparently the old sacred bird of the natives called 'Manu amaui' now lost sight of by them. You will get a pair of this in due season as I got several specimens & made notes on its habits. The only others known are 2 young birds got by Rothschild's men, & a single female which was largely eaten by rats.

The other bird was unknown to the natives till I got mine & it now goes by the name I gave it of 'Nuku pololei'. It too was discovered by Rothschild's men & it was a new genus & species which he called Viridonia sagittirostris. They got 4 specimens & I beat them again with this. I made out its habits & anatomy & found Mr R. had classified it utterly wrongly. It is only found in the wet Hilo woods. I have got some other good birds, but these are of course far and away the pick, as they were new to me.

Insects on Kauai & Hawaii were abundant enough until October when the off season began, but they will soon be in again now. I expect to do a lot of work on Maui this season. Molokai & Lanai I have done pretty thoroughly but I shall try to go to the former to try & get you another one or two of that bird I discovered there.

I expect it will be the insect department of your museum which will eventually give it its most renown with outside countries because of the much greater field afforded by them. Birds like antiquities &c can hardly be much increased after a short time while an insect fauna is always yielding new things. For this reason I should never advise the purchase of foreign birds or insects, because sooner or later some one will have to look after this department & it will always be easy to get specimens of birds & insects from any country in return for Hawaiian insects, or indeed for the native birds, except the commonest kinds. In any case a large collection from any one country is not what you want as it seems to me but rather typical specimens from outside countries & as perfect a collection as possible of Hawaiian species. I don't refer to ethnological specimens of which I know nothing.

I see no reason why after my collections are completed, the new Hawaiian species should not be described here say in a yearly 'catalogue' like the British Mus. catalogues. I think a good man could both do the indoor work i.e. the mechanical & scientific (classifying & describing) & also find time to collect a good many new & interesting things each year, & keep the collections in good order.

In this climate it is certain they will require the utmost care after you get them. I say this because I should hate to think that any of my collections went to pieces, when they ought to last for ever practically.

This is particularly the case with the insects & you must remember that the specimens you receive will have a value that none got afterwards will possess, because so many are new & will the <u>types</u> from which the species have been described. If these get destroyed you may replace them but the new ones will never have the value of the originals which have passed through the hands of the specialist who describes them. As it is, you will have at any rate a large number of types of the new species obtained by me & these should be sufficient to enable the Museum to continue to add & describe species for years to come. Your museum if it is to be first rate, must clearly be so on the strength of its Hawaiian collections in which it could & ought to be ahead of any other; its collection from any foreign country can never hope to rival that of larger countries unless perhaps in the case of some of the other Pacific Islands, & most of these have been pretty well searched before they had been interfered with by civilization. Of the insects of these Islands probably 1/3 of the original fauna are extinct now & 20 years hence may clean out many of those left, as also of the birds. The four first birds of Oahu (got 40 years ago) are now utterly extinct & between the mongoose (which swarms there) cats & mynah birds, not to mention the wholesale clearing which is taking place for coffee planting, those on Hawaii must follow before many years. An old native bird catcher who was with me on Hawaii showed me the place where he was catching birds when the 1880 lava flow came down, in fact we camped on that spot. So late as that he was taking 'Mamo' (I think Sam Parker[222] had some of the feathers) while the 'oo' was in hundreds. Now there is no sign of the former & of the 'Oo' you can't see half again, if you walk from morning to night.

With kind regards,
R.C.L. Perkins

---

[222] Parker, Samuel (1854–1920). Grandson of John Palmer Parker, founder of the Parker Ranch on the Big Island of Hawai'i. Minister of Foreign Affairs in the cabinet of Queen Lili'uokalani.

Wai'anae Mountains, O'ahu
7–28 February 1896

After returning from Hilo, Perkins packed up his collections and had them sent immediately to England. He then gathered up his field gear and, as he had said he planned to do in his letter to Bishop, headed west on the island of O'ahu to visit the Wai'anae range where he had collected four years before.

"In Feb^ry 1896 I camped on the Waianae {ocean} side of the Waianae mts., but somewhat South of the position occupied in 1892. From this camp I collected from 1300 ft. upwards, & obtained a good many insects new to me e.g. Blackburnia, of which I had found only fragments of dead examples—these in great quantities—on the other side of the range at about 2000 ft., beneath the highest point of the mountain." *(R.C.L. Perkins letter to E.C. Zimmerman, 14 February 1944, BPBM Entomology Archives).*

The only entry concerning this particular trip in the *Fauna Hawaiiensis* is very brief:

In February 1896 I spent some time in a tent on the Waianae mountains, at a higher elevation than had been possible in 1892. (Perkins, R.C.L., 1913, *Fauna Hawaiiensis* 1: xxxiv).

JOURNALS AND REMEMBRANCES

In February 1896 I camped on the lee side of the Waianae Mountains, somewhat to the south of where I had collected in 1892. I saw only the usual birds, Iiwi, Apapane, Amakiki, and Elepaio and do not remember shooting any specimens, though I carried a gun always. The camp was not very favourably situated, but was chosen because water was available. The weather was very cool and insects generally not abundant, but I collected a good many Carabidae, including fine series of such species as Blackburnia insignis, Metromenus fraternus and others, also Derobroscus micans, &^c. I also obtained some rather good crickets in some numbers, and the usual casually collected specimens of most of the large endemic genera of beetles. Once or twice I made my way to the exact spot where I had collected the unique specimen of Rhyncogonus funereus and several rather good species of the 'Brachypeplus' group, but the trees which were alive but unhealthy in 1892 were now quite dead and dry. A good deal of time was spent in climbing steep and difficult ridges in hopes of something better in the way of birds, but nothing spe-cial was found and the time would have been better spent on more suitable ground for insects. In this month I also made a very brief trip to Kauai[223] (possibly with Koebele) but I have no notes concerning this trip and I certainly made no camp in the mountains.

SELECTED CORRESPONDENCE

Magdalene College
Cambridge
8 February 1896
Robert Cyril Layton Perkins

My dear Perkins,

Your letter of the 10th Jan[y] has not only followed quickly on its predecessor of 29th Dec[r], to which I replied only four days ago, but it has taken even less time on its way and I at once write to thank you for it – though I have not much else to say. I am glad you seem to be well, though fortune does not seem to have other-wise particularly favoured you of late – the one <u>Viridonia</u> always excepted, & that as you say only at a great expense of labour, discomfort, & the rest of it, for which to be sure you have my sincere commiseration. I am also very glad that I was not mistaken in my belief that you would not be alarmed on the score of cholera. I may repeat here I wrote in my letter of the 4th that a week ago today I had a telegram from Wilson "Just off" – but I have not a notion to when he will get to the islands, & he has never told me where to write him—though I suppose Honolulu along would fetch him.

Now I have to set your mind at ease about your notes on <u>Viridonia</u>—they are still safe in my keeping & shall not leave it without your express wish. I told you in my last that I delayed coming to any conclusion about them until I had looked at Rothschild's book, of which Evans had borrowed the part which contains the account of this species. I am also inclined to refrain, since you give me leave, the last sent notes on <u>Drepanididae</u>. There can be no particular good in publishing them now & I am confident you will have more to say on the subject before you have done. I shall therefore for the present put them in my iron closet with other S.I. papers, & they will be ready for the day when they are wanted—but let me tell you that I think they are very good, though I confess I was not able today, looking over your last Kauai & Hawaii skins, to detect so much differences as to rectal bristles between <u>Hemignathus</u> & <u>Heterorhynchus</u> as you make out.

For the rest of your letter I have not any remarks that could be of use to you. The tradition of a Moho in Kauai gives colour to my supposition as to that island hav-

---

[223] There was no trip to Kaua'i in February 1896. Perkins was mistaking this for his January-February trip to Kaua'i in 1897 (see below).

ing been the seat of <u>Crex</u> <u>sandwichensis</u>, as to what we know of things inclines me to believe that the <u>Rallius</u> {= *Rallus*} there would not be the same as that of Hawaii, nor for that matter of that the bird of Molokai (& Lanai) – but about this last we can make no other conjecture even. We may be sure however that Cook's people did not get it. The unknown bird of W. Maui will, I hope, fall to you lot & prove to be something new. I should fear however it will be only <u>Palmeria</u>. It is very sad you have not seen another of the Oahu <u>Hemignathus</u>.

Sharp has shown me your letter to him of 10th Jan^y & I am sorry that you don't seem satisfied about the division of the specimens. I am sure that we did our best to effect it fairly & strictly according to the agreement with the Bishop Museum; but do what you will it follows necessarily that a 3^d set must be in nearly all cases inferior to a 2nd & that to a 1st. As to the division taking place in your absence that was quite unavoidable looking how strong the British Museum's interest is on the Committee. Even if Hickson had been present at that meeting Sharp & I should have had no chance—nor have we in the future, and I am quite sure that the Committee would hardly listen to your proposal of making the division without sending home the whole collection. If Prof. Brigham comes here we will try & arrange the next distribution in his presence.

Now I must leave off & wishing you all manner of good I remain

Yours very truly,
Alfred Newton

Don't forget bird's eggs—no naturalist I believe has ever seen a Drepanid's.

―――――――――――――

Magdalene College
Cambridge, England
24 February 1896
Robert Cyril Layton Perkins

My dear Perkins,

Your letters (from, Hilo of 24th & Honolulu of 30th January) reached me this morning. On the 20th of this month I had a letter from Wilson bearing the postmark "10 Feb. Chicago", so that he was well on his way, & by this time should have reached the Islands, unless he tarried at San Francisco. I replied to him on the 22^d (two days ago) & he will very likely show you my letter. If so, you will see that I have anticipated your request, almost as if I had already read what you have now written, strongly urging him to consult you as to what he should do, & to be guided by your advice – telling him of the small hope you held out of the existence of <u>Pennula</u> &^{c} &^{c}. There is therefore no need for me to repeat the injunction at so short an interval – and I hope in due time to hear from one or other, or both, of you that a good arrangement has been made – whether work is carried on together or separately.

I am much pleased, naturally, to find that you have got some news of <u>Viridonia</u> – curious indeed that there should be only one ♂ for that so seldom happens – and congratulate you accordingly. It is an additional proof of your zeal & persistence of perseverance, and I trust the unhappy native who broke his head in your service will be none the worst eventually. I note what you say about Petrels – they are wonderful birds. This very species (as determined by Salvin) was last year found breeding on the Salvages, between the Canary Ids & Madeira! Pray get what you can –no kind of birds suffer more from ravages by cats & other introduced pests.

I am glad to learn that the skins reached the Bishop Museum safely & that they looked better than you anticipated. I hope D^r. Brigham & the other authorities them are satisfied with them.

That the wrong locality has been intentionally given for the last "Mamo" is quite possible. I can only vouch for having written to you what I was informed, but I can add that several instances of want of veracity on the part of my informant were known to me of old. In some cases they seemed to have no object, but to be simply the result of a habit of inaccuracy, & I know others thought so too.

Your dissertation on <u>Drepanidae</u> & <u>Fringillidae</u> is extremely interesting – & the observations highly valuable, though I can't say you have yet converted me. Indeed my opinions are so vague (on this as on many other points) that I am sure I am not worth converting. I don't attach much importance to the similarity in scent – I think that must be purely local, but its cause is worth investigating. If it were not local, surely we should have other Finches from other parts of the world possessing this peculiar stink? Eggs – if you could get them – might throw some light on the subject, though-I know of many cases in which they refuse to do so. I find it difficult to persuade people that what are called "Families" in the Class <u>Aves</u> (and I dare say in other groups) are of very different rank. There are men, whose opinion as Systematists is not to be lightly overlooked, maintaining that the several groups of <u>Ratitae</u>, or <u>Struthiones</u> as they would call them, form only so many "Families", or even "Subfamilies". I, on the contrary, follow Huxley in regarding each of these groups as forming an "Order" – equivalent in rank to <u>Passers</u>, <u>Accipitors</u> & so on. The men of this kind are mostly those who insist most strongly on the erection of "Families" among the <u>Passers</u> – a group or Order which it is easy to split into 2 divisions – one the "<u>Pseudo-Oscines</u>" of Sclater (= <u>Suboscines</u> Gadow) containing, so far as our knowledge goes, some 2 or 3 Australian forms – & the other <u>true Oscines</u> all the rest. Of these last anybody can easily separate the <u>Hirundinidae</u> (swallows) & then, with not much more difficulty, the <u>Alaudidae</u> (Larks); but to sort all the rest is at -present, & for some time likely to be almost wholly a <u>subjective</u> process. Take one "character" or even two or three "characters" & you bring out a certain result – take "characters" of another kind and your result is wholly different – which set of "characters" is the more worthy, no man knoweth, or perhaps shall know in our time. The true <u>Oscines</u>, are linked together in the most marvellous way. Every one admits that we must have some way of classifying them – if only to avoid confusion but it is chiefly (at least among those who think as I do) as a matter of convenience. "Families" are no more sacred things than are species or genera, or even bigger groups. When a definition can be clearly drawn it is advisable to draw it. If you say that no clear definition can be drawn between Drepanids & Finches, with all my heart put them together – but then it is only fair & reasonable to enquire whether any distinction can be drawn between Finches & Buntings, Tanagers & Goodness only knows what beside – also on the other hand, between <u>Drepanididae</u> & <u>Coerebidae</u> – for there is obviously much external resemblance between these groups. Thus you will see the question is a big one, & not to be answered without a great deal of investigation, & moreover investigation of a kind that few men have the opportunity of carrying out. I suppose by degrees these points, or some of them, will be cleared up, but I dont expect to see it done in my day, & I always deprecate the announcement of "results" on insufficient ground. I have long admitted that systematic ornithology is in a most confused condition, & it is that fact which made me bring out my book as a "Dictionary."[224] I see a certain framework or scaffolding, to which one may trust oneself, but most of the planks laid upon it are insecure, & if one steps on them one may get a nasty fall. Then too consider that the whole "Class" Birds is possibly only equivalent in rank (if Nature knows such a thing as equivalence in rank) to anyone of the "Orders" of Reptiles, Ichthyosaurs, Dinosaurs or what not, and you will begin to realize that the "Families" of the "Suborder" <u>Oscines</u>, are asteroids compared with planets.

However by all this dont think for an instant that I have any wish to belittle your observations – very far from it. If "collectors" in other parts of the world had been employing their brains in your way we should be in a far better position to tackle these problems, and I can't sufficiently commend you for bearing them in mind. You must keep on covering them, & if fortune favours you, & you may have the opportunity of testing them in some other country with another Fauna. Remember what a time it took Mr. Darwin to see the meaning of thoughts which struck him when he was on his voyage. If he had them published then, they would have encountered much more opposition than they did later (& Heaven knows that was enough) & possibly have been laughed out of existence; but he had the sense to wait till the hour was struck (by Wallace) & then he was able to set them forth in the fullness of his strength. I only hope you will see that in all the above I am only actuated by a wish to see the truth come out if by your means, <u>so much the better for you</u>. I dont care a button if you eventually prove my opinion to be wrong, for I am sure you will admit that it has been formed "according to the evidence" before me – & after all my opinion is only hypothetical. But as a man much older than yourself I am bound to warn you not to be too precipitate. Whether your views be right or wrong, they would, if published just now, be "jumped upon" – & as your experience is <u>almost</u> limited to British Birds & those of the S.I. you would find it a hard matter to defend your position. With more experience you may successfully maintain it, & do a good stroke. I should be very glad of that, for as fate ordained that your lot was to be in some museum put into my hands, it would be brutal for me not to take a sincere interest in your success.

---

224 The *Cambridge Natural History*.

Since I began this Sharp has shewn me your letter to him. of the 31st Jan[y]. with P.S. of 1 Feb[y]. but I don't see that either calls for any particular remark. He has nothing from the Honolulu Museum, in acknowledgment of the birdskins sent (I am thankful they arrived safe) which he & I thought he might have.

We have a man (Gardiner[225] of Caius) going with the Exped[n] to bore the coral the reefs among the Ellice Islands. After it is over he is quite likely to turn up in Honolulu. He is a marine zoologist but a very nice fellow.

With kindest regards & best wishes

I am yours very truly
Alfred Newton

---

225   Gardiner, John Stanley (1872–1946). Irish-born marine zoologist. Fellow of Caius College at Cambridge University. Professor of Zoology and Comparative Anatomy there, specializing in coral reefs. His expedition to Funafuti and Rotuma in 1896–1897 led to him authoring papers on the "Natives of Rotuma" in 1898 and the "Corals of the South Pacific" from 1897–1899.

Kona, Hawai'i Island
March–April 1896

Expecting the arrival of Scott Wilson, Perkins traveled to Kona, where the two were to rendezvous at the Greenwell ranch and Perkins show Wilson the places he collected. Wilson's presence in Hawai'i, this his second trip to the islands, was a disappointment to Perkins. The mysterious and moody Wilson apparently showed no enthusiasm for collecting any birds and there was not the stimulating discussion of Hawaiian birds and Wilson's previous experiences in the islands that Perkins had hoped for. Even the attempt to specifically preserve some precious rare birds in spirit to enable the examination of the tongue was foiled by Wilson's unexplained actions:

> "Scott Wilson met me at the Yates' boarding house & I took him up to my camping spot – I had finished there – but I don't think he got any Rhodacanthis or any bird of consequence. Henry & Arthur Greenwell had at some time obtained for him a couple of Rhodacanthis & Chloridops & preserved them in alcohol. They showed me this before Scott Wilson came up from Honolulu to meet me in Kona. It was for this reason I did not pickle any specimens myself for Gadow to dissect. Gadow eventually never saw Wilson's specimens, as I of course was sure he would, but when he got back to England Wilson had these specimens (coll^d. by the Greenwells) taken out of the container & skins made of them! He knew quite well I had made a beautiful set of skins just before he came to see me." *(R.C.L. Perkins letter to G.C. Munro, 7 October 1951, BPBM Archives, MS SC Munro Box 13.3).*

Perkins was also disappointed in the lack of birds that were so abundant when he visited there in 1892:

> "In 1896 I took my tent & camped in the places where you & I had collected in 1891–92 {= Munro in 1891; Perkins in 1892} in the expectation of getting the smaller species of Rhodacanthis. You had told me when I was on Kauai the exact ground where you had obtained this, apparently in company with R. palmeri. Not only did I not find the smaller bird but palmeri was also absent there & from all the other places where I found it in 1892. The Koa trees were entirely defoliated there by the caterpillars of the genus Scotorhythra. After two weeks or so I shifted my tent down to almost 3000 ft. near the lower dairy. There palmeri was in some numbers, always in the tops of the Koa trees & difficult to get sight of. The Koa were in perfect condition & free from the caterpillars." *(R.C.L. Perkins letter to G.C. Munro, 7 October 1951, BPBM Archives, MS SC Munro Box 13.3).*

During this time in Kona, Perkins announced on 6 April 1896 to Christina Greenwell that he was engaged to Zoe Atkinson. He had a cold the last few days he was in Kona and stayed at the Yates boarding house during his illness.

Having been informed in a letter from Prof. Newton that Scott Wilson was again visiting the islands for the purpose of collecting some nests and eggs of the birds, I had advised him to proceed to Kona on his arrival in Honolulu. This district in 1892 had proved such a paradise for a large number of native passeres, that I thought it would be the best locality for his purpose. I myself left Honolulu a short while before he was due to arrive there, in order to look for the best spots in advance, but owing to his delay in Town[226] I was in Kona for a considerable time before his arrival. I made two camps on this occasion, first at 4,000 ft. where I found the Koa trees greatly defoliated by the caterpillars of Scotorhythra, and birds less abundant than in former years, the Palila (Loxioides) being now hardly to be found at all and no Rhodacanthis to be seen or heard; secondly I fixed my tent at about 3,000 ft. {lower dairy} where the trees were in better condition and birds much more numerous. Rhodacanthis was quite numerous in the tops of the loftiest trees and Psittacirostra in great numbers, with most of the ordinary birds in 1892 I had never seen or heard the former so low down in the forest. It was not until I was nearly due to leave that Wilson arrived and I went over the best ground with him. I had already shot some very fine specimens of Rhodacanthis, in better plumage than those obtained in the summer of 1892. On one occasion standing beneath a very large and very tall Koa I called into this tree nine fully adult males of this fine bird, all at one time, and shot several of them. A good many birds were building their nests at this time, and I found a pair of Phaeornis so engaged, but the nest was incomplete. I directed Wilson to this nest but unfortunately after I left he was unable to find it again and the opportunity of getting the eggs was lost.[227] I did not see or hear a single Oo in the locality where it had been common in 1892, but except this and the Loxioides, other birds were still very numerous. I noted that some of the Naio trees were full of the larvae of Plagithmysus perkinsi and also of Aegosoma but I saw no living beetles of either. In the Koa trees were many larvae of Neoclytarlus nodifer, but only a few of the beetles occurred. Lower down I noticed the larvae of Plagithmysus also in Broussonetia, Pelea and Metrosideros, but as I was anxious to get to Maui as soon as possible having been delayed in Kona longer than expected, I was unable to take along any wood of these trees for the purpose of breeding the beetles.

---

[226] "Town" = Honolulu.
[227] Further details on this are found in correspondence: "In the same place I found a nest of Phaeornis, practi-cally complete, & marked on a fence that it was in a tree only a few yards from my mark. Wilson intended to col-lect all the nests & eggs he could rather than the birds themselves on this visit of his, but just before he returned to England, I met him again one day on Kauai & he told me he could not find my Phaeornis nest!" (*R.C.L. Perkins letter to G.C. Munro, 7 October 1951, BPBM Archives, MS SC Munro Box 13.3*).

SELECTED CORRESPONDENCE

Magdalene College
Cambridge, England
20 March 1896

My dear Perkins,

Your letter of 22^d Feby reached me yesterday & the day before that the box containing your Hilo collection of bird skins (51 in all) arrived in capital order. It is a comfort to have seen <u>Viridonia</u>! No doubt you are right in considering it a true Drepanid, but its bill is curiously pointed & hard, for which there must be some good reason. I dont see much resemblance to "<u>Heterorhynchus</u>", for the slight inequality in length is not more pronounced than one finds in several other forms of various kinds by no means allied. About this, however there is no use in speculating. Enough that it is a very peculiar looking bird.

My last letter to you was on the 24$\underline{th}$ Feby. in answer to yours of the 24$\underline{th}$ & 30$\underline{th}$ Jany. It told you of my having heard from Wilson two days before & I have since (12$\underline{th}$ March) had a letter from him dated 26$\underline{th}$ Feby. telling me of his having seen Bishop at San Francisco before this I hope you may have met, & agreed with him as to your <u>several</u> proceedings wrote rather despondingly – thinking there were no more worlds to conquer, but that no man can say, & there must be at least a chance of <u>Crex</u> <u>sandvicensis</u> (in Kauai?) to say nothing of <u>Drepanis</u>, <u>Ciridops</u> & even <u>Chaetoptila</u> – so I hope you will stay his backslidings & banish his fears. He is very impressionable – luteum in manu figulina – and generally amenable to reason. But to continue your letter. Not only are the <u>Chasiempis</u> skins better than usual, but the whole lot shews that you have wonderfully improved on your earlier performances, and these last will bear comparison with the very best handiwork. I remember when I was in the West Indies finding the advantage of skinning birds as soon as they were shot – though even then a small Dove was a trial. You should be thankful that the Columbidae are what Sclater calls "Lipotypes" in your fauna.

How very sad to read of what has befallen that Happy Valley from which you were before excluded. One could almost wish that the Coffee insect (or fungus was it?) would wreak the vengeance of nature upon the destroyer.

I thought you had satisfied yourself that the supposed smaller <u>Rhodacanthis</u> was a bonus.

In answer to your question how long we are likely to keep you in the islands I can only say that in the first place it depends on how long you are willing to stay, & next on how the Bishop Trustees "stump up". It is a curious thing that they have never written to Sharp, acknowledging the arrival of the bird skins we sent them though we know from you that they had got them, & I confess their silence makes me at times uneasy. The Committee have money to bring you home whenever you really desire to return (which I hope will not be yet awhile), and if they harken to

Sharp & myself they will keep that money (or enough of it) till you want it for that purpose. I have not seen Sharp for the last few days – I think he has been in London "Recording,"[228] & have not yet shewn him your last letter, nor do I know whether he has heard from you by the last mail – but I don't doubt I shall see him shortly. I quite understand your wish to have a summer in England, or part of one at least, but please bear in mind that your great ornithological victory was gained in June, & if I remember right on the very anniversary of Waterloo.

You will have to take out a patent for your newly improved cartridge. I am very glad to think that it will save the waste of bird life caused by the old method. I dont know whether you remember a man you might have met in my rooms of a Sunday evening – by name, Chance – He was here the other day, & told me a younger brother of his is a dead shot with a catapult at anything within 20 yards, & that the birds he so killed were quite uninjured for collecting purposes. I remarked that I only wished he was with you!

I congratulate you on the recovery of your native boy. It would have been unpleasant to me to think that I had indirectly had a hand in the loss of a human life. I suppose if he had been white he would have died.

I believe I have nothing else to tell you. The last time I saw Evans he assured me that the next part of 'Aves Hawaiiensis' should be out before Easter; but I was to see the final proofs, & they have not reached me yet, while Easter is within a measurable distance. He has been very busy all the Term with pupils & his own book. Since October life here has been rendered miserable by the new sewage works, & one street after another has been blocked up. Just now we are being victimized, & I can only obtain access to my fellow creatures by crossing a chasm on a perilous bridge. With best wishes, I am

Yours very truly
Alfred Newton

Kind remarks to Wilson if he be with you. I wrote to him a week ago. I ought to have remarked on the beautiful series of <u>Loxops</u>. I have not compared them with those before sent, but they strike me as being of a lighter shade – if so is it due to locality or season?

---

[228] Editing the *Zoological Record*.

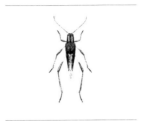

West Maui and Haleakalā, Maui
May 1896

Perkins had only a few days in between trips when he arrived in Honolulu from his Big Island trip. He left Kealakekua on 6 April, taking the steamer to Māʻalaea on the south shore of the Maui isthmus. He stayed a short while (6 days) on Maui and then caught the S.S. *Kinau* on 12 April and headed to Honolulu. For the next few days on Oʻahu, he packed his collections to be posted to England, wrote letters to Sharp (1) and Newton (3), and made arrangements for a trip back to Maui to do more concentrated collections. He left Honolulu on 18 April and arrived back at Māʻalaea, Maui to begin his next collecting adventure.

On this trip, Perkins again visited his favorite hunting grounds of the northern windward forested slopes of Haleakalā. Sharp was prophetic in his early letters to Perkins foretelling that Perkins would indeed enjoy Maui, for Perkins traveled to Maui on seven occasions during *Fauna Hawaiiensis* surveying, five of these in the year 1896 alone. On this particular trip, rather than focus on birds, Perkins spent his time collecting insects.

> "R.C.L. Perkins, the naturalist is camping on Haleakala's slope above Olinda, and is seeking not so much birds as insects. There are some most gorgeous moths near the summit of the mountain." (*Hawaiian Gazette* 1896 (12 May): 3).

Although he arrived on Maui in mid-April, his remembrances transcribed below do not begin until May. No doubt he went to Wailuku to visit Brother Matthias and possibly they tried collecting in west Maui but bad weather (a common occurrence there) prevented them from doing so. It is apparent from the wording of this chapter that Perkins had no notes at hand and was relying purely on memory, thus the scratchy and sparse details.

JOURNALS AND REMEMBRANCES

I again camped in the upper part of the forest during May of 1896, though I probably arrived on the island during the preceding month. All the Maui birds were present as usual in much the same numbers as on previous occasions. I had hoped that before I left, the summer-loving Elateridae would be out in some numbers, but I was too early for these, only two species being secured. It may be observed that none of my visits to Haleakala included a season of the year when these were numerous, so that I must have altogether missed many species. Roughly speaking the season for these beetles, or at least for the vast majority of the species, may be said to be from May to September inclusive, the actual period of their abundance varying somewhat according to the weather and also to the altitude in the mountains. Otherwise insects were much as usual and I collected many specimens of beetles some of the better species amongst these e.g. Prodisenochus terebratus (this date not mentioned in F. H.) [I think a brief paper on collecting on Haleakala, published in the Entom. Monthly Mag., of which I have no copy at hand, referred to this trip.]

I also did some collecting in West Maui Mts., sometimes in company with Bro. Matthias, and I made great efforts to find the bird Phaeornis which was reputed to have formerly occurred in the Iao Valley. Indeed it would be very remarkable if this genus which occurred on all the other islands (though not collected on Oahu after Byron's expedition) should have been always absent from Maui. On one occasion I was on the top of the mountain, making the ascent from the neighbourhood of Waihee, staying out one night on the way up. The weather was unfavourable, and I collected little or nothing, as I saw no birds other than common species — the Ou, Vestiaria, Himatione, Chlorodrepanis and Oreomyza — but many plants that were altogether new to me. On the sandhills Rhyncogonus vestitus which on my earlier visit (in 1894) was found in countless numbers, was very scarce, if it occurred at all, and I wondered whether it was being destroyed by the great flocks of mynah birds now frequenting the locality. There were swarms of larvae and imagines of Deilephila lineata on the sandhills and the caterpillars of P. cardui feeding on the Kikania.

SELECTED CORRESPONDENCE

Cambridge, England
1 May 1896
Robert Cyril Layton Perkins

Dear Mʳ Perkins,

Your last lot of things by parcel post arrived quite safely last week while I was in London. The Prognathogryllus very nice but I am afraid will shrivel very much when taken out of spirit. The one Brachymetopa appears to me different from the other previous species.

I have just seen the Plagithmysus of the Blackburni group – but remarkably reduced in markings – found by d'Albertis 25.II.74, different from anything we have received, it is labelled "W. Honolulu" whether this means W. Oahu, or just outside Honolulu to the west I do not know but I fear it may now be extinct.

Yours very truly,
D. Sharp.

Moloka'i
4 June–20 June 1896

On 4 June, Perkins boarded an inter-island steamer and made his way to Kaunakakai where he spent a few weeks once again in the mountains of Moloka'i. He revisited his collecting areas of 1893 in the East Molokai mountains, primarily to get better-conditioned specimens of the recently described *Drepanis funerea* for the Bishop Museum. This because the only skins they had up to that time were the worst set of the first specimens he collected for the Sandwich Islands Committee. This bothered him because he had no influence in the selection of specimens during the distribution, which took place in England while he was in Hawai'i.

He also wanted to collect further land shells while there, but was dismayed at the damage to them that rats had caused. Perkins reminisced briefly about this to his friend George Munro:

> "There is no doubt that rails at one time existed on Molokai (see Bryan's paper p. 86). Meyer with whom I talked much about Darwin's theories &c assured me that when he first came to Molokai the natives told him of the wingless birds there & offered to get him specimens but he was not then interested. He regretted that very much when he knew they would have been worth. They described to him 2 kinds one was apparently larger than the other & one was redder (ula) than the other. I should think that the rats which were eating up all the land shell creatures in some parts of Molokai in 1896 would have exterminated the rails!" (*R.C.L. Perkins letter to G.C. Munro, 21 March 1948, BPBM Archives, MS SC Munro Box 13.3*).

Journals and Remembrances

In May {error, = June} I visited Molokai as I particularly wanted to secure one or two good skins of the black <u>Drepanis</u>, with the aid of the small .22 cartridges I was now using. I now proved what a boon it would have been to me to have used the contrivance adopted from Henshaw, (see Kau & Puna notes of 1895) when collecting in the densest forests. The report was so small that birds that were in the same bush as the one shot at were not even scared, and the slight smoke from the cartridge was all retained in the barrel of my 20 bore. On the several visits I made to the best localities for the <u>Drepanis</u>, I saw the bird on nearly each occasion but most of them I did not attempt to shoot at.[229] I did not see any Oo in the locality and was not surprised at this, as it was evident from my experience in 1893 that this bird changed its haunts at different seasons, since in that year it appeared suddenly where I had neither seen or heard it on many previous days. Now, as I had expected it was absent.

The large dying Olapa tree which had yielded me my series of the fine Nitidulid beetle <u>Goniothorax</u> <u>conicicollis</u>, <u>Xyleborus</u> <u>molokaiensis</u> and various endemic Staphylinidae, was still standing, but entirely dead, barkless and devoid of any insects. Some fine Carabidae, which I had not met with previously were collected e.g., <u>Deroderus</u> <u>puncticeps</u> and <u>Atrachycnemis</u> <u>perkinsi</u>. On this occasion I paid little attention to land-shells, having given a good deal of time in 1893, but the pretty little shell <u>Laminella</u> <u>depicta</u> was as abundant as ever in the high forest. On the whole this was a successful trip, as I obtained again several species of insects, of which I had previously taken only a single or very few specimens, as well as quite a few novelties.

SELECTED CORRESPONDENCE

Magdalene College
Cambridge, England
15 June 1896
Robert Cyril Layton Perkins

My dear Perkins,

I wrote to you last on the 23[d] May since which I have not heard from you, nor did I expect to do so. I write now mainly to tell you that I start tomorrow on my cruise (which will take me a month or thereabouts) & therefore you will not be surprised if you should not hear from me in the meanwhile. But I also have to tell you that Prof[r]. Brigham was here about a fortnight ago. By bad luck or bad management on his part he missed seeing Sharp, & I did not see so much of him as I should have liked, for I found him very agreeable, and well disposed to help the Committee in every way — Especially as regards the publication of your discoveries, which he thinks there will be no difficulty in getting the Bishop Museum Trustees to undertake. It was very stupid of him not to give Sharp & myself notice of when he was coming as in that case we should have been able to shew him much more civility. As it was he only called on Sharp the day of his arrival, & did not come to me till the next day — that of his departure. I was pleased to find that he had a

---

[229] Correspondence from Perkins gives further details: "The <u>Drepanis</u> was not at all rarer, when I spent a very short time camping in Molokai in <u>1896</u> (June), than in 1893, & I believe I shot at least 3 specimens in fine condition." (*R.C.L. Perkins letter to G.C. Munro, 21 March 1948, BPBM Archives, MS SC Munro Box 13.3*).

high opinion of you – only complaining that you did not go enough into Society! —or amuse yourself as others do a thing I can <u>well</u> understand, & don't blame you for in the least. On the whole I think he liked his visit which after all is the great point – but I am very sorry he did not see Sharp.

Hickson is here for a few days, as Exam[r] for the Nat. Sc. Trips, & came to see me last night. As treasurer of the Joint Committee he wants an acknowledgment from you of the 2[d] £200 you have received (as I suppose by this time) from the Bishop Museum Trustees, & I hope you will not fail to let him have one. There is nothing else that I can think of worth writing to you; and, though I shall leave this open till tomorrow morning, in case of anything turning up, I shall now say good bye, with my best wishes & remain

Yours very truly
Alfred Newton

16 June. I have left this open to the last but have nothing to add, except that I saw Sharp yesterday, & he told me he had no news.

Kaua'i
14 July–9 August 1896

In between the Moloka'i trip and this trip to Kaua'i, Perkins spent a few weeks in Honolulu. There is no correspondence from Perkins during this period to pinpoint his locations; however, a short article in one of the local papers gave details of an aborted collecting trip on O'ahu on 11 July with Albert Koebele.

> "Professor Koebele was up in Palolo Valley with R.C.L. Perkins on Saturday {11 July} but it rained throughout the whole day so that collecting was impossible. However, Professor Koebele had a lot of the fungus poisonous to Japanese beetles and took this occasion of scattering the seeds of kindness: broadcast. He says the beetles are especially fat in the Palolo region." (*Hawaiian Gazette* 1896 (14 July): 4).

To Breed the Fungoid of Japanese Beetles

Take any ordinary tight fitting shallow box with cover so arranged as to be easily removed, place on bottom about one inch of clean sand or sifted soil which should always be kept slightly moist. The innoculated beetles are spread over the surface of the soil and such beetles collected during evenings placed with them. Care should always be taken to keep the collected beetles in healthy condition. Fresh food should be provided for them every evening. After a few days it will be noticed that the collected beetles begin to die, their legs are outstretched and hard, from all the joints the White Mycelium appears which after a couple of days comes into fruit which looks grayish-green. At this stage both living and dead beetles can be taken out daily and scattered under bushes, etc., upon which the beetles feed.

A. KOEBELE,
ENTOMOLOGIST.

BPBM Entomology Archives

Small flyer given out to the public by Koebele to help with the control of the Japanese beetles.

The remembrances below by Perkins are rather brief and do not include daily journal entries. During this trip, Perkins was joined on Kaua'i by Koebele and additional information on the localities visited can be gleaned from Koebele's unpublished field notes.

From Koebele's field notes it appears that he spent most of his time in the lowlands of Kīlauea while Perkins headed for the higher campsite outside of Līhu'e. Koebele was primarily interested in collecting insects associated with the sugar crops and other alien pests, but apparently also collected in Līhu'e on a few occasions on that trip (possibly near Perkins camping locale).

> "R.C.L. Perkins, the naturalist, has been spending a few days on Kauai finding 'bugs' of interest where other people supposed there was nothing." (*Hawaiian Gazette* 1896 (28 July): 4).

Two trips were to Kaua'i made by Perkins during this time. The first to Līhu'e and parts west did not prove as fruitful as Perkins may have hoped. Upon his return on the inter-island steamer *Iwalani*, he gave a short report to the local newspaper:

NATURALIST RETURNS
Lihue Not a Good Place to Find Birds and Insects

> R.C.L. Perkins the naturalist who has done so much good work on the islands in the line of taxidermy and entymology returned from Kauai on the steamer Iwalani Sunday morning after a short stay at Lihue where he went to gather what he could in the way of birds and insects. He says that Lihue is a very lovely place and that the woods at that place are very fine but they are so dense that it would take a couple of natives with very sharp axes to penetrate so as to be able collect anything at all.
>
> Mr Perkins returned to this city on business and will take a steamer soon for Makaweli. He is thoroughly acquainted with this field and is sure that he will come back soon all laden with good things in the line of birds and beasts of various kinds. (*Hawaiian Gazette* 1896 (28 July): 4).

Between 8 August and 18 August, Perkins was back in Honolulu. He collected insects with Koebele in the mountains in back of Honolulu on 10 August (*Koebele field notes, BPBM Archives, MS Document 143*).

JOURNALS AND REMEMBRANCES

In July and August I was on Kauai chiefly for the purpose of collecting certain insects which had not been in season during my other visits — viz. the Elateridae. Nearly all the species of this family are essentially summer insects and especially so at higher elevations in the mountains.

I camped for some time in the mountains some miles west from Lihue, but in a very unsatisfactory locality. The dense masses of stag-horn fern made it most difficult to get around in the absence of any trails and I only stayed so long because I had taken up two or three weeks supply of food. I obtained very few insects of note, the most interesting being the fine Rhyncogonus, R. squamiger. No doubt this and many other good things could have been obtained in numbers but for the difficulties of the locality. Birds were fairly numerous at a good elevation, but I saw neither <u>Heterorhynchus</u>, nor <u>Phaeornis palmeri</u>, though all the other forest species were present.

Leaving this camp where I had only come across a single Elaterid, I proceeded to the plateau behind Waimea, where I found some half dozen species of these beetles, all new to me. Most insects, however, were less abundant than in May and June. Some special attention was given to collecting the very remarkable Bembidiids amongst which were <u>Nesocidium rude</u>, <u>Nesomicrops kauaiensis</u>, <u>Metrocidium admirandum</u> and <u>Macranillus caecus</u>. These turned up in a vain endeavour to discover the presence of the 'Cyclothorax' group of ground beetles on Kauai, since they are found in such situations as one would search for some of these <u>Cyclothorax</u> on the other islands.

During this trip M^r. Francis Gay came up to his mountain house with a considerable party, including Scott Wilson, who occupied a tent with me near the house. Wilson, however, seemed to have lost interest in the birds, and did not accompany me at all when I was collecting. On this occasion, though I carried a gun, I hardly used it, except that I may have taken a few birds in very juvenile plumage.

SELECTED CORRESPONDENCE

Magdalene College
Cambridge, England
17 July 1896
Robert Cyril Layton Perkins

My dear Perkins,

You will have been prepared by my last letter to you (15, 16 June), which told you of my approaching departure on a cruise to the Hebrides &^c for some delay in my reply to any that might shortly arrive from you.

I returned a few days since, and find two or practically three (for yours of the 4th June to Sharp is as much to me as to him) to acknowledge & thank you for. I have not seen him since I came back; and, as I hear is not at the Museum today, I expect I shall not see him before I have to post this, but he informed me, when enclosing your letter, that he had written to you, telling you not to be unhappy about the German "Professor" — I am much of the same opinion. I wish you had mentioned his name, but I have written to an old friend of mine {Hartlaub} at Bremen whence the man appears to come to ask about him. I think he will most likely turn out to be no "Professor" at all, since you say he has no English, & according to my experiences all German Professors speak it. A more serious business perhaps, though at present I don't see how it will affect you or the

Committee, is what you write about <u>Drepanis funerea</u>. There I wholly agree with you & shall not only take care to follow your advice (given in your last letter – 20 June – to me) but fully commend you for your cautious answer to Meyer. It seems to me that the last, being Bishop's agent, is in duty bound to let his sons' spoils go to the Honolulu Museum – certainly not to send them to Knudsen so long as the Trustees want them. I have little doubt that you are perfectly right in your surmise as to the <u>moving power</u> & whence it comes. Whether the <u>motive</u> is precisely what you suggest seems not so certain – but if you be right, what a fine joke it would be for you to send to the Hawaiian journal a note making a new genus <u>Rothschildia</u> for <u>D. funera.</u> Its validity would never be admitted by anyone else, and the name as a generic term be preoccupied for all future time!!! While you were about it you might invent another new genus for something else & call it <u>Gualteria</u>!!!

Now to go to your letters in order. I am sorry you should have lost any of mine, but I only hope there was nothing in it, or them, that could do harm even if published on the housetops. From Wilson I have a letter dated Kona, 10 May, which seems to have been a long while on its way. Therein he told me of his want of success in the matter of <u>Chloridops</u> & <u>Rhodacanthis</u> I hope he will do better with <u>Ciridops</u> – to say nothing of <u>Crex</u> <u>sandvicensis</u> for he said he was going to Kauai, and with his hound he really ought to flush that long-sought prize. I am very glad you have got an entire <u>Pseudonestor</u> in spirit. That ought to determine its place. By this time you must know that I am full of prejudices, & one of them is that <u>Pseudonestor</u> is not a Drepanid, while another is that Drepanids are distinct from Finches! But you should also have known me long enough to be aware that I can shed my prejudices, as a snake sheds its skin; and so, when you have proved your case, with or without Gadow's assistance, I shall glide out glossy & smooth to congratulate you on being right after all. That this may come to pass is quite possible. I always uphold the outdoor observer provided that he be a trained man, & of course no one will doubt your training why you <u>must</u> be the best authority on the ornithology (indeed the zoology in general) of the Sandwich Islands & a far better one than ever there has been before, or perhaps will ever be again.

I am very sorry you had so rough a time of it on Haleakala, but you may depend upon it you will have pleasure in remembering it in time to come &c. Its very name will recall Halelujah. So much for letter no. 1.

No. 2 is that addressed to Sharp, & I have thought it so important that before returning it to him I have copied for myself all in it that relates to ornithology; but I have already remarked upon it at some length. You may be sure that I am as much annoyed as you can be at this Hebrew interference but it is all of a piece with other things that I hear. The old medieval belief that Jews stink, about the truth of which Sir Thomas Browne was unable to satisfy himself, is pitifully true in the moral sense, and all the golden waters of Tring reservoir will fail to purify them.

Letter no. 3. (20 June) On this I have also partially remarked. I congratulate you on the acquisition of the 3 more specms of <u>D.</u> <u>funerea</u> & you may be sure that Sharp only shall know of the fact till the clouds roll by, for I quite appreciate your point. I can only repeat that the right thing for Meyer to do would be to send his sons' specimens to the Bishop Museum trusting to the Trustees for reward. But I grieve over what you tell me of the cattle following your trail, & what is sure to come of it though indeed I anticipated such a fate for the species when I named it. You did well to get the particular <u>Lobelia</u> on which it feeds, but I presume it is a known species - otherwise I suppose I shall have to send it to Kew.

Be under no alarm about Mervyn Powys.[230] If he should go out, he will be sure not to trouble himself or anybody <u>much</u>. He has many excellent qualities – but I believe is lazy to the extreme point, though A.H. Evans found in Shetland that he could be made to work well when a definite task was given to him. But then he was younger & had not taken unto himself a wife, who I suppose will accompany him. My notion is that if you were to set him a job, he would do it, & would put up with a considerable amount of hardship to attain it – but without directions he would simply "loaf", going out after Plover & the like – however he is a keen sportsman & he might be turned to account in the matter of the great Duck question which wants clearing up, & to which you have not yet been able to apply yourself. Thus if he does go out, some use may be made of him – but depend upon it he will want sharp locking after. I might say the same of S.B.W. who is still <u>ever/more</u> a creature of impulse not his own, but of any other person who happens to give him a shove – for he is just like a billiard ball that always runs as it is hit, but if it cannons against another or strikes a cushion it may go whither no one can say.

I forget whether I mentioned to you in my last letter the departure of Barrett-Hamilton (whom you must have seen often in my rooms) on the Bering Sea Seal Commission. I thought he might <u>turn up</u> in Honolulu, but I see by the papers that he & the rest of the Commissioners were taken up in the U.S. ship Albatross to the Pribylof Islands – so that if he should appear in your group it will be later. He is so thoroughly bent upon Mammals that your fauna will have little charm for him – but you might catch him a Mouse or a Rat that has been brought in from some other place & would interest him deeply.

Now I will wish you all manner of good & so remain

Yours very truly,
Alfred Newton

B.-H. might also say how the Mongoose is to be got rid of, for he is very clever at trapping.

---

230 Powys, Mervyn Owen Wayne (1866–1942). English soldier and part-time naturalist. Son of the Reverend Edward Victor Robert Powys (vicar of Kensing, Kent), he graduated with an M.A. from Cambridge in 1892. Eventually became Lieutenant in the 4th Battalion of the Northants Regiment.

Hawai'i Island
18 August–15 September 1896

Perkins traveled to Hawai'i Island accompanied by Albert Koebele. There are no writings of these trips except Perkins's brief recollections below. From references to labels on specimens and ancillary accounts one can paint a vague picture of Perkins traveling with Koebele to conduct surveys between Kona, Ka'ū, Puna, and Hilo. On 18 August, Perkins boarded the Inter-Island Steam Navigation Company's *W.G. Hall* with Koebele and landed in Kealakekua Bay on 19 August to start their collecting in and around the Kona area. They were in the Kona area for only a week or so in mid-August, when they went on to Kīlauea, most likely catching the steamer *W.G. Hall* to take them around South Point to Punalu'u where they would then debark and travel by carriage up to Kīlauea caldera. They collected in the Volcano area, 'Ōla'a, and eventually ended in Hilo.

On 7 September, Perkins was at Volcano House and is reported in one of the local papers to have collected a new beetle.

> "Prof. Perkins found a new species of beetle in the Koa forest today {7 September}. It is about the size of a pin head and an entirely new thing to him." (*Hawaiian Gazette* 1896 (15 September): 3).

During this time in early September, specimen labels show Koebele to have captured an *'akialoa* (*Hemignathus obscurus obscurus*) near Kīlauea in September. On 15 September, Perkins and Koebele departed from Hilo via the *S.S. Kinau* to take them to Maui for a one-month trip there collecting on Haleakalā (see next chapter). Perkins returned to the Big Island in late November and December for an additional collecting trip.

Additional collecting information of the first trip in August and early September is noted in Koebele's unpublished field notes. Here dates and localities are given along with biological annotations for various species he collected from 1885 to 1901. In these notes, mention is made of a specimen of *Aegosoma reflexum* {now *Megopis reflexa* (Coleoptera: Cerambycidae)} taken at light in 'Ōla'a in August 1896 (note no. 1465) and a specimen of *Aspidiotus* sp. {Homoptera: Diaspididae} (note no. 1527) taken in Volcano on 7 September 1896 (*Koebele Collecting notes, BPBM Archives, MS Document 143*). No mention is made in Koebele's notes about the *Plagithmysus* specimens referred to by Perkins in his remembrances below.

JOURNALS AND REMEMBRANCES

I have no special records of this trip, when I again visited the Volcano at Kilauea and part of the time was accompanied by Koebele, who was examining the 7 coffee plantations which had sprung up in Olaa, where many clearings had been made in the dense forest. The two Plagithmysus — P. bilineatus and P. vitticollis var. longulus were in great abundance and I collected the aberrant Neoclytarlus abnormis. The weather in Olaa was very wet. Of the last named species, though it is recorded as a unique, I obtained at least three individuals found at rest sheltering on the underside of large felled trees. I do not know what became of the other specimens, but is possible that one at least may be amongst Koebele's insects, perhaps unmounted. When the coffee planting was started in Olaa Koebele had maintained that it would never be a success in that district and that it was useless to persuade people to attempt its cultivation there. He was of the same opinion, when he went through the district on this occasion and told me that it would soon be given up. The most interesting beetle found on this occasion in Olaa was the aberrant Gonioryctus, G. oppositus, which I collected again in the winter months, when again, I believe, I was accompanied by Koebele.

SELECTED CORRESPONDENCE

Magdalene College
Cambridge, England
21 August 1896
Robert Cyril Layton Perkins

My dear Perkins,

This is only to let you know of the safe arrival of the two little boxes of birdskins, & 3 bottles of spirit specimens, announced in your letter of 20th June to which I replied on the 28th July – the last time I wrote to you. There are 26 skins in all and a nicer little lot never arrived. I am equally pleased with the contents of the bottles, for somehow I had not understood there was a whole Pseudonestor, and I am greatly delighted thereat. I shall get Gadow, (who is just back from boiling himself & his wife at Wildbad & looks all the better for the process) to examine its organs as soon as possible. The Lobelia flower too is all right, & I dare say will make a good illustration for your book when you write it. I am wondering whether it had any colour (I mean the flower) when it was put into spirit it has none now, but it preserves its form. The body & tongue of Viridonia are also to the fore, but I think its relatives are very obvious – the nestling Himatione may be much greater interest.

So far I am well pleased, but I should like to have heard of some further success without being sanguine I yet live in hope. According to one letter you would be about now in the <u>Ciridops</u> country – I heartily wish you luck there. That & <u>Crex sandwicensis</u> are all the novelties I fear that are now possible & either would be a triumph, the last especially. Some months ago you had a rumour of <u>Acrulocercus apicalis</u> – but I suppose rumour lied as she is in the habit of doing.

On the 12th of this month I received one envelope directed by Wilson bearing the Honolulu postmark of July 21 so far as it was legible. It had not been gummed down & its contents were a letter I wrote to him in May last. I imagine he must have been hurried, & in his hurry have put the wrong thing into the envelope but the result is that I know nothing more of him, his doings or his plans than when I last wrote to you. Part VI of his book is out at last but contains several blots. It may be the Jews will not hit them, but I am sorry all the same.

I have not seen Sharp this week i.e. since the arrival of your last box; but notes have passed between us & as he mentions nothing wrong I doubt not all is right. He is very busy, I take it "recording" – at least he not long since & said be should be. I believe be is going to change his house – not being satisfied with drainage or something of that sort. By the way the whole of the town has been turned upside down during the last 12 month, by new sewers & the job is not over yet.

I intend going to the British Association at Liverpool next month – but our Committee is not going to ask for a new grant, though we must be reappointed to carry on the business.

News I have none & so good bye

Yrs very truly,
Alfred Newton

My 'Dictionary' is drawing to a close - Laus Deo!

Cambridge, England
4 September 1896
Robert Cyril Layton Perkins

Dear M^{r}. Perkins,

Your letter of Augt. 10$^{\underline{th}}$ is duly to hand – chiefly about Orthopteran – though I have written two or three times within the last few days I had better reply about the Orthops. at once. I forget whether you were here when the specimens came back or not; but there was something queer about it: unfortunately owing to the way Gray had entered it we could not say how many specimens were sent, but

Brunner said he retained all & yet there was one third less specimens than I expected. Brunner is beyond suspicion but I cannot keep thinking there was something wrong in some way or other.

It is no good sending anything in the way of documentation at present to him as he has <u>no specimens</u>. I deferred, with his permission, sending him the specimens for his share, till we send him the whole lot. When we do so we will now arrange them beforehand so as to know exactly what we do send. We can do that easily now; indeed either you or I could now work them out with greater ease, than either Hym. or Col.

I think we shall find that on referring to de Borman's list I was right about the no. of earwigs; I also think them of much more importance than you do; the question of the constancy of the immigrant fauna when quite naturalised being of great interest.

The Plagithmysus paper is in type, but I cannot send for a copy at present; the numbers mentioned as found of some of the commoner species are not correct as Gray has just turned out some more of two or three species.

I am sorry you had such poor luck in Kauai; but I have no doubt that in addition to the bad season, there has been much extermination there, as in Oahu; probably both were formerly richer than Maui; but those ants; it is no good cursing them, for like the jackdaw they would be nothing the worse, but I should like to do so.

I saw Meyrick for a few minutes in London last week; he says working these things is as if we were doing those of another planet. I retain your Prognathogryllus memo. for the present. With best wishes

Yours very truly,
<u>D. Sharp.</u>

Excuse scrawl: I am extremely busy just now. You might send me Mr. Bishop's address, as I ought to send him a copy of Plagithmysus paper, having thanked him for generosity in it.

Haleakalā, Maui
16 September–18 October 1896

In between his trip to the island of Hawai'i in mid-August and late November 1896, Perkins made a trip back to his favorite collecting spot of Haleakalā. On this trip, he was accompanied by Koebele.

"As it was necessary for me, after I met him {= Koebele}, to do further work in East Maui, I persuaded Koebele to accompany me and share my tent, since he was anxious to obtain some knowledge of the forest insects, concerning which there were complaints. After spending some weeks in the high, wet forest of the windward side, we left our tent, and carrying as few impedimenta as possible, we worked about the summit and through the crater to the lee side, sleeping in the open or in natural shelters where available. Being lightly clothed we were a good deal troubled by the sharp frosts at night, which appeared abnormally cold after the fine hot weather of the daytime. I have referred to this, the first of several hard trips we made together, as it gave me the first opportunity to see what a very accomplished field worker Koebele had become. He was particularly expert at collecting difficult beetles, and had no doubt learned many wrinkles from his friend E.A. Schwarz, of Washington, in early years." (Perkins, R.C.L., 1925, *The Hawaii Planters' Record* 29(4): 361).

Although there are no notes by Koebele of this collecting trip, one of the local newspapers gave readers a brief update on Koebele's and Perkins's whereabouts:

"Professor Koebele and R.C.L. Perkins, the "buggist" are doing Maui. Mr. Perkins will finish his labors here in a few months and leave for his home in England in March." (*Hawaiian Gazette* 1896 (29 September)).

Perkins gives a few additional details of his Haleakalā trip in correspondence:

"Unfortunately one of those {diaries} concerning my best collecting trips were destroyed. I had a very good one on Haleakala in the autumn (?96) when I got specimens of all the Maui birds & saw many specimens of the better species without shooting them. On this trip I spent a week in a hole in the bottom of Haleakala crater, as Bro. Matthias thought he saw a Hesperiid butterfly on one occasion in the crater by Kaupo Gap, but I failed to find anything of the sort. It froze hard there most nights." *(R.C.L. Perkins letter to G.C. Munro, 23 April 1936, BPBM Archives, MS SC Munro Box 13.3).*

"I spent a week in a hole in the crater there {Haleakalā} in October with sharp frost every night, but the heat very great in the day. There was a small pool of water on the side of the crater close to the hole in which I slept. It was amusing to see the number of 2 or 3 species of white-banded Odyneri which came to drink at the edge of this. The water was ice-cold but did not freeze, although there was snow in the gulches at 9000 ft. & a tank at the summit had ice too thick to break so I melted snow to make coffee on the way up & down. After drinking the wasps would fall over as if quite dead, but after a while would recover in the sunshine & fly off. This happened each morning, when I went to get water for coffee. The cave or hole in the floor of the crater was swarming with Onisci." (*R.C.L. Perkins letter to E.C. Zimmerman, 14 October 1945, BPBM Entomology Archives*).

JOURNALS AND REMEMBRANCES

In October 1896 I camped for a considerable time at about 5,000 ft. on Haleakala and did a good deal of work at various points for some miles Eastward in the windward forest entering from the upper edge towards the forest that lies above Wailua, as I had done in '94 and '95.

For some time Koebele shared my tent with me and I collected a good many birds which were in very good plumage and abundant. I also shot specimens of all the better species for Koebele, who wanted to obtain some. [These I believe subsequently went to the B.P. Bishop Museum with some that he had collected in Samoa or Fiji]. We also did a good deal of beetle collecting, sharing specimens collected to some extent. Amongst these I collected local species such as Atrachycnemis sharpi, Disenochus fractus and many others. Plagithmysus finschi on the Koa and funebris on the Mamani were abundant, but pulvillatus on the Ohia was rare, though its larvae were numerous. When I left I carried down a supply of Pelea wood, much affected by larvae, as I had seen no sign of the beetle. This wood subsequently yielded a series of P. collaris, when left in a bag hung up in a damp cellar in Honolulu. They were emerging on Christmas day. Neoclytarlus pennatus was abundant on Koa, the larvae as usual being sought for by the bird Pseudonestor.

On this occasion I spent about a week in the bottom of the crater, living in a hole or cave in the floor. Brother M. Newell had informed me that some years previously he felt sure he had seen a skipper butterfly (Hesperiid) in the very early morning at the mouth of the Kaupo gap, when he went through the crater. Though I visited the spot on several occasions soon after daybreak I failed to find anything that could even have been mistaken for such a butterfly and it is possible that what he saw was some species of Noctuid such as Agrotis microreas, which I have seen flying briskly in the morning sunshine in localities on Hawaii not very dissimilar from the one he gave me. However, though in the crater it was very hot in the daytime there were hard frosts each night and, if it exists, the butterfly might not have been in season. On the summit there was thick ice on the water in the well, and the many wasps which visited the spring in the side of the crater whence I obtained my water, after drinking this, lay as if dead until the hot sun revived them.

The full diary of this interesting trip is not to be found, which I regret, as the number of birds shot and records of their habits was contained therein. On this occasion I brought back to Honolulu a number of flowering silverswords, hoping to breed a species of Heteramphus of which I had found fragments towards the summit of the mountain on a previous visit, the plants containing beetle larvae. These plants, however, yielded only a vast number of a Trypetid fly and crippled specimens of a Phycitid moth, Koebele's office in the Govt. building being very hot & quite unsuited for breeding mountain insects. For this reason, I removed the <u>Pelea</u> wood (above-mentioned) to a damp cellar.

SELECTED CORRESPONDENCE

Magdalene College
Cambridge, England
9 October 1896
Robert Cyril Layton Perkins

My dear Perkins,

I was very glad to have your letter of 17th Sept. two days ago, for a longish interval had passed since I had heard from you – your preceding letter being that of the 20th June; but certainly you had but little to write about <u>to me</u> in the meanwhile. Sharp has also let me see your letters to him if the 7th & 16th Sept., & delighted I am to find that you are not dissatisfied with your captures since your former letters – & above all that you have not been (so far as the evidence goes) endangering your precious life or limbs any more. I suppose that on some previous occasion you have mentioned Mr. Koeble {Koebele} (if that be his name) but my memory is becoming so treacherous that I can't call to mind who he may be; but it is good to think that you have fallen in with some one who you say is a good collector & can work with him.

I am glad also that you got my letters of the 21st August, though I dare say it contained nothing of any particular value to you – except the acknowledgement of the safe arrival of that particularly valuable little lot of skins. Gadow came back from his boiling in German waters much improved in health, though still far from what he ought to be, & after stopping here a week or ten days went off to brace himself on the Welsh hills – where I suppose he still is. However he is bound to return very shortly, & then I must try to fix his attention on <u>Pseudonestor</u> its affinities.

I have a letter from Wilson at Nikko in Japan dated 2[d] Sept. – but no enlightenment as to that which he didn't send me – as I have already informed you. He says that he only got (through some mistake of the Post Office) mine of the 17th July the day he left Honolulu – but what day that was I don't know. I need not tell you that I am disappointed at what he did – or didn't. However, he says he has eggs of <u>Vestiaria</u> & <u>Himatione</u> <u>virens</u> – & one must be thankful for small miracles. I have no doubt he has enjoyed himself, & with that he seems to be content. I do so wish you had been able to get him between your finger & thumb, on his arrival, for then you might have squeezed him into the right shape, but <u>Dîs aliter visum</u>![231]

---

[231] Latin = "the gods had another idea."

I do hope your next attempt at Ciridops may be successful, & I can't say how thankful I am to you for making another – though how the dog (my blessing on the honest beast) is to help you catch it I don't well see – but he (or she, as the case may be) may secure Pennula, & that would be no small triumph – By the way in which Wilson writes I am sure he never really tried for the Kauai Crex – & he seems to have forgotten all about Anas wyvilliana till it was too late. You have not recently mentioned that mysterious bird, & I again commend it to your notice. I am at a loss to make out your bird introduced from China – but to draw a bow at a venture I would suggest Garrulax sinensis or something of that sort. I suppose they ought to be able to make it out at the Bishop Museum.

At the Brit. Ass[n] meeting at Liverpool some 3 weeks ago, when speaking to our Report, I "fetched" the audience by your account of the bit of Kauai (?) which you thought to find such a good hunting ground, & found the imported ants had cleared off everything almost. It even stirred Poulton, who was in the chair of S.D. & for a few minutes he became animated on the subject.

I don't know that there is anything more to tell you, except that Shipley's paper on Arhynchus hemignathi the parasite you found about the bottom of H. procerus is published. I have asked him to let Sharp have a copy for the Bishop Museum. It is the type of a new family of Acanthocephala & seems to be really an interesting creature – only its other "host" is yet to be made out, & that is probably a bark-haunting insect.

Now pray take care of yourself, for your life is very valuable to the Committee, & we had much rather that you would not risk it, and so believe me with all good wishes to be

Yours very truly,
Alfred Newton

When you next write, which I hope will be before long, please to give me some intimation, however rough, of your future plans. When I meet members of the Committee they always ask where you are & what you are going to do next. To question No. 1 I generally answer "In the Sandwich Islands" & to No. 2 "To stay there for the present" but this does not always content them. Which shews how difficult it is to please them.

Hawai'i Island
21 November–early December 1896

After returning to Honolulu on 18 October, Perkins once again packed up his Maui collections and arranged for them to be sent off to England. He then sat down to write letters to his various correspondents including Newton and Sharp in late October and early November and met the U.S. government ornithologist Leonhard Stejneger[232] during his visit to Honolulu from Washington, D.C. Perkins planned an early November departure on the *W.G. Hall* for the island of Hawai'i.

> "R C L Perkins, the naturalist, will leave for Hawaii on the W G Hall Friday {6 November}, to be gone two months." (*Pacific Commercial Advertiser* 1896 (4 November)).

However, a persistent cold kept him in Honolulu until a few weeks later.

> "R C L Perkins did not leave for Hawaii yesterday. He is still suffering from a severe cold." (*Pacific Commercial Advertiser* 1896 (7 November)).

On 20 November he boarded the inter-island steamer *W.G. Hall* for the overnight trip to the Big Island, stopping along the way at Kawaihae, Kealakekua, and finally at Punalu'u.

By this time, Perkins knew he was scheduled to return back to England in a few months and was already planning his future as is evident in the writing to his friend and colleague E.B. Poulton.

The journal of this particular trip "Olaa and Kilauea 1896" was one of the lost journals and Perkins does not include this trip among the remembrances he wrote in 1936. Thus, exact localities and dates for Hawai'i Island can only be traced through correspondence and collecting labels.

In mid-December, Perkins boarded the *W.G. Hall* for the return trip from Punalu'u to Honolulu but stopped off on at Mā'alaea, Maui where he did collecting in

---

[232] Stejneger, Leonhard Hess (1851–1943). Norwegian-born vertebrate zoologist. Stejneger emigrated to the United States in 1881 after the failure of his family business in Norway. He worked at the Smithsonian under the supervision of ornithologist Robert Ridgway. He was employed under various titles at the Smithsonian, eventually becoming the head curator of biology. Although he started out working primarily on birds, he gained his greatest reputation with reptiles and amphibians.

Lahaina and on the slopes of Haleakalā. He boarded the ship on its next pass through on 18 December and returned to Honolulu that same afternoon. No field-work was conducted again until he left Honolulu on 30 December for Lahaina again, where he remained until returning to Oʻahu on 5 January 1897. This latter trip apparently did not result in much collected material.

> "Have just returned from Maui. Was only one day up the mts & then walked up & down so did little. Am going over to Kauai to see if I cant get a bit more lively. I expect to leave here about March 1ˢᵗ." (*R.C.L. Perkins letter to A. Koebele, 5 Jan 1897, California Academy of Sciences Archives, Koebele Collection*).

Selected Correspondence

Puna, Hawaii, Hawaiian Islands
24 November 1896
Edward Bagnall Poulton

Dear Profʳ Poulton

I expect you will be surprised to hear from me after so long a time, but I do very little letter writing out here, outside the necessary reports. I was very sorry I could not come over to Oxford in the 4 months I was at home {in England after his first expedition to the Hawaiian Islands}, but then it was only just as I was about to leave again – & that suddenly & unexpectedly – that I heard from you, & I had hardly seen my own people. I have nearly finished here now, as I expect to leave at the end of February only I shall stay for a while in California & then pay a visit to Washington. I met Stejneger in Honolulu the other day – their bird man – & I want to see Howard & Ashmead as to getting my parasitic Hymenoptera worked out. I feel now that I have done the Hawaiian things as well as one naturally would, unless making a lifelong business of it, so I shall leave with no regret. Questions of general interest that cannot be decided from my collections will probably remain unanswered – not that I think I have got by any means all there is, but such an all round sample as leaves no doubt of the nature of the fauna.

I have been working up the Orthopteran specially for some time. Little Hawaii does not show up so badly – for a country supposed to have the most meager fauna on earth – for I have beaten that of our British species in this group (Orthopteran). Practically all belong to 3 types which have evolved extraordinarily as is the case with all the other insects, as well as the birds & Mollusca. My own group the aculeates show this well nearly all belonging to 3 or 4 types wonderfully evoluted in different directions. The fossores 2 genera – <u>Mimesa</u> about 6 species – <u>Crabro</u> about 30 – wasps – <u>Odynerus</u> only with about 60-100 species – bees – <u>Prosopis</u> about 30 species. Of course there are other odds & ends – imported ants & a few probably natural but recent immigrants which have become slightly modified, but have not yet evolved other species.

The "goodness" of the species surprises me. I expected the endemic species would run much more into each other, but this does not seem to be the case, unless in mollusks & Lepidoptera – groups in which colour is so much used & which have not yet been worked out on good structural characters.

I shall take a good rest when I get home & hope to visit Oxford again, though except yourself, I don't suppose there is a person should I know in the place. At Cambridge I now know quite a lot of people & shall have to be there some time getting off specimens to the people who are working them out. This will take some time as although it is hardly like collecting in S. America or the Malays or even England for that matter(!) I have got a lot of stuff together (I suppose over 50,000 specimens) & it will take a good time to mount & sort all these. After this I may give up zoology, or if I continue it will be to go to S. America as a pure collector & collect special rarities in butterflies & birds for sale, without doing anything scientific in any way. My friend Koebele in California is very anxious to do this for 5 or 6 years, if we can stand it, there being much money in the business, if you collect the right things & let everything else alone.

He is a fine collector & absolutely without rival as an economic entomologist. I think there is something in it, as he is willing to throw up a lucrative appointment to go & that purely for money considerations, not scientific. It is certain I must begin to look out for myself, for I have now worked 7 years for love & failing the S. America business I may get into some business in Honolulu, now I am well known as being energetic, which is more than can be said for most residents here. I have no faith in English zoological demonstrators at £150 a year (about a cabmans' wages here). It seems to me that at home they consider the "workman as worthy of his hire" & rarely make the hire worthy of the workman, while here they do consider the latter case & if you reside in one spot living is therefore cheap here – more so than Cambridge for instance. It is journeying from place to place & employing native help that makes collecting so expensive. However, thanks to the cooperation of the Honolulu Museum, we have not for some time been in danger of the work falling through & I have enough to last me till my time is up. In fact we have had no grant from the Royal Soc. or British Assoc. for over a year now; the Museum here having supported me entirely for that time. I think I did a good stroke of business for our people when I made the arrangement especially as we are likely to get further aid for publications &c.

I caught a nice Hemiptera today – an Emesiid – with predatory front legs like Mantis – indeed its expanded body & narrow thorax &^{c} with the {?tilted} fore leg held up make the resemblance to a small species of Mantis very extraordinary. I have other Emesiids of the same type, but this is much bigger than any of my others, which are smaller than an average sized gnat.

It is clear the fauna here is going to turn out, as composed of odds & ends from very different regions. Walsingham told me he expects nearly all the Microleps were of Australian type – the aculeates certainly are not, but I suspect their nearest relatives will be in Texas or Mexico &^{c}., the birds are chiefly what Newton calls "Columbian" with sprinkling of Australian & New Zealand types – the earthworms are Oriental – & the endemic crickets one genus Oriental the other two allied to Australian forms. I expect however ultimately these "alliances" will prove very resolute in the case of the highly endemic fauna, & the islands will stand alone as a distinct region.

I expect you will be too busy to write so I shant be disappointed this time if I don't hear, but if you should do so my address is always simply Honolulu, Hawaiian Islands. It takes 3 weeks for a letter to come at least & I leave about the end of March.

This should arrive rather before Christmas but I send you my best wishes for the season & remain,

Yours very truly,
R.C.L. Perkins

"The Athenaeum"
{London, England}
28 December 1896
Robert Cyril Layton Perkins

My dear Perkins,

Your letter from Puna of 23ᵈ Novʳ. reached me on Christmas day, & very welcome it was, being written evidently in such much better spirits than its predecessor (of I forget what date) to Sharp, and I most heartily hope your anticipations of being again "fit" have turned out to be correct. I cannot recollect it, &, being away from home, have no memorandum of when I last wrote to you; but I think it cannot have been much more than a fortnight since I besought you to have no hesitation whatever in coming home at once if you thought it desirable, or even if there were a question of its being desirable or not. We can't let you sacrifice yourself to a punctilio and we know you to be of more value than many Drepanids – whether they are "Sparrows" or not! I am glad you have seen Stejneger (who, as I think I mentioned when I last wrote seems rather to have avoided Barrett-Hamilton) for he is a good man in many ways. Perhaps he has not more "fads" than other people, but some he has certainly – doubtless be would say the same of me. I have however yet to learn that he is a better judge of anatomical (internal) characters than Gadow. I suppose from what you say that Stejneger would <u>make</u> the {illegible} big-billed 'Finch'* of the Bonin islands a Drepanid.

{Newton's footnote:}
*I forget its precise name just now. I think it has had 3 given to it. Well, we shall see in due time! I rather think Gadow has seen the tongue of <u>Chloridops</u> – I am quite prepared to see that some one should propose to make all Finches

Drepanids, just as it has been proposed to make all wrens Timelias. So soon as I go back to Cambridge I will have your spirit things looked to. It is undoubtedly a great pity I did not know of Formalin except as a preservative for marine creatures – & that only some time last summer, just before I went on my cruise; but what I saw of it then convinced me that it might be used to advantage in other groups.

Your letter I will forward to Sharp that he may see (inter alia) what you say about Shipley's paper. Now accept my best wishes and adjurations to do nothing hazardous – & so believe me

Yours very truly,
Alfred Newton

I expect to be at Cambridge again about the 5th or 6th Jany. Should you see Dr. Brigham again pray give him my kind regards.

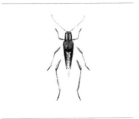

January and February 1897

The remembrances reproduced below are a mixture of various trips to Maui, Kaua'i, etc. during the first two months of 1897. Additional details of some of the trips are found in correspondence:

"I have no diary now of the camp I had in the mts some miles from Lihue & of the August collecting at Kaholuamano. Nor of a successful bird trip there in the autumn when I saw plenty of the Heterorhynchus, more than I saw in all the other times together, nor of the time when I camped in a tent — of Gay's — somewhere between Hanapepe & Makeweli gulch — the time when in a gale of wind & torrential rain the tent came down on me in the middle of the night. This was in Feb^y. & I saw about half a dozen Heterorhynchus always adult ♂ & ♀ together, & I think I shot & killed one ♀, but did not attempt to kill the others. There were very many dead Carelia shells in this tract." *(R.C.L. Perkins letter to G.C. Munro, 23 April 1936, BPBM Archives, MS SC Munro Box 13.3).*

JOURNALS AND REMEMBRANCES

In this month {sic} I did a considerable amount of collecting on the Waianae coast, but did not go into the true forest, as I wanted some of the coast Hymenoptera. I then went to Lahaina[233] where I had a comfortable room, but had to feed at a Chinese store, the food being very poor, dirty and unpalatable and I had much better have camped in my tent. As usual I worked entirely on foot mostly on ridges N. of Lahaina, and in very hot and dry weather found the climbing very laborious, before any fair collecting grounds were reached. I saw no birds except very common species and on the whole had very poor collecting with the maximum of fatigue.

The most interesting beetles obtained were a new Rhyncogonus (R. lahainae) and a small Neoclytarlus of the fragilis group not mentioned in the F.H., this being found on Koa. The very pretty little cricket Paratrigonidium roseum, which lives on the Ohia, was no doubt common, but I only managed to get hold of one of those I saw, it being a very strong and active leaper, I should have done much better on this trip, but I was tired and in need of a rest before I started. Leaving Lahaina I went back to Kauai about the end of the month. I took no tent with me on this occasion but M^r.

---

[233] Perkins memory apparently failed him here as the evidence of insect labels and passenger lists shows that Perkins went to O'ahu and worked in the Waianaes AFTER being on West Maui in early January (he left Maui for O'ahu on 5 January and did not return to Maui again until September 1901). He was on O'ahu for only one week (5 January–12 January) when he traveled to Kaua'i.

Francis Gay had one fixed up at about 2,000 ft. in the mountains in the Makaweli district. I did not collect above 3,000 ft. on this occasion, and although I carried a gun I shot almost no birds, though most of the Kauai species were numerous enough. On one ridge between Hanapepe and Makaweli I noticed several Heterorhynchus hanapepe one of which I shot on account of the locality. This was 1,000 ft. below the elevation at which I had previously seen it and all the specimens seen were in Koa trees, while the former ones I collected were none of them seen in that tree. Hemignathus procerus was fairly common, as was the Oo-aa. There were very high winds at this time, and one night in a gale of wind and torrents of rain accompanied by thunder and lightning my tent crashed down on me and in the dark I managed to make my way down to a small shack which I had noticed at a lower elevation. This was in the region of ants, and I had great trouble in keeping myself free from the swarms of Pheidole when lying on the floor at night and my food at all times. Though further from good collecting ground, I continued to occupy this in preference to the tent, as the strong winds continued. A good many insects new to me were obtained from this camp. A fine batch of Rhyncogonus nitidus under the partly loosened bark of a diseased Straussia, the individuals all touching one another and quiescent, Plagithmysus permundus attracted to small Bobea trees, the bark of which I injured to attract the beetle, after noticing the burrows, — P. equalis in hundreds on Koa trees after patches of bark had been sliced off, Atelothrus transiens in abundance were particularly noticeable. On this occasion I collected a number of the small endemic Staphylinidae, Oligota and Diestota, a notably metallic species of the former in large numbers, but the box containing these must have been lost as they were not included in Sharp's work in the 'Fauna'. The small Nitidulid, Cillaeopeplus perkinsi occurred under bark with some of these Staphylinids, and in its own habitat, Apetasimus involucer was common but many being wet and dirty I did not take a large number [dead specimens of Carelia were abundant in this area, but all the shells were white and bleached & I could find none fresher].

Although the weather was far from satisfactory for bees, wasps some very interesting new species were found, the unusually coloured Odynerus xanthorhoes and the two fine bees Nesoprosopis perspicua and andrenoides. This was my last trip in the islands before I returned to England to work at the material so far collected. In March I did some collecting in California, then collected with Koebele in Arizona and Mexico, and after a short stay in Washington where I first met W.H. Ashmead,[234] reached England in May. Howard was away from Washington when I was there, and Riley who was one of the Committee by whom I was sent out to Hawaii in 1892 had died some time previously the former now occupying his position at the Bureau. I had several talks with Schwarz[235] to whom I think Koebele owed a good deal of his success as a collector of beetles.[236]

---

[234] Ashmead, William Harris (1855–1908). American entomologist, specializing in injurious insects and parasitic Hymenoptera. He began his employment in the Division of Entomology for the U.S. government in 1887 as their field entomologist. In 1895 he became Assistant Curator in entomology at the U.S. National Museum. During his career he described over 3,100 species of insects and published 250 papers.

[235] Schwarz, Eugene Amandus (1844–1928). German-born entomologist, specializing in beetles. Schwarz came to America in 1872 where he worked at the Museum of Comparative Zoology at Cambridge University as assistant to Herman A. Hagen. He was there only a short time since, soon after starting work there, he traveled on various collecting trips and eventually became an entomologist at the U.S. National Museum, where he remained employed until his death.

[236] An entry in Munro's diary gives a bit more information: "Mr. Perkins was here for a few weeks, camped above Waika, and got some good insects. He is leaving now for England." (Munro diary, 16 February 1897, BPBM Archives, MS SC Munro Box 13.2).

In mid-January 1897, the local newspaper, the *Hawaiian Gazette*, reported Perkins impending departure:

> "R.C.L. Perkins, who has spent three years in the islands collecting specimens of birds and insects for two English societies, will sail in six weeks for London. During his stay in this country he has visited all of the islands and traversed all of their forest belts on his scientific explorations. The result has been that he will ship to England several boxes of stuffed birds and insects mounted and named. In Hawaii Professor Perkins has discovered 56 specimens of small and six of large birds. He states that these are not to found in any other part of the world and are new to science. Some are of beautiful plumage and will undoubtedly create considerable notice in the museums to which the specimens will ultimately find their way. Professor Perkins says that his work in Hawaii has been eminently satisfactory ..." (*Hawaiian Gazette*, 1897(12 January): 1).

SELECTED CORRESPONDENCE

Honolulu, Oahu, Hawaiian Islands
5 ~~December~~ *January 1897*
Albert Koebele

Dear Koebele,

Have just returned from Maui. Was only one day up the mts & then walked up & down so did little. Am going over to Kauai to see if I cant get a bit more lively. I expect to leave here about March 1st.

Have just heard from Sharp. He or rather Dr Haviland is setting up a termitarium at Cambridge as they find the species breed well etc in confinement. They are trying to find out all about the different forms found in a nest as it is of great biological importance. Haviland in an enclosed note says "The chief object is to find out what conditions determine the appearance of the different forms? How the king fertilizes the eggs or the queen"? He particularly wants the Californian "Termopsis" which seems to be a very peculiar species. He says "If possible 4 or 5 colonies with queen king & workers. Is there a nest? or do they live in wood? A good supply of food if it consists of some particular wood."

If you know the Californian species & where it is common & are still at home when I come up we could get him some & I would take the nests over with me. Sharp says he believes it is common in California & a very peculiar form.

By the way I suspect we were a little early for Cerambycids at the Volcano. I found I got lots in beautiful condition in October 1892 {in Kona}.

If you don't send your crickets on to Bruner before this reaches you I should like the loan of the Oahu specimens you collected with me. I am very poorly off for these as I have only 2 or 3 of each kind & any little helps in working out. You can of course have your specimens back after they are returned to me. I have lots of material from Hawaii & Kauai & fair from Molokai. My Maui & Oahu specimens are very poor. I have 2 distinct Maui species but only 1 solitary female of each! I of course mean the little brown crickets which are so difficult to work out. I have spent hours over them now & know of at least 12 species. The big green Locustids are easy. I have got a new one since you were here. It is only half as big as the others. Best wishes

Yrs very truly,
R.C.L. Perkins

Magdalene College
Cambridge, England
25 January 1897
Robert Cyril Layton Perkins

{Note under the date in Perkins's hand:}
This was apparently the last letter I received from Prof. Newton before I returned to England. I was very tired after some hard work on foot in the mts of W. Maui, to the west of Lahaina in Jan., & felt I needed a rest.

My dear Perkins,

Your letter of 15th Decr has been rather long on its way & only reached me yesterday. Sorry indeed I am that you can't give a better report of yourself; but I do hope you are running no great risk in staying on, for as I have before written to you your health should be your first consideration. Of course I must report your forced inactivity in regard to bird-collecting, but with that one must put up—& it is a consolation that you are still able to employ yourself usefully in regard to insects.

I wrote to you last on the 28th Decr from London, having there received your letter of 23^d Nov^r—about which Sharp subsequently told me you had been enquiring in a letter of 26–30 Novr. which he shewed me afterwards. On my return to Cambridge I found your last consignment arrived—including the bird skins from Maui (Pseudonestor, Loxops aurea &^{c}) which were all right according to your previous advice—indeed there were 2 more (L. coccinea juv.) than you had advised—also the bird lice, of which Sharp has taken charge.

I notice what you say as to trying to get some more ducks, & I hope the Xmas gunners will have hearkened to you to some purpose. I am not going to suggest to any one else the invention of bogus genera—but I thought you yourself seemed to have an inclination that way, & if you indulged it you would at least have some excuse, while I am sure no one would suspect you of wanting to curry favour with the Jew.

I have not seen Wilson, or heard from him very lately. He wrote that he wanted me to see his birds nests (2 I think), & he might just as well have sent them for me to look at, or brought them to London for that purpose while I was there. I have not, however, pressed him as I have been, & still am, much too busy with other things of more importance.

There is no news to send you, except it be that I saw Flower while in town, & was very sorry to find him but imperfectly recovered from what was almost a complete breakdown, owing to over work. I believe he is now gone away into Cornwall for a change, but that I fear will hardly be enough for him, & I feel sure that he ought to have put the sea between himself & the B.M. for I dare say he will be as much pestered with correspondence & business as if he were at home, & his life is too valuable to everybody for him to play tricks with. Here all goes on much as usual. Last week I had a visit from Stirling[237] (an old pupil of mine) of Adelaide, & the discoverer of the big fossil bird which he calls <u>Genyornis</u>. It would seem to be most nearly allied to the {illegible}, but not to be in the line of that bird's descent. We are having what some people call seasonable weather, but it is of the kind you may congratulate yourself you are not enjoying—for it would not be good for a cold in the chest & a rheumatic leg.

Since writing the above I have read your letters of 15-26 Dec[r] to Sharp, and am much pleased to find you were able to report yourself better. I am afraid you may not be returning to Hawaii; but I don't doubt you have decided for the best, & it seems possible that this may be the last letter you will get from me in the islands. I notice particularly what you say as to the offer likely to be made to you, & I am glad you will be prudent as to accepting it. Sharp will not write to you at present, but expresses his satisfactions at all you have been doing, & sends his kind regards.

With my own I am,

Yours very truly,
Alfred Newton

Honolulu, Oahu, Hawaiian Islands
20 February 1897
Edward Bagnall Poulton

Dear Prof[r] Poulton,

I have just received your letter of Jan[ry] 25th which was extremely welcome. I have finished my last collecting trip & leave here shortly. Though I shall stay some time in America I shall be home by the end of April & hope to see you before you go

---

237 Stirling, Edward Charles (1848–1919). English-born anthropologist, paleontologiost, botanist, physiologist, and artist. Taught physiology at the University of Adelaide and later became director of the Australian Museum (1884–1912).

to the States. It is certainly curious how I have identified with Cambridge. Out here & in the States, until I tell them, nobody knows I ever had anything to do with Oxford. However nothing could exceed the kindness with which I have been treated there & I have a great admiration for many of the men. On the whole they seem to me more practical than with us.

I shall be busy with Hawaiian things for fully 6 months after I return, but hope in that time to finish off my Hymenoptera. I have much splendid material that I shall be able to rival Saunders' work on the British species & his is far ahead of anything else. There is only one genus of endemic bees but it has evolved about 30 or 40 species! One genus of wasps with 60 or more species! Two of fossores with 6 or 7 & about 30 species respectively! It is much the same with other groups. The species are naturally much more difficult to separate than those of the most difficult genera, because I see no reason to doubt that all descended directly from one or at the most 2 or 3 different species. I think when we get out all the results it will be a great work but that cannot for at least 2 or 3 years. This is bad for me as I can write nothing of general interest till this is done, most of the genera as well as species being new in the Leps &c & by that time of course I can't tell where I may be & there will be nothing to prevent anyone with a slight knowledge of the islands' collecting results & writing it up.

In spite of what you say as to professionalism I think I should be simply collector but only because my one idea would be to get as much as possible as quickly as possible so as to get out of it & if you once get into observing you cant do half as much practically. You see Wallace & Bates did not require to get so much to make a good thing of it, because everything was new in those days & novelties of really fine things are now comparatively scarce.

The English appointments make me sick, a cabdriver makes twice as much here & lives as cheaply because he does not require by nature of his calling to put on any show.

There is a peculiar buzzard {= hawk} here which is omnivorous, {eating} caterpillars, mice, birds & spiders, especially a huge yellow & black spider with very strong sticky webs. These get so wrapped around the legs and body of the bird that great lumps of dirt &c &c stick to the former, sometimes so that it cannot even fly! I find here that similar localities can produce similar appearance in insects very different structurally, where there is no question of mimicry & I noticed that such cases will largely curtail the supposed instances of Bates' theory, but the whole matter wants well working out at home. All sorts of questions of this kind have turned up with regard to the Hawaiian fauna & it is here owing to the less complex conditions that they may be most advantageously studied.

I think it must be fine to have such a grand collection as the Hope,[238] to work at, & makes me quite envious, for after all I expect my forte is rather study work than collecting. So many are good at the latter & so few at the former, as I know from

---

[238] The Hope Entomological Collection at Oxford University.

the confusion made by the greatest authorities in the Hawaiian birds, but this is between ourselves. If my unhappy stomach will allow, I hope to entirely remodel the classification of the H.I. birds on the way home. I know Holland very well by reputation & am very glad you have gotten someone who can do good work. They (I was going to say "we") have a glorious coll. of Brit. Acul. Hym. at Cambridge all the great varieties nearly – the whole filling a big cabinet. Many of them are wrongly named but I can put all right in a day or two. They come very easy after the H.I. species. Think of 35 or 40 sp. of Prosopis here probably all spring from one ancestor! & the continentalists dont even understand the European species, though they are a heterogenous lot!

If you ever see or hear of Garstang please remember me to him. I wrote to him once when I first wrote to you but have heard nothing. It is quite likely my letter miscarried, as many have. I should be very sorry to lose touch with him, the more so as he first informed me of the proposed H.I. collecting. I don't even know where he is now.

I have been much out of sorts for 4 or 5 months now & am badly in want of a complete rest. I have lived here so very roughly & in much poor food (everlasting canned goods) when camping, I am much run down. Besides, I have done all my rough work myself nearly i.e., cooking, hauling wood, cutting through the dense forests, pack carrying where a horse can't go &c &c for nearly 5 years. I much prefer to camp entirely alone to having natives & nearly always do so. Besides it much lessens the expense which is great enough anyhow! I could have been comfortable with about £300 a year additional & even then I shouldn't have been more expensive than a surveyor here would be under similar conditions.

I received the paper (your Pres. address) for which many thanks. I see "Nature" here, but I daresay the two are not quite identical.

With kind regards to yourself and Mrs. Poulton, believe me

Yours very sincerely
R.C.L. Perkins

{Postscript:} There are relatively few parasitic species here (Ichneumonidae, &c). This is natural for when a species has arrived here with individuals already attacked the probability of a strange parasite finding a suitable host must be unfortunately small. People at home are surprised at lack of par. Hym. To me it is natural.

It is interesting to notice that a small section of bees (Prosopis) has become parasitic on other species. I think I pointed out in a short & very poor paper I had read at Oxford that most parasitic bees were merely derivatives of the genus they attacked. Here we have in its most primitive condition for the par. spp. of Prosopis and cannot probably be distinguished as a genus from the other species & are quite of the Hawaiian type, only they have around the superficial appearance of Sphecodes, a genus modified from & parasitic on Halictus. (the paper I refer to was in the Midland Naturalist or some such name). I had no copies to give away.

Return to England
March 1897–May 1900

On 9 March 1897, Perkins left Honolulu for San Francisco on board the steamer S.S. *Peru*. In planning this trip, Perkins had hoped to stop *en route* in Washington, D.C. to meet L.O. Howard and W.H. Ashmead. On the way there, he took a rail south and met up with Albert Koebele in California (Koebele had already been on the mainland ahead of Perkins, collecting in southern Arizona). The two collected together in Arizona and in Mexico, searching for biological control agents to introduce into Hawai'i.

> "In 1897, I joined Koebele in California and accompanied him to Arizona and Mexico where he hoped to obtain some natural enemy for the mealybug of the alligator pear. This had now become an unsightly pest, having been introduced since the earlier years of my collecting. The complaints about Lantana were already numerous and some preliminary investigation was made of the plant in Mexico, but at this time no attempt was made to introduce any of the insects attacking it." (Perkins, R.C.L., 1925, *The Hawaii Planters' Record* 29(4): 362).

After a few weeks with Koebele, Perkins continued his train trip eastward through New Mexico and southern Texas to New Orleans. After traversing the U.S. mainland for nearly two months, he finally boarded a ship in New York that took him to England where he arrived in early May and stayed at his father's residence in Raglan, Wales before going up to Cambridge to begin his work on the collections.

Perkins's activities while in England for the next few years can be assembled from the few sentences in his remembrances and the scanty records of correspondence from him to and from others during that period. Most of the time he was processing his collections and sorting and packing the specimens to be sent to the Bishop Museum and elsewhere. His letters to the Bishop Museum Trustee Rev. Hyde discussed the storage cabinets required to properly preserve and maintain the insects being sent back to Honolulu and the arrangement of them in the space allotted at the museum.

JOURNALS AND REMEMBRANCES

After leaving, the Islands in March 1897 on my arrival in England I began work on all the material so far collected in June or July of that year, the material being, in D[r]. Sharp's care in the Museum of Zoology at Cambridge.

I continued at this work with some short intermissions until the end of 1899, when unexpectedly I was asked if I would return to Hawaii for a further period. While at Cambridge I described the aculeate Hymenoptera, Orthopteran, Neuroptera and such beetles as are dealt with in Vol. ii, pt. 3, pp.117–270 of the "Fauna". Brunner v. Wattenwyll had already described in Proc. Zool. Soc. some of the earlier collected Orthopteran, but agreed that I had better complete the work, as I had acquaintance with the habits, and natural appearance of many of the species, this appearance being often much changed in dry specimens. McLachlan in 1894 had undertaken to do the Neuroptera and could have done these much better than myself, who had no special knowledge of the group, but as the collection still remained untouched four years later in the rooms of the Ent. Soc. London, where he had asked me to leave them for him, D[r]. Sharp asked me to bring them back to Cambridge and work at them there. I was working at the anobiids then I left for my last period of collecting in Hawaii, but I had not nearly completed this work.

SELECTED CORRESPONDENCE

{Raglan}
Monmouthshire, Wales
10 May 1897
Charles McEwen Hyde

Dear D[r] Hyde,

Your letter of March 12th is to hand. I only arrived in England a few days ago since I visited Cambridge on the way to my father's place here. Letters written here or to the Cambridge address given you will always get me. The above is perhaps the best now, as I may do some work at Oxford, it being my old University.

I will act with pleasure for the Trustees in division of specimens and see that your interests are fully regarded & if in England at the time the insect collections are divided will see to the forwarding of the Honolulu share myself. If not the Committee here will see that they are properly dispatched.

You will bear in mind that the size of the cases you require is still undecided. Though M[r] Brigham declared against cabinets very emphatically I privately in S. Francisco strongly recommended M[r] Bishop to get one (or more if necessary) good cabinets for such valuable specimens & hope he may arrange the matter diplomatically with the Trustees. I am formally dead against the box or rather case system of keeping a collection unless for difficult insects of no special value. If however nothing further is arranged M^r. B. will insist on cases & in that case you must let me have the exact measurements length & breadth (external measure) you require. In any case the collections will have to be sent in plain packing boxes just as I sent them from the Islands (only arranged & named) & this transferred to their permanent place. I did a good deal of collecting in California & Arizona with Koebele & got some things I expect of great importance for comparison with Hawaiian species. I also conferred with the people at Washington as to getting certain groups worked out there, & made satisfactory arrangements. Moreover they allowed me to pull about all the collections of the groups I myself am studying, which was a great advantage. It is now probable that I shall not only do the bees & wasps myself, but also the group containing the crickets, roaches, earwigs &^c &^c that which includes dragonflies, termites, ant-lions, &^c &^c. This is a much more extensive lot than I had bargained for, but owing to the study I have made of them in life Dr Sharp thinks I have an advantage over the specialist we had originally intended to give them to. With kind regards

Yrs very truly
R.C.L. Perkins

---

1 Bateman St.
Cambridge, England
18 November 1897
Edward Bagnall Poulton

Dear M^r. Poulton

I am still in Cambridge working at the Hawaiian beasts & shall be here at any rate till nearly Christmas time. I hope some time before then to get to Oxford for a day or two – probably on my way to Monmouthshire – & to see you there unless you are likely to be off to America or elsewhere again. I have got through a lot of work on the Hawaiian insects which are of extraordinary interest. The aculeate Hymenoptera I have done, as well as nearly all the Orthopteran & I expect to go on with the Neuroptera shortly. These orders mean a lot of work for me, as I was no specialist at the latter two & consequently a lot of work is necessary before one is competent to start working out the species.

On the whole things turn out just as I should expect in the islands a very few types with great evolution of species of each. I am somewhat conservative in my views, so when I look upon things as quite natural, Sharp regards them as extraordinary. Some very interesting points come out as regards colour, variation &^c &^c & in the islands one has these questions reduced to the simplest form, so that if they cannot be understood from the Hawaiian insects they are never likely to be at all. As an instance I may say that there are over 80 good species of one genus of wasps <u>Odynerus</u> (sensu latiori). Really an utterly heterogenous group. The colour of these varies according to the islands, those on each island being reduced to one or more types. The most extreme case is found on the island of Kauai the most distant from the others. There all the mountain species are of exactly the same superficial appearance. This is not because they are more nearly related to each other than they are to outside species for a species A may be closely related to a species on another island A´ & a second B extremely remote from A structurally, yet very closely allied to a species on another island B´. Nevertheless A & A´ resemble each so closely that superficially no one could tell them apart. This to my mind makes it clear that insects extremely different structurally, can under similar conditions become indistinguishable superficially.

There is no question of warning colours in the matter because there is nothing to warn, for the beasts in question whether coloured or entirely black are not touched at all by birds as I know from the hundreds of dissections of the latter I made, & moreover there are very few birds that in any case would be likely or able to catch such things. Such cases seem to me of extreme interest and importance, & there is probably no collection that could throw so much light on variation as the Hawaiian one.

I have done very little collecting this year as the few days I got off I devoted to trout. After 5 years absence it was a great joy to get hold of a rod.

{copy of letter ends here}.

---

1 Bateman St.
Cambridge, England
7 December 1897
Edward Bagnall Poulton

Dear M^r. Poulton

Many thanks for your letter. I have had no time to write lately, being very busy. Although when it first came under my notice I suspected that the question mentioned would be explained in the way you say, I find the evidence will not allow of it. For these reasons (i) the birds of the islands are extremely specialized, so much so that many of them depend on almost a single species of insect or fruit for food. (ii) the only bird likely to eat the creatures in question is a species of fly-catcher. (iii) on one of the islands where no flycatchers exist or even are likely to have existed the insects tend to form a uniformity of colonizing peculiar to that island. (iv) on some of the islands even the sculpture which can have no significance like the colours, tends to become similar in creatures very widely removed from one another, & in points which are certainly more stable than colouration.

I read a short account of the case to the Phil. Soc. here yesterday with a few other notes. I cannot tell you anything about the disposal of the specimens yet as we do not know ourselves what is to be done with them. In any case I have no say in the matter at all presumably. The B.M. have had my first & best set of birds which are very valuable & complete & we worked for £500 for working out the insects & they were to have the first set of all the types. However they have refused us the money after accepting birds which we could have got that for selling them! The original arrangement was that the B.M. was to have the whole first set of everything, the person who works out the group the second, & the Honolulu Museum the third. This would practically leave nothing to the Committee. There will be difficulty in financing the Committee on the first set of specimens & we may have to do this, I should like to do so, as after so much money has been spent, if the B.M. don't choose to give us such an insignificant sum (we haven't had a farthing from them) they dont deserve anything. Unfortunately they have got the birds & the Microleps (or will have the latter), as Lord Walsingham has already promised these minus the third set for the Honolulu Mus, which aided us greatly financially. We can't get the things worked out without money, & the B.M. people themselves are utterly incompetent to do so, the Hawaiian creatures being probably the most difficult study that could probably be undertaken. If you want to see species-formation in all its various stages, you have it here, but you can understand with minute creatures of extreme variability how difficult systematic work becomes under the circumstances – but then the interest of it!

I have learnt more of such processes from the study of these creatures than I supposed could possibly have been found out from and existing fauna.

With kind regards,

Yours very truly,
R.C.L. Perkins

University Museum of Zoology
Cambridge, England
15 June 1898
Charles Reed Bishop

Dear M^r. Bishop,

I have lately received a letter from D^r. Hyde together with one from yourself. The former I enclose herewith as it contains nothing that it is necessary to preserve. Of course the somewhat indefinite offer therein made is tempting on account of the interest I have in the H.I. fauna. I have written to D^r. Hyde at some length & tried to make clear the position. As matters now stand I have been working for the Committee going on for 7 years & am likely to continue into the eighth, if I finish the work I am now engaged on, & as I am progressing as fast as can be expected I have little doubt I shall manage to do so. it would be folly for me to give up my connection with the Committee here, for the sake of working temporarily for the B.P. Bishop Museum or any Museum or private person.

Both the members of the Committee & others interested in the Hawaiian fauna, have assured me that they will do everything in their power to advance any interests & with such backing I feel quite content to wait for a suitable position. I would not sunder my position with the Committee that is not permanent as I cannot go on forever, on 2, 3, 4 or 5 years collecting job, as the case may be. Nothing suitable turning up in the course of this year I shall probably visit the islands next spring & collect on my own account, but such new things as I get will be given to the museums here, because I cannot afford to lose the connection. I can pay expenses well on things that I have already discovered, as a good many are only known by one or two specimens.

Most of the colonial museum positions are filled by men of this country & should one sufficiently attractive become vacant, I should go for this. In many ways I should even prefer it to an English one. Even if I had finished my work here I should defer the journey to the Island till the Spring, because the month of June is the best of all then July, & the winter except for special things unprofitable, & I should not like the expense of wintering out there, while getting but few species of any account. If I wanted to go on a two or three years collecting trip I should probably go elsewhere than the H.I. & on my own account. A good collector, who will risk his health &c can to-day easily clear a couple of thousand pounds a year in a rich country, but the risk is considerable, & in any case it cannot be done for many years together, as all the countries with the finest & richest faunas are unhealthy. The more they are so the better the price the things fetch. I have seen box after box of a single species of butterfly sold at Stevens auction room in Covent Garden at two to five pounds a single specimen. Hawaiian things being mostly small are much less valuable commercially but there are quite a lot of which one could sell at quantity at 2 1/2 to 5 dollars apiece, & by taking numbers of these one could do fairly well. Probably I should make the whole lot up into typical collections as illustrating the fauna of the H.I. & dispose of them on the continent & to private people. With kind regards

Yours very truly,
R.C.L. Perkins

Of course the Committee here will have nothing to do with any future work I may make. They never aimed at a complete knowledge of the Hawaiian fauna, which work can only be obtained by permanent residents after many years, certainly not of this generation. It will be likely if there is any native fauna left sufficiently long for this to happen.

University Museum of Zoology
Cambridge, England
9 September 1898
Charles McEwen Hyde

Dear Dr Hyde,

I have just received your letter of Aug. 16th announcing arrival of case of insects. I was greatly surprised to hear of this, as the cases sent to me via the States always took 3 months & generally more! Only a few days ago I wrote a formal letter to the Trustees saying that the case might be expected by the time that letter arrived. Probably the quick passage is due to the fact that I got the agents here to see that the case was not left lying around on the way, as in that case the contents would be liable to be damaged.

The boxes which you seem to admire are only of the rough kind that I always took around for collecting purposes. They are not good enough for permanent lodging of specimens, but will be useful for further collecting by the addition of a few screws. Otherwise in the damp mountains they will come to pieces in short order, being only glued & dovetailed. I could get off another lot of the same extent immediately were I not just now pressed for time. I have been away on holiday (needless to say collecting!) & we have had the International Congress of Zoologists & Physiologists here for a week, which has been another delay, & I may go to the British Association meeting now on at Bristol, as they partly defrayed the expenses of the Hawaiian trips. I have up to the present paid all bills for the Bishop Museum i.e. carriage of birds, care of insects, boxes for same &c but will later on send the receipts in to the Trustees.

Dr Sharp tells me he has written more than once about the assistance offered by you in printing results of my collecting but I daresay you have now received his letters. I will probably send a lot of Lepidoptera (moths) in the next lot. I will not undertake to get them relaxed & spread here as it can only be done at some deterioration of the specimens & owing to the damp air at sea the wings will be sure to fall out of position again. You could have it done out there, but it will be very ill advised to do so; they should be replaced by degrees by specimens set immediately on capture if wanted for show, & themselves kept carefully for types, as they vary so in the same species, they are very difficult to determine, & it will be impossible to do this from description alone, if the specimens come to grief in any way.

I had a long talk with Meyrick (at the Congress here) who worked them out & he told me it was the toughest job he ever had in his life, which I can quite believe from my experience in other groups. I am thinking of shortly leaving here & going to London to work on Godman & Salvin's great work (the Biologia Centrali-Americana) which is far from complete. in any case I have done more than my share of the island beasts for it is almost unheard of for one man to make a study of more than one of the great orders of insects, & I have completed 3 &

started on a fourth (the beetles). Many of the big Continental entomologists came & looked through my collection but we could not persuade any of them to help in working it out. It was "magnifique mais très difficile" & they would have none of it! It is safe to say that of the three orders I have worked out, if I had not done so, you would have had your share all unnamed (or at least in two of them) for no one here or on the continent or in America would tackle them. I should only have been too glad to get part off my hands, & gone abroad again before now, if it could have been arranged, but my first collection of Neuroptera was four years in the hands of the greatest specialist on that group, & he never even started on them, so I fetched them away & did them myself.

He (McLachlan) was also at the Congress here & seemed sorry he had not done them, but had they remained with him 20 years it could have been the same, as it was with the West-Indian expedition. I receive a consignment of insects by this post from the islands but I think nothing very special.

D^r. Stejneger was the only American over here I knew, but we had a vast number of the greatest European Zoologists, & the Congress was a huge success. With kind regards

Yours very truly
R.C.L. Perkins

University Museum of Zoology
Cambridge, England
18 November 1898
Albert Koebele

Dear Koebele,

It seems to be ages since I have heard of or from you & I have no idea where you are at the present time. I am still here, working at the beetles. I get on very slowly, have not even finished curculionids yet, & not touched anything else. We hope to get a first volume published before long, containing the aculeate Hymenoptera, macroleps, & some other things. It is quite likely that I may come out to the islands again next year. I have no fear of being anticipated in most of the things as they are so difficult no one would work at them, & if I had not done so they would have been left as they are for years probably. I did a little collecting this year & got some good bees & wasps but I get out very little & should be glad to get off on another trip. This is however impossible until we get on with the publishing of the Hawaiian things. I have envied you often, probably away in Mexico, Texas, or somewhere, amongst those lovely Hymenoptera.

Mind you write & let me know where you are & what you are doing. I think you once asked me the names of some Hawaiian things. At that time I could not tell you, but probably I could give you names of a good many things now. With kind regards to you and Mrs. K. if you are at home.

Yours very truly,
R.C.L. Perkins

---

1 Bateman St.
Cambridge, England
19 February 1899
Edward Bagnall Poulton

Dear Prof^r Poulton

Very many thanks for your letter & information.

I have never seen any of the Hymenoptera in the coll. & no doubt that of W.W. Saunders named by Smith is valuable, the more so as Smith's descriptions are often faulty. I could probably do some good work if I returned to Hawaii now, as in working out the collections a number of interesting questions have turned up, which can only be solved there, & by some one familiar with the insects themselves, & their habits. Most of the native species are rare, many of the most peculiar & interesting very rare. You can walk through lovely forest all day in many places & hardly see an insect unless it be a foreign thing.

You will find that the wasps of Chili exhibit a case like the special Australia forms, & I think there are no true vespae in Chili, but the Odyneri (Eumenidae) are quite special & resemble Vespidae in general appearance.

How very rarely a species can have reached the Hawaiian Is. from outside (nearest land is 2000 miles) can be judged from this fact: of some 165 endemic species of Acul. Hymenoptera no less than 125 are found to be restricted to one (or two) of the islands. Those most widely separate are only 60 or 70 miles apart, several are only separated by channels 9 miles wide.

The amount of endemicity of a given island is directly proportional to the length of the channel between it & its neighbour, roughly speaking. Facts of this sort are certainly interesting & the fauna is of great import for throwing light on various questions concerning evolution. I will write again shortly. In great haste & with kind regards

Yours very truly,
R.C.L. Perkins

1 Bateman St.
Cambridge, England
27 April 1899
Edward Bagnall Poulton

Dear Prof^r Poulton

Yours of the 3rd just reached me after I had been out to post the specimens of <u>Astata</u> <u>stigma</u> & the forceps to Oxford. I hope I may get through the Curculion-idae in about a fortnight, & whether I shall go on with the Hawaiian fauna after that is doubtful. I have suffered in health so much from the last two years close indoor work, after five years of camp life, that I have some thought of giving up for a time at any rate. Possibly I may go to the coast for a time & write up a small book on the zoology of the Is. on my own account or I may to my father's at Raglan Mon. & do likewise. I am putting on all the work I can now to finish off (I have already dealt with 90 species of the genus <u>Proterhinus</u>, & not finished!) what I am working at, for it is clear I cannot keep on in such conditions as I have been accustomed to. I will however write again before long. With kind regards to M^{rs}. Poulton & yourself

Yours very truly,
R.C.L. Perkins

University Museum of Zoology
Cambridge, England
21 February 1900
{Bishop Museum Trustee}

Dear sir,

This is to inform you that I have dispatched <u>two</u> <u>cases</u> containing a large number of species of insects pinned in boxes as follows:

1. The rest of the Hymenoptera – that is the bees & ants.
2. Most of the remainder of the Macro-Lepidoptera.
3. Neuroptera (family Chrysopidae)
4. Neuroptera (fam^s Odonata & Myrmeliontidae)
5. Orthopteran (complete)
6. Beetles (fam. Curculionidae complete)

The whole of these lots occupy two dozen or more boxes, & should be carefully examined on arrival for loose and broken specimens &^{c}.

Had it not been for the outbreak of plague I should probably myself have been in Honolulu before the date on which you receive this letter.

Yours very truly,
R.C.L. Perkins

PART FOUR

Third Expedition (1900–1901)

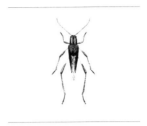

Collecting, Chiefly O'ahu
1900–1901

Perkins's final collecting expedition to the Hawaiian Islands did not start off as planned. He had wanted to come earlier, but was delayed a few months, necessitated by an outbreak of bubonic plague in Honolulu in early 1900.

He sailed from England to New York, and then traveled overland by rail to San Francisco. There he boarded the S.S. *Australia* and arrived in Honolulu on 30 May 1900. Though this was his third trip to the islands, his arrival still made the Hawaiian press:

PROFESSOR PERKINS HERE
EMINENT NATURALIST AGAIN IN TOWN
Comes to the Islands to Gather and Study Butterflies and the Like — to be Here a Year

Prof. R.C.L. Perkins, the naturalist, returned to Honolulu today after an absence of several years in England. As before, he is sent out by the Royal Society, and comes to make further entomological researches in the Islands.

"I have been in England since I left Honolulu nearly four years ago," said the Professor this morning, "and have been hard at work all the time upon specimens taken from here at the time of my former visit.

"As before, I am sent out by the societies at home to gather and mount them. It is my intention to be in Honolulu quite a long time and in the Islands about one year. My stay may be even longer than that, for the work before me is quite extensive."

"My attention will be turned especially to this" — the Professor pointing to a cabinet in which were mounted numerous butterflies and the like. He went on to say that he would not on this visit have anything to do with birds. His intention is to gather a complete line of butterflies and insects as may be found in the Islands."

One of the first calls made by the naturalist this morning was upon Prof. Koebele, the local entomologist. The latter opened up his collection of butterflies, and the two men busied with them for a long time. Some of the specimens were new, and were only located by means of what may be called a "bugicon" or dictionary of flies and bugs. (*Hawaiian Star* 1900 (2 June)).

Professor Perkins is stopping at the Arlington. The visitor is not a stranger in the Islands. It may be added that he is one of the most famous men in his line in the world. (*Hawaiian Star*, 1900 (6 June): 1).

Perkins third collecting trip was not to be accompanied by the daily entries in journals that so became a part of his activities during the first trip and less so on the second trip. It was not a high priority of the third trip to discover anything new nor to provide reports in order to procure further grant funds, so journal writing was not considered by Perkins to be a necessity.

"... I returned to the islands early in 1900. In this and the following year my work was almost entirely confined to Oahu. I rarely carried a gun, and paid little attention to anything but insects and mostly limited my observations to certain groups of these. Very little indiscriminate collecting was attempted. Beetles such as are easily obtained by indiscriminate collecting, beating of trees or sweeping these, were almost all collected by special search, as I wished to obtain a more certain knowledge of their habits and particularly of the restriction of species to one food-plant, the variation of individuals found in company and that of different colonies. Practically all the specimens obtained were mounted, when freshly killed, and to a large extent examined at the time. Observations were made in widely separated localities and in both mountain ranges. During this period I had facilities for working the specimens in the office of my friend Mr. A. Koebele, the Government entomologist of the islands, who accompanied me on a number of my trips. Although, as has been said, my latter work was more of a special nature, yet more new species than might have been expected were obtained." (Perkins, R.C.L., 1913, *Fauna Hawaiiensis* 1: xxxiv–xxxv).

Apparently Perkins's last year of collecting had him rather distracted at times; in distinct contrast to the earlier years:

"I was disappointed in regard to Mr. Perkins. I went to Wailuku and remained here two weeks expecting him to come up. I had a nice time on Maui, spent three days in the Iao Valley collecting Hymenoptera. Was well pleased with what I got. Have some new things I believe. I suppose Mr. Perkins has gone back by now." *(M. Newell letter to A. Koebele, 27 August 1901, BPBM Archives, MS Group 91 Box 1).*

Perkins spent some time collecting in the mountains near Honolulu and especially Tantalus. It was at this locality that he found numerous endemic species including flightless forms. Shortly after he collected in 1900 and 1901 he returned there with Walter Giffard:

"That little {flightless} Nesidiorchestes was common under the same tree as the little {flightless} Emperoptera fly. I took Giffard there as it was also a habitat of Metromenus fugitivus & cuneipennis & other Carabids, while Apetinus explanatus, the Nitidulid, was very common. There were also many predaceous flies & the flightless Nabis there. At the time Giffard was only much interested in some of the beetles, & he went there many times for these afterwards he told me. Scores of the more obscure Dolichopodids were always present, darting on to the minute exposed larvae when one disturbed the leaves & surface soil. I don't think I took any of these flies there, nor of a fair-sized Mymarid, no doubt Polynema, which flew around, but was very difficult to see on account of poor & broken sunlight." *(R.C.L. Perkins letter to E.C. Zimmerman, 21 November 1948, BPBM Entomology Archives).*

The collection of the flightless *Emperoptera* was explained further by Perkins in an interview with E.C. Zimmerman:

"A flightless dolichopodid was found by Perk, 'by the hundreds' hopping about beneath a certain Elaeocarpus tree on Tantalus, & in the damp leaves nitidulids were extremely abundant together with several carabids. (Perk gave me instructions on how to find the tree, & when I returned to Honolulu I found that tree, but when I searched for what was a new EMPEROPTERA, all I could find were swarms of ants)." *(Notes by E.C. Zimmerman of R.C.L. Perkins interview, August 1949, E.C. Zimmerman letter to N.L. Evenhuis, 20 November 2002).*

In addition to his many collecting trips to the mountains near Honolulu in those last months (as well as in earlier and later years), Perkins also collected around Waikīkī:

"In wet years in autumn & winter at Waikiki I did a good deal of collecting on Diamond Head. There were still native endemic plants there, dwarf bastard sandal, & some composites & quite a lot of endemic insects, including numerous bees, & wasps, & some leaf hoppers, moths, &c. In dry years when the slopes were all dried up most of these things disappeared entirely & must have laid dormant until rains came & the Ilima was all in flower." *(R.C.L. Perkins letter to G.C. Munro, 12 December 1951, BPBM Archives, MS SC Munro Box 13.3).*

"In 1901–02 I collected a great deal on the lower part (not the steep part) of Leahi {= Diamond Head}. The tufts of grass & Ilima which grew thickly in the open parts amongst the Kiawe trees & one or two endemic Composites or other plants produced quite a few endemic insects. In the soil in parts were great numbers of land shells, of course often broken. It was on Diamond Head that I collected the yellow-marked Odynerus wasp which I think was the first ever described from Hawaii & I had never even seen it when I described the species in the Fauna Vol. 1. but I gave de Saussure's French description. I don't think I found it elsewhere than on D. Head. The locality was only good after there had been good rains." *(R.C.L. Perkins letter to G.C. Munro, 17 July 1952, BPBM Archives, MS SC Munro Box 13.3).*

The Sandwich Islands Committee, reporting annually to the British Association for the Advancement of Science since its inception in 1890, continued in 1900 and 1901 to request funds for Perkins and for annual reappointments of the Committee to continue to oversee the work of Perkins while in the Islands. All requests for funding were granted until 1901, when the Committee's request was refused. The Committee continued to exist for another year, but the lack of funding no doubt caused Perkins to make his decision to quit the survey.

"This Committee was appointed in 1890, and has been since annually reappointed. Last year a grant from the Association was asked for by this Committee, but was not accorded. The Committee were consequently for a time without the funds necessary to enable them to retain the services of Mr. Perkins, on whom they relied to complete the working out of the extensive collections.

Last June {1902} the Committee received for its work a grant of £200 from the Government Grant Committee of the Royal Society. In the meantime Mr. Perkins had accepted an appointment in the Sandwich Islands, and there is now little prospect of his speedy return to England as a consequence work has been suspended to a considerable extent." *(Rep. Br. Assoc. Adv. Sci. 1902: 284–285).*

What appears below is a short synopsis of his collecting activities during those 18 months from June 1900 until December 1901, when Perkins formally ceased to collect for the Committee.

JOURNALS AND REMEMBRANCES

My collecting in 1900 and 1901 was nearly altogether confined to Oahu. On various occasions I had the pleasure of Koebele's company in different localities. During this time Ashmead of the Smithsonian Institute at Washington, visited the islands for a considerable time and did some collecting with Koebele and myself on Oahu before proceeding to the other islands. He was under the impression that he would be able to make a fairly comprehensive collection of the insects of all Orders of each island during his stay, but I told him this would be impossible for any man, I do not know whether he published any results. I also had the pleasure of meeting Marlatt[239] who also visited the islands but did no collecting.

My object on this my last period of collecting for the Committee was not so much the acquisition of new species as to make some special investigation of the habits and variation of species especially of some of the very difficult genera of Coleoptera. As it happened my efforts in this direction were largely frustrated by accident.

It was expected that at the end of my collecting I should return to Cambridge to see the finish of the Fauna Hawaiiensis but my marriage and the offer of work first as Inspector of introduced plants, and subsequently as Entomologist to the Board of Agriculture and later H.S.P.A. Experiment Station prevented this. The material that I had collected very carefully had been nearly all mounted up when fresh and was sent on to England. Batches of <u>Proterhinus</u> and of different species from special trees, and batches of such beetles of one species collected from different trees for the study of variation were specially numbered by myself as well as labelled with the usual data. Unfortunately when I returned for a trip to England in the summer of 1907 the cards had been cut up and the individuals separated without the preservation of my own numbers, these having been made to follow on from the numbers used for previous collections. Consequently only the usual data were generally available, and my own notes which I had retained were largely useless.

This unfortunate result was entirely my own fault, as I should have notified D^r. Sharp that the specimens should not be renumbered, or I should have sent my notes with them. But I was always expecting to get over to Cambridge & attend to the matter personally, while as it turned out I was away from England for 7 years, before I went on vacation & examined the specimens.

---

[239] Marlatt, Charles Lester (1863–1954). An economic entomologist who succeeded L.O. Howard as chief of the Bureau of Entomology in Washington, D.C. He specialized in sawflies and scale insects. Marlatt's trip to Hawai'i at this time was a stopover on his trip (at his own expense) to Japan in search of natural enemies of the pestiferous San Jose scale.

SELECTED CORRESPONDENCE

Magdalene College
Cambridge, {England}
"Mayday MCM" {= 1 May 1900}
Robert Cyril Layton Perkins

My dear Perkins,

Sharp gave me your last letter to him some days ago, & I have been intending to write to you ever since, but I have somehow or other had so much to do that I could not find time; but since you are not to leave till the 11th of this month, the delay was not so much signified, & really beyond bestowing on you my parting blessing I don't know that there is much to add to what I said when last we met. Of course it is not for me to "teach my grandmother" & you really know far better than I what is wanted & what you have to do to get it. I would only beseech you to make every effort to clear up that Duck mystery – to which I confess I don't see any clew at all for I can't believe in the Salvadorian theory of hybridism to account for it. We also want an adult (♂ & ♀) Nycticorax – since R.B.S. {= Sharpe} impounded the one you got before. One would like also to know something certain about the introduced species – what they primarily are, how they get on, & what mischief they do in cutting out the native species & so on. I should like to know whether California Carpodacus Finch ever puts on its breeding plumage – all those that Scott Wilson go were plainly dressed, & he foolishly threw them away, so that we have not one here or perhaps a single one. It has always seemed to me a species that might make its way to the islands naturally, even though some be known to have been imported.

You will not neglect the tongues of those big* Finches Rhodocanthis &^c. – if it be to prove your own views, & it would be a great glory if you could come upon the Oahu Hemignathus Loxops & Phaeornis. Be sure that any letters from you will be most welcome, so pray write as often as you can, & let us know how things go with you. You must also remember me in fit terms to M^r. Bishop, if you should see him as I suppose you will try to do, & so I remain with the best of wishes

Yours very truly,
Alfred Newton

{Newton's footnote}:
* (All birds of this group would be well to bottle – people in years to come will want to work them out again.)

Honolulu, Oahu, Hawaiian Islands
17 June 1900
Edward Bagnall Poulton

Dear Prof. Poulton,

Your note was forwarded here to me. Those New Orleans sp. were taken in Apr. /97 but I don't know how near to New Or. A train broke down ahead of us at Day Creek & caused some delay & I got out & picked those few things up at rest while we waited, but I did not know exactly where we were. A good way from New Orleans probably.[240]

I should like to see your Majorca bees some time. The heat here is terrible just now but I shall get up in the mountains soon. I hope to breed nearly all my material this trip. With kind regards

Yours very truly
R.C.L. Perkins

Magdalene College
Cambridge, {England}
9 October 1900
Robert Cyril Layton Perkins

My dear Perkins,

I have an impression that I wrote to you some months ago, but I can not be sure about it. Sharp has shown me various letters received from you at diverse times, & I formed the virtuous resolution that I would write to you before long. Your last letter to him (5 Sept[r]. I think) complaining that you heard but little from any one at home makes me no longer delay, for I never knew of you making such a complaint before, & always supposed that in your secret heart you looked on letters as a bore, & would sooner be without them.

I have little or nothing that is worth writing to tell you. It seems to us that your latest conclusion is that you may have worked up about one half of the entomology of the Islands, and of the rest probably one half will have been extirpated before you can get hold of it! This shews a nice state of things, especially as Mr. Bloxam "the naturalist" of H.M.S. 'Blonde' reported that with all his care he could only find 3 or 4 species of <u>Coleoptera</u> & that the islands were decidedly deficient in Insect life!!

Your last letter especially delighted me, though I was of course unable to appreci-

---

[240] Day Creek is actually in Texas, a few miles west of Texarkana, about 200 miles northwest of New Orleans.

ate the entomological part, because it shewed you to be keener than ever – in fact so keen on bug-hunting that I hardly dare suggest that there are still a few birds about which we should like to know some more. Letting alone the little "dicky birds", which I need not name to you – there is that puzzle about the Ducks or Duck to be solved – & I hope you will manage to do this. It is all very well for people (Salvadori for instance) to say that Anas wyvilii is a hybrid but if so between what species? & are the hybrids fertile? I will not go so far as to say that the Ornithology of the islands is in such a state as you represent the entomology to be in; but I do say that there is plenty that we don't know about it, and I don't expect that the forthcoming part to complete the Hebrew Gospel will instruct one very much, though I try to prepare myself for finding many surprises in it. It is to be out I am told before the end of the year, so that any trouble it may involve will belong to the coming century.

The bird world has been very stagnant for the last six months, though there has been a rather unusual number of silly books published. Little Pycraft[241] has turned out a very nice little book on Birds in general – a most amazing shilling worth – but it contains many bad mistakes, most of which could be set right with a single stroke of the pen – will be I hope in a 2ᵈ edⁿ. which the book well deserves.

Wiglesworth, who you may remember, applied to the Joint Committee to be sent out when you were appointed, writes to me that he at last sees his way to start on an investigation of Polynesian birds, & hopes to be off to Fiji next month. I am sure I wish him all success, but I fear that he may be disappointed in some of his results. Most of the islands have been more than skimmed and I suspect there is not much that is of great interest to be obtained. He will not confine himself however to Fiji, but go to as many other groups as he can.

I was greatly pleased to gather from your letters that your health remains good, & trusting that it will so continue I wish you all prosperity & remain

Yours very truly,
Alfred Newton

---

[241] Pycraft, William Plane (1868–1942). Pycraft was a zoologist specializing in osteology at the British Museum of Natural History. In addition to the the popular book referred to above *The Story of Bird Life*, published in 1900, Pycraft also published many other popular books such as *The Story of Fish Life* (1901) and *The Story of Reptile Life* (1905), and *The History of Birds* (1910). The Piltdown scandal at one time implicated Pycraft but he was cleared when it was evident that his being crippled would have kept him from clandestinely entering the site to place the bones.

Magdalene College
Cambridge, England
26 February 1901
Robert Cyril Layton Perkins

My Dear Perkins,

It is some time since I had a letter from you, but Sharpe {sic} has from time to time shewn me those he has received—among them your last two written at the end of January. In one of them you enquire about the places visited by the naturalist of Beechey's voyage. I have been looking into his narrative & made a few extracts, which Sharpe {sic} I believe will send you, but you will see that information such as you desire is not forthcoming. George Tradescant Lay, the naturalist in question, was seriously ill when the 'Blossom' arrived at Honolulu {20 May 1826}, and was left there when she sailed {1 June 1826} northward (Bering Strait) being picked up on her return the next year {26 January to 4 March 1827}, and taken off—apparently recovered. How he occupied himself while in the islands, & whither he went there is nothing to shew. He subsequently contributed to the "Fishes" of the "Zoology" of the voyage, when that was published, & thereto appended a curiously worded note of apology, which amounts to an admission of discharging his duty very imperfectly. Some allowance must be made for his ill health, and also for his having been apparently more of a botanist than a zoologist. He may have made notes or kept a journal, & if so these may still exist. I will try to find out something about him—he is probably long since dead; but at present I know nothing. However I was unexpectedly successful in recovering Bloxam's notes—not that they were worth much—& may have the luck to succeed again.

One of your last letters very much relieved me, that in which you said you had been collecting the lizards, for it had been on my conscience for sometime that we had done nothing in regard to the Reptile, and of course they are bound sooner or later to suffer, if they have not already suffered, like the rest of the fauna. Pray get as many as you conveniently can—scincs & all—who could have been at the trouble of introducing scincs I can't imagine, nor can I conceive how they should have introduced themselves—

I believe that when I last wrote I reminded you about the Ducks, as being one of the bird-puzzles still left. Pray try to solve it. This can only be done by getting males in their breeding plumage, as they will be just about the time this reaches you. If it cost money to buy them, they must be bought & I must stand the shot. I have just now been buying a pair from the Jew's agent (Rosenberg)—at 24/ cash! & the male is in "eclipse" {i.e. post-nuptial} plumage-for they were both killed as the labels shew on the 7th August, on Niihau. The female you got at Halemanu, Oahu, in February /92 is said by Salvadori to be quite different from the type of A. wyvilliana, & I believe he is right. Palmer got at least one female killed early in the year, which I saw & it really had the look of being a hybrid, but between what species I can't say. Please apply yourself to this business.

Remember too that we want to get an adult Night-Heron, & I should much like an owl—for Rothschild in the concluding part of his book (which by this time has probably reached Honolulu)—reorganizes it as a distinct sub. species. If you can get them through or from anyone I will pay anything within reason for them. I don't want you to waste your time over them, as that is too valuable. You are obviously far better employed when sticking to your insects, & I do hope you will thoroughly clear up Oahu. That would be a good job!

On the supposition that you will have seen the last part of Rothschild's book there is no use in telling you what is in it. A.H. Evans met him not long since & in talking to him about it discovered that he had a very imperfect knowledge of its contents and even of S. I. birds in general or particular. A long while ago I surmised that Hartert was the real author, for I felt that the questions of nomenclature were treated in a way that Rothschild could not manage, & now it seems that I was right. Rothschild has plenty of ability, but it is not of that sort. It is rather diverting to read what he (or Hartert) writes of the avifauna generally & the conclusions at which he announces that he has arrived, and then to see that essentially they are the same as others have reached before yet I will be bound that he will be given credit for them all! Plagiarists are the most despicable kind of Naturalists.

We were a little disturbed by one of your former letters in which you spoke of having taken a chill, or something of that sort, but as you do not mention your bodily condition in the later letter I trust all is well with you, & especially that you are no longer troubled as you were here about two years ago. So with all good wishes I remain

Yours very truly,
Alfred Newton

Magdalene College
Cambridge, England
15 March 1901
Robert Cyril Layton Perkins

My Dear Perkins,

As you told Sharp you wanted to find out something about the places where the Insects now in the Brit. Mus. from the 'Blonde' {= 'Blossom'} voyage were taken I have been trying to find out concerning Mr. Lay who was ostensibly the "naturalist" on board that ship. As I wrote to you some ten days or a fortnight ago he was left at Honolulu very sick while the ship went to the north, & was picked up on her return some nine or ten months afterwards.

I think I gave you the precise time, taken from Beechey's narrative of the voyage, but I have not the work {book} at hand at any rate it does not much matter, for he was in Oahu long enough to have done some good work, had his health allowed him, & he been competent. Finding from his own admission in the 'Zoology' of the voyage that he evidently did but little as a Zoologist, I thought he might be a proficient botanist, I therefore wrote to Hooker as the most likely man to know anything of him, but he replies that he can tell me nothing more than that in his father's {Sir W. J. Hooker's} correspondence, now at Kew, there are only 2 letters from Lay, and they give the impression of his being 'a very poor locater or creature & no botanist at all'! He only wrote about the expenses of and impediments 'to collecting'. So there my enquiries are for the present at an end, but I don't mean to lose sight of the business, & trust that something may turn up, as it did in the case of Bloxam's papers, though I should fear that no notes or journals of Lay's, if they exist, would be worth much.

Since writing to you I have received the Report for 1899 of the Director of the B. P. Bishop Museum which contains some 'Field notes on the Birds of Oahu' by Mr. Alvin Seale collector for the Museum. {p. 33} Now could you not induce this gentleman, when he has supplied the wants of the Museum, to obtain for me some of the specimens we still want? I would pay any reasonable price for them. There is the short-eared owl which he says is "quite abundant" near Honolulu, yet we have not a single example. Then there is the Night-Heron which he says is 'common about the marshes in the vicinity of Kahuku'. You know how much I have wanted an adult. He also says of Anas wyvilliana that it is 'fairly common the island among the tule swamps and ponds near the coast.' This bird is still surrounded by mystery, & the mystery is only to be solved by a good series of specimens & especially drakes in breeding plumage. Surely Mr. Seale might procure me some specimens of all these three without much difficulty—to say nothing of the sea-birds (e.g. Anous hawaiiensis) which you did not get? It seems too that there is also a regular taxidermist – a Mr. Bryan. Of course I don't wish to intercept any specimens that are desirable for the B. P. Bishop Museum; but, when that is sufficiently furnished with time, I should like to have of the surplus, & I think that my attempts to get the Avifauna of the islands (to say nothing of their Zoology at large) worked out justify me in thinking that it would not be misapplied—especially as I am willing to pay for it.

I can think of nothing to tell you by way of news—Sharp (whom I have seen since I wrote the foregoing) says he is very well, but he looks overworked, & so with the best of all good wishes I am

Yours very truly
Alfred Newton

I am beginning to get about a little, but I have had rather a bad time of it for some months past.

Magdalene College
Cambridge, England
26 April 1901
Robert Cyril Layton Perkins

My dear Perkins,

Your letter of 28 March reached me three days ago, & though its contents were not of the most hopeful character I was glad to get it. A week or two after I wrote that to which it was in answer I wrote to you again, with more information (not much) concerning Lay, who cannot I think have been the good collector you set him down for. How like the Brit. Mus. to have lost some of his types! The boasting of all concerned with that establishment is beyond belief.

Sharp has shewn me other letters of yours, & I hope your anxiety as to money affairs has been set at rest. We are applying for a continuation or reappointment of the Joint Committee, but are not asking for any grant.

I do hope you have been able to do something about the ducks. That is the greatest mystery in the ornithology of the islands. According to the Curator of the B. P. Museum there are plenty near Honolulu, only preserved by a 'gun club'. What is the condition in which they live? Can they be semi-domesticated—for in that case hybrids might well occur? You really should attempt to solve this problem.

I wonder the B. P. Museum has not subscribed for Rothschild's book; but I don't suppose any one else in the islands would care to pay the price for it. It is certainly not good, however pretentious it be. Finsch complains of Wilson's being rather too much the work of an amateur, but that is just what a German would say. He is vastly pleased with the duplicates we sent him & complains of the Berlin people, that they overlooked 2 or 3 new birds he got to publish his field notes—but I have my doubts as to their being worth very much, as he never gave me the notion of being a good out of door observer. In a Museum nothing escapes him.

The best part of your letter is that which told me that you were none the worse for the rough work you had been having, & with all good wishes believe me to be

Yours very truly
Alfred Newton

In my last letter I asked you to arrange if you could for some bird skins from the Museum 'taxidermist' on my own account to complete our series.

Magdalene College
Cambridge, {England}
12 July 1901
Robert Cyril Layton Perkins

My dear Perkins,

I have not seen Sharp since his return but he sent me your paper on Drepanids a few days ago & I have lost no time in placing it in A.H. Evans' hands for publication in the <u>October</u> 'Ibis'. This I hope will be soon enough for you, & moreover I have told Evans that if he has it set up in type at once, he will probably be able to send you a proof for corrections (I do not know whether you are aware that he is Editor with Sclater of that journal) but you will have to lose no time about it.

I have read the paper & see that it is one of much merit, though there is a good deal in it with which I can't agree. However I consider that it certainly ought to be printed, for no one has a better claim than you to set forth opinions on the subject whether right or wrong, & moreover in regard to your long & excellent services to the S.I. Committee I think it only due to you that it should appear as being "communicated" by that Committee. I have therefore added a foot note to that effect, but otherwise I have not touched a word. I dare say the Editor may, at his discretion, modify some of the expressions for, though the views you express may be mature, I think it may have been written out rather hastily, but such alterations, if any, will I believe be only verbal & not affecting your opinions. This is one reason why I am most anxious that you should have the opportunity of seeing & correcting the proof.

It seems to me that in regard to one branch of your hypothesis you have started from a basis which is very questionable. Is it quite certain that there are any birds that find honey to be <u>of</u> <u>itself</u> a food on which they can subsist? So far as my knowledge goes this, with the possible exception of the S. African <u>Indicator</u> (honey guide), cannot be said. All the <u>Nectariniidae</u> <u>Corbidae</u> & <u>Trochilidae</u> have been in succession shewn (so far as examples of each have been examined) to live on insects, which being attracted by the "nectar" are drawn out by means of the "brush" or "tubular" tongue. Of course the honey extracted with them is swallowed by the bird, but it has been proved that hummingbirds die of hunger if in captivity insect food is not supplied to them.

I am rather sorry to see that you adopt so much of the Hartert nomenclature where it differs from that given by Wilson. This is a very minor point, & questions of nomenclature are not worth the ink that is often shed upon them – but I did take some trouble with Wilson's names, & <u>continue</u>? to think that my judgment in this matter is of more weight than Hartert's – for he is a very ill read man, & has taken up opinions on the subject of nomenclature which are not held by the majority of ornithologists in this country at least. Here I write intentionally of Hartert for I <u>am credibly</u> informed that Rothschild is only the nominal author of that book, & hardly knows one Sandwich Island bird from another, which of my own knowledge I am sure that he is wholly ignorant of all (or most) nomenclatural difficulties.

I shall not trouble you with more now – I do hope you will be successful in getting me the birds we want to complete our series & with the very best wishes for
your continued health & welfare I remain

Yours very truly,
Alfred Newton

I ought to add that I am greatly pleased with your comparison of the Birds &
Beetles. Nobody in the world but you could have done it.

Magdalene College
Cambridge, {England}
23 August 1901
Robert Cyril Layton Perkins

My dear Perkins,

Your letter of the 1st was very welcome this morning & tomorrow being the regular mail day I write at once to thank you for it. I heard from Evans that he had
sent you a proof of your paper for "The Ibis" & I trust it may have reached you
safely, in which case it ought to get back with your corrections in time. He sent
me another copy, but beyond noting some obvious printer's errors I did not venture to alter it. I was much pleased to read it in type, for though there is a good
deal to which I, as yet, cannot agree, I am not so conceited as to suppose myself
infallible, & still less to question your perfect right to express yourself as you like
on a subject which you must know far better than anyone else. Moreover it is a
most suggestive paper, whether your views be right or wrong, & one of a kind of
which we have of late years had far too few. Indeed I should call it one of the best
papers of its sort I have ever read.

Your letter I shall send on to Evans, & if he does not get your proof back in time
I shall suggest his extracting that part relating to honey as birds' food, & adding it
as a postscript to the paper or he might do this to advantage even if he does
receive your proof – but that will be for him to judge. I am always for letting everybody have his say, whether I am convinced by it or not. I must own that what you
now write is rather staggering to my belief, for I never question your ability as an
observer of the right sort; but I had certainly thought that the case of the
Humming-birds had shewn that birds could not live on honey alone for more
than a comparatively short time, & I should like to have some good physiologist's
opinion as to the life-sustaining qualities of honey.

I am wondering what your generic or subgeneric characters for <u>Paroreomyza</u> will
be.

I have not seen Sharp for the last week & I hope he is not ill again. He was attacked after his return from his holiday in the New Forest by "shingles" – a most disagreeable complaint, & for a while was quite on the shelf, but when I last saw him he seemed recovered.

I have been much grieved by the death of poor Wiglesworth of dysentery in Fiji. You will remember him as your competitor for the job you have had so long in hand, & he was bitterly disappointed at not getting it. If he had been sent out when he first volunteered his services, the Committee would have scored the successes (or some of them) that were achieved by Palmer & Co. though it is possible that he might have succumbed to the work; but otherwise I am sure we have had no reason to regret the delay that occurred, since it brought you to the front. Still his fate is sad. He was bent on exploring somewhere, & Polynesia in particular. For years he could not see his way to get out, & he occupied himself in mastering the subject so far as books & specimens go – i.e. of Birds, for he had no taste for entomology, though he would have tried to do his duty in that way also. At last his chance came, & he speedily fell a victim! There may be some consolation in the thought that no one but himself was responsible for his going, indeed I believe his own people did not like the notion of it. I am sorry you have been neglected by your correspondents Sharp & myself excepted, & with all good wishes, I remain

Yours very truly,
Alfred Newton

You don't say anything about supplying the gaps in our Bird Collection, but I hope still.

Waialua, Oahu, Hawaiian Islands
6 October 1901
George Campbell Munro

Dear Munro,

Alas! I am afraid I shall not visit you on Molokai after all. I don't know when you get your papers but if you have already got last Saturdays 'Star' you will now know that I am married at last. I expect now to return to England very soon, for my collecting days are done, & I am not sorry for this. I hope you will send me those bird skins as I promised Newton to get them but you must let me pay you for

A WEDDING AT WAIALUA

MISS ATKINSON MARRIED TO R. C. L. PERKINS.

A Host of Friends Will Extend Good Wishes—Was a Very Quiet Affair. The Bride and Groom.

WAIALUA, Oahu, October 5.—Miss Zoe L. S. A. Atkinson, eldest daughter of Mr. and Mrs. Alatau T. Atkinson, was married last evening at 6 o'clock to R. C. L. Perkins.

The marriage took place at the Waialua Hotel in the presence of Colonel and Mrs. Curtis P. Iaukea and the father and mother of the bride. The ceremony was performed by the Rev. Oili of the Waialua church.

Few couples will receive heartier good wishes or from a wider circle of friends than Mr. and Mrs. Perkins. The bride has lived almost all her life in Honolulu and has always been a favorite among her large circle of friends, and an active spirit in the social life of the community. In her profession as a teacher she has shown both zeal and ability and has achieved an enviable position.

The groom is a scientist of international reputation to whom Hawaii owes very much.

Hawaiian Star, Saturday 5 October 1901.

them, as I shall not feel justified in taking them other wise. I return to Honolulu the day after to-morrow and should be glad of the skins at once. Put whatever price you like on them & I will send you an order, as I must get these. Our marriage was determined so very suddenly as it took place here on Friday night & we only made up our minds the day before! We came out here because Mr & Mrs A were staying here already & they knew nothing about it till I arrived in advance at noon on Friday to make the necessary arrangements, my wife coming on the evening train, when we are married at once in the hotel by the kanaka farm. I must get time to write you again so with that – wishes to Mrs Munro & yourself I am

Yours always
R.C.L. Perkins

Honolulu, Oahu, Hawaiian Islands
13 November 1901
George Campbell Munro

Dear Munro,

I am intending to come up to Molokai – alone of course – in about 2 weeks time. I do not know whether it will be convenient for you to take me in at that time or not. If not do not hesitate to say so as a little since I met one of the Meyer's boys over here, & he invites me to stay with them, so you must not in any way inconvenience yourself. I am going off the day after to-morrow in a tent to the Waianae mountains with Sam Wilder. I especially want to look at the variation of the Oreomyza here. It is very different to any other species of the 'Akikiki' but having a strong thick bill. Its male is quite bright yellow but I never shot one in this plumage as mine were got in summer. I have not yet shot a single bird since I came to the islands this time. In haste & with best wishes.

Yours very truly
R.C.L. Perkins

Honolulu, Oahu, Hawaiian Islands
22 November 1901
George Campbell Munro

Dear Munro,

Thank you for your letter of the 14th. I have been collecting in the Waianae mountains, so did not get it till my return. It is not likely I will leave here for Molokai before the beginning of December if so soon, as I want to finish off here.

I have been studying the 'Oreomyza' of this island ('Akikiki') as there is something curious about it. In the Waianae range the adult ♀ is light yellow beneath, but in the other mountains I have not been able so far to find this form of dull ♂ ♂ like the ♀. This bird by the way is not a true Oreomyza, only the old Kauai form & that of Hawaii belonging properly to that genus.

I call the other 4 species Paroreomyza.

| Oreomyza bairdi | Kauai |
| Oreomyza maua | Hawaii |

subgenus Paroreomyza montana	Lanai
" newtoni	Maui
" flammea	Molokai
" maculata	Oahu

In Oreomyza proper ♂ & ♀ adult are nearly alike, in Paroreomyza they have little resemblance to one another.

My wife is still teaching here so is not likely to accompany me to Molokai as the vacation at Christmas is short, & she probably would not like to be away at that time. Your foreign snipe was probably 'Wilson's snipe' from America, or the 'Painter snipe' both of which have been known to visit the islands. I have to get specimens of the Hawaiian 'noddy' ("naio") Anous hawaiiensis. It is distinct from the common Anous stolidus & is peculiar to this group. It is found the other side of the pali here at the coast. With aloha nui.

Yours very truly
R.C.L. Perkins

GLOSSARY

'a'ali'i (*Dodonaea viscosa*) — a fairly common low-growing native Hawaiian shrub.

Acacia — a genus of legume trees. The genus for the *koa* tree (*Acacia koa*).

Acalles — a genus of Hawaiian weevils of the family Curculionidae (Coleoptera).

Achatinella — a genus of strikingly colorful land snails endemic to the island of O'ahu. Those referred to by Perkins as "Achatinella" from islands other than O'ahu are now placed in other genera. The unfortunate predation by introduced snails as well as feeding by rats coupled with uncontrolled collecting by shell collectors resulted in the virtual devastation of this once speciose genus.

Acrulocercus — old name for an endemic genus of honey eaters, the *'ō'ō*. Current genus name is *Moho*.

Agrion — see *Megalagrion*.

Agrotis — a speciose genus of Hawaiian moths including native and alien armyworm or cutworm moths (Lepidoptera).

āholehole — the Hawaiian name for the young stage of the Hawaiian flagtail (*Kuhlia sandvicensis*), a silver perch-like fish.

'akakane (*Loxops coccineus*) — a Hawaiian honeycreeper. More commonly known as *'ākepa*.

'ākala (*Rubus hawaiensis*) — related to the raspberry, *'ākala* is the Hawaiian name for a native Hawaiian plant bearing edible fruit that grows as medium-sized shrubs with reduced thorns.

'ākia — endemic shrubs of the genus *Wikstroemia* (Thymelaeaceae). Native Hawaiians crushed the plant and scattered the plant bits onto tidepools, where fish would soon float to the surface, affected by the toxins in the plant.

'akialoa (*Hemignathus*) — a Hawaiian honeycreeper with a very long down-curved bill. Used as a source of green feathers in featherwork. Species currently referred to as *'akialoa* are *H. obscurus* (Hawai'i Island) and *H. ellisianus* (other islands).

'akialoa nukupu'u — see *nukupu'u*.

'akikiki (*Oreomystis bairdi*) — the Kaua'i creeper. This small honeycreeper has reduced populations now confined to the Alaka'i area. In Perkins's time its distribution probably extended almost island-wide.

'alalā (*Corvus hawaiiensis*)— the Hawaiian crow. Common throughout the islands in Perkins's time, its natural curiosity and feeding preferences — fruits and other commercial crops — soon led to its virtual extinction from hunting and trapping by farmers. Its natural diet consisted of *'ōhelo* berries and *'ie'ie* fruits. When humans invaded its native habitat and started agricultural crops, its diet changed to accommodate the easier resources. Recently, a rigorous captive breeding program has saved the last few individuals but releases into the wild have proven unsuccessful. The Hawaiian name means "cry like a young animal" and refers to its call resembling the crying of a young child.

alani (*Melicope clusiifolia*) — this endemic Hawaiian plant occurs as shrubs or trees in the wet forests on all of the major islands, especially on Oʻahu and Hawaiʻi, the latter where it can be found in the forests near the Kīlauea volcano. It can grow to 25 or 30 feet in height. The leaves were used for scenting *tapa*.

Aleurites — a genus of the family Euphorbiaceae that contains the *kukui* or candle nut tree (*Aleurites moluccana*).

Allobophora — a genus of earthworms.

Alucita — a genus of microlepidoptera (moths) (Lepidoptera).

Alyxia — see *maile*.

ʻamakihi — a Hawaiian honeycreepers. Three species are recognized today: Kauaʻi ʻAmakihi (*Hemignathus kauaiensis*); Hawaiʻi ʻAmakihi (*Hemignathus virens*) [also on Maui and Molokaʻi]; Oʻahu ʻAmakihi (*Hemignathus flavus*). Also known as *ʻamakiki.*

ʻamakiki — see *ʻamakihi.*

Amastra — a genus of native Hawaiian land snails.

Anas — the genus name for a type of duck.

Anatidae — the family name for ducks and geese.

Anax — a genus of dragonflies (Odonata). Two species of this genus occur in Hawaiʻi. *Anax junius* and *A. strenuus*. The giant *Anax strenuus* is the largest dragonfly in North America (including outlying states and provinces).

Anchonymus — a genus of ground beetles of the family Carabidae (Coleoptera).

Andrena — a genus of bees (Hymenoptera).

Anisodactylus — a genus of ground beetles of the family Carabidae (Coleoptera).

Anisolabis — a genus of earwigs (Dermaptera).

Anobiidae — a family of beetles including the deathwatch and cigarette beetles (Coleoptera).

Anotheorus — a genus of weevils (Coleoptera).

Anous — a genus of birds commonly called noddies.

ʻapapane (*Himatione sanguinea*) — a red Hawaiian honeycreeper found on all the main Hawaiian Islands and is abundant in native *ʻōhiʻa* forests, although it occasionally visits exotic forests. It forages in the forest canopy for nectar and insects. It also frequents flowering *koa* and *māmane* and has been observed feeding in pines and flowering eucalyptus. Its feathers were used in Hawaiian featherwork.

Apetasimus — a genus of nitidulid beetles (Coleoptera).

Apterocis — a genus of ciid beetles (Coleoptera).

Apterocyclus — a genus of stag beetles of the family Lucanidae (Coleoptera).

Apteromesus — a genus of ground beetles of the family Carabidae (Coleoptera).

Archips — a genus of microlepidopteran moths (Lepidoptera).

Astelia — see *paʻiniu*.

Atelothrus — a genus of endemic Hawaiian ground beetles of the family Carabidae.

Atrachycnemis — a genus of Hawaiian ground beetles of the family Carabidae.

ʻauku — see *ʻaukuʻu.*

ʻaukuʻu (*Nycticorax nycticorax*) — the Black-crowned Night Heron. It is native to Hawaiʻi and found almost worldwide. It is a predator and feeds on small rodents, fishes, insects, and even small chicks of other birds.

ʻawa — see *kava*.

Bactra — a genus of microlepidoptera of the family Tortricidae. Includes native species and species purposefully introduced for weed control in Hawaiʻi.

Banza — a native katydid (Tettigoniidae) that is composed of eleven species in Hawaiʻi. The species referred to here is probably *Banza deplanata* or *B. molokaiensis*, both of which occur on East Molokaʻi.

Baryneus sharpi — an endemic Hawaiian ground beetle of the family Carabidae (Coleoptera) found on East Maui.

Barypristus — a genus of ground beetle of the family Carabidae (Coleoptera).

Begonia — a genus of native, introduced and cultivated plants of the family Begoniaceae.

Bembidion — a genus of ground beetle of the family Carabidae (Coleoptera).

Blackburnia — a genus of endemic Hawaiian ground beetle of the family Carabidae

Bobea — a genus of trees of the family Rubiaceae known as ʻahakea in Hawaiian.

Brachypeplus — a genus of beetles of the family Nitidulidae (Coleoptera).

Brontolaemus — a genus of beetles of the family Cucujidae (Coleoptera).

Broussonetia — see *wauke*.

Buteo — see ʻio.

Calandra — a genus of weevils of the family Curculionidae (Coleoptera). Some species have, since Perkins's time, been transferred to the genus *Sitophila*, but one introduced species, the coconut weevil, is now in the genus *Diocalandra*.

Callipepla californica — the California Quail. This is one of two species of quail currently found in Hawaiʻi; both alien species. It was introduced to the Hawaiian Islands before 1855, probably for hunting.

Callithmysus — an old genus name for endemic Hawaiian long-horned beetles of the family Cerambycidae (Coleoptera) now placed in the genus *Plagithmysus*.

Campodea — a genus of small, white, bristle-tailed arthropods in the order Diplura.

Campsicnemus — a genus of long-legged flies of the family Dolichopodidae (Diptera); very diverse in Hawaiʻi (approximately 150 species).

Campylotheca — an old genus name of plants now treated in the native composite genus *Bidens*.

Capsidae — an old name for a family of leaf bugs (Heteroptera) now called Miridae.

Capua — a genus of endemic Hawaiian moths of the family Tortricidae now placed in the genus *Spheterista*.

Carabidae — a family of beetles commonly called ground beetles (Coleoptera).

Carelia — a genus of land snails.

Carpodacus — the genus name of the common House Finch, an alien species in Hawaiʻi.

Cerambycidae — commonly known as "wood boring beetles," their vernacular name referring to the habits of the grubs that bore into trees; or "long-horned beetles" or "longicorns," referring the conspicuously long antennae of the adults.

Chaetoptila — the genus name of the extinct Hawaiian honeyeater called kioea (*Chaetoptila angustipluma*). After the crow, the largest bird known in from the Hawaiian Islands. Only 4 specimens exist in museum collections.

Chalcididae — tiny parasitic wasps, usually less than 2 mm in length (Hymenoptera).

Chalcolepidus — a genus of click beetles (also known as wire worms) of the family Elateridae (Coleoptera).

Chalcomenus — a genus of Hawaiian ground beetles of the family Carabidae (Coleoptera).

Chasiempis — a Hawaiian endemic genus of Monarch Flycatcher. See ʻelepaio.

Cheirodendron — a plant genus known in Hawaiian as ʻōlapa. Usually found in association with ʻōhiʻa trees.

Chelodynerus — a genus of wasps of the family Vespidae (Hymenoptera).

Chloridops — a genus of Hawaiian honeycreepers with massive finch-type beaks. The species *Chloridops kona* (the Kona Grosbeak) was discovered in 1887 by Scott Wilson and last seen in the 1890s by Perkins. It is thought by some to have gone extinct due to bird malaria.

Chlorodrepanis — an outdated genus name for the ʻamakihi, a Hawaiian honeycreeper. The current genus name is *Hemignathus*.

Chrysopa — a genus of predaceous insects, commonly called lace-wings, of the family Chrysopidae (Neuroptera).

Chrysopidae — a family of insects containing lace wings (Neuroptera).

Cibotium (*hāpu'u*) — a genus of large tree ferns. There are six species of *Cibotium* in Hawai'i.

Cillaeopeplus — a genus of nitidulid beetles (Coleoptera).

Ciridops — a genus of small Hawaiian honeycreepers including the now extinct *'ula-'ai-hāwane* (*Ciridops anna*), which in historical times, was found only on the Big Island.

Cis — a genus of minute tree-fungus beetles of the family Ciidae (Coleoptera).

Cistela — a genus of beetles of the family Tenebrionidae.

Cistelidae — an old name for a family of beetles (Coleoptera) now called Tenebrionidae.

Clermontia — a genus of Hawaiian lobelioids of the family Campanulaceae.

Clytarlus — the genus name used in Perkins's time for Hawaiian long-horned beetles now mostly known in the genus *Plagithmysus*.

Clytus — a genus of long-horned beetles of the family Cerambycidae.

Coenosia [= *Lispocephala*] — a speciose Hawaiian genus of predaceous flies of the family Anthomyiidae (Diptera).

Coleoptera — the order of beetles.

Coleotichus blackburniae — the spectacular iridescent-colored koa bug (Heteroptera). This native "stinkless stinkbug" is an increasingly uncommon sight on *a'ali'i* bushes and koa trees. It was once more plentiful, but the parasitic fly introduced to help control its cousin, the southern green stink bug *Nezara viridula*, often missed its mark and parasitized this harmless bug because of its similar shape.

Colias — a genus of butterflies of the family Pieridae, nonnative in Hawai'i.

Collembola — an order of arthropods commonly called springtails.

Colpocaccus — a genus of Hawaiian ground beetles of the family Carabidae now placed in the genus *Blackburnia*.

Colpodiscus — a genus of Hawaiian ground beetles of the family Carabidae.

Corvus — a genus of crow. The only surviving Hawaiian species (*Corvus hawaiiensis*, the *'alalā*) is close to extinction. Historically, there were at least 2 more species of crows on O'ahu, Moloka'i, and Maui. See *'alalā*.

Cossonidae — now a subfamily (Cossoninae) of weevils (Curculionidae). Characterized by the long body and long, curved snout.

Crabro — genus of wasps whose Hawaiian species are now placed in the genus *Ectemnius* (Hymenoptera).

Crambidae — a family of moths (Lepidoptera).

Crambus — a genus of moths of the family Crambidae (Lepidoptera).

Crex — a genus name of birds also known as crakes. The name was at one time applied to the flightless rail from Hawai'i Island.

Cyclothorax — a genus of ground beetles of the family Carabidae (Coleoptera).

Dacnitus — a genus of endemic Hawaiian click beetles of the family Elateridae (Coleoptera). The only species (*Dacnitus currax*) is only known from the island of Kaua'i.

Danais — genus of nymphalid butterflies including the monarch (*Danais plexippus*) (Lepidoptera).

Dasyuris — a genus of inch-worm moths of the family Geometridae (Lepidoptera). The Hawaiian species are now placed in the genus *Megalotica*.

Datura — a genus of solanaceous plants (Solanaceae).

Deilephila — a genus of hawkmoths of the family Sphingidae (Lepidoptera). The species *lineata* and *calida* mentioned by Perkins are now placed in the genus *Hyles*.

Deinocossonus — an endemic Hawaiian genus of weevils of the family Curculionidae.

Deinomimesa — a genus of wasps of the family Sphecidae (Hymenoptera).

Dermestidae — a family of beetles (Coleoptera). Many are major pests of stored products and museum collections of natural history specimens.

Derobroscus — a genus of ground beetles of the family Carabidae (Coleoptera).

Deropristus — a genus of ground beetles of the family Carabidae (Coleoptera).

Dicranopteris — see *uluhe*.

Diestota — a genus of rove beetles of the family Staphylinidae (Coleoptera)

Diptera — an order of insects including flies, gnats, and mosquitoes.

Disenochus — a genus of ground beetles of the family Carabidae.

Distoleon — a genus of ant lions; see Myrmeleontidae.

Dodonaea — see *'a'ali'i*.

Dolichopodidae [= *Campsicnemus*] — a family of long-legged flies (Diptera).

Dolichopus — a genus of long-legged flies common throughout the Hawaiian islands.

Dracaena — a genus name sometimes used for species of the genus *Pleomele* (*hala pepe*). The use by Perkins for this plant being found at the head of Nu'uanu Valley in the 1890s probably refers to either *Pandanus* or *Pleomele* and not true *Dracaena*.

Drepanidops — a genus name suggested to Perkins by Newton for the Black Mamo (*Drepanis funerea*) discovered by Perkins on Moloka'i. The name was never used.

Drepanididae — the family of Hawaiian honeycreepers. Treated as a family in Perkins's time in Hawai'i, it was classified as a subfamily of the Fringillidae (finches) for many years. Recently, some taxonomists have reinstated it to full family rank.

Drepanis — genus of Hawaiian honeycreepers including the species discovered by Perkins on Moloka'i (*Drepanis funerea*), which went extinct only a few years later. See also *mamo*.

Dromaeolus — a genus of false click beetles of the family Eucmenidae (Coleoptera).

Drosophila — commonly known as pomace flies. This genus of flies is one of the best examples of adaptive speciation in Hawai'i. There are over 800 species of this genus in Hawai'i, which is roughly three-fourths of the species known worldwide. These flies are favorite subjects of evolutionary and population biologists as well as geneticists in learning how life evolved in such a remote place as the Hawaiian Islands.

Dryophthorus — a genus of ground beetles of the family Carabidae (Coleoptera).

Dyscritomyia — as genus of calliphorid (blow) flies endemic to the Hawaiian Islands (Diptera). Maggots of some species are thought to feed on native snails.

Elaeocarpus — a genus of large trees of the family Elaeocarpaceae.

Elateridae — a family of beetles commonly known as click beetles or wireworms. The immature grub stage feeds on the roots of grasses and can be a major pest of turf grass.

'elepaio (*Chasiempis sandwichensis*) — an endemic genus of Monarch Flycatcher; three subspecies are recognized. The Hawaiian canoe makers regarded this bird as a guardian spirit that would show them which *koa* trees were best for canoe making.

Embia — a genus of insects known as webspinners in the family Embiidae (Embioptera).

Emperoptera — a rare endemic Hawaiian genus of long-legged flies whose species are flightless (Diptera). Five species have been described, but only one is known to still survive.

Endodontidae — an endemic Pacific family of ground-dwelling snails. They are the most diverse land snail family in the Pacific but their ground dwelling habits make them easily susceptible to predation by ants.

Eopenthes — a genus of click beetles of the family Elateridae (Coleoptera).

Eristalis — a syrphid fly or flower fly whose larvae are commonly referred to as rat-tailed maggots (Diptera).

Eucnemidae — the family of false click beetles (Coleoptera).

Eucymatoge — an old name for a genus of inch worm moths of the family Geometridae (Lepidoptera) now placed in *Eupethecia*.

Eunitidula — a genus of sap beetles of the family Nitidulidae (Coleoptera).

Eupelmus — a genus of parasitic wasp of the family Eupelmidae (Hymenoptera).

Eupethecia — One of the more unusual moths in Hawai'i, caterpillars of some endemic species are carnivorous predators instead of being leaf-eating herbivores like most caterpillars.

Fornax — a genus of false click beetles of the family Eucmenidae (Coleoptera). Hawaiʻi has one endemic and one nonnative species. The species Perkins was referring to was probably the endemic species *Fornax longicornis* Blackburn, which is found only on Maui.

Freycinetia — a genus of climbing vines in forests called *ʻieʻie* in Hawaiian.

Fringilla anna — see *Ciridops*.

Fringillidae — the family of finches.

Fulica — a genus of coots in the family Rallidae. The species in Hawaiʻi (*Fulica alai*, the Hawaiian coot) is a federally endangered species. Its Hawaiian name, *ʻalae keʻokeʻo*, refers to its white beak and frontal shield.

Geometridae — a family of moths, the caterpillars of which are known as inchworms (Lepidoptera).

Glyptoma — a genus of rove beetles of the family Staphylinidae (Coleoptera).

Gnatholymnaeum — a genus of ground beetles of the family Carabidae (Coleoptera).

Gomphus — a genus of dragonflies of the family Gomphidae (Odonata). The specimens referred to by Perkins were initially misidentified by him as belonging to this genus. They are now in the genus *Nesogonia* (Libellulidae).

Gonioryctus — a genus of sap beetles of the family Nitidulidae (Coleoptera).

Goniothorax — a genus of sap beetles of the family Nitidulidae (Coleoptera).

Gracillaria — a genus of moths of the family Gracillariidae (Lepidoptera). The species mentioned by Perkins (*Gracillaria epibathra*) is now placed in the genus *Philodoria*.

Gryllidae — a family of insects commonly called crickets (Orthoptera).

Gunnera — a genus of plants with enormous round leaves in the family Gunneraceae. On Mt. Kaʻala there is a seep on the eastern slope that is thickly covered with these plants and is known by the name "Gunnera Springs," an old collecting ground for many botanists and entomologists.

hau (*Hibiscus tiliaceus*) — a tropical Pacific plant brought to Hawaiʻi by colonizing Polynesians and grows near the shoreline. It is used for canoe-making, firewood, fertilizer, and medicine.

Helix — an genus name for land snails. The specimens Perkins referred to are now in the family Endodontidae (*q.v.*) under another genus name.

Hemerobiidae — a family of insects commonly called brown lace wings (Neuroptera).

Hemignathus — see *ʻamakihi*.

Hemiptera — an order of insects known as true bugs.

Herpestes javanicus — the Small Indian Mongoose; this sly predator was an ill-advised introduction in 1883 into the Hawaiian Islands meant to help control rats in the sugar cane fields. Unfortunately, the mongoose did not stay in the cane fields (where it did a good job of controlling rats) but soon spread to other habitats and food sources in the form of the eggs of ground nesting birds. Soon after their introduction to the islands, most of the ground nesting birds had extremely reduced populations and of those, the rails had gone extinct.

Hesperiidae — a family of butterflies known as skippers (Lepidoptera).

Heteramphus — a genus of endemic Hawaiian weevils of the family Curculionidae (Coleoptera).

Heterocrossa — a genus of carposinid moths of the family Carposinidae (Lepidoptera). Species in Hawaiʻi are now placed in the genus Carposina.

Heterorhynchus — an old genus name for the *ʻakiapōlāʻau*. Now placed in the genus *Hemignathus*.

Hillebrandia — an endemic Hawaiian genus of begonias (Begoniaceae) with a single known endemic species (*Hillebrandia sandwicensis*).

Himatione — see *ʻapapane*.

Holcobius — a genus of cigarette beetles of the family Anobiidae (Coleoptera).

Holochila [= *Udara*] — old genus name for the native Hawaiian lycaenid (see *Udara*).

Homalota — a genus of rove beetles of the family Staphylinidae (Coleoptera).

Homoptera — an order of sap sucking insects including planthoppers, leafhoppers, scales, and mealy bugs.

Hydrophilidae — the family of water scavenger beetles (Coleoptera).

Hylaeus (*Neosoprosopis*) — native bees of the family Colletidae (Hymenoptera).

Hymenoptera — an order of insects including ants, bees, and wasps.

Hypenomyia — a genus of parasitic flies of the family Tachinidae (Diptera).

Hyposmocoma — a diverse genus of Hawaiian moths with perhaps as many endemic Hawaiian species as in Hawaiian *Drosophila*.

Iapyx — a genus of arthropods of the order Diplura.

Icerya — a genus of the bug family Margarodidae (Homoptera). The cottony cushion scale (*Icerya purchasi*), introduced to the United States with acacias from Australia, became a serious damaging pest to citrus crops in California in the 1870s. Successful introduction of natural enemies to control it created enthusiasm for using the method biological control for mitigation of pest animals and plants.

Ichneumonidae — family of parasitic wasps (Hymenoptera).

'ie'ie (*Freycinetia arborea*) — *'ie'ie* are climbing vines once dominant in Hawaiian forests. After the introduction of cattle and other invasive aliens, the *'ie'ie* has been severely reduced in numbers throughout the island chain.

'i'iwi (*Vestiaria coccinea*) — a scarlet red Hawaiian honeycreeper with a long bill for probing deep into flowers to sip nectar. It was a major source of bright red feathers for Hawaiian featherwork.

'iliahi (*Santalum paniculatum*) — sandalwood. In Hawai'i, varying in size from small shrubs to trees, were harvested for their pleasant odor and shipped to China where they were used in incense and fine woodworking. Captain John Kendrick, a Boston fur trader, who used it as an adjunct to the already existing sea otter fur trade from the California coast, initiated the sandalwood trade in Hawai'i in 1791. The trade in Hawai'i reached its peak between 1810 and 1820, when the fur traders realized that it was much more profitable than furs and eventually sent ships to Hawai'i solely for the wood. The price of sandalwood at that time was upwards of $125 per ton (equal to about $1600 per ton in current [2006] dollars). It is estimated that the total sales of the wood from Hawai'i reached 3 to 4 million dollars during its heyday when over 1400 tons of sandalwood were shipped to China each year. Export of the wood brought money to the Hawaiian *ali'i* (royalty), who, controlling the sandalwood land, forced their people to labor in the forests cutting trees and transporting the wood to the harbors by hand. Some of these laborers, hoping to quickly end the trade of this tree and put an end to their hard labor, would pull out any sandalwood seedlings they would find. The forests were virtually gone by 1839, and the export of sandalwood from Hawai'i ended in 1840. Today, no forests of sandalwood survive. Only a few solitary sandalwood trees exist scattered throughout the Hawaiian Islands.

'io — Hawaiian name for the endemic Hawaiian Hawk (*Buteo solitarius*). The species is currently on the federal Endangered Species List. Fortunately, its numbers are increasing. The *'io* is the only raptor in Hawai'i that has survived into historic times. Its former range included Kaua'i, O'ahu, and Moloka'i as shown by fossil remains, but in modern times has only been known from the Big Island.

Isoptera — an order of insects commonly known as termites.

Itodacnus — a genus of click beetles of the family Elateridae (Coleoptera).

Japyx — see *Iapyx*.

kākāwahie (*Paroreomyza flammea*) — a Hawaiian honeycreeper commonly known as the Moloka'i Creeper. Thought to be extinct, it was last seen in 1963 in the Pelekunu area of Moloka'i.

kāmaʻo (*Myadestes myadestinus*) — also known as the Large Kauaʻi Thrush, it is the largest of the Hawaiian thrushes. Last seen in 1992 and thought to be extinct due to avian malaria.

kava (*Piper methysticum*) — a tropical evergreen shrub with large heart-shaped leaves and woody stems. Its thick roots are mashed or ground and made into a cold beverage used similarly to alcohol. It has a long history of ritual and recreational use in Polynesia and is now a common herbal product.

kiawe (*Prosopis pallida*) — mesquite, algoroba. The first tree in Hawaiʻi was grown from seed on the Catholic Mission grounds in downtown Honolulu in 1828 by Father Alexis Bachelot (1796–1837). The seeds were obtained from a tree on the grounds of the Jardin du Roi in Paris. Some have claimed that all *kiawe* trees in Hawaiʻi derive from this single individual but there have been separate purposeful introductions since 1900. In Hawaiʻi, the tree is used for windbreaks and charcoal production.

kīkānia (*Datura stramonium*) — Jimson weed, thornapple. An introduced invasive and toxic plant. It is native to North America but has been introduced into many areas of the Pacific as an ornamental where it spreads naturally.

koa (*Acacia koa*) — the *koa* tree is one of the fastest growing trees in Hawaiʻi and occupies a vegetational zone above the more common *ʻōhiʻa* trees.

koaiʻa (*Acacia koaia*) — a tree that is closely related to *Acacia koa*, but has denser wood. It is a small tree with a straight trunk and round canopy.

kōlea (*Pluvialis fulva*) — this bird, commonly called the Pacific Golden Plover, migrates in August to Hawaiʻi where it stays until April, then returns to its breeding grounds in Alaska and Siberia.

kopena — a Hawaiian name for crickets.

kōpiko (*Psychotria mariniana*) — a plant of the coffee family that grows as a small tree in mesic to wet forests on Kauaʻi, Oʻahu, Molokaʻi, Lānaʻi, and Maui.

kukui (*Aleurites moluccana*) — candlenut. This species of tree from the spurge family, found throughout the Pacific, is used by Hawaiians in medicine, and its hard nuts when cured and polished are used in lei making

Labetis — a genus of comb-clawed beetles of the family Tenebrionidae (Coleoptera).

Labia — a genus of nonnative earwigs of the family Labiidae (Dermaptera).

Labrocerus — a genus of dermestid beetles of the family Dermestidae (Coleoptera).

Laemophloeus — a genus of beetles of the family Cucujidae (Coleoptera).

Laminella — a genus name of Hawaiian landsnails of the family Amastridae.

lantana (*Lantana camara*) — a nonnative plant of the verbena family introduced into Hawaiʻi as an ornamental and escaped to quickly spread into the more drier areas of the main Hawaiian Islands becoming a serious invasive pest, the control of which was the main focus of the some of Perkins's early work for the Hawaiian government after his collecting for the Sandwich Islands Committee was completed.

Lasiurus cinereus semotus (*ʻōpeʻapeʻa*) — the Hawaiian Hoary Bat. One of only two mammals native to the Hawaiian Islands (the other is the Hawaiian Monk Seal). In certain areas, it is commonly seen at dusk catching insects on the wing. This Hawaiian subspecies of the Hoary Bat is on the Federal Endangered Species List.

Lathridius — a genus of square-nosed fungus beetles of the family Lathridiidae (Coleoptera). The species referred to by Perkins (*nodifer*) is now placed in the genus *Aridius*.

lehua — the Hawaiian name for the flower of the *ʻōhiʻa* tree.

Lepidoptera — an order of insects that includes moths and butterflies.

Leptogenys — a genus of ponerine ant in the family Formicidae (Hymenoptera).

Leptogryllus — a genus of bush crickets with 29 species endemic to the Hawaiian Islands. When Perkins was surveying for the Sandwich Islands Committee, only one species was known from Hawaiʻi.

Leucania — a genus of armyworm moths in the family Noctuidae that are found as a pest of corn, sugar cane, and other grasses (Lepidoptera). Native Hawaiian species are now placed in the genus *Pseudaletra*.

Leurocorynus — a genus of rove beetles of the family Staphylinidae (Coleoptera).

Ligia — a genus of primarily marine littoral invertebrates called wharf roaches in the family Ligiidae (Isopoda). Terrestrial inland forms occur on Kaua'i and O'ahu.

Lineodes — a genus of moths in the family Crambidae (Lepidoptera).

Liophaena — a genus of rove beetles of the family Staphylinidae (Coleoptera).

Lispinodes — a genus of rove beetles of the family Staphylinidae (Coleoptera).

Lithocolletidae — a family of leaf miner moths (Lepidoptera). The species referred to by Perkins (*Philodoria splendida*) as possibly being in this family is now placed in the family Gracillariidae.

Locustidae — family of insects commonly called grasshoppers.

loulu — the Hawaiian name for the fan palms of the genus *Pritchardia*.

Loxioides — see *palila*.

Loxops — a genus of Hawaiian honeycreepers with conical, finch-like bills crossed apically.

Loxostege — a genus of moths in the family Crambidae (Lepidoptera). Hawaiian species are now placed in the genus *Udea*.

Lycaenidae — a family of butterflies commonly called "blues" or "hairstreaks." Hawai'i only has one native species of lycaenids, *Udara blackburniae*.

Machilis — a genus of jumping bristletails of the family Machilidae (Archaeognatha).

Macranillus — an old genus name for ground beetles of the family Carabidae (Coleoptera). Species are now placed in the genus *Bembidion*.

maile (*Alyxia oliviformis*) — a vine endemic to the Hawaiian Islands that is found at elevations from 50 to 2000 meters in the forests of all the main islands except Ni'ihau and Kaho'olawe. It imparts a pleasant fragrance when its leaves are crushed. It is one of the favorite plants used in lei making and other festive decorations.

māmane or *mamani* (*Sophora chrysophylla*) — *māmane* are shrubby trees that in some cases make up the dominant element of subalpine areas on East Maui and the Big Island comprising what is known as the *māmane/naio* vegetational zone. Its seedpods, buds, and flowers are a staple food for the endangered native *palila*, who may also eat insects that live in the tree and feed them to their fledgling young. Additionally, its wood serves as a host medium for certain long-horned beetles of the genus *Plagithmysus* (Cerambycidae).

mamo — the Hawaiian name for two endemic Hawaiian honeycreepers of the genus *Drepanis*, now all extinct. The Black Mamo (*Drepanis funerea*) was discovered by Perkins. The Hawai'i Mamo (*Drepanis pacifica*) was highly prized by Hawaiian feather-workers for its rich golden feathers.

Margaronia — a genus of moths of the family Pyralidae (Lepidoptera).

Mauia — a native Hawaiian genus of fungus weevils of the family Anthribidae (Coleoptera).

Mauna — a genus of native Hawaiian ground beetles in the family Carabidae (Coleoptera).

Meconemus — a genus of fungus weevils of the family Anthribidae (Coleoptera).

Mecostomus — a genus of ground beetles of the family Carabidae (Coleoptera).

Mecyclothorax — a speciose genus of ground beetles of the family Carabidae (Coleoptera).

Megachile — a genus of bees sometimes known as "leaf-cutting bees."

Megalagrion — these endemic Hawaiian damselflies (referred to in Perkins's journals as *Agrion*) comprise over 20 species in the islands, including half a dozen that are currently considered near extinction and as of this writing are being considered for federal protection.

Meliphagidae — a family of birds commonly called honeyeaters. In Hawai'i, these were the *'ō'ō* and the *kioea*.

Metrarga — a genus of seed bugs of the family Lygaeidae (Heteroptera).

Metrocidium — a group of ground beetles of the family Carabidae (Coleoptera). Now considered a subgenus of *Bembidion*.

Metromeni — plural for specimens of the genus *Metromenus*.

Metromenus — a genus of ground beetles of the family Carabidae (Coleoptera).

Metrosideros — see *'ōhi'a*.

Mimesa — an old genus name of wasps of the family Sphecidae (Hymenoptera). Now *placed* in the genus *Nesomimesa*.

Mirosternus — a genus of cigarette beetles of the family Anobiidae (Coleoptera).

Moho — the genus of native Hawaiian honeyeaters (Meliphagidae) more commonly known as the *'ō'ō*.

mokihana — the Hawaiian name for one of the species of the genus *Melicope* (*M. anisata*).

Myllaena — a genus of rove beetles of the family Staphylinidae (Coleoptera).

Myoporum — see *naio*.

Myriapoda — a group of arthropods including centipedes and millipedes.

Myrmeleontidae — commonly called ant lions. In most parts of the world, ant lions are noted for the habit of the predaceous immature stages to produce a small sand pit in which they trap falling insects. The native Hawaiian ant lion (e.g., *Distoleon wilsoni*) differs in that it does not form a sand pit.

Myrsine — a genus of plants also known as *kōlea* in the family Myrsinaceae.

naio (*Myoporum sandwicense*) — bastard sandal, or bastard sandalwood. An indigenous species (found in the Cook Islands and Hawai'i) of small tree having an odor similar to that of true sandalwood. It was shipped to China as a substitute when the sandalwood supply in Hawai'i (*vide infra*) was exhausted in the early 1800s, but it was not accepted.

Nasturtium — a genus of plants in the mustard family Brassicaceae.

Neoclytarlus — a genus of long-horned beetles in the family Cerambycidae (Coleoptera). Now placed in the genus *Plagithmysus*.

Nesamiptis — an old genus name for moths of the family Noctuidae (Lepidoptera) now placed in the genus *Hypena*.

Nesocrabro — a group of wasps of the family Sphecidae (Hymenoptera) now treated as a subgenus of *Ectemnius*.

Nesogonia — an endemic genus of dragonflies of the family Libellulidae (Odonata).

Nesomedon — a genus of rove beetles of the family Staphylinidae (Coleoptera).

Nesomicromus — an old genus name of brown lacewings of the family Hemerobiidae (Neuroptera) now placed in the genus *Micromus*.

Nesomicrops — a group of ground beetles of the family Carabidae (Coleoptera) now treated in the genus *Bembidion*.

Nesoprosopis — see *Hylaeus*.

Nesotocus — a genus of weevils of the family Curculionidae (Coleoptera).

Neuroptera — an order of insects containing lace wing and ants lions. During the time Perkins was in Hawai'i, it also referred to damselflies and dragonflies, which are now placed in the order Odonata.

Newcombia — a genus of now rare land snails.

Nezara viridula — a species of pestiferous true bug commonly known as the stink bug (Heteroptera).

Nitidulidae — a family of beetles commonly called sap beetles (Coleoptera).

Noctuidae — a family of moths whose pestiferous caterpillars are known as cut worms and army worms (Lepidoptera). There are many native species in the Hawaiian Islands.

nohu —the Hawaiian name for the puncture vine, *Tribulus*.

noju — see *nohu*.

nuku puʻu (*Hemignathus lucidus*) — Hawaiian honeycreepers (Drepanididae) with a long, narrow curved upper beak and a short, robust curved lower beak. Three subspecies are recognized from Kauaʻi, Oʻahu, and Molokaʻi. All are thought to be extinct. The Oʻahu population was the one that Newton was obsessed with obtaining and Perkins felt obligated to achieve on behalf of his patron, although his efforts were fruitless. It was last collected in 1837 in Nuʻuanu Valley.

nukupololei — the Hawaiian name Perkins coined for the *Viridonia* he collected on the slopes of Mauna Kea that the native Hawaiians did not know and for which they had no name. Perkins's Hawaiian name was never subsequently used by Hawaiians or ornithologists. The genus name *Viridonia* is now included in the genus *Hemignathus*. Perkins's use of this genus name applied only to the Greater ʻAmakihi (*Hemignathus sagittirostris*).

Numenius — a genus of curlews and whimbrels.

Nysius — a genus of seed bugs of the family Lygaeidae (Heteroptera).

Odonata — an order of insects containing damselflies and dragonflies.

Odyneri — a tribe of wasps containing the genus *Odynerus*.

Odynerus — a genus of wasps of the family Vespidae (Hymenoptera).

ʻōhiʻa lehua — see *ʻōhiʻa*.

ʻōhiʻa or *ʻōhiʻa lehua* or *lehua* (*Metrosideros polymorpha*) — the *ʻōhiʻa* tree is the most common and dominant tree in Hawaiian forests. Its species name is more than apt as it takes on a variety of sizes depending where it grows. It can range from a tiny 2 inches in the Alakaʻi Swamp of Kauaʻi to large three-story trees in mesic forests of the Big Island.

ʻōhiʻa ʻai (*Syzygium malaccense*) — this plant is commonly known as mountain apple. It is a plant brought in with the Polynesians and is a member of the myrtle family (Myrtaceae).

ʻōhiʻa hā (*Syzygium sandwicensis*) — this member of the myrtle family (Myrtaceae) is related to the mountain apple but its uses by Hawaiians were primarily for medicine, canoe building, house construction, and dyes.

ʻōlapa (*Cheirodendron* spp.) — these native Hawaiian plants of the family Araliaceae are often seen growing in association with *ʻōhiʻa* trees in forests. The Hawaiian name means "dancer" and refers to the "dancing" or flapping of the leaves in even the slightest wind.

Oligota — a genus of rove beetles of the family Staphylinidae (Coleoptera).

olomaʻo (*Myadestes lanaiensis*) — the Hawaiian name for a smallish brown solitaire known from Maui, Lānaʻi, and Molokaʻi, now thought to be extinct due to avian malaria. It was last seen on Molokaʻi in the 1980s. The Maui population was only seen in the 1860s. The Lānaʻi population disappeared in 1933.

ʻōmaʻo (*Myadestes obscurus*) — Hawaiian name for this common Hawaiian thrush formerly known from all the main islands. Now known only from the island of Hawaiʻi.

ʻōʻō — the Hawaiian name for the extinct honeycreepers of the genus *Moho*. All species are now extinct.

ʻōʻō-āʻā — the Hawaiian name for the Kauaʻi *ʻōʻō* (*Moho braccatus*). It is thought to be extinct and was last sighted in the 1970s.

Oodemas — a genus of weevils of the family Curculionidae (Coleoptera).

Ophion — a genus of wasps of the family Ichneumonidae (Hymenoptera).

Opostega — a genus of moths of the family Opostegidae (Lepidoptera).

Oreomyza — an old genus name for small, short-tailed Hawaiian honeycreepers. These birds are now treated in the genus Perkins proposed for them: *Paroreomyza*.

Orneodes — a genus of moths of the family Alucitidae (Lepidoptera) now treated in *Alucita*.

Orthostolus — a genus of sap beetles of the family Nitidulidae (Coleoptera).

Otiorhynchinae (-ini) — a group (subfamily: -inae; tribe: -ini) of weevils of the family Curculionidae (Coleoptera).

ʻōʻū (*Psittirostra psittacea*) — this green-yellow honeycreeper (Drepanididae) was at one time common throughout the main Hawaiian Islands. Probably extinct now on all islands.

Oxyura — an obsolete and antiquated classification division of tiny parasitic wasps including those in Proctotrupidae, Scelionidae, and others (Hymenoptera).

paʻiniu (*Astelia*) — a lily-like Hawaiian endemic plant of the family Liliaceae usually found in mesic forests. Some native insects and other invertebrates live in the water held in its leaf axils.

palila (*Loxioides bailleui*) — a finch-billed Hawaiian honeycreeper (Drepanididae) on the federal Endangered Species List and currently found only on the slopes of Mauna Kea on the island of Hawaiʻi. In Perkins's time it ranged southward into the Kona forests above the Greenwell Ranch. The species is restricted to the *māmane/naio* scrub forests where the adults feed almost exclusively on the *māmane* seed pods. Fossil remains show that the *palila* once inhabited Oʻahu and Kauaʻi.

Palmeria — the genus for the crested honeycreeper (*Palmeria dolei*) or *ʻākohekohe*. It was declared an endangered species in 1967 and the population is still considered endangered. It is now known only from the slopes of Haleakalā volcano on Maui, but also occurred on Molokaʻi in Perkins's time.

Panaphelix — a genus of leafroller moths of the family Tortricidae (Lepidoptera).

Pandanus — a genus of screw pine (Pandanaceae) common throughout the Pacific. In Hawaiʻi it is known as hala and its leaves are used in weaving.

Pantala — a genus of native Hawaiian dragonflies (Odonata) including the widely traveled *Pantala flavescens*, which can migrate thousands of miles over Pacific waters looking for new breeding grounds.

Parandra — a genus of rather bulky long-horned beetle of the family Cerambycidae (Coleoptera).

Parandrita — a genus of flat bark beetles of the family Cucujidae (Coleoptera).

Paratrigonidium — a genus of crickets of the family Gryllidae (Orthoptera). Only one endemic species (*Paratrigonidium pacifum*) is known in the genus in Hawaiʻi and is found on all the main islands in the Hawaiian chain. The over 150 species formerly in this genus during Perkins's time are now placed in three other genera (*Trigonidium*, *Laupala*, and *Prolaupata*).

Partulina — a genus of native Hawaiian land snails of the family Achatinellidae.

Pelea — a genus of plants now known in the genus *Melicope*.

Pennula — an old genus name for the extinct Hawaiian Rail (*Porzana sandwichensis*). It was a small, flightless rail and is known only from 7 museum specimens. Perkins searched in vain for this bird while in Hawaiʻi, but it had probably gone extinct before his arrival.

Pentarthrum — a genus of wood-boring weevils of the family Curculionidae (Coleoptera).

Perdicella — a genus of land snails of the family Achatinellidae.

pewee — common name of a group of birds in the genus *Contopus*, the name referring to the sound of its call.

Phaeornis — an old genus name for Hawaiian thrushes now treated in the genus *Myadestes*. See e.g., *ʻōmaʻo, olomaʻo,* and *kāmaʻo*.

Pheidole — a genus of ants (Formicidae) including the bigheaded ant (*Pheidole megacephala*). This species of ant alone has probably caused more damage to the native invertebrate fauna of the Hawaiian Islands than any other introduced animal. It has a habit of scouring the area for any small prey to take back to its nest. Ganging up on prey they are able to capture larger items. Many flightless insect species are thought to have gone extinct due to the introduction of this ant.

Philodoria — a genus of leaf mining moths of the family Gracillariidae (Lepidoptera).

Phlyctaenia — a genus of webworm moths of the family Crambidae (Lepidoptera).

Phycitidae — a family of moths including the cactus moth *Cactoblastis cactorum*, sometimes treated in the family Pyralidae (Lepidoptera).

Pison — a genus of wasps in the family Sphecidae (Hymenoptera).

Plagithmysus — an endemic Hawaiian genus of long-horned beetles (Coleoptera) containing some of the larger native beetles in Hawai'i. Many of the species of these beetles in Hawai'i have had their populations reduced or extirpated and are now very rare.

pohā (*Physalis peruviana*) — the Hawaiian name for a plant also known as Cape gooseberry. Seeds of this native Brazilian plant were brought from Australia to the Hawaiian Islands before 1825 and it quickly became naturalized and spread throughout the island chain. Its fruits are edible and are used in salads and preserves.

Polistes — a genus of paper wasps (Hymenoptera). All species in Hawai'i are non-native.

Pompilidae — a family of wasps (Hymenoptera) that commonly paralyze spiders and use them as prey for their growing larvae.

Ponera — a genus of ants of the family Formicidae (Hymenoptera).

Pritchardia — a genus of fan palms known in Hawai'i as *loulu*.

Proctotrupes — a genus of parasitic wasps of the family Proctotrupidae (Hymenoptera).

Prodisenochus — a genus of ground beetles of the family Carabidae (Coleoptera).

Prognathogryllus — a genus of crickets of the family Gryllidae (Orthoptera). There are over 30 endemic species of these crickets in Hawai'i.

Progonostola — a native Hawaiian genus of inch worm moths of the family Geometridae (Lepidoptera).

Promylaea — a genus name of crambid moths now treated as a subgenus of *Mestolobes* (Lepidoptera).

Prosopis [animal] — bees currently classified as the subgenus Hylaeus (Nesoprosopis).

Prosopis [plant] — mesquite, commonly known in Hawai'i as *kiawe*.

Prosthetochaeta — an old genus of blow flies (Calliphoridae), the Hawaiian species of which are now treated in the endemic Hawaiian genus *Dyscritomyia* (Diptera).

Proterhinus — speciose genus of beetles of the family Belidae (formerly placed in Aglycyderidae). There are over 150 native species known from Hawai'i with many more awaiting naming and description.

Protoparce — a genus of sphinx moths (Sphingidae) including the tomato horn-worm (Lepidoptera). The endemic Hawaiian species *blackburni* is now placed in the genus *Manduca*.

Pseudobroscus — a genus of ground beetles of the family Carabidae (Coleoptera).

Pseudonestor — a monotypic genus of Hawaiian honeycreepers (Drepanididae) commonly called the Maui parrotbill (*Pseudonestor xanthophrys*). Once thought to be extinct, it was rediscovered in 1950. Its former range included Moloka'i and Maui; it is currently restricted to high elevation rainforests of East Maui.

Psidium — the genus of guava plants introduced into Hawai'i in the early 1800s. One species is now a major pest in Hawaiian forests where it has displaced native species and limits understory growth.

Psittirostra — a genus of Hawaiian honeycreepers (Drepanididae). The '*ō'ū* (*Psittirostra psittacea*) is the only species in the genus.

Psocidae — a family of insects including book lice and bark lice (Psocoptera).

Psyllidae — a family of plant sucking bugs (Homoptera)

Pteris — a genus of ferns in the family Pteridaceae, commonly called brakes.

Pterophoridae — the family name for plume moths (Lepidoptera).

Pterophorus — a genus of plume moths of the family Pterophoridae (Lepidoptera).

pua — the Hawaiian name refers to a number of plants but in the context of Perkins's notes, he could be referring to the *pua kenikeni* (*Fagraea berteroana*), which was introduced into the islands in the late 1800s.

Pycnophion — a genus of ichneumon wasps of the family Ichneumonidae (Hymenoptera).

Pyralidae — the family of pyralid moths (Lepidoptera).

Pyrameis tammeamea — see *Vanessa tameamea*.

Pyrausta — a genus of moths of the family Crambidae (Lepidoptera). The species Perkins was referring to (*dracontias*) is now placed in the genus *Udea*.

Rallus sandwichensis — one of several old names for the extinct flightless rail whose common name is the Hawaiian Rail. See *Pennula*.

Rhabdoscelus obscurus — commonly known locally as the "cane borer." A weevil introduced to the Hawaiian Islands from the South Pacific sometime before 1865. After it became established, it soon attacked a variety of palms, papayas, and bananas, but was commonly known as a severe pest of sugar cane by the time Perkins arrived in the islands.

Rhodacanthis — the genus name for the koa finches. Both species (the Lesser Koa Finch and Greater Koa Finch) are now extinct.

Rhyncogonus — a genus of Pacific weevils of the family Curculionidae (Coleoptera) that have a diverse number of endemic species in Hawai'i.

Rubus — see *'ākala*.

Salda — a genus of shore bugs of the family Saldidae (Heteroptera).

Santalum — see *'iliahi*.

Sarcophaga — genus of flies known as carrion flies in the family Sarcophagidae (Diptera).

Satyrium — a genus of hairstreaks or blues of the butterfly family Lycaenidae (Lepidoptera).

Sclerodermus — a genus of wasps of the family Bethylidae (Hymenoptera).

Scoparia — a genus of crambid moths (Lepidoptera). Hawaiian species are now treated in the genus *Eudonia*.

Scotorhyrtha — a genus of inch worm moths in the family Geometridae (Lepidoptera) with numerous endemic species in the Hawaiian Islands.

Scymnus — a genus of ladybird beetles of the family Coccinellidae (Coleoptera).

Sierola — a speciose genus of parasitic wasps of the family Bethylidae (Hymenoptera).

Smilax — genus of native Hawaiian vine in the family Smilacaceae.

Sophora — the genus for the *māmane* tree (*Sophora chrysophylla*) in the family Fabaceae.

Sphecodes — a genus of the bee family Halictidae (Hymenoptera). The genus does not occur in Hawai'i.

Sphingidae — family of moths commonly known as hawk moths or sphinx moths (Lepidoptera).

Sphinx — genus of sphinx moths (Lepidoptera).

Staphylinidae — family of beetles commonly known as rove beetles (Coleoptera).

Stemorrhages — a genus of moths of the family Crambidae (Lepidoptera).

Straussia — plants now placed in the genus *Psychotria*. See *kōpiko*.

Styphelia — an old genus name for the *pūkiawe* plant now known as *Leptecophylla tameiameiae*.

Suttonia — an old genus name for plant species now treated in the genus *Myrsine* (*q.v.*)

Sympetrum — a genus of dragonflies of the family Libellulidae (Odonata).

Syrphidae — family of flies commonly called flower flies (Diptera).

Tachinidae — family of parasitic flies (Diptera). Many have been introduced into areas as biological control agents against pest insects.

Talis — a genus of crambid moths (Lepidoptera). Hawaiian species are now placed in the endemic genus *Tamsica*.

Tettigoniidae — family of insects known as long-horned grasshoppers or katydids (Orthoptera).

Thoracophorus — a genus of rove beetles of the family Staphylinidae (Coleoptera).

Thriscothorax — an old genus name for ground beetles of the family Carabidae (Coleoptera) now treated in the genus *Mecyclothorax*.

Thysanura — order of arthropods known as silverfish.

Tineidae — family of moths commonly called clothes moths (Lepidoptera).

Tipulinae — subfamily of flies known as crane flies in the family Tipulidae (Diptera).

Tortricidae — a family of moths some of whom are commonly known as leafrollers (Lepidoptera).

Tortrix — a genus of leafroller moths in the family Tortricidae (Lepidoptera).

Totanus — a genus of birds commonly called sand pipers and redshanks, some of whose species are treated now in the genus *Tringa*.

Tribulus — see *nohu*.

Trichopterygidae — a family of feather-winged beetles (Coleoptera) also known by the family name Ptiliidae.

Trypetidae [= Tephritidae] — family of flies known as fruit flies (Diptera).

Udara— genus of lycaenid moths containing the endemic Hawaiian species *Udara blackburniae*.

'ūhini — Hawaiian name for endemic katydids of the genus *Banza* (Orthoptera).

'ula-'ai-hāwane (*Ciridops anna*) — a small but striking Hawaiian honeycreeper (Drepanididae), with black, crimson, and gray plumage. The name *'ula-'ai-hāwane* roughly translates in Hawaiian to "the red bird that eats in the *hāwane* palm." It was reported only the Big Island but fossil remains show that it also inhabited the forests of Moloka'i. The live bird was perhaps never seen by Western ornithologists. The five specimens that exist in museums were all taken by native bird catchers.

'ūlili (*Heteroscelus incanus*) — the Wandering Tattler is a common coastal migrant whose home is in the Pacific Northwest and Alaska. It migrates southward to California and Mexico and even across the Pacific to Hawai'i, Australia, and South Pacific Islands.

uluhe (*Dicranopteris linearis*) — false staghorn fern. This fern forms thick mats that can be deceiving as they will grow over gaps in trails and obscure the true terrain underneath it. Perkins stated the following concerning it: "I found the Staghorn fern a great trial on Oahu & elsewhere (e.g. near Lihue on Kauai) where it grew to a great height. In some parts of Oahu great numbers of {the wasp} *Polistes macauensis* would nest in it & when one was forcing through the fern one would break down a nest & get fiercely attacked. One could escape stings by lying down flat on the ground." (*R.C.L. Perkins letter to E.C. Zimmerman, 22 August 1948, BPBM Entomology Archives*).

Vaccinium — a genus of plants in the heath family (Ericaeae), called *'ōhelo* in Hawaiian.

Vanessa tameamea — the Kamehameha butterfly, a member of the family Nymphalidae and the unofficial state insect of Hawai'i. It is one of only two endemic butterflies found in Hawai'i. Very similar in appearance to the Red Admiral (*Vanessa atalanta*) found in the continental United States. Older references referred to this species in the genus *Pyrameis*.

Vestiaria — see *'i'iwi*.

Viridonia — an old genus name for the Hawaiian honeycreeper commonly called the Greater 'Amakihi. Perkins called it the "Green Solitaire." It is currently classified as *Hemignathus sagittirostris*. Last seen in 1901, it is presumed extinct.

Vitex — a genus of shore-inhabiting plants in the verbena family (Verbenaceae) found throughout the Pacific from Hawai'i to India.

Waltheria — a genus of plants of the family Sterculiaceae.

wauke (*Broussonetia papyrifera*) — native to Asia, this plant, also called paper mulberry, is an important part of Polynesian culture and essential to native Hawaiians in *tapa* [or *kapa*] making for clothes and mattings.

Wikstroemia — see *'ākia*.

Xanthocorynus — a genus of rove beetles of the family Staphylinidae (Coleoptera).

Xanthogramma — a genus of flower flies of the family Syrphidae (Diptera).

Xanthorhoe — a genus of inch worm moths of the family Geometridae (Lepidoptera). Hawaiian species are now placed other genera including *Fletcherana* and *Progono-stola*.

Xanthoxylum — see *Zanthoxylum*.

Xyleborus — a genus of shot-hole borer beetles of the family Curculionidae (Coleoptera).

Xyletobius — a genus of beetles of the family Anobiidae (Coleoptera).

Zanthoxylum — a genus of plants known as prickly ash (sometimes spelled *Xanthoxylum*) in the family Rutaceae.

Literature Cited

Kent, H.W. 1965. *Charles Reed Bishop, Man of Hawaii*. Pacific Books: Palo Alto. xvi + 365 p.

Manning, A. 1986. The Sandwich Islands Committee, Bishop Museum, and R.C.L. Perkins: cooperative zoological exploration and publication. *Bishop Museum Occasional Papers* **26**: 1–46.

Rothschild, M. 1983. *Dear Lord Rothschild, birds, butterflies, and history*. Hutchinson: London. xx + 398 p.

Scott, H.B. 1956. Robert Cyril Layton Perkins 1866–1955. *Biographical Memoirs of the Fellows of the Royal Society* **2**: 215–236.

List of Biographical Information on R.C.L. Perkins

Anonymous. 1955. *Daily Telegraph* (4 October).

Anonymous. 1955. *Honolulu Advertiser* (1 October): B5.

Anonymous. 1955. Dr. R.C.L. Perkins. *The Times, London* (5 October): 11d.

Anonymous. 1956. Obituary notices: Robert Cyril Layton Perkins. *Devon Association Transactions* **1956**: 210–211.

Black, A.C. & Black, C. 1961. *Who Was Who, 1951–1960*, p. 865.

Fullaway, D.T. 1956. Biographical sketch of Dr. R.C.L. Perkins. *Proceedings of the Hawaiian Entomological Society* **16**: 45–46.

Hall, W.J. 1956. The President's remarks: Robert Cyril Layton Perkins. *Proceedings of the Royal Entomological Society* (C) **20**: 73.

Harvey, J.M.V., Gilbert, P. & Martin, K.S. 1996. *A catalogue of manuscripts in the Entomology Library of the Natural History Museum*. Mansell: London. p. 159–160.

Liebherr, J.K. & Polhemus, D.A. 1997. R.C.L. Perkins: 100 years of Hawaiian entomology. *Pacific Science* **51**: 343–355.

Manning, A. 1986. The Sandwich Islands Committee, Bishop Museum, and R.C.L. Perkins: cooperative zoological exploration and publication. *Bishop*

Museum Occasional Papers **26**: 1–46.

Munroe, G.C. 1956. Robert Cyril Layton Perkins, F.R.S. 1920, M.A., D.Sc. (Oxon), F.Z.S., F.E.S. *Elepaio* **17**(3): 19–20.

Perkins, J.F. 1971. Perkins, Robert Cyril Layton. In: Williams, E.T. & Palmer, H.M., eds. *Dictionary of National Biography 1951–1960.* p. 806–807.

Sachtleben, H. 1956. Entomologische Chronik: Dr. Robert Cyril Layton Perkins. *Beiträge zur Entomologie* **6**: 458–459.

Scott, H.B. 1956. Robert Cyril Layton Perkins 1866–1955. *Biographical Memoirs of the Fellows of the Royal Society* **2**: 215–236.

Scott, H.B. & **Benson, R.B.** 1955. Obituary: R.C.L. Perkins, D.Sc., F.R.S. (1866–1955). *Entomologist's Monthly Magazine* **19**: 289–291.

APPENDIX

Appendix

Archival Resources and Credits

The following is a list of the archival sources used in this study. These sources either possess documentation and/or imagery of or about Perkins or have ancillary information germane to the life and times of Perkins while in Hawaiʻi or England.

The journals and remembrances reproduced here derive from the Bishop Museum Archives (except for the copy of the original diary of the first 1893 Molokaʻi trip that derived from the Royal Zoological Society, London) as does the correspodence from Sharp and Newton to Perkins and letters from Perkins to Bishop, Brigham, Judd, and Hyde. The letters from Perkins to Zimmerman are held in the Bishop Museum Entomology Archives. Other credits for documents reproduced or transcribed and used in this book are annotated below.

Bishop Museum Archives, Honolulu
Bishop Museum Registrar (letters from R.C.L. Perkins to Mrs. E.C. Zimmerman)
Bishop Museum Department of Natural Sciences:
    Entomology Collections (information on labels of insect collections)
    Vertebrate Zoology Collection (information on labels of bird collections)
California Academy of Sciences, San Francisco — Koebele Collection (5 January 1897 letter from R.C.L. Perkins to A. Koebele)
Cambridge University Museum of Zoology, Cambridge
Hawaii State Archives, Honolulu
Hawaii Volcanoes National Park Archives and Library, Volcano (Volcano House registry and visitor's book)
Hawaiian Sugar Planters' Association, ʻAiea (Perkins biographical information)
Kauaʻi Historical Society, Līhuʻe (Halemanu House)
Kona Historical Society, Captain Cook (Greenwell Ranch information)
Natural History Museum, London (Perkins correspondence and copies of journals)
Oxford University Natural History Museum Library, Oxford (letters from R.C.L. Perkins to E.B. Poulton)
University of Hawaiʻi at Mānoa, Hamilton Library, Honolulu—Hawaiian Newspapers

INDEXES

Terms indexed here include English and Hawaiian common names and scientific names of plants and animals and the full names and vital dates (where found) of persons mentioned in the text as well as in correspondence (through p. 380). Terms in subsequent chapters including the glossary are not included. Plurals are used for all common names in the index although the singular may have been used in the text. Diacritics are not included so as to keep with the original orthography of the journals and correspondence.

INSECTS and Other ARTHROPODS

BIRDS

SNAILS/SLUGS

OTHER ANIMALS

PEOPLE

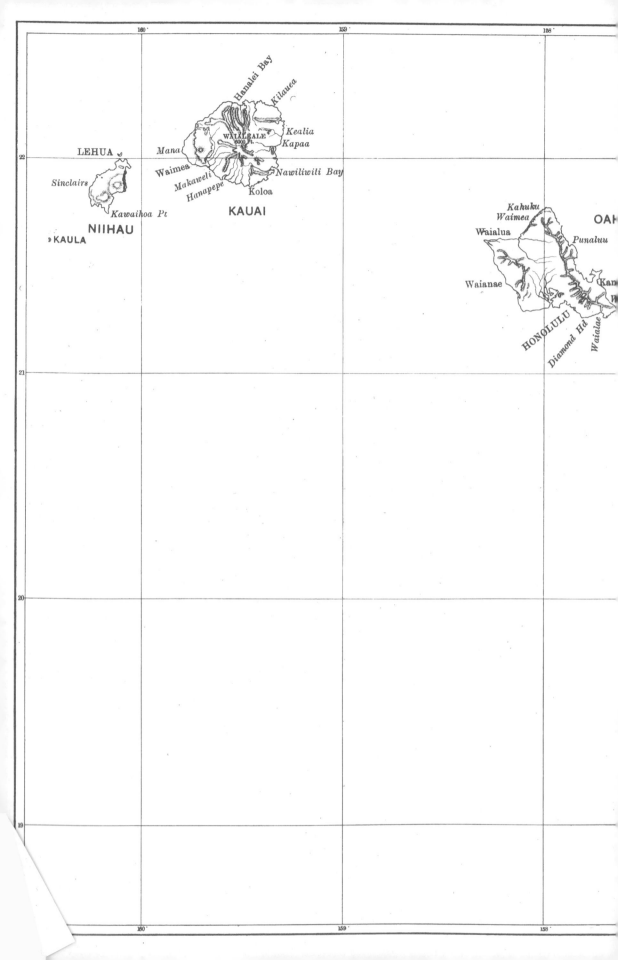